CW00498736

SUBJECTIVITIES

June 1991

For David,
With thanks & affection,
Regenia

A Barnardo boy, circa 1888. By Permission of the Barnardo Photographic Archive.

SUBJECTIVITIES

*A History of Self-Representation
in Britain, 1832–1920*

REGENIA GAGNIER

New York   Oxford
OXFORD UNIVERSITY PRESS
1991

Oxford University Press

Oxford New York Toronto
Delhi Bombay Calcutta Madras Karachi
Petaling Jaya Singapore Hong Kong Tokyo
Nairobi Dar es Salaam Cape Town
Melbourne Auckland

and associated companies in
Berlin Ibadan

Published by Oxford University Press, Inc.
200 Madison Avenue, New York, NY 10016

Oxford is a registered trademark of Oxford University Press

Library of Congress Cataloging-in-Publication Data
Gagnier, Regenia.
Subjectivities : a history of self-representation in Britain,
1832–1920 / Regenia Gagnier.
p. cm.
Includes bibliographical references.
ISBN 0-19-506096-2
1. English prose literature—19th century—History and criticism.
2. Autobiography. 3. Self in literature. 4. Subjectivity in
literature. 5. Working class in literature. 6. Social classes
in literature. 7. Autobiographical fiction, English—History
and criticism. 8. English prose literature—20th century—
History and criticism. I. Title.
PR788.A9G34 1991
828'.80809—dc20   89-26641 CIP

9 8 7 6 5 4 3 2 1

Printed in the United States of America
on acid free paper

Acknowledgments

I was blessed to have passed my youth in the San Francisco Bay Area in the 1960s, dividing my adolescence between rock concerts in Golden Gate Park and Black Panther parties in Oakland penthouses. In pursuit of these activities I saw people with more varied histories and goals than I have ever seen since. Because of these experiences and the analyses of them that came later, I will probably always intuitively respond with equal warmth (and probably incoherently) to romantic communitarianism and the possibility of sudden revolution. The conclusions of this book, however, lead in other directions.

They lead to the slowness of history. Reading hundreds of autobiographies written at the end of lives spanning a century, when the writer takes his or her last opportunity to impart to later generations whatever wisdom he or she has to bestow in this life, I have often called this study a gerontology. I doubt whether I have been able to represent how excruciatingly moving it has been to read the stories of human freedom unfolding in the lives of Victorian workers, women, and writers: to hear the languages of emancipation take hold of the lives of Chartists or suffragettes or the sons and daughters of imperialists and capitalists, or to see a founder of the middle-class monolith *Punch* transvaluate Victorian values through his intimate contact with the poorest of London's poor. Walter Benjamin's "Angel of History" was propelled violently from the pile of wreckage that was the past into a future toward which his back was turned; but in reading these lives, one is repeatedly reminded that the democratic revolutions of the West are just 200 years old and that positive (i.e., liberating) ideology takes time to make sense in the life of the individual, especially when it is offset by many—very many—material deprivations and counter ideologies. Perhaps 200 years, maybe six generations, are not long in the history of freedom. Individual lives of conflict and community show how long ideas take to take root and how much they matter.

After those to history, my most pressing and deeply felt acknowledgments are to an institution. I am deeply grateful to the English Department of Stanford University, who individually and collectively treat its new members with a decency I would have thought impossible in a modern bureaucratic setting. Special thanks are due to three of my colleagues, Herbert Lindenberger, Diane Middlebrook, and Robert Polhemus, who hired me and criticized me with a passionate objectivity. The other institutions within the institution that have perfected my intellectual environment are the Cultural Studies Group, the Feminist Theory Seminar and Institute for Research on Women and Gender, and the Stanford Humanities Center, groups of colleagues who have shown me, term after term, the rewards of cooperative, interdisciplinary work. The Pew Memorial Trust contributed travel grants without which the research for this work could not have been done.

I also owe much to individuals, whose criticisms of the manuscript have reshaped it through and through. Patrick Brantlinger has supported this work at many times and in many forms. His critical acumen and knowledge of the period are unfailing. I've never met him, but will say in print that I would like to. Paul John Eakin gave me a valuable correspondence on autobiographical theory. I imagine that he must look kindly and wise. Russell Berman, Eckart Förster, David Millar, Carol Nathan, Leonard Nathan, Harriet Ritvo, and Brackette Williams gave me strong readings of several sections at critical stages. Charles Altieri wrote me a passionate defense of liberalism that I felt obliged to answer. A warm thanks goes to Anne Humphreys, whose expertise on Henry Mayhew and Victorian journalism is second only to her generosity. I am also very grateful to some anonymous readers of the manuscript, whose criticisms were invaluable in the final stages.

Even brief conversations with some people can be of great significance in an author's thinking about a topic. Such were lunch, dinner, and drinks, respectively, with Stuart Hampshire, Stephen Jay Gould, and Philip Kitcher.

Many students are cited in the pages that follow. Three former graduate advisees in particular, now professors themselves, have repeatedly challenged me with their commitment, hope, and intellectual courage. This work bears the imprints of Mary Jean Corbett, Lydia Fillingham, and Victor Luftig.

And finally acknowledgments go to my J. S. Mill and Sidney Webb, John Dupré, who helps me believe in the lack of distinction between private desire and public good. He has read every word and contributed enough of his own that this might truly be said to represent Our Partnership.

This book is dedicated to the memory of my brothers, Shane and Steven Gagnier, who were strong in body and generous in mind.

Parts of the following chapters have been previously published in the following journals, to which I am grateful for permission to reprint: Introduction in *The Stanford Humanities Review* 1/2 (Winter 1990); Chapter 1 in *Textual Practice* 3/1 (Spring 1989); Chapter 2 in *Representations* 22 (Spring 1988); Chapter 4 in *Victorian Studies* 30/3 (Spring 1987); Chapter 5 in *Browning Institute Studies* 16 (1988) and in *Women's Studies* 15/1–3 (1988).

Palo Alto   R.G.
December 1989

Contents

SUBJECTIVITIES

Introduction

Pragmatics, Rhetoric, and Cultural Studies

Subjectivities: A History of Self-Representation is a comparative analysis of subjectivity and value across social class and gender in nineteenth- and early twentieth-century Britain. I have attempted a cultural and material analysis of Victorian subjectivity—of what it was like to be a Victorian gentleman, lady, midwife, carpenter, mudlark, barrister, or nurse. In doing this I have simultaneously asked questions of value: What are the varieties of human desire? What is the nature of the society that can provide for such desires? And what kind of subjectivities have we today valued? Developing from my own disciplinary situation, the study has also evolved as a critique (an examination of the scope and limits) of the kind of subjectivity we have valued in imaginative literature. I view the completed project as a historical study of possible subjects, of human possibilities in antagonism and participation. My texts, or primary sources, are hundreds of autobiographical works by women and men from early nineteenth- through early twentieth-century Britain with a predominant focus upon the Victorian period. The "self-representation" of the title, then, refers literally to autobiography and more broadly to an axiology of the self: the systems of values, expectations, and constraints that come into play when one represents oneself to others in the concrete circumstances of daily life.

Although this work could not have been imagined or written without the honorable recuperative work of social historians in Britain and the United States, for which I am very grateful; and although I have tried within my abilities and resources to be as accurate as possible about the historical production and reception (or lack of reception) of the texts, my approach to them, like my interest in them, is literary, or more precisely, rhetorical. Even with the writers about whom we "know" a great deal, like Orwell—whose prep school, historians tell us, was not so very nasty as it appears in his autobiographical "Such, Such Were the Joys," I am interested in self-representation for the writer's specific ends rather than conformity to the facts per se. The study is concerned with the pragmatics of self-representation. Instead of evaluating the truth of a statement, pragmatism considers what it does. Thus pragmatism seeks to locate the purpose an autobiographical statement serves in the life and circumstances of its author and readers.

In writing of how people situate themselves in the world, nothing is self-evident, neither the aspects of the world and Nature that one would think salient, nor "the self" itself, about which literary criticism has been unfortunately provincial. Since Ramus, Chaim Perelman tells us in his massive and missionary *New Rhetoric,* modern rhetoric has primarily concerned itself with stylistics (Scotland perhaps provides exceptions). Although I will by no means eschew stylistics in the analyses that follow, I value rhetoric rather as Aristotle and Perelman did, as a practical discipline that sees speech or writing as aiming at persuasive action upon a particular audience, even if—as in a few upcoming instances—the audience is only one's divided self. More importantly, I value rhetoric as the study of the possibility of human communities with shared values though not necessarily values based upon some "objective" (i.e., universal) reality.[1] Indeed, I take it that no such universality characterizes value in our modern (and postmodern) world.

The rhetorical inquiry is comprised of the analysis of a particular set of circumstances, the judgments made thereof, and the persuasion to accept the judgment and its appropriate action, and it is centrally concerned with value. Thus classical rhetoric was divided into three parts: the deliberative (having to do with political assemblies), the forensic (having to do with legal jurisdiction), and the epideictic or encomiastic (having to do with praise or blame). Despite the fact that the texts I discuss are written compositions, I want to resist the postromantic literary tradition that excludes everything but the rich and ornate linguistic "display" that was once the domain of the epideictic. The lack of privacy and leisure of many of the writers render it expedient to recall the Rhetoric of Isocrates, that which was useful, which pertained to practical skills and the active (as well as contemplative and self-reflective) life. This was the rhetoric that allowed Isocrates in 354–353 B.C. at the age of eighty-two to write his *Antidosis.* Although it purports to be written for a trial, its "real purpose is to show the truth about myself, to make those who are ignorant about me know the sort of man I am."[2] Sounding like any number of nineteenth-century workers, Isocrates thus produced what is generally accepted as the first Western autobiography of an "ordinary" person.

What needs to be added to the study of rhetoric to prevent it from tending toward mere academic "appreciation" is the self-conscious interpretive dimension of a more recent development: cultural studies. Cultural studies not only seeks to specify the historical meaning of a text but also takes account of how meaning, or reception, changes through time and through the mediation of interpreters and interpretive institutions. For example, I concur with theorists like Adena Rosmarin in *The Power of Genre* that genres like "autobiography" are not classes but classifying statements; and I choose to expand the class to include self-representation previously excluded from literary analyses of "autobiography."[3] Like the self-representation of the primary texts (the "autobiographies") themselves, the designation of a genre is meant to serve a pragmatic end. The authors of the bibliography *The Autobiography of the Working Class,* one of my main sources for working-class writers' texts, collected disparate texts by disparate workers under the classification "working-class autobiography." In doing so I take it that, like the "autobiographers" themselves, they acted rhetorically and pragmatically in terms of audience and purpose, the audience being interested scholars and readers with the purpose of reviving voices that had been excluded from historiography. In writing about the selves represented herein the critical practice prescribed by the critical genre is neither "canonoclasm" nor even canon-reformation, but cultural criticism.

My goal is not an exhaustive study of nineteenth- and early twentieth-century autobiography, nor of the fine distinctions of social hierarchy in modern Britain: I have read only about three-quarters—and some of these only in published excerpts—of the 804 working-class writers listed in the aforementioned bibliography. Also, despite following many leads in secondary sources and the autobiographies themselves of public- and boarding-school graduates, I still meet Anglophiles who speak lovingly of a school memoir unknown to me—readers whose very devotion supports my argument for the communal function of school memoirs. I have ranged chronologically more than most historians would consider wise because my interest is less in periodicity than in how people respond to highly stratified yet mobile societies and in the continuous reformations of hegemonic and counterhegemonic borders. By *hegemonic* I mean that which possesses the cultural supremacy of one social bloc over others and thus prevents the full development of other cultural forms. As I shall elaborate in Chapter 1, hegemony appears in autobiography in the form of master, or broad cultural, "narratives" that determine how people see their lives. For example, such narratives include ideologies of gender—of masculinity and femininity—that make women and men write their lives in terms of romance and financial success, whether or not their acutal lives are conducive to such pursuits. They also include narratives of the Enlightenment that legitimize workers in seeing their lives as the pursuit of "bread, knowledge, and freedom," and thus make their autobiographies read much like that of John Stuart Mill, a son of the middle-class intelligentsia, or Beatrice Webb, a daughter of one of the wealthiest capitalists in England. There are also narratives of family that make working-class people obsessed with parents they never knew and others, such as Samuel Butler and Florence Nightingale, obsessed with parents and a family system they knew and hated. In general when I write of *gender* in the chapters that follow, I do not mean men and women so much as master "narratives" that shape the way people see their lives.

A highly stratified society under the pressures of industrialization and the democratic revolution is particularly rich in terms of the master narratives that manifest themselves in individual lives and autobiography. Any discursive "autobiographical" or collective "move," as I shall elaborate in Chapter 1, will contain participatory or antagonistic codes, and often it will contain both. The cultural critic must situate the "I" or "we" of social participation or antagonism with unwavering attention to differing, often subtly nuanced, codes and contexts. What is crucial in the cultural critic's analysis is that she or he be sensitive to the participatory or positive, in Raymond Williams's sense, articulations of individuals and groups as well as to the negative or antagonistic articulations that Marxists have traced so brilliantly. Such participatory and antagonistic discourses, which often develop in an individual life, provide a plethora of alternatives to subjectivity in the limited sense in which it has come to be taken in literary studies.

A corollary of cultural studies is the study of texts as means in the elaboration of a nonreductionist understanding of cultures rather than ends in themselves. The text is only one "moment" in a circuit of production, circulation, and consumption of cultural artifacts, and its meaning depends upon its relation to the other "moments." As Richard Johnson writes in a recent article entitled "What is Cultural Studies Anyway?":

> All cultural products, for example, require to be produced, but the conditions of their production cannot be inferred by scrutinizing them as

"texts." Similarly all cultural products are "read" by persons other than professional analysts (if they weren't there would be little profit in their production), but we cannot predict these uses from our own analysis, or, indeed, from the conditions of production. As anyone knows, all our communications are liable to return to us in unrecognisable or at least transformed terms. . . . To understand the transformation, then, we have to understand specific conditions of consumption or reading. . . . In our societies, many forms of cultural production also take the form of capitalist commodities. In this case we have to supply specifically capitalist conditions of production and specifically capitalist conditions of consumption. Of course this does not tell us all there is to know about these moments, which may be structured on other principles as well, but in these cases the circuit is, at one and the same time, a circuit of capital and its expanded reproduction *and* a circuit of the production and circulation of subjective forms.[4]

Johnson also locates the specific domain of cultural studies in "historical forms of consciousness or subjectivity" (43), a topic to which I shall turn in the next section.

I have attempted to comprehend the texts of workers, former public- and boarding-school pupils, and Victorian celebrities within a materialist, or situationally conscious, analysis of Victorian culture. I have tried to mark the conditions in which the texts were produced, whether as a relatively isolated event or part of a larger public event of representation, especially by seeing how conventional literary forms and figures are transformed by, or adapt to, concrete situations. I have tried to trace the reception, or meaning, of the texts, both within their own historical moment as well as within ours. In addition, by drawing upon historiography and ethnography, I have tried to understand something of the lived cultures of these people who can only provisionally and pragmatically be approached in terms of analytic categories like "class" and "gender."

Social historians, anthropologists, and, above all, feminist scholars have insisted upon fine distinctions and sensitivity to difference, often against theorists of a homogenizing Power who ignore differences in generalizing about "the Subject" or "the State." Within this tradition of attentiveness to difference, cultural critics still have to grapple with the difficulty and delicacy of the applications of history to the texts of the imagination. I consider all writing about one's self, whether called autobiography, memoir, confession, or (as I call it) rhetorical projects embedded in concrete material situations, to be within the category of texts of the imagination. As that most rational of men Thomas Henry Huxley said in the preface to his own no-nonsense autobiography (it was nine pages in length): "All autobiographies are essentially works of fiction, whatever biographies may be."[5] What is common to all autobiographical writing discussed in these pages is the survival of differences in the writers' imaginations, even where past and present readers have most expected to find conformity.

The remainder of this Introduction will situate the two key terms of the study, *subjectivity* and *value*. In doing this at the outset I not only acknowledge the theorists who have informed the work, but provide a grammar of relevant concepts for the six chapters that follow—concepts like, "Unger's continuum of personality," "Nagel's 'what it is like to be' a thing," "liberal autonomy," "Bourdieu's critique of Kantian aesthetics," and gender as social dimorphism rather than, for example, biological males and females. In this way there will be fewer theoretical digressions to interrupt the analyses of the "subjectivities" under question.

Subjectivity

> The blessed will not care what angle they are regarded from.
> W. H. AUDEN, "In Praise of Limestone"

For the purposes of this study *subjectivity* has to be taken in its broadest range of senses, for it is precisely the categories of subjectivity that are under interrogation. First, the subject is a subject to itself, an "I," however difficult or even impossible it may be for others to understand this "I" from its own viewpoint, within its own experience. Simultaneously, the subject is a subject to, and of, others; in fact, it is often an "Other" to others, which also affects its sense of its own subjectivity. This construction of self in opposition to others, it will be seen, is as characteristic of groups, communities, classes, and nations, as it is of individuals, as in the self-conception of Chartists, or "the working classes," or schoolboys, or ladies, or, today, "Women," or "the Third World." Third, the subject is also a subject of knowledge, most familiarly perhaps of the discourse of social institutions that circumscribe its terms of being. Fourth, the subject is a body that is separate (except in the case of pregnant women) from other human bodies; and the body, and therefore the subject, is closely dependent upon its physical environment. Finally, subjectivity in its common Cartesian sense—and despite the efforts of intellectuals to deconstruct the dichotomy—is opposed to objectivity: the particular or partial view (the view in and for itself) is opposed to some other (if only hypothetical) universal view (the view from nowhere and for no one, the view that contains all possible perspectives). Furthermore, in writing or self-representation (like autobiography), the *I* is the self-present subject of the sentence as well as the subject "subjected" to the symbolic order of the language in which one is writing—the subject is subject to language, or intersubjectivity (i.e., culture).

Each of these usages of the term will be familiar to readers of cultural and social theory, but as I have been eclectic in my use of that theory in order to regard subjectivity from as many "angles" as possible, I shall specify some of the key considerations and vocabularies informing the book. A major issue in social theory today is the relation of subjects to social structures and systems (e.g., institutions, bodies of knowledge, language). Of course Michel Foucault's work has been significant here, but so has that of many others from very different perspectives. Foucault's rejection of humanistic subjectivity—autonomous creativity, genius, etc.—in favor of "the author function" (social practices differentiating and privileging some discourses above others) opened new avenues for the study of subjectivity as an effect of institutional practices.[6] In his later work, Foucault attempted to distinguish the subjectivity of ancient Hellenic culture from that of our modern period, articulating the difference between a public and aesthetic "care of the self" and a Christian and, later, psychoanalytic cult of the "true self," a self that could only be revealed through an agonized process of self-decipherment: "Christianity substituted the idea of a self which one had to renounce, because clinging to the self was opposed to God's will, for the idea of a self which had to be created as a work of art."[7] Foucault then asked, "But couldn't everyone's life become a work of art? Why should the lamp or the house be an art object, but not our life?" However hollow Foucault's aestheticizing of the self sounds in the late twentieth century—as mere nostalgia for an autonomous community of honorable men or the private luxury of an aesthete's regime of self-regulation in a finely "disciplined" world—it remains a rejection of the bourgeois, Cartesian subjectivity that "could only be revealed."

Yet this later Foucault inspired by an aesthetic care of the self has been less influential than the earlier theorist of modern institutional power. Like Lacan and Althusser, Foucault is best known for locating the sites where individual subjects and institutional power meet and for emphasizing the determinant character of institutional power in the construction of the subject. This post-structural conception of subjectivity claims that the *I*, the apparent seat of consciousness, is not the integral center of thought but a contradictory, discursive category constituted by ideological discourse itself. Hence concepts like "the death of the author" and the "interpellation of the subject" by ideological and repressive apparatuses. The discourses Foucault analyzed represented what Althusser called the Ideological State Apparatuses (ISAs), such as the law, medicine, family, and educational institutions and their bureaucracies.[8] Yet however suggestive such work has been for the subject's constitution in and through representation, reliant as it is upon the discourses of power it has had little to say about (1) how subjects mediate (i.e., transform) those discourses in their everyday lives, or (2) how subjects see themselves to the extent that they are not entirely identified with those institutions. (Possible exceptions are Foucault's superb editions of the "autobiographical" writings of the French peasant Pierre Rivière and the hermaphrodite "Herculine Barbin.")[9] Granting the subject's social embeddedness, an embeddedness most pronounced when one begins to write, one must also grant—at least this study has taught me to grant—the subject's mediation (i.e., transformation) of structures and systems, including systems as large as language or the State. Understanding subjectivity from the bottom rather than the top, without reintroducing an autonomous subject, requires perspectives in addition to Foucault's and Althusser's.

In this sense, I have found "practice" theorists like Raymond Williams, E. P. Thompson, Anthony Giddens, and Pierre Bourdieu more helpful.[10] The practice theorists have reintroduced agency into disciplines preoccupied with systems and structures without abandoning a recognition of the shaping power of social structures or retreating to a methodological individualism. For example, Giddens proposes a "duality of structure" that both constrains and enables agency, saving the reflexive, acting subject, and rejecting accounts that see it merely as a series of moments brought about by the intersection of the dominant signifying structures. With a duality of structure, one can comprehend the relations of dominance and resistance, participation and antagonism, and thereby explain the coappearance with modern social institutions of their reflexive counterparts in social movements: the labor movement in relation to the development of capitalism, ecological movements in relation to industrialization, free speech movements in relation to the control of information, peace movements in relation to militarization, feminism and gay rights in relation to patriarchal heterosexism.[11] Each of these movements showing the reflexivity of modernism has extensive implications for the subjectivity of its members. While concurring with poststructural insights that subjectivities are produced by the social, and are not given, the practice theorists often emphasize a more positive version of the death of the Cartesian subject. Rather than the obliteration of human agency, they often see a liberation into the social, into the possiblities of more participatory social life.

Another related and fruitful approach to subjectivity was what I came to call *material culture* studies; that is, analyses of the relation of physical circumstances to subjectivity. Indispensable here, of course, were Marx and Veblen; but also useful were Mary Douglas and Baron Isherwood's "communications approach to consumption," Donna Haraway's work on the technological "cyborg," and Elaine Scarry's work on the honorable place of artifacts and technology in any consideration of human life and value[12] (see especially Chapter 2). Pursuing the relationship of material culture and subjectivity also led to a consideration of the physical body and subjectivity, a pairing again familiar to readers of current social theory. In this capacity I have found Anglo-American philosophy of mind and personal identity useful, especially Thomas Nagel's questions about "what it is like to be" a thing.[13] Nagel claims that the "objectivity" of physicalists (proponents of the view that mental states are states of the body) can only be a partial description in a world of experiencing subjects, that physicalism alone cannot describe human experience insofar as experience necessarily entails a point of view and raises the question of what it is like to be the thing with that point of view. Since this study is centrally concerned with how subjects see themselves in response to the material and cultural "facts" of their lives, I have found Nagel's challenge to physicalists to attempt something like an empirical phenomenology—an external analysis of subjectivity—highly suggestive.[14]

Ultimately, however, although I am deeply sympathetic to Nagel's critique of physicalism, I believe that his view of "what it is like to be a thing" remains open to the usual criticisms of dualism. Rather than some unique point of view that is difficult if not impossible of access to others and is housed within a physical body, I would emphasize the shared aspect of consciousness or point of view. Again and again in the pages that follow, "the self" is not an autonomous introspectible state—a Cogito or a unique point of view—but is instead dependent upon intersubjectivity, or the intersubjective nature of language and culture. Following

Wittgenstein, Naomi Scheman debunks the religious Cogito and secular empiricism with the logical necessity of a context preceding a "self":

> We can, I think, maintain that our twinges, pangs, and so on are particular events no matter what our social situation, but it does not follow that the same is true for more complex psychological objects, such as emotions, beliefs, motives, and capacities. What we need to know in order to identify *them* is how to group together introspectible states and behavior and how to interpret it all. The question is one of meaning, not just at the level of what to call it, but at the level of there being an "it" at all. And questions of meaning and interpretation cannot be answered in abstraction from a social setting.[15]

Sheman concludes that humans have "emotions, beliefs, abilities and so on only in so far as they are embedded in a social web of interpretation that serves to give meaning to the bare data of inner experience and behavior."

The practical consequences of this view were presented vividly in a work of fiction. Tom Wolfe's *Bonfire of the Vanities* (1988) is the story of the humiliation (or radicalization) of a Wall Street bonds dealer after he inadvertently but fatally injures a black student in the Bronx and becomes a "media event." At one point the narrator explains the protagonist's subjective dissolution like this:

> The Bororo Indians, a tribe who live along the Vermelho River in the Amazon jungles of Brazil, believe that there is no such thing as a private self. The Bororos regard the mind as an open cavity, like a cave or a tunnel or an arcade . . . in which the entire village dwells and the jungle grows. In 1969 José M. R. Delgado, the eminent Spanish brain physiologist, pronounced the Bororos correct. For nearly three millennia, Western philosophers had viewed the self as something unique, something encased inside a person's skull, so to speak. This inner self had to deal with and learn from the outside world, of course, and it might prove incompetent in doing so. Nevertheless, at the core of one's self there was presumed to be something irreducible and inviolate. Not so, said Delgado. "Each person is a transitory composite of materials borrowed from the environment." The important word was *transitory,* and he was talking not about years but about hours. He cited experiments in which healthy college students lying on beds in well-lit but soundproofed chambers, wearing gloves to reduce the sense of touch and translucent goggles to block out specific sights, began to hallucinate *within hours.* Without the entire village, the whole jungle, occupying the cavity, they had no minds left.

He cited no investigations of the opposite case, however. He did not discuss what happens when one's self—or what one takes to be one's self—is not a mere cavity open to the outside world but has suddenly become an amusement park to which everybody, *todo el mundo, tout le monde,* comes scampering, skipping and screaming, nerves a-tingle, loins aflame, ready for anything, all you've got, laughs, tears, moans, giddy thrills, gasps, horrors, whatever, the gorier the merrier. Which is to say, he told us nothing of the mind of a person at the center of a scandal in the last quarter of the twentieth century.[16]

As "Sherman McCoy of the McCoy family and Yale and Park Avenue and Wall Street" moves into prison as a militant "professional defendant" he learns that *"Your self . . .* is *other people,* all the people you're tied to, and it's only a thread" (587). One of the most interesting contrasts in the following pages is, I believe, that between writers who do claim an autonomous introspective "self" and those who do not—a distinction that appears strongly class-based.

Because it would seem to many a necessary component of a study of modern subjectivity, I should say a word about the place of psychoanalysis in this study. I take psychoanalysis as a theory to be the great reflexive critique of liberal dreams of autonomy and progress; its claims for the exigencies of personal histories have been confirmed in particularly intimate ways in some of the cases that follow. Furthermore, language, the medium of self-representation, is here a central category of analysis, and psychoanalysis, especially as used by Lacan, Althusser, and feminist critics, has been essential in describing the subject's social interpellation through language and ideology.[17] After recognizing the importance of personal history and language generally in the constitution of the subject, however, I have not found any one, or any unalterable, structure of coordinates of that constitution, whether penis, "phallus," father, or mother. In general regarding psychoanalysis I have trusted to the lessons of postmodern feminist theory.[18] I have not trusted dichotomies presupposing gender or class warfare and I have been wary of the notion that there are universal modes of human interaction (such as domestic or public, kinship or political). Rather I have tried to uncover the symbolic and social processes in nineteenth- and twentieth-century Britain that made these domains appear "natural." For example, rather than assuming the (middle-class) centrality of familial relations in psychic development, I have looked into the economic or social conditions that make nuclear and nonnuclear kin relations strong and those that make community, peer, or neighborhood ties more important.

As for feminist psychoanalytic critiques of subjectivity per se, following Luce Irigaray's view that all theories of "the Subject" have always been appropriated to the masculine, one of the aims of this study is precisely not to define subjectivity (or women's alleged relegation to the status of objects) through the eyes of Irigaray's "Western philosophical tradition from Plato to Freud," but rather to assume no definition of subjectivity as a general category in analyzing a range of subjectivities: to explore the practical constitution of selves rather than some a priori notion of "the Self." In this I am much closer to Nancy Armstrong's project in *Desire and Domestic Fiction* to provide a history of subjectivity, or more precisely a history of subjectivities, in everyday life rather than a study of some ideal form of subjectivity, either masculine or feminine.[19] That everyday life in this period is inevitably "gendered" and "classed" life means that gender will impact upon this history in a myriad of concrete, but often different, ways.

Value

AESTHETIC VALUE

> In the ethno-poetics and performance of the shaman, my people, the Indians, did not split the artistic from the functional, the sacred from the secular, art from everyday life.
>
> GLORIA ANZALDÚA, *Borderlands: La Frontera*[20]

The South African "security expert" (distinguished from three "literary experts") called upon to determine the subversive content of Nadine Gordimer's *Burger's Daughter* (1980) explained his judgment as follows: "The question regarding literary value is to what extent literary merit can compensate for a negative judgment when taking other considerations into account. On the one hand one can presume that with a good work of literature the writer primarily intended to create literature and merely chose a certain subject and certain sentiments as a medium."[21] Here the "security expert" reduces the writer to "artist," whose "intent" is to "create literature," and thereby disqualifies her as an activist (a reduction consistent with some of Gordimer's published pronouncements on the role of the writer). He simultaneously reduces literature to a disinterested aesthetic: whereas politics and propaganda narrowly take sides, literature is full and many-sided, showing the "free play" of the imagination. The ban on *Burger's Daughter* was lifted when it was proven to be "serious literature"; that is, serious literature allows for multiple interpretations and does not "take sides." Its qualification as "literature" disqualified it as taking an ethical stance toward its subject matter. The remainder of this introduction will first consider the axiology of autonomous aesthetics that underlies the historical reception (or lack of reception) of the texts discussed in the following chapters and then take up the relation of aesthetic value to broader notions of value and the self.

To illustrate the parameters of the aesthetic inquiry I shall use Pierre Bourdieu's polemic against the Kantian ("pure") aesthetic. Accusing the French educational establishment of merely reproducing bourgeois ideology and therefore reproducing the status quo, Bourdieu argued that aesthetic "distinction," or taste, was solely a product of education, family, and the social trajectories of economic class and status (what he calls the "habitus"—in classical rhetoric, one's specific ethical disposition toward the world). Thus he traces the establishment's aesthetic preference for form and style to its distance from economic necessity, and the blue collar taste for content ("realism") and moral or recreative agreeableness to engagement with material conditions.

> Popular taste applies the schemes of the ethos, which pertain in the ordinary circumstances of life, to legitimate works of art, and so performs a systematic reduction of the things of art to the things of life. The very seriousness (or naivety) which this taste invests in fictions and representations demonstrates a contrario that pure taste performs a suspension of "naive" involvement which is one dimension of a "quasi-ludic" relationship with the necessities of the world. Intellectuals could be said to believe in the representation—literature, theatre, painting—more than in the things represented, whereas the people chiefly expect representations and the conventions which govern them to allow them to believe "naively" in the things represented. The pure aesthetic is rooted in an ethic, or rather, an ethos of elective distance from the necessities of the natural and social world, which may take the form of moral agnosticism (visible when ethical transgression becomes an artistic *parti pris*) or of an aestheticism which presents the aesthetic disposition as a universally valid principle and takes the bourgeois denial of the social world to its limit. The detachment of the pure gaze cannot be dissociated from a general disposition towards the world which is the paradoxical product of conditioning by negative economic necessities—a life of ease—that tends to induce an active distance from necessity.[22]

As will be seen shortly in the comparative studies of classic texts and those of working-class autobiographers (and their reception), much of

Bourdieu's complex material analysis will be relevant to cross-class differences of taste, and I shall add gender as another differentiating mechanism. It is important at the outset, however, to understand what is at
stake in a critique of the "pure" aesthetic.

Bourdieu claims that a "pure" reading of Kant's *Critique of Judgment*
(1790) (i.e., a reading of the Third Critique as an autonomous work)
obscures Kant's concealed opposition between high and low culture. I
believe, rather, that Kant and Bourdieu have two distinct notions of
value and that both are of interest to the cultural critic. I shall briefly turn
to Kantian taste and then return to Bourdieu. Kant distinguishes between
three kinds of judgment. The first kind of judgment is objective, or predicated upon an object (the table is brown). The second is subjective, or
predicated upon the subject (the wine is pleasant, it gives me pleasure, I
like it). The third kind of judgment, a judgment of taste, is neither objective nor subjective in this sense. It is not objective because not addressing
a property of an object, and not subjective because it has nothing to do
with any interest I have in it.

> Interest is what we call the liking we connect with the presentation of an
> object's existence. Hence such a liking always refers at once to our power
> of desire, either as the basis that determines it, or at any rate as necessarily
> connected with that determining basis. But if the question is whether
> something is beautiful, what we want to know is not whether we or any-
> one cares, or so much as might care, in any way, about the thing's exist-
> ence, but rather how we judge it in our mere contemplation of it (intuition
> or reflection). . . . We can easily see that, in order for me to say that an
> object is *beautiful,* and to prove that I have taste, what matters is what I
> do with this presentation within myself, and not the [respect] in which I
> depend on the object's existence. Everyone has to admit that if a judgment
> about beauty is mingled with the least interest then it is very partial and
> not a pure judgment of taste. In order to play the judge in matters
> of taste, we must not be in the least biased in favor of the thing's exis-
> tence but must be wholly indifferent about it. (Part I, Division I, Book I,
> Sec. 1)[23]

The judgment of taste is subjective in that it expresses an experience I
have alone and it is objective in that everyone will agree with it *as if* it
were about an objective property. Because the experience itself is independent of the demand that everyone agree with it, Kant provides the
phenomenology of it in Book I, "The Analytic." This experience is the
"free play" of imagination synthesizing perception and concept.

There are two aspects of cognition for Kant: perception and thought (concepts). When we recognize something *as* something we cognize, fitting our perceptions to our store of concepts. In the case of a beautiful object, the concept does not fully exhaust the perception: the beautiful object or work is *inexhaustible.* The experience of the beautiful, then, the feeling of disinterested pleasure, is the pleasure of *free play.* The imagination is the synthesis of new perception not entirely contained by old concepts or, put differently, "X is beautiful" denotes the harmonious free play of imagination and cognition when one has been confronted with an object.

Kant's view may be illustrated by a Victorian example. Following Winckelmann and Hegel, many nineteenth-century writers on aesthetics, from Benjamin Robert Haydon on the Elgin marbles in 1808 (Haydon's *Autobiography* published in 1853) to Walter Pater in *The Renaissance* (1873; 1893), remarked upon the aesthetic effects of Greek sculpture, which they often attributed to its lack of cognitive and affective content— its "pure" form. Unaware that the colored pigmentation of the eyes had eroded through time, aesthetes like Pater wrote eloquently of the vacant gaze of colorless eyeball, which no cognitive mapping could constrain and which engendered the free play of the spectator's imagination: "In proportion as the art of sculpture ceased to be merely decorative, and subordinate to architecture, it threw itself upon pure form. It renounces the power of expression by lower or heightened tones. In it, no member of the human form is more significant than the rest. . . . The eyes are wide and directionless, without pupil, not fixing anything with their gaze, nor riveting the brain to any special external object."[24]

The free play of imagination that occurs when one is confronted with an object that holds for one no "interest" and that one's concepts cannot fully exhaust may well be the nature of many people's aesthetic experience—many people do respond with recognition to such descriptions. Yet in what is for many a less persuasive section of the Third Critique, called the *Dialectic,* Kant explains why it is imperative that judgments of taste command *universal* assent, and he thereby brings the phenomenological experience in line with his larger, logical, project. We bestow upon our subjective experience the universality that accords it objective status by establishing the beautiful as the symbol of the morally good. In what is perhaps the most famous sentence in aesthetic philosophy, Kant maintains just this:

> Now I maintain that the beautiful is the symbol of the morally good; and
> only because we refer the beautiful to the morally good (we all do so nat-

urally and require all others also to do so, as a duty) does our liking for it
include a claim to everyone else's assent, while the mind is also conscious
of being ennobled, by this [reference], above a mere receptivity for pleasure derived from sense impressions, and it assesses the value of other
people too on the basis of [their having] a similar maxim in their power
of judgment. (Part I, Bk. II, Div. II, sec. 59)[25]

Moreover, the judgment of taste stands in the same relation to empirical
judgment that practical reason governed by the Categorical Imperative
bears to desire: the relationship of freedom, or what ought to be, to necessity, or what is. Thus for Kant, who provided a critique (an examination
of the scope and limits) of our power to cognize beauty, the beautiful is
the symbol of freedom. When the beautiful ceases to be referred to the
moral good, it ceases to command universal assent.

For Bourdieu, who provided a sociology of the institution of the
artworld, the artworld and the experience of the beautiful have become
decoupled so that taste has come to be institutionalized in a manner that
excludes and oppresses rather than the symbol of a freedom that can be
(in Kant, ought to be) shared universally. That is, the "disinterested" aesthetic no longer refers to freedom but is reduced to a class-based preference for form. Like other pragmatists, Bourdieu denies that aesthetic
value is a property of objects, subjects, or psychological processes
between subjects and objects, but is rather a product of the dynamics of
sociocultural systems. Because different acquired tastes tend to be experienced as internal and natural, they often function to legitimate social
distinctions (e.g., "disinterested" highbrow or "interested" lowbrow).
The second significant difference between Kant and Bourdieu is, of
course, Kant's idealism: for Kant, value consists in freedom from necessity, symbolized by the free play of the imagination. From the same tradition as Kant came the formal or procedural freedoms of liberal thought
(freedom of speech, of dissent, right to vote, etc.). For Bourdieu, value
consists in material satisfaction insofar as value is the Good, and is
merely an effect of institutional power insofar as value is a social practice.
From the tradition informing Bourdieu came the substantive freedoms
of socialism or communitarianism (freedom from starvation, from
homelessness, etc.) In the rest of this section I shall consider the "liberal"
conceptions of the self and its freedoms that have been fundamental to
our aesthetic judgments of modern imaginative literature. The purpose
of such a critique is to indicate what we have excluded by such an
aesthetic.

VALUE AND THE SELF

"The self is hateful. You cover it up, Mitton, but that does not mean that you take it away. So you are still hateful."

"Not so, because by being obliging to everyone as we are, we give them no more cause to hate us."

"True enough if the only hateful thing about the self were the unpleasantness it caused us."

"But if I hate it because it is unjust that it should make itself the centre of everything, I shall go on hating it."

"In a word the self has two characteristics. It is unjust in itself for making itself centre of everything: it is a nuisance to others in that it tries to subjugate them, for each self is the enemy of all the others and would like to tyrannize them. You take away the nuisance, but not the injustice.

"And thus, you do not make it pleasing to those who hate it for being unjust; you only make it pleasing to unjust people who no longer see it as their enemy. Thus you remain unjust, and can only please unjust people."[26]

PASCAL, Pensées (1662)

[The President] used the hateful epithet to describe the Democrats no fewer than 22 times.... [The Vice President] described his opponent as "a liberal wimp with a liberated libido who would liberally dismantle our defenses so that liberalizing Communist liberalizers could liberate Liberia and set up a libertine state on our shores." . . .

Dukakis was not to be denied. While Bush called for the reduction of capital gains taxes on unearned income, Dukakis demanded their elimination. "Why should our citizens be required to pay income taxes on income they didn't earn?" he cried.

When Bush proposed a graduated income tax ranging from three percent in the highest brackets up to fifty percent in the lowest, Dukakis came out for a Child Labor Act that would promote child labor "in order to get our kids off the streets."

. . . By November Dukakis looked like the most illiberal candidate in history and thus a shoo-in. It was then that Bush unleashed his ultimate weapon: a 1977 photograph of Dukakis extending a 25-cent piece to a scruffy mendicant lounging on a corner. . . . It was obvious that the election would be a mere formality, for everyone agreed that the Dem-

ocratic candidate was unfit to be president now that he had
shown what he was made of—everyone, that is, but one ignorant little boy.

"If it means helping poor people and caring about the
unfortunate," the ignorant boy asked his mother, "what's so
wrong with being a lib . . .?"

But before he could finish his question, his mother washed
his mouth out with soap, spanked his bottom and sent him to
bed.

ARTHUR HOPPE, "The Dread L Word,"
San Francisco Chronicle, August 17, 1988

In this section I will argue that the modern aesthetic has arisen, and
shares the assumptions of a particular "human nature," with liberal political theory. The terms *liberal* and *liberalism,* however, are clearly in transition at present, and are used more widely and in more mutually contradictory senses than was even *individualism* in the nineteenth
century.[27] It will thus be useful to survey briefly the contemporary usages.
The range is apparently from intellectually serious positions that have
little to do with each other, such as Adam Smith's free market economics
and J. S. Mill's social tolerances and procedural freedoms of speech, dissent, and vote (see Chapter 6), to intellectually unserious positions such
as the president's usage of the term to mean communists, perverts, and
baby-killers. Many of my students call themselves liberals meaning that
they advocate the "classic free-market liberalism of Adam Smith." These
often also espouse the notion of a "good" liberalism as a liberal democracy (as opposed to some totalitarian State). Most of my colleagues in the
humanities call themselves liberals meaning that they support the free
market, procedural freedoms, and a degree of human rights and social
welfare. Great liberal philosophers like John Rawls or Ronald Dworkin
intend by "liberal" social tolerance, procedural freedoms, and social justice that may extend to socialism[28]; and the Critical Legal Studies Movement (to be discussed in detail later) intends a certain conception of
human nature as rational, individualist, and autonomous. Clearly—and
it is very important in qualifying the critique of liberal procedural rights
that follows—all those liberals, like Joseph Raz, for whom autonomy,
not rights, is the central demand of the doctrine of liberalism, *and* for
whom the promotion of the conditions of autonomy for all its citizens is
a duty of the State, will be exempt from many of the criticisms that follow.[29] For Raz, who wants to defend liberalism from the kinds of charges
I take up in the following pages, liberalism's effort consists of trying to
expand the domain in which agents "create their own lives through pro-

gressive choices from a multiplicity of valuable options" (265). To the extent that Raz and others like him stress the collective aspect, and material conditions, of liberal rights, they are not subject to the criticisms of procedural rights and autonomy that follow.

Presumably all liberals (left, right, and center) who identify with the term support social and religious tolerance and the procedural freedoms of speech, dissent, and the franchise. Accepting this shared assumption, we can proceed to map a continuum of liberalism that would have made sense to the Victorians as well as to the ignorant boy in Hoppe's satire: a continuum plotting the degree of concern for social justice for even the least advantaged members of a society. On such a continuum, left liberalism would represent a primary concern for social justice (called *socialism*) on the one pole and right liberalism would represent no concern for social justice (called *free-market capitalism*) on the other pole. In between, centrist liberals balance free-market economics with concern for those who get lost along the way in the form of modest welfare programs, though often only so long as taxes do not get raised. It is significant that centrist liberals conceive of social justice for the least advantaged in terms of the absence of pain, while left liberals conceive of it as equal opportunity to exploit to the fullest the procedural freedoms, and right liberals conceive of it as the successful having the unqualified rights to grow more successful.

What is clear in this mapping is that the shared assumption of support for "equality" defined as merely theoretical access to the procedural freedoms is by and large enough to satisfy the sense of social justice of both centrist and right liberals . Here is where the conception of human nature that I will argue has been central to post-Enlightenment aesthetics enters with its privileging of rationality, individualism, and autonomy from material circumstances. The feminist philosopher Alison Jaggar discusses the intellectual foundations of liberal theory; I quote at length because the concepts of normative dualism, abstract individualism, and liberal rationality will recur frequently in ensuing chapters.

> Liberal political theory is grounded on the conception of human beings as essentially rational agents, where rationality is a "mental" capacity. The classical liberal theorists were metaphysical dualists; that is to say, they believed that the human mind and the human body represented two quite different kinds of beings, each irreducible to and connected only contingently with the other. Contemporary liberal theorists are not committed explicitly to metaphysical dualism, but their political theory rests on a

kind of dualism that I call "normative dualism." Normative dualism is the belief that what is especially valuable about human beings is a particular "mental" capacity, the capacity for rationality.[30]

Hence their concern, one might interject here, with formal or procedural, rather than substantive or material, equality. Jaggar continues:

> A second feature of the liberal conception of rationality is that it is conceived as a property of individuals rather than of groups. Like normative dualism, this view of rationality is connected with an underlying metaphysical assumption. The assumption in this case is that human individuals are ontologically prior to society; in other words, human individuals are the basic constituents out of which social groups are composed. Logically if not empirically, human individuals could exist outside a social context; their essential characteristics, their needs and interests, their capacities and desires, are given independently of their social context and are not created or even fundamentally altered by that context. This metaphysical assumption is sometimes called abstract individualism because it conceives of human individuals in abstraction from any social circumstances. It is easy to see how abstract individualism influences the liberal conception of rationality as an essential characteristic of human individuals. It does not force liberals to deny that the presence of a social group may be an empirical prerequisite for an individual's learning to exercise her or his capacity to reason, insofar as one's ability to reason is inferred primarily from one's ability to speak and speech develops only in groups. But the metaphysical assumption of human beings as individual atoms which in principle are separable from social molecules does discourage liberals from conceiving of rationality as constituted by or defined by group norms, let alone as being a property of social structure. Instead, they identify as rational only individuals who are able to act in quite specific ways.

Jaggar goes on to describe liberal rationality as the assumption that each human individual will be motivated by the desire to secure as large an individual share as possible of the available resources, or, in Utilitarian terms, to maximize her or his individual self-interest. Jaggar calls this tendency of liberal theory—often, admittedly, qualified in moral philosophers like Locke and Kant—the *assumption of universal egoism*. Feminists on the left in the United States and Britain, and Critical Legal Scholars, have criticized liberal theory for its political skepticism, solipsism, a priori individualism, and its pessimistic view of rationality (see Chapter 1). Here I shall illustrate the ideological consequences of liberal theory for subjectivity with one of the early promoters of liberal theory and one of its Victorian victims. I have chosen Locke as an example of the former because in him the implications of normative dualism, abstract individualism, and liberal rationality for a class society divided between mental and manual labour are very clear. The fact that Locke wrote prior to industrialization only shows the *problem* of his undisputed influence on subsequent liberal theory in Britain and the United States.

In Locke's *An Essay Concerning Human Understanding* (1689), the *self* is "that which is conscious of pleasure and pain" (Bk. 2, Ch. 27, Sec. 26).[31] This consciousness of pleasure and pain is housed within a body that entirely circumscribes the self and its interests: "In this personal identity [i.e., the self, not the body] is founded all the right and justice of reward and punishment; happiness and misery being that for which everyone is concerned for *himself,* and not mattering what becomes of any substance, not joined to, or affected with that consciousness" (Bk. 2, Ch. 27, Sec. 18). Here Locke comes close to what Jaggar calls "universal egoism," or "rational" self-interest. In his *Second Treatise of Government* (1690), Locke defines the body as the original property ("Though the earth and all inferior creatures be common to all men, yet every man has a property in his own person" [Ch. 5, Sec. 27, p.15]), which is in turn defined by its capacity to labor in the service of the mind's desires for happiness ("the labor of his body and the work of his hands, we may say, are properly his" [Ch. 5, Sec. 27, p.15]).[32] Thus the self is identified with the mind that desires and that owns the body that labors. Just as the self is prior to the body that works for its needs (i.e., the mind commands the body), so, for Locke, the State, the collective self, commands the consent of the bodies within its domain: ". . . for it would be a direct contradiction for any one to enter into society with others for the securing and regulating of property, and yet to suppose his land, whose property is to be regulated by the laws of the society should be exempt from the jurisdiction of that government. . . . They become, both of them person and possession, subject to the government and dominions of that commonwealth" (Ch. 8, Sec. 120, p.62): "When any number of men have so consented to make one community or government, they are thereby presently incorporated and make one body politic" (Ch. 8, Sec. 95, p. 49).

The liberal state's concern with procedural rather than substantive rights derives from such definitions of the body as merely the instrument and accessory of the self defined solely by its consciousness. The liberal state defends the desires and rights of the mind (free speech, right to vote, right to dissent, etc.) rather than those of the body (freedom from star-vation, sickness, cold, homelessness) and thus maintains the original devaluation of the body implicit in normative dualism. The conse-quences of liberalism's ignoring substantive differences in material situ-ation to the way people see themselves in liberal society are evident. As Jaggar says, liberal rationality is normative as well as descriptive. Individ-uals who fail to maximize their self-interest are regarded as deficient in fulfilling their uniquely human potential. This is Locke's view of laborers, who were not permitted material conditions conducive to Reason. Here Locke insists upon normative dualism, the capacity to be "free" of embodiment:

> [Laborers'] lives are worn out only in the provisions for living. These men's opportunity of knowledge and inquiry are commonly as narrow as their fortunes; and their understandings are but little instructed, when all their whole time and pains is laid out to still the croaking of their own bellies, or the cries of their children. It is not to be expected that a man who drudges on all his life in a laborious trade should be more knowing in the variety of things done in the world than a packhorse, who is driven constantly forwards and backwards in a narrow lane and dirty road, only to market, should be skilled in the geography of the country. (*Essay* 4, 20, 2)

Laborers under classical liberal political theory become the body of the state, directed by the possessors of wealth (freedom from necessity) who are capable of achieving distance from, and control over, that body.

Henry Mayhew's *Morning Chronicle* interviews with London laborers cannot unproblematically be called "autobiographies," but they do give a sense of what it was like to live on the physical side of Locke's dualism (see Chapter 2). Mayhew records the testimony of a latter-day Adam Bede in the metropolis: "We are used for all the world like cab or omni-bus horses. Directly they've had all the work out of us we are turned off, and I am sure after my day's work is over, my feelings must be very much the same as one of the London cab horses. As for Sunday, it is *literally* a day of rest with us, for the greater part of us lays a bed all day, and even that will hardly take the aches and pains out of our bones and muscles. When I'm done and flung by, of course I must starve."[33] In the next inter-view a seventy-nine-year-old carpenter explained that men delayed wear-ing spectacles as long as possible, for glasses signified that a man was too old to work and ensured that he would be fired. The very symbol of the thinker and reader in the upper classes signified destitution for workers.

The best that they could say was that they, like God, were builders rather than thinkers, and that they too required a Sabbath for rest.

Perhaps most important, because closest to my own objectives in attempting a literary method for exploring human possibilities in participation and antagonism, is the critique of liberalism by the legal theorists who have come to be known as the Critical Legal Studies Movement (CLS).[34] The fundamental problematic of liberalism as CLS defined it is the relation of atomistic individuals in pursuit of self-interest to the state or society, created as a social contract. In its rejection of liberalism, CLS commenced a re-examination of the subject's relation to the state in the service of radical social change. It first attacked the dualistic foundations of liberal thought (distinctions between state of nature and social order, subjective and objective, private and public) in order to propose that we deal with the problem of human association, or autonomy and relatedness, in other ways. For example, Robin West, both a sympathizer with, and a feminist critic of, CLS, has argued (following the work of Nancy Chodorow, Carol Gilligan, and Dorothy Dinnerstein on the extensive implications for theories of autonomy and relatedness of the fact that women bear primary responsibility for the nurturing of children) that the autonomous individual of liberal legalism—individuals who create value by satiating their subjective desires with choices subject to consensual constraint—is an essentially *male* creation of political theory.[35] Positing that women, for both biological and cultural reasons, have been at least as other-regarding as self-regarding and that the constraints upon their co-called choices may not necessarily have been attributable to consent, West observes that the liberal theory of the human being with its apparatus of liberal (procedural) rights may definitionally exclude half of humankind. Liberal legalism posits one kind of subjectivity—of human beings who maximize their individual self-interests limited by rights arrived at consensually—to the exclusion of women, for whom connectedness to others is prior to individuation. Thus other-regarding, women provide for others' needs at least as much as their own. West further critiques liberalism's fetishizing of "consent," arguing that if a being (like a woman) is culturally constructed to "give," its generosity cannot be construed as consent. In general, CLS saw no distinctive mode of legal reasoning that could be contrasted with political dialogue, and it accordingly asserted that law *was* politics. It rejected liberalism for entailing limited possibilities for human association and social transformation, insisting rather that human possibility was a product of history rather than nature and that it could therefore be changed.

CLS's positive plan for social transformation came largely in two distinctive forms, but they shared a common basis in their claims of provisionality. Roberto Unger analyzed the nature of the self's relation to others in *Knowledge and Politics* (1976) and *Passion: An Essay on Personality* (1984) and then the nature of the society in which the self could flourish in *The Critical Legal Studies Movement* (1986) and his massive three-volume *Politics* (1987).[36] He proposed four kinds of rights for collective self-government in the new social organization that would protect society from rigidifying into the kind of static hierarchy that has come, according to CLS, to be protected by law. In proposing a rather determinate social form (based upon immunity, destabilization, market, and solidarity rights), however, Unger has repeatedly insisted upon its provisional character, its ability to change as its subjects—he calls them "superliberal" subjects—would change under the new regime. Another CLS theorist, Duncan Kennedy, has a more postmodern vision of the law. Recovering it for everyday life, Kennedy's "experimental" law practice would look more like legal "alternatives," storefront lawshops, and community action projects.[37]

In sympathy with CLS's critique of the liberal conception of human nature (even if it does not always credit liberalism's kinder, gentler advocates), I want in this study to provide alternative images of possible subjects in many situations of autonomy and relatedness, antagonism and participation. This returns us to cultural studies. Like CLS, *cultural studies* is more an "attitude" than an organic movement; but also like CLS, it includes some common practices loosely shared by its proponents. Like CLS's assertion that law is politics, cultural studies considers that the production of the literary canon, the consumption, or meaning, of imaginative literature, and the status of the literary community's cultural capital are within the realm of politics. Like CLS's *trashing* (a technical term for what cultural critics call *deconstruction*), cultural studies has deconstructed such knots of ideology in literature as mind/body, subjective/objective, self/other, public/private, and extraordinary/everyday. Like CLS, it has considered that deconstruction that merely works on the status quo is ultimately a conservative practice. Like CLS's positive program to transform the law by reintegrating it with everyday life, cultural studies wants to reintegrate the extraordinary (called *Art* or *Literature*) with the ordinary (called *popular culture*). Like CLS's critique of the liberal subject, cultural studies reevaluates subjectivity, situating the "literary subject" in relation to other past, present, and even future forms as a product of culture rather than nature. Like CLS's assault on hierarchy, cultural studies replaces Culture with a capital "C" as an elite cultural capital with a pluralistic, diverse conception of cultures. And like CLS's utopian goals, it finally wants to understand the place of aesthetics in ethics and politics. For example, another feminist theorist of CLS, Drusilla Cornell, has suggested that the moment of ethical commitment may be aesthetic in orientation, demanding not only the capacity for judgment but also the ability to dream of what-is-not-yet. For Cornell, the ethical cannot be reduced to the aesthetic, but neither can it do without the aesthetic. Elsewhere, following Derrida and Adorno, she calls this collaborative process of the ethical and aesthetic the dream of relations beyond indifference and domination.[38]

In another example of the simultaneously critical and utopian approach to art, Unger proposes a rapprochement of the extraordinary or art and the everyday. He urges us to transform the modern realms of private life and ideals—Art, Romantic love, Religion—from their mystifications under current conditions into tools for the transformation of ordinary life, so that imaginative literature, for example, would not be the realm of artistic alienation (say no to society) and sublimation (a dream of freedom, autonomy, personality), but rather a window upon possibilities of other social relations:

> The extraordinary representation of the ideal in art, religion, and love has a two-faced significance for everyday life. On the one hand, it can offer the self temporary refuge. In this sense, the extraordinary is a mystification, the aroma that sweetens the air of the established order. Its very availability makes the absence of the ideal from everyday life seem tolerable and even necessary. Because the sacred, art, and love are separated out from banal events, everything in the ordinary world can become all the more relentlessly profane, prosaic, and self-regarding.
>
> Nonetheless, the extraordinary also makes it possible to grasp the ideal, and to contrast it with one's ordinary experience of the world. In this sense, the extraordinary is the starting point for the critique and transformation of social life. It poses the task of actualizing in the world of commonplace things and situations what has already been encountered as a divine liberation from the everyday. . . . In the course of this actualization both the extraordinary and the everyday must be changed. The final and most important change would be the disappearance of the distinction between them.[39]

Of course, unlike legal critics, cultural critics have no such elevated notions of literature. By studying a wide range of Victorian autobiography across social class and gender, I came to understand *precisely in contrast to other subjectivities*—a contrario, as Bourdieu would say—what I call the *literary subject:* a mixture of introspective self-consciousness, middle-class familialism and genderization, and liberal autonomy. The modern literary subject assumed individual creativity, autonomy, and freedom to create value by satiating its subjective desires as a right; it considered self-reflection as problem-solving, and thus valued reading and writing; and it developed in a progressive narrative of self in gendered familial relations and increasing material well-being. This was the self of Victorian literature as it was studied in the academy. Subjects who did not assume creativity, autonomy, and freedom; who expressed no self-consciousness; who did not express themselves in individuated voices with subjective desires; who were regardless of family relations; and who narrated no development or progress or plot never appeared in literature courses. In short, what appeared was private individuals and families in pursuit of private gain for whom society was generally an obstacle to be surmounted. The dominant political ideology in the West for the past four centuries has held that the especially valuable thing about human beings is their mental capacity and that this capacity is a property of individuals rather than groups; that rational behavior is commensurate with the maximization of individual utility; and that essential human characteristics are properties of individuals independent of their material conditions and social environment. It is therefore hardly surprising that what has been saved from everyday language as Literature also participated in this ideology. This is to say that Art is not an uncontaminated locus of the Ideal.

Yet if one guards against the sublimation of literature, one can begin Unger's project of reintegrating art and the ordinary, breaking down the distinction between the ideal and the everyday—with the end, of course, to make the everyday more ideal. As legal critic Robert Gordon has said, predicting the assimilation of CLS into respectable law schools, when CLS has deconstructed liberal legal theory, legal critics can begin to decode the vernacular, giving us accounts of how law has been imbricated in and helped to structure the most routine practices of daily life.[40] This decoding of the vernacular, or locating the law in the discourses of everyday life, rather than the elevating of literature, is where legal critics and cultural critics will meet with most promise in the future.

In the decodings included in the following chapters, I employ Unger's continuum of personality. Rejecting a dualism of fact and value, reason and passion, Unger has developed a moral idyll of the relation of the self to others. He sees the generative polarities of the passions, the source of "personality," as the two poles of longing for others and fear of others. Personality can be mapped upon a continuum in which fear and antagonism on one pole—call it the right—are contained by fixed hierarchical relations that lead to a condition of stable, if uncreative, social relations. Trust and participation, on the left pole, represent the vulnerability and risk of nonhierarchical social relations. The life of the passions, or personality, may be seen in the way women and men participate in or resist Unger's "moral idyll," which rejects the pole of fixed relations for the pole of risk and vulnerability, for a world of encounters in countless combinations of longing and fear. Often, in reading Victorian autobiography, I have found it useful to adapt Unger's continuum of personality to discourse, locating a text between the poles of discursive participation and antagonism with other cultural narratives including, but by no means limited to, the "master" or culturally dominant narratives mentioned earlier.

Unger has been rightly criticized for his superliberalism, or his romantic view of the self's possibilities, and for his communitarianism, or his romantic view of the groups.[41] My point in using his work here has been that although cultural critics, like CLS, can no longer take subjectivity as uniform or universal, the continuum of personality from fear to trust, from autonomy to relatedness, from antagonism to participation, can be adapted in terms of discourse to clarify the historical and intersubjective constitution of subjectivities.

The ensuing chapters explore subjectivity and value through analyses of autobiographical writings. Chapter 1 illustrates with detailed examples how antagonistic and participatory cultural narratives shape the lives and autobiographies of working people. Taking up the critique of Cartesian dualism and liberalism's abstract individualism, Chapter 2 explores the consequences to our understanding of subjectivity and value of a consideration of the body and its material context through the writings of pregnant working women, the upper-class nurse and reformer Florence Nightingale, and Henry Mayhew's interviews with male and female London laborers at midcentury. What is striking about the "mind" or personality is not its uniqueness or autonomy, but is rather its profound dependence upon intersubjectively shared meanings and its vulnerability to the deprivations of the body. Using fictional and nonfictional representations of the poor by middle-class writers, Chapter 3 examines the perpetuation of bourgeois subjectivity and values through time and shows why we ought to read the poor's own self-representation. The contrast between the reformist sociologists, with their obsession with numbers, and the canonical novelists, with their obsession with individual character that led to stereotyping and tokenism, is instructive concerning the limits of the literary imagination in furthering human solidarity. Chapter 3 also specifies the kinds of representation working-class writers labored under when they attempted their own self-representation. Chapter 4 is entirely devoted to the diverse and heterogeneous autobiographical writing of self-identified members of Britain's working classes, both women and men. Its positive goal is to indicate the variety of forms and rhetorical functions of working-class autobiography, and its critical goal is to indicate the ways in which working-class autobiography alters the genre of autobiography as it has been conceived in literary studies and indeed alters our notions of subjectivity itself. Using public and boarding school memoirs, Chapter 5 explores the making of middle-class identities through the institutions of school and family and begins to elaborate the particular kind of subjectivity that came to be identified with—the particular "self" claimed by—imaginative writers. It contrasts this "literary subjectivity" with alternative male and female participatory or collective forms of consciousness. Chapter 6 situates some of the period's classics in terms of this literary subjectivity that arose in opposition to Church, family, and school or State. It then explores "other possibilities" for subjectivity and value as represented in the autobiographical writings of Ruskin, Mill, Darwin, Huxley, and Webb—writers who resisted the characteristic features of literary subjectivity for more co-operative social visions. I conclude with a brief summary and reflection upon subjectivities in the 1990s.

1.

Situating Subjectivities

A comparative study of Victorian autobiography across social class and gender will situate *precisely in contrast to other subjectivities* what I call the *modern literary subject:* a mixture of introspective self-reflexivity, middle-class familialism and genderization, and liberal autonomy. In the first section of this chapter I shall propose a literary method for exploring other possibilities of autonomy and relatedness, or participation and antagonism, and redefine autobiographies as rhetorical projects embedded in concrete material situations. Next, using several texts by working-class writers, I shall explore some articulations of participation and antagonism to illustrate the significance of discourse and ideology, or broad cultural "narratives," in the way people interpret their lives.

Rhetorical Projects in Participation and Antagonism

Since the nineteenth century, professional writers and literary critics have attempted generic definitions of autobiography, encouraging readers to take some forms of self-representation as proper autobiography and others as life, perhaps, but not Art. Such determinations were concurrent with developments in literary professionalism. Despite the marketing developments of 1840–1880 that resulted in the institutionalizing of authorship—for example, specialist readers at publishing houses, literary agents, author's royalties, the Society of Authors, and so forth—literary hegemony, or a poweful literary bloc that prevented or limited "Other" discursive blocs, did not operate by way of the institutional infrastructure, rules, and procedures of the ancient professions of law, medicine, and clergy. By (or through developments in) the nineteenth century, those ancient professions effectively exercised monopolies (through professional associations and a "service" ethos justifying collegial control and autonomy from the market) over each profession's cognitive base (knowledge and techniques) and institutional training and licensing. The fruits of professionalization included a security and respectability that differentiated professionals from other members of society.[1]

From the second half of the eighteenth century, when the democratic revolution combined with the effects of printing, writers had attempted to "commodify" literary talent in the same way. In his *Essay on the Manners and Genius of the Literary Character* (1795), Isaac Disraeli makes the literary character independent of local or historical environment, locating the writer's special commodity in his unique psychology.[2] After Disraeli, the so-called Romantic poets, with their unconsciously commodifed image of the poet, as in Wordsworth's Preface to the second edition of the *Lyrical Ballads* in 1802, aimed at privileged professional status without the institutional apparatus of the learned professions. In *The Prelude* (1805; 1850), subtitled *Growth of a Poet's Mind,* Wordsworth tentatively specified the meticulous—and idiosyncratic—training program of the poetic sensibility, to be legitimated with great bravura in Shelley's poets in "A Defense of Poetry" (1821; 1840)—"the unacknowledged legislators of the world." Mary Jean Corbett has argued that with the sublimation of the poet the "literary character" sought self-determined valuation rather than subordination to the market; recognition of literature as a specialized and special service offered by the possessor of poetic knowledge for the edification of others; and a measure of social independence and economic security. Like Disraeli, the Romantics felt the need to distinguish "true artists" from the more populous tribe of scribbling tradespeople.[3]

With the exception of Keats, who died young enough to truncate his agonistic relations with a "free market" that granted the poetic "gift" of the son of a stablekeeper no special privilege, the Romantic poets were of sufficient means to enjoy the homely privileges of the gentry amateur. In 1802, eighty percent of the English population lived in villages and farms; by 1851 half the population was urban, and by 1901 eighty percent lived in towns.[4] Within Victorian bourgeois ideology specialized knowledge and services came to be seen as within the public sphere. The person who "worked" at "home," within the private sphere, was either payed very little, as in working-class women's "sweated" homework, or nothing, as in middle-class women's household management. This contradiction for the literary men who worked at home contributed to their fear of "effeminization" within a society that conflated "public" with masculine for the middle class and differentiated this competitive market-place from the private "feminine" space of the home.

Dickens's work of what is called *autobiographical fiction, The Personal History and Experience of David Copperfield* (1850), did for the middle-class novelist what Wordsworth had done for the poet, and more: it introduced the professional author to an extended market—Dickens was the most popular writer of the nineteenth century—and reclaimed and colonized the home as *his* domain. Dickens's competitive product, a "critical" reflective sensibility ("Nature and accident had made me an author," writes David in Chapter 48, entitled "Domestic"), was commodified in *David Copperfield* as *the* autobiography of the self-made author: it showed the buying public who the man writing "really" was.

Yet in contributing to the ideological distinction between mental and manual labor (David vs. the Peggotty family) that caused problems for working-class subjectivity in ways that I shall specify, Dickens also contributed to the division of labor along lines of gender. He showed that behind every David Copperfield writing at home, there was an Agnes Wickfield, a perfect household manager, for whom homemaking was as effortless as writing was for David.[5] David's "progress" to worldly success follows a sequence of relationships with unsuitable women, until child-like and incompetent mother and first wife, vulgar nurse, excessively independent aunt, and flirtatious, class-aspiring Little Emily are supplanted by the "good angel" Agnes, who even as a child is introduced as "a little housekeeper" with "a little basket-trifle hanging at her side, with keys in it."[6] Agnes Wickfield Copperfield is the prototypical wife who cares for the material needs of the writer and who in later lives would type the manuscripts. Moreover, the writer David was to be distinguished from lesser "hack" writers like Mr. Micawber (whose wife is disorganized and whose imprudently large family is banished to Australia); Mr. Dick (the "blocked" hysteric who lives with the "divorced" and sterile aunt); and Uriah Heep (the sweaty-palmed charity-school lad who had presumed to compete with David for Agnes). Dickens launched *David Copperfield* with his new periodical *Household Words,* whose very title conflated the themes of the novel, domesticity and writing.[7]

A vast cultural production relegating women to household management while "authors" wrote contributed to the difficulties of middle-class women aspiring to literary careers. As sociologist of literature Terry Lovell points out in *Consuming Fiction,* women comprised two-thirds of the number of publishing novelists during the eighteenth century, when the trade was both low status and low paying. By the 1840s the social status of novelists had risen, but women comprised only twenty percent.[8] Increasingly, men and professionals, especially professional men, worked in the abstract realm of mental labor, and women and workers, especially women workers, worked in the immediate, concrete material. Agnes, as it were, types the manuscripts of David's *oeuvre*. Women, like workers, mediate for men between conceptual action and its concrete forms: "lady typewriters" (as late-Victorians called them, conflating the women with their machines) reproduced men's ideas; Beatrice Webb's "social investigators" walked door to door collecting data for male analysts; Florence Nightingale's nurses made doctors' prescriptions into medicine and administered it to the stricken; and working-class cooks and cleaners cleaned and cared for the domus. That it should be any other way seemed funny in Britain even in the 1960s. One of Monty Python's most popular skits represents a convocation of charladies discussing the views of J.-P. Sartre, whose wife is also a charlady.

Of course the literary character was not restricted to novelists. In the celebrated Victorian autobiographies, having a woman at home is necessary to the self-conception of authorial men (see Chapter 6). In John Stuart Mill's *Autobiography* (1873), the great radical philosopher retires to Avignon (to get sufficient distance and perspective upon English society) with his stepdaughter Helen Taylor as secretary. In John Ruskin's *Praeterita* (1885–1889), the social critic retires to Brantwood with "Joanie" Severn and calls his last chapter, before madness silenced him forever, "Joanna's Care." Charles Darwin's obliging wife and family enabled the scientist to withdraw for the last forty years of his life from bothersome social engagements (that made him ill, he says) into secluded work and domesticity at Down (*Autobiography,* 1887).

In her edition of his *Autobiography,* Darwin's granddaughter Nora Barlow includes some notes Darwin scribbled in two columns as he deliberated whether or not to marry. On the plus side, the advantages of marriage, he listed "constant companion, (friend in old age), who will feel interested in one, object to be beloved and played with—better than a dog anyhow—Home, and someone to take care of house. . . . Imagine living all one's day solitarily in smoky dirty London House.—Only picture to yourself a nice soft wife on a sofa with good fire, and books and music perhaps." On the negative, "Not MARRY" side, he listed, "Perhaps my wife won't like London; then the sentence is banishment and degradation with indolent idle fool" and "I never should know French,— or see the Continent,—or go to America, or go up in a Balloon."[9]

In Samuel Butler's autobiographical fiction *The Way of All Flesh*

(1873–1878; pub. 1903), the only woman the narrator approves of is a rich aunt who offers the protagonist a room of his own in which to develop his aesthetic and muscular interests and then conveniently dies leaving him her fortune. Now if we return to Disraeli we find a chapter on "The Domestic Life of Genius" in which we are instructed that "the home of the literary character should be the abode of repose and of silence" (234), where "the soothing interruptions of the voices of those whom he loves [may] recall him from his abstractions into social existence" (236). And there are additional chapters upon "the matrimonial state of literature" and "a picture of the literary wife" who silently mediates between social and material distractions while the detached and isolated literary character produces abstract thought.

Even reading, although it unquestionably empowered men of all classes, was dangerous for women. In her brilliant autobiographical essay "Cassandra" (1852) Florence Nightingale writes contemptuously of the autonomy denied women in the practice of their being "read aloud to," a practice she compares to forced feeding (see Chapters 2 and 5).[10] At the turn of the century Lady Florence Bell interviewed 200 workers employed at her Middlesborough iron foundry. She found that even within reading families the man read considerably more than the woman because "he has more times of leisure in which he feels he is amply justified in 'sitting down with a book'."[11] Reading often competed with sewing for wives, an impediment only occasionally alleviated when husbands read to their wives while they sewed. "Nearly all of the women," Bell observed, "seem to have a feeling that it is wrong to sit down with a book," and she tellingly reflects, probably self-reflexively, that "Even among the well-to-do this idea persists a great deal more than one would at the first blush admit" (301). When women worked outside the home, many working-women's autobiographies indicate, reading was perceived by employers to interfere with their work and consequently often jeopardized their jobs. Because of the sexual division of labor, reading and writing threatened rather than advanced women's work. The subject of reading, like writing, was properly male, to whom women ministered.

Feminist scholars have largely been occupied with the struggles of middle-class women writers.[12] Yet, like the historical subjects themselves, they have rarely questioned the Victorian distinctions between mental and manual labor that had first excluded women, and they have rarely attempted to demystify the individualist "creative imagination" that women, as producers of concrete material life, had historically been denied.[13] That is, in Gayatri Spivak's terms, they have been mesmerized by a female subjectivity formulated within the ideologies of meritocratic individualism and "the creative imagination."[14]

On the problem of the subjectivity of women writers, most instructive is the paradox of Virginia Woolf, who consistently expressed both a genuine communitarianism and a limited individualist aesthetic. Especially in *A Room of One's Own* (1929) and *Three Guineas* (1938), Woolf made the most eloquent case of her generation on the historical constraints upon women writers and the necessity of community for literary greatness. She concludes her peroration to women at Newnham and Girton colleges in 1928, a peroration that eventually became *A Room of One's Own,* with the cultural conditions necessary to produce a female counterpart to Shakespeare:

> She lives in you and in me, and in many other women who are not here tonight, for they are washing up the dishes and putting the children to bed. But she lives; for great poets do not die; they are continuing presences; they need only the opportunity to walk among us in the flesh. This opportunity, as I think, it is now coming within your power to give her. For my belief is that if we live another century or so—I am talking of the common life which is the real life and not of the little separate lives which we live as individuals—and have five hundred a year each of us and rooms of our own; if we have the habit of freedom and the courage to write exactly what we think; if we escape a little from the common sitting-room and see human beings not always in their relation to each other but in relation to reality; and the sky, too, and the trees or whatever it may be in themselves; if we look past Milton's bogey, for no human being should shut out the view; if we face the fact, for it is a fact, that there is no arm to cling to, but that we go alone and that our relation is to the world of reality and not only to the world of men and women, then the opportunity will come and the dead poet who was Shakespeare's sister will put on the body which she has so often laid down. Drawing her life from the lives of the unknown who were her forerunners, as her brother did before her, she will be born.[15]

Throughout the essay Woolf insists that masterpieces are the product of cultural participation, "not single and solitary births . . . [but] the outcome of many years of thinking in common, of thinking by the body of the people, so that the experience of the mass is behind the single voice" (68–69). She insists that greatness does not come from "little separate lives which we live as individuals" bound by the respective constraints of social class—either "washing up the dishes" or obsessively preoccupying the self with interpersonal relations in "common sitting-rooms." Yet despite her visionary communitarianism, her implicit faith in the liberal dualism of mind and body ("the single voice" and "the body of the people") remains unquestioned and her aesthetic excludes the possibility of genius among manual laborers: "For genius like Shakespeare's is not born among labouring, uneducated, servile people. It was not born in England among the Saxons and the Britons. It is not born today among the working classes" (50). "The experience of the mass" must be "behind the single voice," but in Woolf's aesthetic that voice is rigidly autonomous from the experience.

In one of the most revealing cultural confrontations in modern British history, Woolf's 1931 Introduction to the autobiographical accounts of the Women's Co-Operative Guild illustrates the cross-purposes of Woolf's aesthetic and other uses of literacy.[16] Having been asked to write a preface, Woolf begins with the problem of prefaces for autonomous aesthetics—"Books should stand on their own feet" (xv)—and solves the problem of introducing the Co-Operativists' writing by writing not quite a Preface but rather a personal letter to the editor, another upper-class woman, Margaret Llewelyn Davies. Woolf wants the Co-Operativists to be individualists. ("Their writing lacks detachment and imaginative breadth," she remarks, "even as the women themselves lack variety and play of feature" [xxxvii].) She wants them to develop the self-expression and choices for things that are ends in themselves like "Mozart and Einstein" and not things that are means like "baths and money" (xxv–vi). In short, she wants for them rooms of their own, private places for private thoughts, detached, as Bourdieu would say, from the necessities of the natural and social world.[17] Some working-class women, indeed many upper domestic servants—the most ideologically "embourgeoised" workers—did want such pleasures of private life; but the Guild women's autobiographical writing indicates that they primarily wanted something different, communality; and distance from the necessities of the natural and social world ("our minds flying free at the end of a short length of capital" as Woolf puts it [xxv]) had not led middle-class women to change society in that direction.

Rather than aspiring to the *family* of Shakespeare (Woolf's bourgeois metaphor of sibling rivalry is telling), the Co-Operativists are especially grateful to the Guild for transforming shy, nervous women into "public speakers" specifically trained to transgress the confines of domestic space (32, 48–49, 65, 110–101, 141): a woman can write forever in a room of her own without ever learning not to go dry-mouthed and shaking in public. Woolf writes sympathetically about the production of the Co-

Operativists' texts, "a work of labour and difficulty. The writing has been done in kitchens, at odds and ends of leisure, in the midst of distractions and obstacles" (xxxix), but confined by her own aesthetics of individualism and detachment, she cannot imagine that "the self" can consist of a communal, engaged, and dialogical consciousness as well as an individual, detached, and "imaginative" one (just as an autobiography can be collective, "Life as *We* Have Known It," as well as individual). To the contrary, if such a world is possible—and here Woolf's socialism is in tension with her aesthetic—she cannot imagine herself within it: "This force of theirs"—the Co-Operativists are always "they" to Woolf's editorial "we"—"this smouldering heat which broke the crust now and then and licked the surface with a hot and fearless flame, is about to break through and melt us together so that life will be richer and books more complex and society will pool its possessions instead of segregating them—all this is going to happen inevitably—but only when we are dead" (xxix).

Social historians (not to speak of socialist feminists) have made this point somewhat differently to middle-class feminists. The issue concerns normative dualism, the belief that the especially valuable thing about human beings is their mental capacity and that this capacity is a property of individuals rather than groups ("Mozart and Einstein"), and classical economic rationality, the belief that rational behavior is commensurate with the maximization of individual utility.[18] Showing the astonishing "strategies" of married working-class women living along the poverty line in the late-nineteenth and early-twentieth centuries—working part- or full-time outside the home, using children's wages, controlling household budgets, using the products of their families' allotments, and borrowing both goods and cash—Elizabeth Roberts writes that the women's "individual concerns were of little importance to them. They appear to have found their chief satisfaction in running their homes economically and seeing their children grow up. Their major preoccupations were (throughout the period) feeding, clothing and housing their familes."[19] In an article in the same collection, Diana Gittins writes of the three interrelated and often overlapping occupational spheres for working-class women from the mid-nineteenth century through the second world war—paid work, unpaid domestic work in extended families, and marriage—as "strategies for survival, but survival for the household generally rather than for the individual women."[20] In addition, I have already discussed feminist critiques of liberal rationality from the perspective of women's "other-regardingness," or the cultural consequences of female reproduction and nurturing.[21] My reading of working women's autobiography confirms that for many of them such strategies for the family household were, again, indistinguishable from self-actualization. (For familialism vs. individualism among middle-class women, see Chapter 5.)

Moreover, nonindividualism comes in the form of communalism as well as familialism. Victorian working-class autobiography suggests that the other-regarding subjectivity of women at home with their families was the least conducive to the consitution of writing subjects. Contrary to the claims on behalf of a room of one's own, their autobiographies suggest that writing women were those whose work took them out of the home. Although some working people wrote to understand themselves, with the characteristic splitting of the subjective self from the objective world that gave rise to the intense introspectivity of literary artists, most wrote unselfconsciously, without the introspective or aesthetic ends that characterized the literary artists of Woolf's generation. They wrote to record lost experiences for future generations, to raise money, to warn others, to teach others, or to relieve or amuse themselves. One pragmatic William Tayler, footman to a wealthy London widow in 1837, wrote his autobiographical journal "to improve my handwriting" (i.e., as an exercise in practical self-help for social mobility).[22]

Such pragmatic uses of literacy have little to do with the literary aesthetic as it is represented in literature departments or with the autobiographical canon in particular, which has centered on such extraordinary spiritual lives as Augustine's or Rousseau's *Confessions* (for comparatists) and Carlyle's *Sartor Resartus* or Newman's *Apologia Pro Vita Sua* (for Victorianists). Criteria we may deduce from such canons include a meditative and self-reflective sensibility; faith in writing as a tool of self-exploration; an attempt to make sense of life as a narrative progressing in time, with a narrative typically structured upon parent–child relationships and familial development; and a belief in personal creativity, autonomy, and freedom for the future. This is autobiography as the term is usually employed by literary critics, and—even with early texts like Augustine's, in which personal uniqueness is premissed upon the Grace of God—it is also compatible, if not identical, with bourgeois subjectivity, the dominant ideology of the nineteenth and at least the first half of the twentieth century. It adds the assumption of *abstract individualism,* or the belief that essential human characteristics are properties of individuals independent of their material conditions and social environment, to assumptions of normative dualism and liberal rationality.

Modern literary critics have made deviation from this model of auto-

biography a moral as well as an aesthetic failure. Despite Georges Gusdorf's "discovery" in 1956 that the "self" of modern literary autobiography was limited by culture and history, in 1960 Roy Pascal claimed
that "bad" autobiography indicated "a certain falling short in respect to
the whole personality . . . an inadequacy in the persons writing, a lack of
moral responsibility towards their task."[23] Pascal's stance belongs with
that of James Olney in *Metaphors of Self* (1972); both are apologists for
the primacy of individualism as represented by a literary tradition. Even
more recent and properly deconstructive theorists of autobiography in
the 1980s, like Paul Jay, Avrom Fleishman, and Michael Sprinker, privilege what they intend to deconstruct by employing such notions as "the
end of autobiography."[24] For the organic, self-regarding, typically male
and middle-class self of literary autobiography was always only one "self"
among others, even before it was dispersed under the conditions of postmodernism. Feminist critics and theorists of women's autobiography,
like Estelle C. Jelinek, Sidonie Smith, Shari Benstock, Bella Brodski,
Celeste Schenck, Susan Groag Bell, and Marilyn Yalom have exposed the
masculine bias of much of this theory, if often remaining within its class
and literary assumptions.[25] Rather than privileging the customary literary
associations of autobiography, or honoring the customary distinction
between literary autobiography and other "non," "sub," or "extra" literary self-representation, I shall consider all autobiography as rhetorical
projects embedded in concrete material situations.[26]

Discursive production must be understood in terms of the multifarious purposes and projects of specific individuals or groups in specific
material circumstances. For example, I have often found it useful to
adapt Unger's spectrum of personality (from longing to be with others to
fear of others) to discourse, locating a text between the poles of discursive
participation and antagonism with others.[27] All autobiographical
"moves" in my sense are "interested," whether or not they are as inten-
tionally political as those of the Guild Co-Operativists or Chartists. All
display the features of two contexts, as cultural products in circulation
with other cultural products (e.g., some music-hall performers wrote specifically for their writing's exchange value) and as articulations of participatory and antagonistic social relations. Sometimes these articulations
are simultaneously participatory and antagonistic. Writers like Annie
Kenney in *Memoirs of a Militant* (1924) and William Lovett in *Pursuit
of Bread, Knowledge, and Freedom* (1876) are participatory with their
respective movements, Suffrage and Chartism, while antagonistic to the
hegemonic disourses of sexism and classism—*hegemonic* again meaning

dominant with respect to other discourses, preventing other discourses their full development and articulation. I read autobiography rhetorically, taking language as realist, not in the sense of metaphysical realism, direct isomorphism with reality (Thomas Nagel's "the view from nowhere"), but realist in the sense of projecting objectively real articulations of power in particular communities. Like reading itself, writing is a function of specific and community interactions.[28]

I want to emphasize that when I say *power* I intend its feminist as well as its Foucauldian associations: empowerment, "power to," as well as "power over." Autobiography is the arena of empowerment to represent oneself in a discursive cultural field as well as the arena of subjective disempowerment by the "subjecting" discourses of others. In the postmodern world we live in, "autobiography" as bourgeois subjectivity may be dead except in academic or psychoanalytic circles; but as long as there is society, even cyborg society, there will be rhetorical projects of participation and antagonism in concrete material situations.[29] It is the responsibility of protectors of speech not to disqualify subhegemonic articulations, like women's, like workers', by evaluating them out of the game.

Gendered, Classed Subjects and Cultural Narratives

There is no "typical" Victorian working-class life or autobiography; rather the forms of autobiography were as multifarious as the British laboring classes themselves. Chapter 4 will consider these forms and their sociocultural appurtenances in detail; in this section I want to suggest how ideology, or broad cultural narrative, operates in the self-conception of a small number of working-class writers. It will illustrate a general tendency in the study to see aspects of ideology and counterideology, participation and antagonism, as manifested in complex interrelations and overlappings in autobiographical narrative. In Chapter 4, in the context of the full range of working-class autobiographies, I shall conclude this discussion with an adaptation of Dependency theory. In this adaptation, hegemonic and counterhegemonic effects upon subjectivity provide "intertextualities" of subtle and diverse kinds.

The loose "generic" groupings of autobiography that may be made according to the rhetorical approach outlined earlier indicate some uniformity in how texts are written, read, and historically assessed in terms of the participatory modes of value and consensus and the antagonistic modes of resistance, domination, and appropriation. Thus in nineteenth-

century Britain, when working people began to include their occupations
in titles of their work, as in *Memories of a Working Woman, Confessions
of a Strolling Player, Narrative of a Factory Cripple, In Service,* and *Autobiography of a Private Soldier,* "memories" often came from southern
agrarian workers who hoped to preserve local history for members of the
community or domestic workers whose trade declined radically after the
first world war, "narratives" from organized northern industrial workers
who sought to empower other workers and compete historically with the
bourgeoisie, and "confessions" from transients like stage performers who
hoped to gain cash by giving readers immediately consumable sensation.[30] In other words, gender, socioeconomic status, rhetorical purpose,
status of labor, and geography were often heavily significant in the forms
the autobiographical writing took.

The second point regarding autonomy and relatedness in working-
class autobiography is that whether the writer was a factory operative
(38% of the working population in 1861), agricultural laborer (18%),
miner (4%), or domestic servant (19%—half of the population of women
workers), being a significant agent worthy of the regard of others, a
human subject, as well as an individuated "ego", distinct from others,
was not a given.[31] In conditions of long work hours, crowded housing,
and inadequate light, it was difficult enough for workers to contemplate
themselves, but they had also to justify themselves as writers worthy of
the attention of others. Most working-class autobiography begins not
with family lineage or a birthdate (conventional middle-class beginnings),
but rather with a statement of its author's ordinariness, encoded in titles
like *One of the Multitude* (1911) by the pseudonymous George Acorn, a
linguistically conscious furniture builder who aspired to grow into an
oak. The authors were conscious that to many potential readers they were
but "social atoms" making up the undifferentiated "masses." As radical
journalist William Adams put it in 1903, "I call myself a Social Atom—
a small speck on the surface of society. The term indicates my insignificance. . . . I am just an ordinary person."[32] Depending upon the author's
purpose in writing, such rhetorical "modesty" could in fact signify any
point within an affective range extending from defensive self-effacement
through defiant irony, as in the "Old Potter" Charles Shaw's splendid
"We were a part of Malthus's 'superfluous population.'"[33] In Chapter 4,
I examine the sources of this rhetorical modesty in the writers' struggle,
as *Homo laborans* rather than *Homo cogitans,* to present themselves as
subjects worthy of the attention of others; their simultaneous resistance

to embourgeoisement; and their competition with representations of themselves in middle-class fiction and its implicit, broadly Cartesian, assumptions about the self.

Beyond the problematic relationship of author to audience, the second way that working-class autobiographies differ from classic spiritual autobiographies is in form. The classic realist autobiography includes such elements as remembered details of childhood, parent–child relationships, the subject's formal education, and a progressive developmental narrative of self culminating in material well-being and "fame" within greater or lesser circles (whether the Old Boy's place among Old School fellows or John Stuart Mill's place in the democratic revolution). Most workers' autobiographies deviate from this narrative pattern for fairly obvious reasons. To state only one obvious case among the most sensational, in *A Cornish Waif's Story,* which will be discussed later, Emma Smith was born in the workhouse, raised by a child molester, and educated in a penitentiary.

First, most of the writers were working outside the home by the time they were eight years old, so the period of "childhood" is problematic, the remembered details often truncated to the more common "first memory." This first memory is often traumatic; its significant positioning within the first paragraphs of the text operates and resonates differently from the evolutionary narrative of childhood familiar to readers of middle-class autobiography. Second, as will be demonstrated in detail, parent–child relationships among the working classes often differed from those in the upper classes. Third, since the subject's formal education competed with the family economy, in most cases it was not limited to a particular period. In many working-class examples, education often continues throughout the book, up to and including the time of writing. Fourth, most working-class autobiographies do not end with success but rather *in medias res.* In this context it is worth noting that with the exception of political- and religious-conversion autobiography most working-class texts do not have the crises and recoveries that are common to "literary" autobiography, just as they do not have climaxes. The bourgeois climax-and-resolution/action-and-interaction model presupposes an active and reactive world not always accessible to working-class writers, who often felt themselves passive victims of economic determinism. Working since the age of nine, Mrs. Wrigley writes a life consisting of a series of jobs, mentioning in the one sentence devoted to her marriage its maternal character and her childlike relations with her employers: "I was sorry to give up such a good home, and they was sorry for me to leave but my young man wanted to get married for he had no mother."[34]

Perhaps what is most fundamentally "missing," however, in much working-class autobiography is the structuring effect, apparent in any middle-class "plot," of gender dimorphism. In Britain, middle-class boys experienced and wrote of an ordered progress from preschool at home to childhood and youth at school and university, through the Raj, diplomatic corps, or civil serivce, or through domestic life with equally genderized wives and daughters (see Chapter 5). Middle-class women wrote of early life with fathers and afterlife with husbands. These two patterns—as central to the great nineteenth-century realist novels as to Victorian autobiography—represent middle-class gender construction of masculinity and femininity, public power and domesticity. Whereas boys learned "independence" through extrusion from mothers and nannies, and paternalism through elaborate forms of self-government in public schools, middle-class girls under constant supervision by parents and headmistresses learned to be dependent upon and obedient to husbands. (Needless to say, many also rebelled against this pattern. See Chapter 5 and, for an early critique, Cecily Hamilton's trenchant and witty *Marriage As A Trade* [1909].) On the other hand, from the time they were old enough to mind younger siblings, to their minding the children of the upper classes, to their noncompanionate (economically oriented) marriages ("because my young man had no mother"), working-class women learned to be self-reliant and responsible for dependents, and their husbands learned to be "matronized." "What I needed was a man who was master in his own house upon whom I could lean," writes Emma Smith, longing for middle-class femininity. "Instead of this", she continues, "I always had to take a leading role."[35] This account of gender inversion—strong mother who somehow "gets by" for her family and dependent, disempowered, or absent father—remained relevant when the historian Carolyn Steedman was growing up in working-class South London in the 1950s.[36]

This difference in the practical sex-gender system leads to the major structural difference of working-class autobiography, but there are transclass similarities according to gender as well. Working women refer far more frequently to their husbands or lovers and children (their personal relationships) and working men to their jobs or occupations (their social status), characteristics that conform to feminist accounts of women's other-regardingness. Traditionally prevented from speaking in public, even women like the Guild Co-Operativists, who write with the explicit purpose of political reform, speak from within a material economic realm; yet politicized men, even before they gained full male suffrage in

1885, were accustomed to public speaking (for example, in pubs) and argued within the discourse of national politics.[37] Comparatively isolated within their homes or other's as domestics, the Co-Operativists learned to internalize rhetorical values acceptable to the middle class, such as the catechism, and criticized personal injustices and inequalities within marriage and the family. On the other hand, from early experience in public and on the job with others, the men write movingly of specific material deprivations but predominantly of the "rights" of workers and the class struggle, explicitly attacking class structure.

This different understanding of injustice—one local and immediate, the other systemic—leads to different formulations of political goals. The Co-Operativists see politics as a forum for domestic demands, like baths for miners or peace for one's remaining son. The male radicals want what the middle class has. In effect, these may not be different goals: the middle class has baths and sons comparatively safe from war, but because the women reason from personal example and moral lesson and the men launch discourses articulated within the democratic revolutions of the United States and France, even the politically motivated autobiographies are often informed differently by women and men.

Such differences are attributable to the relative isolation of working women as they were driven from the factories from the 1840s and the highest paying and most independent employment consigned to men as principal breadwinners. Yet gender in working-class autobiography also shows itself as ideological hegemony—in Antonio Gramsci's sense of popular consent to the political order. I shall now turn to some of the texts in which gender functions as an ideological "narrative" influencing the ways that working-class writers understand their experience.

In such texts one reads the cost of bourgeois—especially familial or gendered—ideology to women and men who were not permitted bourgeois lives. They were often written by people with lives of unmitigated hardship, for whom writing is a form, more or less successful, of therapy. They are not trying to sell their work so much as to analyze and alleviate their pain, yet their narratives are derived from models, often literary models, more suitable to the conditions of middle-class authors. Unlike other working-class writers, these have extensively adopted middle-class ideology: they have accepted the value of introspection and writing as tools of self-understanding; they seek to write their lives as middle-class narratives, especially with respect to the development of parent–child relationships and material progress; and they believe that writing and self-understanding will help them succeed. Although they attempt self-analysis, however, their experience cannot be analyzed in the terms of their acculturation. This gap between ideology and experience leads not only to the disintegration of the narrative the writer hopes to construct, but, as the analyses will show, to the disintegration of personality itself. Characteristic of such texts are the authors' layered revisions of their experience, which contribute to an unusual density of signification. Literary readers will find them the most "literary" of working-class writers.[38] Here I shall focus upon the writers' attempts to structure their lives according to dominant gender ideology.

The struggle between ideology and experience is inscribed both micrologically and macrologically in James Burn's *Autobiography of a Beggar Boy* (1855). At nine years old, Burn tracks down his biological father in Ireland, where the boy is humiliated to wear rags, endure lice, and work in isolation. In a fit of humiliation and self-hatred, and a parody of primogeniture, he runs away, calling the dirt he associates with his father his patrimony: "I had neither staff, nor scrip, nor money in my pocket. I commenced the world with the old turf-bag. It was my only patrimony. In order that I might sever the only remaining link that bound me to my family, I tore two syllables from my name [i.e., from McBurney, his father's name]."[39] This minute detail of the boy's insufficiency to meet a cultural code—his castration of his father's name as sign of his lack of father and patrimony in a partriarchal and propertied culture—prefigures the larger narrative distortion reflecting the insufficiency of his experience to meet his society's master narrative, or ideology, of male progress.

When Burn summarizes the lesson of his life for his son at the end of his book (199–200), the summary corresponds to his preceding narrative only up to a point: he writes of his thoughtless wandering until he was twelve years old, of parental neglect ("I had been blessed with three fathers and two mothers, and I was then as comfortably situated as if I never had either one or the other" [1606]), and of his lack of social connection for long periods. This summary corresponds to the episodic structure of his preceding story and to the fragmented nature of his childhood as itinerant beggar on the Scots Border. Yet then Burn refers to the "grand turning point" of his life, when he learned a trade as hatter's apprentice. In fact, only a nominal change occurred with his apprenticeship: since there was no work, he was permitted to call himself a hatter rather than a beggar while on tramp for 1,400 miles (135). He makes much of a change of status from unemployable to employable, although no material change occurs—he remains unemployed. Also articulating an ideology more compatible with upper-class situations, he continues to insist upon the great happiness of his domestic life, despite the necessity of living apart from his family for long periods of tramping and the deaths of his wife and twelve of his sixteen children. The summary concludes with the assertion of his relative success in remaining respectable as a debt collector to the poor, a respectability that was reinforced by the bowdlerized edition of 1882, in which he finally obliterated all references to sexual experiences and bodily functions.

This summary male middle-class narrative, beginning with the imaginary "grand turning point" of his trade, occludes, first, Burn's political activity (for which he was well known), and, second, much of his past. With the threat of the General Strike in 1839, he had turned against the Chartists and had begun to conceive of his prior activism as "madness." In revising his life this "madness" is excluded along with earlier madnesses, such as the madness of Scottish and Irish poetry. Due to its link with supersition and supernaturalism—and despite his opinion that English poetry is "dull and lifeless" in comparison—Burn must reject it as irreconcilable with "useful knowledge" (192–98). Similarly, the lively Dickensian style of the first two chapters shows his affection for society on the Borders, its lack of social differentiation and its extreme linguistic diversity. Yet this too disappears from his summary. He is left attempting to reconcile his proprietorship of taverns and spirit cellars with his hysterical temperance and passing over the details of his job as debt collector to his former Chartist friends. Everything that must be repudiated in the service of class mobility—social tolerance, epistemological pluralism, the aspect of freedom of life on the Borders as a beggar boy—is expunged from the summary. Yet in dutifully obliterating or rewriting his past, there is no indication that Burn is comfortable with his present or future. As he puts it, "Amid the universal transformation of things in the moral and physical world, my own condition has been tossed so in the rough blanket of fate, that my identity, if at any time a reality, must have been one which few could venture to swear to" (56); or, "All our antecedents are made up of so many yesterdays, and the morrow never comes" (185).

Moreover, despite the seasonal difficulties of the hatting trade and high unemployment among artisans in Glasgow in the 1830s and 1840s, and despite an active and successful tenure as spokesperson for hatters in the Glasgow United Committee of Trades Delegates, Burn blames himself for his failure in business by personalizing his class background as his individual incompetence. Assuming a liberal and masculine ethic of autonomy and progress, he concludes that he was personally deficient in the struggle to maintain either self or social position, and he therefore believes himself uneducable: "Although my teachers have been as various as my different positions, and much of their instruction forced upon me by the necessities of my condition, yet I have always been a dull dog" (196). Assuming individual responsibility for conditions beyond his control and de-identifying with other workers, he remains merely isolated, neither materially and socially middle-class nor identifying with his own. The disturbing power of the first half of the text, with the boy's mystical worship of his stepfather; the disintegration of the later sections; the emphatic progress and rationality in tension with the obsessive memories of early days; and the mystified transition from anger against a negligent father to guilt as an unworthy native son: all contribute to a nightmare of sociopsychic marginality. Nonetheless, the book was received as a gratifying example of self-improvement and respectability among the lower classes.[40] Today we can see it as releasing all the phantoms of an ideology of familialism, autonomy, and progress upon a child who was deprived of a family and a chance. Unlike other working-class writers, Burn attempts to narrate his experience according to upper-class models. The price he pays is narrative and psychological disintegration.

Whereas Burn's story shows the effect of Enlightenment narratives, presumably from his days as a Chartist, and masculine "success" stories combining with familial narrative, women's narratives of this type are correspondingly dominated by familialism and romance. In his *Annals of Labour,* the social historian John Burnett cites Louise Jermy's *Memories of a Working Woman* as an example of a successful transition from a low-paying millinery position into domestic service and ultimately marriage.[41] Yet Jermy herself sees her life as a series of episodes failing to conform to her expectations of family and romance. Born in 1877, she is motherless before her second birthday. Her childhood and health are "bartered" by her father and stepmother when she is taken from school to do mangling (cloth-pressing) at home in order for her parents to buy a house. Her adolescence is isolated, "not like other girls," between illness and an apprenticeship at fourteen to a dressmaker in "sweated" conditions (long hours in confined and crowded space, few and short breaks, low pay). Her education is continually frustrated as her stepmother destroys her books, and while in service to a married couple at Birmingham University "anything like deep thinking produced the dreadful headaches" (93).

Jermy's romantic life is also a series of noncorrespondences with middle-class norms. A fragile betrothal conflicts with the long hours and the

9:00 P.M. curfew of domestic servants, until her fiancé bolts and leaves her in a severe depression that endures two years. Finally she marries a farm laborer in 1911 but, like many husbands described by working-class wives, he is (in the common terminology) "delicate," ill every Spring, and lives only ten years. Jermy returns to work to raise her two sons.

She suffers from amnesia, ceases in childhood to confide in others, and bears a conviction of her awkwardness and unattractiveness. She leaves the millinery shop not, as Burnett implies, for better wages, but in order to leave home; and she wears black—the "decent black" of domestic servants, as Mayhew put it, "no ringlets, followers, or scandals"—on and off the job.[42] While each episode fails to correspond to its middle-class analogue, Jermy nonetheless adopts—but this is perhaps too tidy a word for a complex process—middle-class standards and conventional narratives as her own. R. H. Mottram introduces *The Memories of a Working Woman* as the first autobiography written by a member of the Women's Institute. Jermy, however, never mentions the Institute: the dominant features of her life, at least prior to the Institute, were perverted familial relations (glorified dead mother, evil stepmother), aborted romance, and pronounced isolation.

In *A Cornish Waif's Story: An Autobiography* the pseudonymous Emma Smith's life is also a sequence of noncorrespondence to middle-class norms. Born in 1894, Smith was the "illegitimate" daughter of one of twenty-three children of a Cornish tin-miner blinded in a mining accident and retired without pension. As a child she is told that her mother is her sister. As accompanist to a Hurdy-Gurdy man, she is sexually molested by a man she calls "Fagin" and his friend Dusty the Sword Swallower. At eleven, she runs away and is sent to a convent penitentiary, a home for "errant" girls: "I was no more a prostitute than Dickens's Oliver Twist was a thief, if I may draw upon a character of fiction to illustrate what I mean. Yet here I was placed in the category, and indirectly it has affected my whole life" (108). Like the tales of "low life" the middle classes had told themselves much earlier (see Chapter 3), Smith constructs her life from the perspective of the ordinary person trapped in the margins of society. Thus the Dickensian "Fagin" is both her exploiter and necessary protector, and her identification with the orphaned Oliver draws upon fiction to legitimate her very real sense of victimization. Later, Smith's extraordinary literary sensibility would, in the manner of Oliver, distinguish her in her own mind from other members of her class.

The convent penitentiary fails to prepare her for her re-entry into society, especially for marriage and a family, while it equally denies her a "speakable" past: her "Home" for errant girls, the closest to "home" she had experienced, jeopardized her chances for ever having a Victorian domus. Upon release, "it was impressed upon me . . . that I was never to talk about the Home or let anyone know where I had come from . . . it was something to be very ashamed of" (133). Working as a servant in a vicarage provides dissonances that are borne out by her own marriage— "Nothing was as I imagined it. The vicar was blessed with an unholy temper. His wife did not get on with her husband and took no pains to hide the fact" (134). Her marriage to a gardener is probably arranged by her employers—"If you have two servants, a man and a woman, the thing to do is to marry them up. Then you have two servants for the price of one" (152)—and she very quickly distances herself as a unique, reflective, psychologically rich self ("a complex piece of machinery") from her husband ("a simple country man"), who, as a transparent product of his class status, fails to fulfill her emotional, intellectual, and romantic aspirations (152–66).

Again with echoes of Oliver and Agnes, she obsessively attempts to reconcile with her mother (from an external point of view, always a nonexistent dyad); aborts an extramarital romance in Australia; and returns with her husband to Cornwall. Yet rather than a parish girl's progress to financial and domestic stability (she is a successful head laundress with three healthy daughters), Smith's is a "hysterical" narrative indicating her nonadjustment to married life and maternity. She is as unwilling a wife as a waif.

If personal identity is a function of a temporal unification of past, present, and future, Smith was as deprived as Foucault's "Herculine Barbin" (who, raised as a girl in a convent, was legally declared to be male as an adult) of the past she had had to repress, and as unprepared for the future entailed by her gender: "I would dream that I was an inmate of a convent . . . I was, or could have been, supremely happy if it were not for the knowledge that somewhere in the background I had a husband and children" (178).[43] After several mental breakdowns, she twice attempts suicide (quietly, like a good servant—and wife, with aspirin and sleeping pills), but is finally convinced by her doctor that her responsibility is to live for her family. In her last paragraph Smith once again mediates her experience through fictional modes, this time apparently unconsciously:

> I should end my life story on a very happy note if I could honestly record
> that I have grown so well-balanced mentally that nothing now upsets or
> worries me. Such, however, is not the case. I am easily worried and upset

over certain things, and for this reason as much as for others, I am anxious to find a little cottage somewhere in Cornwall with a bit of ground upon which we can grow vegetables and flowers. It would be a great thrill to me if my dream cottage had a view of both the sun rising and the sunset, for the sun rising fills me with hope, and the sunset fills me with peace. (188)

Novel-readers will recognize this image of the rose-covered cottage as the standard ending of Dickens's domestic fiction, including the image and final resting place of the adopted orphan Oliver Twist.

It is perhaps worth digressing here on the accessibility of such literary archetypes to working-class writers. By the late eighteenth century there was near universal literacy among male artisans, and as many as a third of the least literate section of the population, farm laborers, could manage to sign their names in the marriage register. Given this generous criterion of literacy, by the 1840s the ratio of readers to writers was somewhere between 1:2 and 2:3; by the end of the century the ratios between name-signing and an adequate reading capacity, and between reading capacity and writing capacity, tended rapidly to converge.[44] In 1840 the national literacy rate for men was two-thirds and for women one-half, the bottom third of the population being cut off not only by its abject poverty but also by its illiteracy. The highest rate for adult males was in London (88%); followed by the far north with 81 percent (Northumberland, Cumberland, Westmoreland, Durham, and the East and North Ridings of Yorkshire); to the lowest, 51 percent, in the group of counties very close to the north and east of London (Bedfordshire, Hertfordshire, Huntingdonshire, Buckinghamshire, Essex, Cambridgeshire, Suffolk, and Norfolk).

Where the literacy rate for men is highest, as in the far northern counties, the gap between men and women is greatest (78 vs. 57%), whereas in the least literate areas, like the three East Anglian counties, it is smaller (52 vs. 46%). By the death of Victoria illiteracy was virtually eliminated throughout England and Wales for both women and men. For Scotland, the source of autobiographies like Burn's and Ellen Johnston's (to be discussed shortly), the estimated figures are much higher: 90 percent in 1800 and still 89 percent by 1855. There education at all levels was on a far larger scale, and social mobility was far greater than in England. (Scotland's democratic Glasgow University is often contrasted to elitist Oxbridge.) Even granting that literacy figures technically refer to the capacity to sign one's name rather than the ability really to use the written word as a means of communication, it is pretty clear that in mid-

Victorian England at least two-thirds of the population had access (even if only being read to) to the broad forms of literary production.

What is common to the texts discussed in this section is the conscious desire on the part of the writers to write their lives according to middle-class narratives and the unconscious distance between those narratives—especially of financial success, familialism, and romance—and the facts of their existence, especially un- and underemployment, nonfamilialism, aborted romance, and noncompanionate marriage: the distance between narratives of relatively autonomous individuals in pursuit of chosen goals and economic determinism. Domesticity, at home and abroad, was a dominant ideological state apparatus; as a contemporary observer put it, Queen Victoria affected domestic bliss to the same degree that Elizabeth I affected virginity.[45] Yet for the working classes, the restricted family was not only the most convenient site of avoidable or unavoidable neglect of children, but also the site of noncompanionate marriage. In *Jipping Street* Kathleen Woodward presents a fairly typical image of an urban working family—psychologically, if not literally, representative of her own—that can be counterposed with that of Victoria's hearth and home. Woodward's grandfather so brutalizes her mother and grandmother that when he kills himself his wife refuses to identify his body at the coroner's; one of the few pieces of decorative matter that Woodward remembers from her childhood is his framed death certificate on her living-room wall. Like many fathers in working women's autobiographies, Woodward's is represented as debilitated and unable to support the family. Her image is of him weeping in bed and her mother "holding him back from the grave."[46] Her mother is strong, protective, indestructible, but not affectionate: "I lived close to my mother, held fast by strong ties which existed without love or affection."[47] Burn, Smith, and Jermy's narratives of disintegrated personality demonstrate that in circumstances of familial deprivation familial ideology can only be assumed at great psychic cost.

Yet not all working-class autobiographers assumed familial ideology at such a cost. It was a cultural commonplace that many male radicals—for example, Thomas Hardy, William Lovett, Thomas Cooper, Robert Blatchford, Robert Lowery, James Watson, and Thomas Dunning—had been raised by women alone ("resourceful widows" was the technical term), and they resisted bourgeois ideology as much as Emma Smith submitted to it. Unlike the previous writers, the male radicals were engaged in communities with common purpose and in the process of rearticulating their common experience through other master narratives (i.e., the progressive narratives of the Enlightenment—as Lovett put it, through their common pursuits of bread, knowledge, and freedom, or material well-being, education, and political emancipation). Emma Smith, Louise Jermy, and the Chartist renegade James Burn, on the other hand, were as isolated, individualistic, or unaffiliated as the middle-class subjects whose ideology they adopted—as isolated but not so autonomous: Smith, unhappy in her marriage, maintained the forms of middle-class respectability and swallowed her pain with her sleeping pills; Jermy was forced to return to work to support her fatherless sons; and as Burn said, whether or not there was work, his children kept him "hostage to the State" (132).

Faced with such difficulties, the emotional health, or functional identities, of working-class writers was not dependent upon their politicization in any rigid sense so much as upon their participation in alternative articulations of their common experience. The indomitable Ellen Johnston, known to working people as Scotch Nell the "Factory Girl," could have been a Jermy or a Smith. Abandoned by her father, a stonemason, "tormented" by her stepfather, "deceived" by two lovers, and ostracized as a fallen woman, the power-loom weaver/poet's brief *Autobiography* (1867) is melodramatically modeled on Walter Scott and "those strange romatic ordeals attributed to the imaginary heroines 'of Inglewood Forest'," and her poems show the effects of literary hegemony, although they are often gender- and class-inverted, as in "Lines to a Young Gentleman of Surpassing Beauty."[48]

Yet Johnston also articulated a common experience of great value to herself and fellow workers: for every epideictic poem to a romantic young gentleman there are many more in praise of working men (she writes, she says, to relieve them from the toils of factory life), and her *Autobiography* concludes not with melancholy and melodrama but with her taking her foreman to court, indicating that the Factory Girl has learned to imitate the middle class in more than literary hegemony. Within the narratives of her own class and local cultures, she publishes proud poems on her "illegitimate" daughter "bonny Mary Auchinvole"; composes many—including love poems—on behalf of less literate co-workers; includes in her volume addresses and songs written for her from other workers (to which she often composes personal responses); goes international with "Welcome, Garibaldi" and "The Exile of Poland"; and writes with irresistible affection for the material life of the factory, as in "An Address to Napier's Dockyard" and "Kennedy's Dear Mill." "The Factory Girl's Farewell" concludes:

Farewell to all the works around,
The flaxmill, foundry, copperage too;
The old forge, with its blazing mound,
And Tennant's stalk, farewell to you.
Your gen'rous masters were so kind,
Theirs was the gift that did excel;
Their name around my heart is twined:
So Gailbraith's bonnie mill, farewell!

Farewell, my honour'd masters two,
Your mill no more I may traverse;
I breathe you both a fond adieu;
Long may you live lords of commerce.
Farewell unto my native land,
Land of the thistle and blue-bell;
Oh! wish me joy with heart and hand;
So Gailbraith's bonnie mill, farewell! (95)

Johnston participated fully in public life in factories in Scotland, Ireland, and England. Familial and romantic ideology, when combined with circumstances unconducive to family or romance, exacted the highest psychic cost to those who lived in isolation. It seems inescapable that the emotional health and flourishing self-image of working-class subjects whose lives did not conform to the patterns of the dominant culture were proportionate to the degree of participatory—as opposed to purely antagonistic—discursive engagement with others beyond the family in the home. The narrative and psychological disintegration of working-class writers who attempted to adopt middle-class narratives of self, and the relatively successful identities of those supported by alternative participatory articulations, indicate the significance and subtlety of discourse and ideology—in this case, of gendered, familial discourse and ideology—in human identity, as well as their insufficiency to override nondiscursive material conditions entirely.

2.

Subjectivity, the Body, and Material Culture

In "A Manifesto for Cyborgs," Donna Haraway signals three boundary breakdowns causing considerable stress in late twentieth-century life, in which the meaning of life—that is, of the word *life*—is part of the stress.[1] These boundary breakdowns are between the human and animal, the human/animal and machine, and, a subset of the second, the physical and nonphysical. Biology and evolutionary theory have claimed that human and nonhuman animals share language, tool use, and social behavior, and that nothing really convincingly settles their separation; advocates of animal rights have repudiated the need for such a separation. The distinction between organism and machine has disappeared with organicism in postmodern life: precybernetic machines were not self-moving, self-designing, or autonomous, says Haraway, adding that they were not selves at all, but only a caricature, like Frankenstein's monster, of the masculinist reproductive dream. Today machines challenge the difference between natural and artificial, self-developing and externally designed; moreover, machines are near the hearts of many of us, prolonging our lives mechanically. The distinction between physical and nonphysical is further eroded by modern microelectronics, which are nothing but signals but are nonetheless, as Haraway says, "a matter of immense human pain in Detroit and Singapore" (70). Sherry Turkle, an anthropologist whose fieldwork is among Hightech Society at MIT, argues that in the nineteenth century when machinery was transparent, when as if in Chaplin's *Modern Times* one could see the wheels and gears and shafts, workers could distinguish themselves from the machine and see the machine as no more than a mechanical threat; today workers in artificial intelligence (AI) have great plans for the machine, which is now our equal. Because AI is invisible but is everywhere (like God) they imagine that the soul inhabits it, that it represents our own Unconscious, the limits of cognitive possibility—our omniscience.[2]

This boundary breakdown, one of the material sources of what is called the *postmodern condition,* signals changing concepts of the self and personal identity beyond the literary intelligentsia's wildest nightmares. (Turkle's training in psychoanalysis in Paris, she tells us, was rendered obsolete at MIT.) It has also, apparently, made scholars sensitive to cultural variation in boundary construction. Some concerned with the Gothic and Gothic moments have written extensively about the psychological state of abjection, or loss of self and absorption by the Other, often in terms of class, race, or gender instability.[3] Others, like Arnold Davidson, Evelyn Fox Keller, and Roberto Unger, have explored the reflexive interactions between historical shifts in legitimating discourse in religion, science, and political economy.[4]

We can now locate some common nineteenth-century topoi within the conceptual frame of psychological, epistemological, and somatological boundaries of the self. Although the monster in Mary Shelly's *Frankenstein* (1818) incorporates a rich literary subjectivity, as eloquent as Milton and introspective as a Romantic poet, it is his ugly synthetic body that defeats him in human community and that ensures that he be denied his reproductive rights—his body, not his reasoning capacity (which is considerable), isolates and defeats him. Fictional images of alterity like the Creole Bertha Mason, the Jew Fagin, and the Oriental Dracula inherit in their physical appearances and animal behavior the Darwinian continuum between human and animal that was theorized in its most aesthetic form in Pater's Mona Lisa, "humanity as wrought upon by, and summing up in itself, all modes of thought and life," or what Pater calls "the modern idea" of the evolution of species.[5] Moreover, literary competence teaches us that fictional characters' bodies represent their emotive conditions and class appurtenances. In utilitarian fashion Jane Eyre and Catherine Linton "gain flesh" according to their precise degrees of happiness or the reverse, and Dick in *Oliver Twist* and Helen in *Jane Eyre* "lose flesh" as their lives are consumed by the workhouse and Lowood charity school. In a sort of reductio ad absurdum of the separate worlds of mind and body, the upper classes *(Homo cogitans)* are represented by their eyes (see the large, dark, and *meaningful* eyes of George Eliot's Maggie Tulliver and Dorothea Brooke), indicators of intelligence and the emotions, and the lower by their bodies, which were increasingly degraded under industrialization but in their "natural" setting sufficed to represent the essential worker. See the preindustrial *Homo laborans* Adam Bede cheerfully singing to the sound of his hammer "shake off dull sloth" and the Eliotian narrator's assurance that "such a voice could only come from a broad chest[ed] . . . large-boned muscular man" with a "flat back" and "poised head."[6]

The same themes appear when we turn from the extraordinary in Victorian fiction to the everyday in the workplace. The Luddites and rick-burners were only the most obvious reaction to the threat of machines to human identity. As early as the seventeenth century, medical science had viewed biological organisms as machines, bones as levers, and the heart as a pump; but Charles Babbage, the eccentric scientist credited with inventing the concept of the modern computer in the early years of the industrial revolution, wanted machines to perform calculations, like humans. Babbage is also, of course, credited with creating the field of operations research, the analysis, for example, of more efficient ways to perform tasks in a factory. Babbage's "operations research," tending as it did to view workers as parts of the factory-machine, further blurred the line between humans and machines.

By considering the effects of material conditions on subjectivity, this chapter will give texture and *body* to the critique of Cartesian dualism and classical liberalism's abstract individualism. One critique of dualism says that one's body and daily physical circumstances provide an ineliminable basis of one's subjectivity.[7] Our pragmatic approach insists that what is important to understanding the physical subject embedded in material circumstances is not some unique experience (a Cogito, or "what it is like to be that thing"), but is rather a complex and specific dialectic between experience and its communication to self and others. One critique of liberalism says that we in the West have cared too little for the actual material circumstances of all our subjects in our on-going struggles for democratic reform. The two critiques together mean that whereas no *philosophical* distinctions can be made between "mind" and "body," *political* distinctions between mental and manual labor—in both their class and gender manifestations—have been liberalism's blind-spot. Thus whereas Mill was inspired by and cited Florence Nightingale's unpublished "Cassandra" in his *Subjection of Women* (1869), his arguments against women's servitude in the domus and exclusion from the marketplace remain eloquent statements of the principles of liberty among rational beings, but Nightingale's own text emerges as an enraged indictment of the *physical* suffering incurred by upper-class women's confinement. In 1867 when Mill asked Nightingale to join the National Society for Women's Suffrage she consequently refused on the grounds that exclusive concentration on the vote might undermine the drive for women's economic independence.

This chapter will explore the consequences to our understanding of subjectivity and value of a consideration of the body and its material context. In the first section I urge that we look at sexuality in material as well as ideological terms—in terms of reproduction as well as discourse and eroticism. Until recently, literature and literary criticism have suppressed discussion of material sexuality in favor of Romance, or in contemporary terms, of Desire. The first part will not be an "eroticized" reading, nor will it be conducive to any voyeuristic "pleasure of the text." In discussing working-class mothers' accounts of pregnancy I argue for the interrelation of body and discourse in an analysis of Victorian subjectivity.

In the second, and major, part of the chapter I examine Henry Mayhew's critique of liberal political economy, free trade, and philanthropy in the context of his engagement with the concrete, material world of the metropolitan poor. In the course of his many interviews with London workers, Mayhew moves from the subjective isolation of the poor to a revisionist evaluation of the centrality of labor in British socioeconomic life that resists the reductionism, essentialism, and determinism that often characterize more abstract theoretical discussions of "poverty." Although Mayhew's interviews most obviously belong with the middle-class representations of the working classes in the next chapter, his sensitivity to the multifarious physical experiences and material circumstances of the poor separates him from the liberal novelists and sociologists that follow. It also led him to reject the novelists' fundamental principles and projects—although, as we shall see, he retained much of their literary method.

In the third and concluding section I argue, with the example of Florence Nightingale, that the association of woman with soma inhibited women's professionalization, while the commercialization of femininity masked women's exclusion from political power. Consequently, women reacted against the material domain of their confinement—the hearth—with a negativity that has been little analyzed. In the three discussions, what is striking about the "mind" or personality is not its uniqueness or autonomy, but rather its profound dependence upon intersubjectively shared meanings and its profound vulnerability to the deprivations of the body.

Working Women's Uncanny World of Childbirth

In 1913 fear of population decline stimulated concern with high infant mortality rates, and political strategists in the Working Women's Co-Operative Guild sponsored a campaign for government support of working-class women's maternity needs. A major component of the campaign was the letters of 386 current or former Guild Officials, covering the experiences of maternity and infant mortality of 400 women in families with normal weekly wages of 11 s. to £ 5. Out of the 386 women who wrote, 348 recalled 1,396 live children, 83 stillbirths, and 218 miscarriages. The high incidence of continuous pregnancy in the context of very low incomes and incessant work was to be contrasted with the concomitants of maternity for middle-class women, which included—for good or ill—medical advice and care during and after the pregnancy and birth, respite from domestic work (indeed many women resented the social expectation of idleness), at least adequate nutrition and exercise, and the ministrations of domestic servants.[8] For a middle-class woman to be deprived of any one of these conditions would have been considered an outrage. Working-class women were habitually deprived of them all.

The correspondents—as Guild officials, considerably better off than many other working women and wives of laborers—were aware of their ironic relationship to Victorian maternity and they refer to it with irony: "The rapture of a babe in arms drawing nourishment from me crowned me with glory and sanctity and honour. Alas! the doctor who attended me suffered from eczema of a very bad type in his hands. The disease attacked me, and in twenty-four hours I was covered from head to foot ... finally leaving me partially and sometimes totally crippled in my hands" (44). Another wrote, "I do not think I was very different in my pregnancies to others. I always prepared myself to die, and I think this depression is common to most at this time" (166). As the causes of their condition they cite inadequate wages; the gender system that dictated women's duty as the satisfaction of their husband's desires and the bearing of children without regard to the women's physical or mental states; and, significantly and insistently, the lack of knowledge, skilled advice, and treatment.

The patent content of the letters overwhelmingly concerns the female body. The correspondents record extreme physical abjection, or loss of boundaries. In their own terminology, they suffered continually from misplacements, womb displacement, falling of the womb, gathered breasts, breasts in slings, childbed fever, husbands' abuse of the organs of reproduction, cold in the ovaries, varicose veins, marble leg, continuous urination throughout pregnancy, untimely flooding, growth of the after-birth inside the mother, confinement in body-belts and leg-bands, severe hemorrhaging caused by sexual intercourse too soon after birth, white-leg, and the psychologically maddening grinding of machinery in the factory, "knowing that it is mostly women and girls who are working in these factories gives you the feeling their bodies are going round with the machinery. The mother wonders what she has to live for; if there is another baby coming she hopes it will be dead when it is born" (42).[9]

There are cases of women who did not know that they were pregnant until they gave birth ("I got very weak yet very stout. I thought it was through sitting so much at the machine" [341]), and of one who, when the midwife arrived for the birth, still "had not the slightest idea where or how the child would come into the world" (187). Furthermore, these women were "easy prey to sexual intercourse" (99) and physical abuse by husbands; typically physically exhausted by work; and often starving themselves in order to save for their families. Their bodies did not provide, in Unger's terms, the natural frontier of the self, one of the three bases of conscious individuality. Rather, the letters overwhelmingly indicate that their bodies were as mysteries to their *un*conscious owners, completely out of their control. The women often represent themselves as subhuman, brutish. "I never felt a woman during pregnancy," one writes, "I have had the doctor's arm in my body, and felt his fingers tearing the afterbirth from my side" [28].

Ironically, however, the self unmade by pain was often made through the experience, the viewpoint in Thomas Nagel's sense, of a particular mode of suffering through time. The letters repeatedly attribute lifelong suffering to ill usage during first confinements. The consequences of material deprivation and abuse are visited onto the children, either through miscarriage or early death, or in the form of what they call "delicacy" (or constitutional weakness), disfigurement, lameness, and retardation. Here particular sensory modalities entail a point of view that functions as identity. Nagel contended that we could only know what it was like to be a bat if we lived in a bat's body in the dark and had sonar intelligence. The letters suggest that reproductive suffering was an essential component of the subjectivity in question: *that* is what it was like to be a working-class woman.

The second point, however, is that by 1913 this passive or somatic subjectivity was presented in order that it be rejected. For, as I shall argue later from Mayhew's interviews with metropolitan labor, subjectivity that is confined to isolation within the body obliterates the greatest part of human subjectivity: intersubjectivity. Contrary to middle-class representations à la Zola of the lower classes as sexually free and savvy, manual laborers during this period represented themselves as more mystified by their bodies than were the middle classes; this was precisely because the bodies of manual laborers were *un*mediated by the professional or mental mediators of legitimate knowledge. The Guild correspondents demand doctors, midwives, and, above all, discussion. They refer to a conspiracy of silence and demand "mothercraft" to mediate the most "natural" of activities. This refrain is too numerous to belabor here, but the following situation is typical:

> Judging from my own experience, a fair amount of knowledge at the commencement of pregnancy would do a lot of good. One may have a good mother who would be willing to give needed information, but to people like myself your mother is the last person you would talk to about yourself or your state. Although mother nursed me with my first child, I never said one word to her about it coming, except the bare date I expected. I felt I couldn't, and outside people only tell you what garments you need, and just the barest information. (114)

The call for mediation between working women and their bodies reflects a profound ideological legitimation—one that was probably inevitable after the 1840s, when organized British workers took the road of Chartism rather than Owenism, reformism rather than socialism. These workers were uprooted from traditional communities and confronting the middle-class requirements of respectability. In a traditional laboring community, there would have been midwives and mothers with stories about maternity that would have been passed on to daughters, and there would have been care of the mother and child. The young women who eventually became Guild members, however, operated under a conspiracy of silence—"say nothing about your body"—that amounted to ignorance with the most appalling consequences to themselves and their descendants. This conspiracy of silence, even between mother and daughter, was adopted from middle-class respectability, in which, however, it was a mark of status rather than ignorance. For middle-class women had professional mediators to speak about, and care for, their bodies, as well as access to an expanding cultural industry about sexuality. While the demands of respectability were preventing working women from sharing knowledge within their own communities, they were simultaneously deprived of medical knowledge externally as their midwives were delegitimated by a professional medical community of doctors they could not afford to see (see the third part of this chapter). In another concrete man-

ifestation of the mind/body dualism, the working women were caught
between respectable silence and the unmediated soma, or ignorance without specialists to intervene. They experienced physical abjection and a
profound epistemological lack.

Significantly, however, the Guildswomen simultaneously broke the
silence and demanded specialists, thus diverging from middle-class ideology in also breaking the boundaries between public and private. That
is, middle-class pregnancy could be publicly invisible because it was privately attended to by specialists. In demanding municipal rather than
philanthropic action, the correspondents rejected the public/private distinction that the laboring classes did not share and that supported the
status quo; and in writing about their bodies, sharing information, and
demanding professional services, they came close to rejecting the distinction between mental and manual labor that devalued the laboring classes
and supported the status quo. Women who had been isolated by their
subjective experiences of pain learned as Guildswomen to articulate that
pain as part of a narrative of progressive demands on behalf of a "we,"
finding community and voice simultaneously. The hegemonic discourse
of healthcare, exclusion from which had left them alienated from their
bodies, was countered by the equally hegemonic discourse of rights.

So the final stage in the story of subjectivity revealed in these letters
is the story—so complex in its twentieth-century developments that I can
only introduce it in concluding this section—of female citizens, in their
own terms "hopeful mothers of the nation." If culture had alienated
working women from their laboring bodies, working women now used
their bodies to change culture. "It is high time that something was done
by the Government to lessen the sufferings of mothers, which has always
been hidden as something not to be talked about" (156). And finally, the
last sentence of the "National Scheme Proposed by the Women's Co-
Operative Guild," "It is by a partnership between the women who are
themselves concerned, the medical profession, and the State that the best
results of democratic government can be secured for the mothers and
infants of the country" (212).

Henry Mayhew's Rich World of Poverty

> Look or listen which way you would, the many sights and
> sounds that filled the eye and ear told each its different tale of
> busy trade and boundless capital.
>
> HENRY MAYHEW, Letter in *The Morning Chronicle* (1849)

> In coarse God Almighty made the world, and the poor brick-layers' labourers built the houses afterwards—that's *my* opinion.
>
> COSTERLAD, *London Labour and the London Poor* (1861)

As organized, self-educated Co-Operativists, the Guildswomen trans-formed themselves from subjective isolation within their bodies to sub-jects with claims upon the State. They won a maternity benefit under the National Insurance Law and a provision for four weeks sick pay at child-birth for the employed. They went on to win the establishment of Munic-ipal Maternity Centres for delivery, pre- and postnatal care. My second illustration of subjectivity, value, and material culture now returns to midcentury, just prior to the Great Exhibition of the Industry of All Nations in London in 1851.

In this section the bodies of the workers will remain central to my discussion of their subjectivity, but I shall extend the physical experience bearing upon subjectivity into the realm of goods, both the goods pro-duced by the London laborers *and* the goods produced by Mayhew in his presentation of them. There are a number of very different accounts of the relationship between goods and subjectivity. For Marx in the second half of the nineteenth century, goods signified commodities with use value or exchange value in complex relationship to the human labour invested in their production. For Thorstein Veblen in 1900, who was concerned with the "conspicious consumption" of the leisure classes, they signified psychological investments, the power of envy as a factor in social motivation and of display as its iconography. For Mary Douglas today, they signify a live information system, a valuable index to com-munity, meaning, and human relationships.[11] Although Mayhew's work was parallel to Marx's in a general labor theory of value, like the later women cooperativists he never went so far as to see wage labor itself as naturally dehumanizing, or occupational specialization as an evil pre-venting the new mode of spontaneous productive activity predicated by Marx and Engels on the socialization of the means of production. Although his informants and then Mayhew himself spoke out against sub-subsistence wages, they were not in principle opposed to wage labor per se.

Mayhew's contribution to Marxist thought is that he located working people centrally in his system of value *after* spending most of his working time with them, whereas Marx culled the lavish documentation of *Cap-*

ital from the reports of British factory inspectors. In recording their own *subjective* responses to the conditions of their existence Mayhew dignified them as the builders, seamstresses, sewer-cleaners, buyers, and sellers of the metropolis, giving them a voice thirty-seven years before *Capital* was translated into English. (Which is not to deny the essential part that Marx's own physical experience had in the production of the theory of materialism: living in a London slum on bread and potatoes, pawning his own clothes, while writing nine hours a day in the British Museum.) With his attention to subjective experience, as well as, like Engels's, to its material culture, Mayhew's work serves as that of an Ur ethnography— a middle-class representation of the poor, to be sure, but one that can be juxtaposed with the political economy of his day.

Scholars are currently directing considerable attention to the "discourses" of Victorian poverty, especially to those of Victorian social science that will be discussed briefly in Chapter 3. Generally in their surveys Mayhew's interviews with hundreds of workers in the midcentury metropolis appear in the role of a Foucauldian power-knowledge, a means of surveillance marking the upper classes' response to their fears of engulfment by the democratic multitude. (Hence the proliferation from the 1830s of discourse on crime, prostitution, infectious disease, degeneracy, etc., with the establishment of statistical societies and city police departments).[12] In most cases, such readings of Mayhew are very selective and do not distinguish between the voice of Mayhew as commentator in isolated passages in his study and that of Mayhew as he came to understand political economy in the course of his interviews. This broader Mayhew, influenced by his "subjects" at least as much as his work influenced them, is the one I shall explore in what follows. I do this not, to be sure, to redeem a dead journalist from new historians and neo-conservatives but rather to insist upon the difference that distinguishes Mayhew's richly reflexive empirical investigation (he is commonly acknowledged as the founder of the technique of oral history) from the work of less empirical social scientists and explorers.[13] It is doubtless the case that the classifying of the world, a large part of Mayhew's project, contributed to its control, but in Mayhew's case, direct and prolonged contact with the poor he interviewed produced effects rather different from those of other social explorers and scientists, especially from the more theoretical and even mathematical political economists for whom "poverty" was more distant and abstract. A proper study of the interface of the voice of the commentator and those of his interviewees, analyzing the entirety of Mayhew's interviews in *The Morning Chronicle* and *Lon-*

don Labour and the London Poor, would tell us a great deal about the relative merits of different kinds of empirical research on the causes of poverty. Such a study is not my purpose in this book, but I hope that this section will be a step toward it.

Mayhew considered his "the office of examining into the condition of the poor of London . . . according as they *will* work, they *can't* work, and they *won't* work" (102). I shall structure my discussion of subjectivity and value in metropolitan labor in a scheme developed first in Marx's account of the alienation of the product of human labor in the *Economic and Philosophical Manuscripts* of 1844 and most recently in Elaine Scarry's "arc of reciprocity" in *The Body in Pain: The Making and Unmaking of the World.* The arc of human making, from human projection in an idea, through the idea's embodiment in an artifact, to the artifact's reciprocal utility for the maker, takes into account the dual character of modern technology, its beneficent as well as its destructive character. Mayhew's "tale of busy trade and boundless capital" represents, *literally,* the making of the working class: what they made, how they made it, and how it returned to remake the makers. I shall therefore discuss Mayhew's contribution to our knowledge of subjectivity and value in terms of (1) the people who made the world, (2) the world that they made, (3) the world that, in the arc of reciprocity, returned to (remake) them, (4) the significance of what Mayhew himself made, and a concluding section on (5) London's streetfolk and value.

Before turning to the argument, however, I shall describe the limited scope of Mayhew's surveys. The *Morning Chronicle* letters provide the closest look we have at London trades from within, yet it is the particularity of these views, their "close-up" effects, that are significant in representing London labor rather than their breadth. For in focusing upon the classic trades Mayhew excluded professional and subprofessional workers, including engineers and clerks. Nor did he interview domestic workers, who represented twenty percent of the working population. As will be discussed in Chapter 4, domestic workers within the workplace were difficult of access to outsiders, a fact that contributed to their susceptibility to embourgeoisement. The sequel to the *Morning Chronicle* letters, *London Labour and the London Poor,* only includes the metropolitan streetfolk—the buyers, sellers, finders, and performers who provided goods and services to the very poor themselves.

Interviews are clearly not autobiography, and Mayhew undoubtedly set the agenda in specifically directing his interviews around wages and working conditions. Yet because of the extensive resources at his com-

mand for the project, the biographies in the *Morning Chronicle* are taken
as accurately representing the stories of the tradespeople as they told
them. They were often interviewed with witnesses and their accounts
were often corroborated by others. On the "street biographies" (as Mayhew calls them) of *London Labour and the London Poor*, Anne Humpherys concludes:

> I am convinced that though Mayhew may have been fooled by some of
> his informants, though under the pressure of deadlines he may have been
> careless and erratic in his checking of individual statements, though occa-
> sionally he may have been drawn to the more picturesque specimens of
> the lower part of the lower classes, he did not deliberately omit informa-
> tion he did not want to hear, nor add other material to clarify or bend the
> interviews, nor distort the stories in other ways. There is too much "extra-
> neous" information in individual interviews and too many statements
> expounding different points of view in nearly all his series. The inclusive-
> ness plus the number reinforces my confidence in the general reliability
> of particular cases. But to repeat, this reliability depends on the total pic-
> ture that emerges from his different series, and to use Mayhew's work
> accurately we must use it in toto.[14]

THE PEOPLE WHO MAKE THE WORLD

Even given the limited scope of Mayhew's work, his eighty-two detailed
articles or "letters" in the *Morning Chronicle* from October 1849 through
December 1850 and their extension in *London Labour and the London
Poor* for a decade later comprise the most extensive single project we have
on material culture and subjectivity in Victorian England and perhaps in
nineteenth-century Europe. In the *Morning Chronicle* letters one sees the
metropolis from the viewpoint of—in Nagel's sense of what it is like to
be—silk-weavers, needlewomen, tailors, boot- and shoemakers, wood-
workers, dressmakers and milliners, hatters, tanners, curriers, men,
women, and children: all worked, or suffered from the lack of work.
Within these distinct trades Mayhew found more distinctions, each with
their own distinct experiences: tailors (23,517), milliners and dressmakers
(20,780) are divided from slopworkers and needlewomen (33,529); boot
and shoemakers (28,574) are divided between masters (2,096) and work-
people (26,478) with the latter divided between "men's-men" and "wom-
en's-men" and clickers, closers and makers; merchant-seamen (7,002—
"in the month of June") are distinguished from the navy (1,092) and distinguished by geography: the Australian trade, West Indian trade, African

trade, the whale fishery of the South Seas, the American trade. Wood-workers are divided between sawyers (29,593); carpenters and joiners (20,000); cabinetmakers (whose number cannot be estimated because the census of 1841 "lumps them with upholsterers," who, Mayhew remarks derisively, "are a totally different class of workmen, operating upon differing materials" [360]); ship- and boatbuilders (2,850); and coopers (4,000). To take only the last category of these, the coopers are divided between wet, dry, white, and general vesselmakers. Dressmakers make gowns and milliners other outward attire. Hatters (3,506) include furriers, curriers, finishers, shapers, stuff-hatters, and silk-hatters. Initially at least, and like the censuses of his day, Mayhew grouped people according to the materials they worked with, believing, with his informants, that consciousness depended upon material environment.

Also like his informants, he further divided labor between the honorable or fair (paying the standard wage) and dishonorable or foul (below standard wage). Each trade has its own sloptrade with dishonorable employers called sweaters, garretmasters, or slaughterhouse masters. All workers are either Society (10%), "the aristocracy" of trade, or Nonsociety (90%) according to whether they pay dues and remain in good standing with their respective unions. Each trade and Union has a price-book established by employers and operatives that regulates wages, and Union members are bound to work for no less. In the terms of political economy, Society wages are thus regulated by custom and Nonsociety by competition among the masters. Flints work for union wage; refractories shirk union regulation yet profess to be union operatives; scabs work for lower wages, break strikes, and so forth.

Such are the people who make the world, according to the divisions, laws, and customs of their crafts, as Mayhew presented them to readers of the paper second in prestige only to *The Times*. In addition to the details of the separate trades, he included sections on the "cultural habits," "social conditions," "views" or "opinions," and "histories" of each trade, indicating, as Sherlock Holmes would do later in his numerous descriptions of suspicious persons, that the craft visibly marked the craftspersons—individually, in neighborhoods, and as a class. Curriers wear very thick blue flannel trousers and jackets, strong shirts, and blue flannel aprons, and "their boots are often the very best" (460). The silk-weavers of Spitalfields, descendants of French refugees after the revocation of the Edict of Nantes, cultivated a legendary love of botany and horticulture that was still evident—amid the deterioration Mayhew found them in—

in their gardens "filled with many-coloured dahlias" (108). The show-room-women in prominent milliners' establishments in the West End wear "silk dresses, with short sleeves, and very small lace caps, with long streamers of ribbon that fall over their shoulders down to their feet" (430); while the women in the workroom itself "are generally short. If there is a tall one amongst them she is usually an 'improver' [i.e., came from the country to learn the trade], and has grown up before she learned her business. Very few of them can be called pretty, for if their features are well formed, they are so thin and pale-looking that their appearance is not very prepossessing" (431, written account to Mayhew by "a lady"). Seamen identifiably clad themselves warmly and cleanly, while slopwork tailors and needlewomen had generally, by the time they met Mayhew, pawned some of their clothes, beginning with underclothing.

Trade also marks social relations. Unlike the workers themselves, the marketplace did not distinguish between child and adult labor, a lack of distinction that strained familial and social relations. Cabinetmakers in the East End had from five to six children per family. "They are generally all at work for them [from the age of six years]," explains a father/employer of the estimated 12,000 juvenile cabinetmakers in the metropolis, "You see our trade's come to such a pass that unless a man has children to help him he can't live at all" (395). A stoker on a steamer has contempt for above-bridge boats guided by "nothing but a parcel of boys, had cheap" (321), articulating a common complaint whereby children, who worked for lower wages, were looked upon as competition by adult workers and received with due hostility. A West End woman's(shoe)man writes to Mayhew with concern for the degree of competiton between children and adult men, "One of the chief evils of our trade. . . . These boys are not apprentice boys, but taken on from ten to sixteen years of age, and instructed in the trade. Thus, a sharp lad will be perfect in two years, and then his labour is brought into the market, to reduce the man to the boy's level" (251). Often hostility deriving from unemployment was directed against the Irish and other immigrants; but industrialization in the 1840s was extraordinary in its tendency to scapegoat children. Children, of course, are always marginal, but they are not usually, or easily, viewed, as they were under such conditions of economic competition, as antagonistic Others.

Many adult workers, however, did pity the children for their peculiar loss of childhood. A London toygunmaker whose entire tin trade had been supplanted by child factory labor in Birmingham empathized with "the poor little things to whom a toy is a horror" (292), and Mayhew himself reflected that it was "curious enough, and somewhat melancholy, to observe the boy working at that which constitutes other boys' play" (282). As adults often viewed children as threats or competition, children did not see themselves as children according to middle-class connotations of child development. The twelve-year-old son of a cooper and impoverished shoe-man—impoverished partly because wages had been driven down by child labor—attributes his work history and independent economic status to needs unmet by his family: "I wanted a few halfpence for myself, but most of all I wanted clothes" (276). As George Gissing and Thomas Hardy would point out at the end of the century, working-class children saw themselves as economic agents, a perception that significantly distinguished them from their middle-class peers.[15]

If parent–child relationships among metropolitan laborers differed from those among the middle classes, so to a great extent did the entire sex–gender system, and this fact contributed to their different subjective experiences. Of the 33,500 needle- and slopworkers in the capital, more than three-fourths, or at least 28,500, were women under twenty: many of these were both mothers and occasional prostitutes. In his later dealings with London's streetfolk and costermongers, Mayhew would find lives and social patterns—including sexual habits, family, and kinship organization—at such variance with those of the respectable middle classes that he would resort to the analytic categories of contemporary ethnography, treating the costers as nomadic tribes distinct from the society in which they appeared. Among them, he would find children for whom "the age of puberty, or something closely resembling it, may be attained at a much less numerical amount of years than that at which most writers upon the human species have hitherto fixed it"; a majority of adults who had never known their own ages; and an eight-year old watercress seller who was so uncanny a mixture of child in physical appearance and woman in experience that he confessed, "I did not know how to talk with her."[16] "I was brought up to the musical profession, and have been a street-performer twenty-two years," a member of a street band told Mayhew, "I'm now twenty-six"—indicting that "rearing" was granted streetchildren at the most the space of four years (III, 173). Mayhew would also quote the father of two performers on the tightrope and stilts whose daughters had performed in public for money before their third birthdays (III, 159).

In *Landscape for a Good Woman,* Carolyn Steedman is as fascinated as Mayhew by the story of the watercress girl. She contrasts it with that of Freud's Dora, a story whose middle-class metaphors are familiar and accessible to readers:

When a thing is presented in Dora's story, it takes on a universe of meaning: a jewel-case, a reticule, a closed door, a pair of pearl ear-rings. In this way, the writing of case-history takes on the dimensions of story-telling: it works by telling us that something is about to be revealed—that the story is already there to tell.

But there is no story for the little watercress girl. The things she spoke to Mayhew about (pieces of fur, the bunches of cress, the scrubbed floor) still startle after 130 years, not because they are strange things in themselves, but because in our conventional reading, they are not held together in figurative relationship to each other. . . . [B]oth narrative and metaphor work by bringing together things that at first seem separate and distant, but which then, moved towards each other through logical space, make a new and pertinent sense. But this shift through space depends on our ability as listeners and readers to accept the new ordering of events and entities which have been made by the plot of a story, or by the use of a metaphor. Where there is not the vision that permits the understanding of these new connections, then a story cannot be told.[17]

Steedman writes of the watercress girl's highly elaborated keeping of accounts—"In this situation her labour was not an attribute, nor a possession, but herself; that which she exchanged daily for the means of livelihood, for love, and food and protection" (136)—and she concludes with the interview's strangeness, its difference from stories like Dora's. Yet the watercress girl's story is not strange like the exotica of distant cultures. Rather, it is strange for its overdetermined marginality to the central story of middle-class childhood, for the way that the two stories that never touch, whose terms are wholly other, are interdependent.

The content and imagery [of the watercress girl's story] demonstrate its marginality to the central story, of the bourgeois household and the romances of the family and the fairy-tales that lie behind its closed doors. . . . [It is] the arena outside the gate, the set of metaphors forged out of the necessary and contingent relationship between all the big houses and the Clerkenwell rooms in which the child grew up. The marginality of her story is what maintains the other's centrality. (139)

THE WORLD THEY MADE

In Mayhew, the world of the metropolitan workers evokes some of the most beautiful language in Victoriana, a language of industry, of ideas transformed into art. Mayhew himself composes an anaphoral "To Penshurst" of the arts and sciences contributing to "the construction of the playthings of the young":

> Optics gives its burning glass, its microscope, its magic lantern, its stereo-scope, its thaumatrope, its phantasmascope, and a variety of others; electricity, its Leyden jars, galvanic batteries, electrotypes, etc.; chemistry, its balloons, fireworks, and crackers; mechanics, its clock-work mice—its steam and other carriages; pneumatics contributes its kites and windmills; acoustics, its Jew's harps, musical-glasses, accordians, and all the long train of musical instruments; astronomy lends its orreries. . . . Nor are the arts and artists that are called into play in the manufacture of toys less numerous. There is the turner, to turn the handles of the skipping-ropes, the ninepins, the peg, the humming, and the whipping tops, the hoop-sticks; the basket-worker, to make dolls' cradles, and babies' rattles, and the wicker-work carts and carriages; the tinman, to manufacture tin swords and shields, pea-shooters and carts, money-boxes, and miniature candlesticks; and the pewterer to cast the metal soldiers, and dolls' cups, and saucers, and fire-irons, and knives and forks, plates and dishes, chairs and table, and all the leaden furniture of the baby-house. (281)

He describes Loo tables ("the carving alone of one of the most beautiful ever made, for the Army and Navy Club, cost, I am assured, £40" [364]), dining tables, card tables; library, sofa, and occasional tables; and the materials of which they are made. He describes dining-room chairs, drawing-room chairs, japanned bedroom chairs; sofas—cabriole, couch, tête-à-tête ("in the form of the letter S, adapted for two persons only, who occupy the respective bends"); sideboards of mahogany and oak; cabinets of oak, walnut, and rosewood; "a perfect masterpiece" of a bookcase, so "pronounced by the trade" (365); chiffoniers, drawers, wardrobes—and here for the only time in almost a million words, Mayhew lapses into the fashionable language of France.

The tradespeople themselves speak lyrically of production that, like the vision of the matchgirl, appears in almost magical radiance. A weaver dying of cholera displays for Mayhew his velvet "for ladies to wear and adorn them, and make them handsome" (115) and Mayhew glosses it as "an exquisite piece that, amidst all the squalor of the place, seemed marvellously beautiful" (115). What Mayhew glimpses—and Bourdieu has theorized—as a working-class aesthetic ensures that, whenever possible, the functional object has a supplementary task to please the eye. He writes of the "strong-man" shoemaker, whose hands "are callous, like horn, from the induration caused by the constant friction of the threads," who yet "expended some time in polishing the sole of a very strong cheap shoe, so as to make it sightly (*or* as they frequently call it, *viewly*)." "This," Mayhew writes, "was the more noticeable, as the work was for no window-show, and the sole, of course, would be dirtied by the first wear; but still, with the poorest, the eye must be pleased" (253). The best paid class of wood-carvers have decorated their society museum with "some of the choicest specimens of the arts" (377)—and Mayhew dignifies his language to accommodate the table "strewn with volumes of valuable prints and drawings in connection with the craft . . . , *The Architectural Ornaments and Decorations of Cottingham, The Gothic Ornaments of Pugin, Tatham's Greek Relics, Raphael's Pilaster Ornaments of the Vatican, Le Pautre's Designs* and *Baptiste's Collection of Flowers* (large folio)" [377]. All this, it must be remembered, is forty years before the philanthropic Kyrle Society took it upon itself to promote the Diffusion of Beauty among the Lower Classes.

Mayhew writes of one "remarkable production," a sort of Book of Kells of working people, the price-book of the cabinetmakers. Embellished with "engravings of all the principal articles in the trade," it lists the price of every article of furniture and of each modification for function and ornament. Mayhew's description is a perfect piece of cultural criticism, of the artifact and its production, its meaning or reception, and the lived social relations in which it is embededed:

> It is a thick quarto volume, containing some 600 pages. . . . The date of this book of prices is 1811, and the wages of the society men have been unchanged since then. The preparation of this ample and minute statement of prices occupied a committee of masters and of journeymen between two and three years. The committee were paid for their loss of time from the masters' and the journeymen's funds respectively; and what with these payments, what with the expense of attending the meetings and consultations, the making and remaking of models, the cost of printing and engravings, the cabinet-makers' book of prices was not compiled, I am assured, at a less cost than from £4,000 to £5,000. (367)

The implicit aesthetic here—Mayhew and his informant's recognition that this book is beautiful—is a functional one, of course, the beautiful, first, according to the labor theory of value. Second, it is beautiful according to its benevolent influence when it enters the circuits of meaning or consumption ("the date of this book of prices is 1811, and the wages of the society men have been unchanged since then"). Yet this apparently functional aesthetic is not entirely at odds with traditional

Kantian aesthetics. Mayhew would confirm his aesthetic in his treatment of the costermongers' temporary theatres ("penny gaffs"). His statement is curiously contradictory in that it begins with the Kantian dictum that "to cultivate the sense of the beautiful is necessarily to inculcate a detestation of the sensual." Yet for Mayhew the beautiful as analogue of the Good leads in a circular fashion from sensuous nature to Kantian freedom and back to the "munificent Creation" of the sensual world:

> It is impossible for the mind to be accustomed to the contemplation of what is admirable without continually mounting to higher and higher forms of it—from the beauty of nature to that of thought—from thought to feeling, from feeling to action, and lastly to the fountain of all goodness—the great munificent Creator of the sea, the mountains, and the flowers—the stars, the sunshine, and the rainbow—the fancy, the reason, the love and the heroism of man and womankind—the instincts of the beasts—the glory of the angels—and the mercy of Christ. (I, 44)

As the series continues and labor, or creativity, comes to be central to human value, Mayhew's laborers would come increasingly to seem made in the image of a munificent Creator. Yet unlike the great price-book, most of the work praised in the *Morning Chronicle* letters did not remain among the workers but passed into the possession of the upper classes, and Mayhew begins to wonder of the shoemaker who polished the sole of the very cheap shoe whether the "working-class" aesthetic was not *more* "disinterested" than traditional aestheticism's. According to Ben Jonson, the walls of Penshurst had been reared with no man's ruin, no man's groan. However unlikely that is, it was certainly not true of the bricklayers' laborers who built and maintained the 300,000 houses of the metropolis in 1850.

THE WORLD RETURNED TO (REMAKE) THEM

Explicating texts from Goethe's *Faust* and Shakespeare's *Timon of Athens* on "the real nature of money" in 1844, Marx observed that propertied subjects took their identity from their power of possession:

> That which is for me through the medium of *money*—that for which I can pay (i.e., which money can buy)—that am *I*, the possessor of the money. The extent of the power of money is the extent of my power. Money's properties are my properties and essential powers—the properties and powers of its possessor. Thus, what I *am* and *am capable* of is by

no means determined by my individuality. I am ugly, but I can buy for myself the most *beautiful* of women. Therefore I am not *ugly,* for the effect of *ugliness*—its deterrent power—is nullified by money. I, in my character as an individual, am *lame,* but money furnishes me with twenty-four feet. Therefore I am not lame. I am bad, dishonest, unscrupulous, stupid; but money is honoured, and therefore so is its possessor. Money is the supreme good, therefore its possessor is good. Money, besides, saves me the trouble of being dishonest: I am therefore presumed honest. I am *stupid,* but money is the *real mind* of all things and how then should its possessor be stupid? Besides, he can buy talented people for himself, and is he who has power over the talented not more talented than the talented? Do not I, who thanks to money am capable of *all* that the human heart longs for, possess all human capacities? ... The overturning and confounding of all human and natural qualities, the fraternization of impossibilities—the *divine* power of money—lies in its *character* as men's estranged, alienating and self-disposing *species-nature.* Money is the alienated *ability of mankind.*[18]

To the extent to which this eloquent account of the relation of property to personal identity was true, it was equally true that dispossession dispossessed of more than property. Just as consumers derive their identity from consumption, so those whose identity depended upon their production were psychologically vulnerable to those who cheapened their work for their own profit. The producer's psychological dependence upon the things she makes is one of the most eloquent aspects of Mayhew's interviews. "That's cotton partly, you see, sir," the dying weaver shows Mayhew the shameful underside of the marvelous velvet, "just for the manufacturers to cheat the public, and get a cheap article, and have all the gold out of the poor working creatures they can, and don't care nothing for the work" (115)—and it is not clear whether the worker or the work is more diminished by the swindle. A boatbuilder is "degraded" and "lowered" by owners who permit rotten ("nailsick") boats to be superficially repaired for profit (411); and after minutely describing the contract system of speculative building a housebuilder speaks of the humiliation of both building and builder (352–53). If the artifact may be seen as the projection of the worker's idea made flesh, the cheapening and desecration of the artifact was the cheapening and desecration of the worker's world.

The arc of reciprocity returned the worker's labor in the form of a weapon or a tool, harming or helping her. Many operatives analyzed the injury and exploitation, as well as the possibility that it might have been otherwise. An experienced sawyer, whose trade had been superseded by steam sawmills, analyzed both the harm and the possibility:

> I look upon machinery as an injury to society generally, because if it drives the hands out of our trade they must go into some other, so that working men is continually pressing one upon another. . . . Supposing a machine do the work of 100 pair of saywers, then of course it throws 200 men out of employ; and these 200 men have families, and they are all benefitted by the employment of the working man's labour. But in the case of machinery only one man is benefitted . . . the money all goes to him and the others are left to starve. . . . We believe machinery to be a blessing if rightly managed. It only works for one class but the time *will* come when it *will* work for all parties. . . . You see, sir, when some are injured by any alteration, they gets compensation; but here is our trade cut up altogether, and what compensation do we get? (334)

The tale told in miniature repeatedly in the *Morning Chronicle* was the irony of creativity gone awry, misappropriated. (For a narrative of actual face to face combat between man and machine, see the *Sufferings of A Factory Cripple* [1841] in Chapter 4.) A Dutch sweated tailor will not marry a woman living in the shop with him because he cannot redeem his coat from the pawnshop and refuses to marry in his shirt-sleeves (120). In an interview so shocking to plague-mad middle-class readers that Charles Kingsley used it in his "Condition of England" novel *Alton Locke: Tailor and Poet: An Autobiography* (1850) (see Chapter 29, entitled "Nemesis"), a starving, tubercular tailor describes to Mayhew how he has pawned his own and his children's clothes and now sleeps under the garments his family manufactures and will sell to affluent clients. Many workers never left the workrooms, had never "been outside the doors and smelt the fresh air for months and months together" (215). Another tailor describes the sweatshop living arrangement, often the destination of immigrants from the provinces and Ireland:

> A sweater usually keeps about six men. These occupy two small garrets; one room is called the kitchen, and the other the workshop; and here the whole of the six men, and the sweater, his wife, and family, live and sleep. One sweater I worked with had four children, six men, and they, together with his wife, sister-in-law, and himself, all lived in two rooms, the largest of which was about 8 feet by 10. We worked in the smallest room and slept there as well—all six of us. There were two turn-up beds in it, and we slept three in a bed. There was no chimney, and indeed no ventilation whatever. (220)

Sweated shoemakers were apparently more brutalized than sweated tailors. Workers starved and watched their children starve in unventilated one-room dwellings with exorbitant rents; many wanted to emigrate but could not save the fee. Men, women, and children, worked, ate, slept, gave birth, and died while others in the same room continued working. A tailor "cursed in my heart such a country as England, which seemed to deny me the only privilege that I felt that I wanted—labour sufficiently remunerative to support my children without becoming a pauper" (264). Seamen swear that, should England war with the United States, they will not fight, for American ships "know how to behave to a man" (321 and passim). Even the best paid class of workers, the draughtsmen carpenters who are "so anxious about the education of their children because they themselves find the necessity of a knowledge of arithmetic, geometry, and drawing," only see them on Sundays, when they can take a meal at home (338).

It is increasingly obvious to Mayhew that environment creates the consciousness of the laborer. In the introduction I cited the provincial carpenter in a London sweater's shop whose self-confessed "feelings must be very much the same as one of the London cab horses" (348). It served there as an example of the psychological cost of classical liberalism's distinction between mental and manual labor. I cite here in full the striking image of the negative significance of spectacles for working people in the words of a seventy-nine-year-old carpenter:

> One master discharged two men when he saw them at work in glasses. . . .
> I used to wear glasses in one employ, and others did the same, and the
> foreman was a good man to the men as well as to the master; and if the
> master was coming, he used to sing out "Take those sashes out of the
> way," and so we had time to whip off our glasses, and the master didn't
> know we were forced to use them; but when he did find out, by coming
> into the shop unawares, he discharged two men. . . . It's no use my going
> to ask for work of any master, for if I hadn't my glasses on he'd see from
> my appearance I was old, and must wear them, and wouldn't hear of giv-
> ing an old man a job. One master said to me, "Pooh, you won't do—you
> were born too soon." (348–49)

Other workers attribute their measures of rational capacity to the unique conditions of specific trades. Union shipwrights are "great politicians" (i.e., organized workers) because they take half-hour lunches in pubs where "one man reads the newspaper aloud . . . a discussion almost invariably follows, and is often enough resumed in the evening" (404). On the other hand, a joiner commented that "joiners' work is noisy, and they can't talk when carrying it on, and that may account for joiners not being such politicians or thinkers as shoe-makers or tailors [who worked in groups and talked as they worked]" (344). Of cabinetmakers, Mayhew himself observed: "When the men are at work there is seldom much conversation, as each man's attention is given to his own especial task, while the noise of the saw, the plane, or the hammer, is another impediment to conversation. Politics, beyond the mere news of the day, are, I am assured by experienced parties, little discussed in these workshops . . . cabinet-makers, as a body, care little about such matters" (366).

Later, in *London Labour and the London Poor,* Mayhew reported the effects of the environment upon the streetfolk without comment. The education of the costermongers' children was "such only as the streets afford; and the streets teach them, for the most part—and in greater or lesser degrees,—acuteness—a precocious acuteness—in all that concerns their immediate wants, business, or gratifications; a patient endurance of cold and hunger; a desire to obtain money without working for it; a craving for the excitement of gambling; an inordinate love of amusement; and an irrepressible repugnance to any settled in-door industry" (I, 26). And he reports that costergirls "cannot settle": "the least restraint will make her sigh after the perfect liberty of the coster's 'roving life'" (I, 46).

In the course of the *Morning Chronicle* series, Mayhew becomes increasingly conscious of the *psychological* deprivation of manual laborers, alluding frequently to the metaphysical as well as physical isolation of labor: "The fancy cabinet-makers are, I am informed, far less political than they used to be. The working singly, and in their own rooms, as is nearly universal with them now, has rendered them more unsocial than they were, and less disposed for the interchange of good offices with their fellow workmen, as well as less regardful of their position and their rights as skilled labourers" (373). The "rationalization," or division into distinct disembedded functions, of trade (another consequence of "regulation by competition") contributed to a moral isolation that Engels had theorized as a principle of modernity itself in 1844 in *The Condition of the Working Class in England* (translated and published in England in 1882). Although the predominant source of *The Condition* was Manchester, where Engels managed his father's factory, he took his key illustration of modern isolation from the slums of London: "[The inhabitants] rush past each other as if they had nothing in common. They are tacitly agreed on one thing only—that everyone should keep to the right of the pavement so as not to collide with the stream of people moving in the opposite direction. . . . The disintegration of society into individuals, each guided by his private principles and each pursuing his own aims has been pushed to its furthest limits in London. Here indeed human society has been split into its component atoms."[19]

Competition among the masters, or economic individualism, translated into isolation for workers, with the extent of their isolation reflected by their frequent ignorance of the competition itself: "There is among the East-end cabinet-makers no society, no benefit or sick fund, and very little communion between the different classes," Mayhew writes. "The chair-maker knows nothing of the table-maker next door, and cannot tell whether others in his calling thrive better or worse than he does. These men have no time for social inter-communication" (382). It was precisely to encourage social intercommunication that Mayhew called his many mass meetings with the poor, introducing them to one another and to the world at large. He addressed fifty ticket-of-leave men, or convicts with commuted sentences, with the "wish to get bodies of men together in a mass, their influence by that means being more sensibly felt than if they remain isolated" (III, 440). He duly seized upon the spectacle of the Crystal Palace and Great Exhibition of the Industry of All Nations in 1851 as the image of cooperative effort. Unlike most of its critics then and now, he did not analyze it primarily as a modernist monument to imperialism, which it undoubtedly also was, but rather, and perhaps equally importantly, as "the first public expression of the dignity and artistic quality of labour that has been made in this country."[20]

WHAT MAYHEW MADE

Satirical, antiestablishment, irreverent, bohemian, Henry Mayhew, son of a successful London solicitor who disinherited him, and renegade from Westminster (he refused to be flogged and ran away at fifteen), was a cofounder of *Punch*. At the height of his career as a journalist with the *Morning Chronicle* letters, he was an obscure bankrupt by 1860 and remained obscure and poor until his death in 1887, the year that *Capital* was translated into English.

He had commenced the *Morning Chronicle* series in 1849 as an effort in social reconciliation—after the revolutionary events of 1848 in Europe, the last flickers of Chartism in England, and perhaps most significantly, the cholera epidemic of 1848, which as E. P. Thompson says provoked an "almost hysteric wave of social conscience."[21] Published in the distinguished *Morning Chronicle,* the letters had an immediate, far-reaching, and dramatic reception. After his most sensational (to middle-class readers) revelation, that of prostitution among the needlewomen (a theme taken up by Elizabeth Gaskell in *Mary Barton* [1848] and *Ruth* [1853]), he convened a meeting of about 1,000 female slopworkers, which was disrupted by Lord Ashley (future Earl of Shaftesbury) and Sidney Herbert, who announced that the slopworkers were poor because they were in excess of demand (the premise of philanthropy and political economy) and that 500,000 of them would be welcomed in the colonies. Successive letters and editorials in the *Morning Chronicle* offered that the surplus women be "filtered" through some Magdalen institution before departure to Australia. The Queen and Prince Albert headed the subscription list. Dickens contributed his views on the topic by sending not only Martha the prostitute but also the fallen little Emily to Australia with the Micawbers in *David Copperfield* (1850). Other social reforms directly responding to the letters included an (unsuccessful) attempt to change the method of payment for ballast-heavers (hired and paid through publicans) and the founding of a Friendly Association of coster-mongers. The *Economist* attacked Mayhew as a communist and (also) advised the poor to control their population.[22]

In the course of his interviews Mayhew had increasingly rejected Malthusian determinism, blaming the evils of poverty rather on unregulated competition. During the year he edited *The Comic Almanac* (1851), an anonymous satire appeared on the Female Emigration Society, expressing what was probably Mayhew's own low estimation of transportation as a solution to poverty. When he began to criticize free trade in favor of protection, his editor began to censor the letters. Forced to repudiate editorial opinion falsely attributed to himself (which, incidentally, confused and distressed some of his working-class readers), Mayhew addressed a public demonstration of 1,500 convened by London tailors, where he called philanthropists "social ghouls and commercial cannibals," the Sheriff of London's own tailoring establishment "a disgrace and an abomination," and the Sheriff himself one of the "really 'dangerous classes.'" One year with the *Morning Chronicle* had provoked an alliance against Mayhew of political economists, free traders, philanthropists, and nervous employers, not to mention jealous fellow journalists.

Yet Mayhew's project had followed three decades of investigation of the working classes, in the cities' local and voluntary statistical societies as well as in the Royal Commissions and Select Committees on the administration of Poor Laws and the Health of Towns. Committed to

the political economy maxim that the adult male worker must be free
from legislative "interference" to the mercies of the free market and fearful that the factory system was destroying the institution of the family,
the authors of the major industrial studies of factories (1833), mines
(1842), and agriculture (1843) had focused solely on the physical and
moral condition of children and women at work. Only the inquiry into
the condition of the handloom weavers (1838–1841) attempted to find
the economic causes of poverty, the economic position of the whole family, net wages, and the extent of unemployment. By way of his interviews
in the *Morning Chronicle* office and homes of the poor, Mayhew under-
took the first "systematic" study of the industrial causes of low wages and
poverty in the metropolitan trades.[23] Only once were his investigations
challenged on grounds of selection or misrepresentation, in the Ragged
Schools case, and the furor of that affair may be attributed to Mayhew's
impolitic attack upon the middle-class panaceas of education and
philanthropy.[24]

Mayhew, who had cultivated an interest in scientific induction since
he was a boy (when he longed to be a research chemist), always
intended—throughout both the *Morning Chronicle* and *London Labour
and the London Poor* series—to write a proper "philosophical" treatise
on the general laws of political economy after he had collected the
"facts." Yet as the "facts" continued to multiply in the unending (and
unfinished) numbers of the two series, he continued to read the political
economists, from Smith, Ricardo, and Mill, to Charles Babbage (*The
Economy of Machinery and Manufacturers* [1832]) and Andrew Ure
(*The Philosophy of Manufacturers* [1835]), to the most ephemeral pam-
phleteers. As it happened, he publicized his conclusions with his data.
Despite disorder and occasional contradiction, one strong statement
emerged: as wages were reduced, families and individuals worked longer
hours, so there was less work for others, who were thrown out of work.
In slopwork, employers forced productivity, trying to get more work from
the same or fewer employees. This increase in productivity resulted in an
artificial surplus and the reduction of wages. As Mayhew put it, "over-
work makes under-pay" (385). Simultaneously, as workers try to increase
their diminishing incomes, "under-pay makes over-work." Marx would
make the same point in his discussion of the working day in *Capital*.
Although his informants themselves often blamed foreign trade, machinery, child labor, and London rents (higher than elsewhere), Mayhew
returned repeatedly to the evils of unregulated competition. He further
insisted that irregularity of employment was inconsistent with the regu-

larity of habits such as domesticity, industry, and temperance. His empirical account of the causes of poverty in the system of regulation by competition distinguished him from political economists, free traders, and philanthropists—or most of the producers of discourse on poverty of his time.

By working within an ethnological rather than the abstract, deductive mode of political economy, Mayhew came to identify the London poor and value itself in concrete and material terms. In the first letter to the *Morning Chronicle* he had identified the poor by the fact of their *pain:* "all those persons whose incomings are insufficient for the satisfaction of their wants—a want being . . . contra-distinguished from a mere desire by a positive physical pain" (102). As a result of the wrappers he appended to the serial numbers of *London Labour and the London Poor,* he published *Low Wages, Their Consequences and Remedies* (1851).[25] There he insists that the determining principle of good and bad wages is "the standard of sufficiency of remuneration." To set a minimal standard Mayhew places the body of the worker with its own primary, relentless economy at the center of value: "The cost of producing so much work can only be governed by the quantity of food required to be consumed during the performance of it. Food is to the human machine what coals are to the steam engine—the motive power. With all muscular action there is destruction of muscular tissue, and if that be not reproduced, the labourer must live on his capital of accumulated strength; and this, if continued, must, of course, end in that physical bankruptcy which is commonly called starvation" (463).

Minimal sufficiency of remuneration further includes the subsistence of the laborer when incapacitated for further work by illness or infirmity. Here Mayhew not only treats the body in its creative capacity, he treats creativity itself in its double sense of mental and manual creation, troping construction with instruction, and claiming that both deserve their "compensation": "What wear and tear is to the thing of brass and iron, so is sickness and accident to the creature of flesh and blood; and what the capital sunk in its *con*struction is to the machine, so is the time and money expended in *in*struction to the workman . . . but there is seldom any allowance made to the labourer for the wear and tear of the machinery of his frame; nor do his wages include any return for the capital and labour sunk in learning his business" (464–65). Continuing to turn the language of the political economists against them, Mayhew projects the minimum standard of sufficiency of remuneration further into the world to include the subsistence of the laborer's family, lest the children "be allowed to run wild and pick their morals and education out of the gutter" (465). Thus beginning with the muscular tissue, flesh and blood of the worker's body, Mayhew presses open his circle of value to include wider and wider circles of life.

He concludes Low Wages, Their Consequences and Remedies with images of the poor and himself not as objective observer but as an anonymous third person among them (. . . "he has heard women tell how they were forced to prostitute their bodies for the bread they could not earn by their labour . . . he has met with men who were forced to rent of their employers rooms they could not occupy . . ." [475]) and, as he began his letters in the Morning Chronicle, with verbs marking his own witnessing and engagement: found, discovered, seen, heard, met with. He counterposes these images and actions, his witnessing of the material world of the poor, with the books of the Economists, where he had found "doctrines" and words perverted from their meanings: "and when he sought, in the works of such as profess to teach the rights of labour as well as of capital, a remedy for the wrongs he witnessed, he found there doctrines only which made the impoverishment and fraud of the labourer part of the necessities and expediencies, if not glories, of the times" (475).

The apparent contradictions within Mayhew are significant here. In his dealings both with needlewomen who were occasional prostitutes in the Morning Chronicle and with women who "were forced to prostitute their bodies for the bread they could not earn by their labor" in Low Wages (i.e., when he had direct contact with the women through interviews), Mayhew was considerably more critical of the social factors contributing to prostitution than when he wrote about prostitutes without the benefit of interviews. In The Criminal Prisons of London (1862) he wavered between sociological and biological accounts of prostitution; and in the great tabular "Classification of the Workers and NonWorkers of Great Britain" in volume IV of London Labour he included all women laborers under the category Those Who Will Work, but all "prostitutes," including all unmarried female domestic partners—"those whose paramours cannot afford to buy the marriage fees" (IV, 27)—as well as professional prostitutes in brothels, under the category of Those Who Will Not Work. These latter would not work due to a "moral defect" in their character comparable to the "intellectual defect" of lunatics and "physical defect" of the young and old (IV, 3), all of whom (lunatic, young, and old), however, were included among the category of Those Who Cannot Work. Wives and children within the home Mayhew did not interview at all. Nor did he consider our modern feminist category of "unpaid childcare" as labor, but rather included wives and children among Those Who Need Not Work, who "derived their support from the head of the family" (IV, 27). Indeed, as Steedman suggests, part of his fascination with the watercress girl was the strangeness of her description of her liminal second job of babyminding, which childcare was a public economic relation as well as private and familial. In minding her baby sister, the seller of cress was both working and caring. Thus in his ethnographic work Mayhew captured the socioeconomic complexity of the daily lives of the poor. Away from his interviewees he often lapsed into the sentimental or biological clichés of the status quo or struggled to make his data fit their statistical taxa.

In his best work, Mayhew rejected the distance of political economy for the witnessing of the making of the world and unmaking of those who made it. He left them solidly in a world where *con*struction and *in*struction deserved equal compensation and where conditions were not discussed without the opinion of those inhabiting them, where objectivity was achieved not by the exclusive "impartiality" of political economic science but by including the very partial viewpoints of those concerned. He also discovered, perhaps most importantly for our discussion of subjectivity, the lie at the heart of classical economic individualism: the separation of mind and body into private and public that allows for procedural rights and freedoms (free markets) without a care for their substance in concrete lives. Mayhew saw that the mind or personality that was traditionally so unique and individual—what the middle classes called "genius"—was dependent upon communication with others, was in fact the most shared aspect of "individual" identity. Alternatively, the body, so common that everyone had one, under conditions of deprivation became the most private and alienating aspect of identity. With workers in society and in isolation, Mayhew learned what the Guild Cooperativists would learn: subjectivity cannot exist without intersubjectivity, whereas bodies in pain exist only as bodies in pain.

LONDON'S STREETFOLK AND VALUE

After the furor over the *Morning Chronicle* letters, Mayhew continued his project with interviews of the London streetfolk in *London Labour and the London Poor* (1861–1862), which are sometimes seen as a decline from his attempt at a systematic analysis of poverty from the inside into his considerable talent as an impressionist of streetlife "character." Part of the problem with the street biographies in *London Labour* is their literary–historical embeddedness. Coming as they did after very popular fictive and semifictive representations of London "lowlife" that romanticized the "freedom" of streetfolk and sensationalized their "violence," and with the "Condition of England" (today "industrial") fiction that exploited them as sources, it was and is difficult not to reduce them to the uncanny or the picturesque on the level of Pierce Egan's *Life in London* (1821), Dickens's *Sketches by Boz* (1835–1836), or G.W.M. Reynold's *Mysteries of London* (1844–1848, modeled on Eugène Sue). Dickens used *London Labour and the London Poor* most famously—or infamously—in his Dustmen, Doll's Dressmakers, Dredgermen, and general theme of commodity circulation, in *Our Mutual Friend* (1865). Mayhew thought Dickens "fatally-facile" and sentimental, yet a line from the section on "London Dustmen, Nightmen, Sweeps, and Scavengers" in the "Street-Finders or Collectors" section of Volume 2 could serve as epigraph to the clandestine energy of that haunting novel on consumption and recycling: "Almost without cognizance of the mass of the people, the refuse is removed from our streets and houses: and London, as if in the care of a tidy housewife, is *always* being cleaned" (II, 177). The crucial difference is that for Mayhew the cleansers of the metropolis are communicative and benevolent, whereas for Dickens they are mysterious and sensation-provoking, simply the willing or unwilling accomplices to the plotting of the upper classes.

I want to conclude my discussion of Mayhew with these four volumes because they reveal a critique of Victorian ideology and a revision of value that were surpassed only by the Marx of *Capital.* The Enlightenment practices of classification analyzed in Foucault's *Order of Things* did not culminate in Mayhew's case in a predictable power-knowledge but in the final obliteration of class boundaries. The road to his final, surprising analysis is one of distinctions multiplied infinitely, until all that remains is not the abstract categories of political economists but the unique "character" singularly embedded in its material world, a world that Mayhew values above all other cultural configurations, classifications, and statistics. He differed from novelists of his class and time in never taking the individual "character" as *representative* of the poor in general, but rather in multiplying their differences between one another ad infinitum. Yet despite his criticism of the status quo, like the novelists who drew so heavily upon his works he was deeply reformist rather than revolutionary. I shall return to these points.

Mayhew begins the first volume, "Of the London Streetfolk," with the "six distinct genera or kinds" of streetsellers, streetbuyers, streetfind-

ers, streetperformers/artists/showmen, streetartizans/pedlars, and street
laborers. The first genus, streetsellers, is subdivided according to the
nature of its products: sellers of fish, vegetables and fruits, eatables and
drinkables, literature and the fine arts, manufactured articles, live animals, and mineral products. These are further subdivided between the
uneducated streetsellers and the educated, or "patterers"—the "oratorical streetsellers" (former mountebanks), whose product is less their wares
than their wit. As one said to Mayhew, "We are the haristocracy of the
streets. People don't pay us for what we gives 'em, but only to hear us
talk. We live like yourself, sir, by the hexercise of our hinterlects—we by
talking, and you by writing" (I, 227). Throughout, Mayhew also incorporates entire sections on national and ethnic divisions: Irish fruitsellers,
Jewish clothesmen (Portuguese ["Sephardin"] and German/Polish), Italian organ boys, French singing women, Indian crossingsweepers, and so
forth.

The divisions are further and more finely articulated in the interviews
themselves, especially in Volume 2, in which streetsellers of dogs are
divided among sellers of terriers, pugs, poodles, sporting dogs, and so on,
and sellers of birds among kinds of birds and birdnests. After describing
the kinds of 43,000 streetsellers, Mayhew takes up the street buyers—of
Rag and Bottle and Marine Shops, of old clothes, of hogs' wash, tealeaves,
and so forth—and the streetfinders or collectors, of "pure" (dog's dung)
and cigar-ends, and so on, including the sewerhunters and mudlarks.
Each "class," no matter how tiny, is distinguished by a voice, a "character," and a habitat. The finders, "who go abroad daily to *find* in the
streets, and carry away with them such things as . . . no one appropri-
ates," include bonegrubbers and raggatherers as well as the sewerhunters
("whose labour is confined to the river, or to that subterranean city of
sewerage unto which the Thames supplies the great outlet" [II, 152]) and
the mudlarks, elderly women and orphans who search among the tidal
recesses and are known for their stupidity ("they may be passed and
repassed, but they notice no one; they never speak, but with a stolid look
of wretchedness they plash their way anxiously about, and occasionally
stoop to pick up some paltry treasure that falls in their way" [II, 173]).
The "public cleansers" are divided between dustmen (for dustbins),
nightmen (for cesspools), sweeps (for chimneys), and scavengers (for
streets), and each category is further subdivided. By the time Mayhew (or
his brother Augustus, or both of them) incorporates material on the street
musicians and artists in Volume 3, he classifies them according to
whether they are skillful or impaired, distinguishing the latter in a kind

of ablative mode, according to the place on the body where they have been maimed: the blind performer on the bells, blind female violin player, blind Irish piper, the blind profile cutters, and the writers without hands. Having begun the *Morning Chronicle* letters by taking his statistics and categories from government reports and censuses, Mayhew used his own classes, categories, and statistics for his work on the streets.

As I indicated earlier with the *Morning Chronicle* letters, such classifying always leads Mayhew to extend the world outward. He must write of the streetstalls of the costermongers, the homes of the street Irish, the rats of the "destroyers of vermin," the "low lodging houses" of the patterers, the theaters of the Jews. He includes an astonishing section of 180 pages in tiny print in Volume 2 on the *streets* themselves: the different kinds of pavement covering them, of traffics traversing them, of waters draining them, of dirt fouling them, and of ways of cleansing them.

Beyond the individual charms of the street performers and uncanniness of the mudlarks, the overwhelming effect of *London Labour and the London Poor* is the *fecund* materiality of the city, a remarkable effect in a study ostensibly about poverty. Unlike some of the other social explorers and scientists who will be discussed in Chapter 3, Mayhew does not present this paradoxical wealth as a threat of engulfment, but rather as a distinctly unMalthusian *productivity*. In Volume 2 he provides a chart "Showing the Quantity of Refuse Bought, Collected, or Found, in the Streets of London" (II, 524–25) (Figure 2.1) indicating the monumental circulation and recycling of everything from copper to women's stays to fishskins in tabular form. Anne Humpherys rightly points out the significance of consumption patterns to an ethnography of the poor's own version of Carlyle's "cash nexus": "A street seller sold tea to the artisan for his dinner; the artisan's wife sold the used tea leaves to a woman who in turn sold them to a rag-and-bottle shop (the cheapest sort of second-hand shop) and ultimately they were made into 'new' tea and sold again to the costermonger's companion."[26] I think of Mary Douglas's "communications approach to consumption," her view that commodity consumption constitutes a live information system and that we can measure social involvement by comparing consumption patterns.[27]

As Humpherys notes, scholars have ridiculed Mayhew's obsessive calculations of horsedung and cattle-droppings annually deposited on the streets of London, not to mention his claim that, were the 12,480 tons of refuse paper annually bought by the street buyers to be distributed in half-ounce letters, it would supply material "for *forty-four millions, seven hundred and twenty-eight thousand, four hundred and thirty letters on business, love or friendship*" (II, 526). Yet with such calculations Mayhew was providing a critique of politicial economy not only from the viewpoint of "the poor" but from the position of their neglected production. Although the London streetsellers were "driven from stations to which long possession might have given them a quasi-legal right ... bandied about at the will of a police-officer ... [told to] 'move on' and not obstruct a thoroughfare blocked with the carriages of the wealthy until to cross the road on foot is a danger," they were nonetheless, for Mayhew, a force of 40,000 turning over £3,000,000 per annum: "They are, in fine, a body numbering thousands, who are allowed to live in the prosecution of the most ancient of all trades, sale or barter in the open air, *by sufferance alone.* They are classed as unauthorized or illegal and intrusive traders, though they *'turn over' millions in a year*" (II, 3).

Mayhew's insistence upon the productivity of the poor reflects what the poor valued in themselves. It is doubly remarkable when one recalls that Mayhew was thus glorying in the multitude and its productivity at a time when the country was still reeling under the "dismal science" (Carlyle's phrase) of Malthus and Ricardo, which saw a humanity groaning under a flood of hungry mouths and predicted another flood of commodities without buyers, and when many social scientists expressed fears of social contagion from the so-called dangerous classes.

The proliferation of his data, the irrepressible individuation of his subjects, prevented Mayhew from ever completing his surveys, but they also led him to a new political economy with labor at its center on the wrappers of *London Labour* and his final classifications obliterating class distinctions at the beginning of Volume 4. In the former, the covers or "wrappers" of *London Labour and the London Poor,* Mayhew published a correspondence column called "Answers to Correspondents." With his customary sensitivity to commodity recycling he called these inscribed wrappers "waste" papers—not bearing the permanency of the interviews making up the text proper—and permitted himself the largeness of view suppressed in his empirical work as well as a dialogical turn almost unique in the production of economic theory. These wrappers indicate how his immersion into the laborers' world, his taking up their viewpoint, as it were, had led him to a revision of political economy, which had previously been characterized precisely by its *distance,* its a priori logic concerning the "mass" it analyzed. "Political Economy," he wrote, "as it stands is super-eminently the science of trading ... the fallacy of the whole appears to consist in ignoring the existence of the labourer and

A TABLE SHOWING THE QUANTITY OF REFUSE BOUGHT, COLLECTED, OR FOUND, IN THE STREETS OF LONDON.

Articles bought, collected, or found.	Annual gross quantity.	Average Number of Buyers, and quantity sold Daily or Weekly.	Obtained of the Street Buyers.	Price per pound weight, &c.	Average Yearly Money Value. £ s. d.	Parties to whom sold.
REFUSE METAL.						
Copper	291,600 lbs.	200 buyers ¼ cwt. each weekly	1-500th	6d. per lb.	7,290 0 0	Sold to brass-founders and pewterers.
Brass	291,600 "	do. ¼ " do.	"	4d. "	4,860 6 8	Do. do.
Iron	2,329,600 "	do. 2 " do.	1-200th	½d. "	2,426 13 4	Do. to iron-founders and manufacturers.
Steel	62,400 "	do. 6 lbs. do.	none	1d. "	260 0 0	Do. to manufacturers.
Lead	1,164,800 "	do. 1 cwt. do.	1-500th	1½d. "	7,280 0 0	Do. to brass-founders and pewterers.
Pewter	291,600 "	do. ¼ " do.	"	5d. "	6,075 13 4	Do. do.
					28,192 13 4	
HORSE & CARRIAGE FURNITURE.						
Carriages	120 "	4 — 30 sets yearly	none	11l. each	1,320 0 0	Sold to Jew dealers.
Wheels (4, from coach-builders)	600 sets	100 — 8 do.	"	25s. a set	750 0 0	Do. to costers and small tradesmen.
Wheels, in pairs for carts & trucks	600 pairs	50 — 12 pairs yearly	"	7s. a pair	210 0 0	Do. do.
Springs for trucks and small carts	780 "	5 — 3 " weekly	"	6s. per pair	234 0 0	Do. to costers and others.
Lace, from coach-builders	1,344 lbs.	12 — 112 lbs. yearly	"	1d. per lb.	5 12 0	Do. to cab-masters and to Jews.
Fringe and tassels, from ditto	2,688 "	12 — 224 " do.	. "	½d. "	5 12 0	Do. to Jews.
Coach & carriage linings, singly	156 "	12 — 13 yearly	"	25s. each	195 0 0	Do. to cab-masters.
Harness (carriage pairs)	60 pairs	12 — 6 pairs do.	"	3l. per pair	180 0 0	Do. to omnibus proprietors.
Ditto (single sets)	144 sets	12 — 12 sets do.	"	30s. per set	216 0 0	Do. to cab-masters.
Ditto (sets of donkey and pony)	41,600 "	100 — 8 sets weekly	harness makers	4s. a set	8,320 0 0	Do. to little master harness-makers.
Saddles	1,040 "	2 — 2 " do.	"	4s. "	203 0 0	Do.
Collars	2,080 "	10 — 4 " do.	"	9d. "	78 0 0	Do. and marine stores.
Bridles	4,160 "	10 — 6 " do.	"	8d. "	138 13 4	Do. do.
Pads	2,080 "	10 — 4 " do.	"	6d. "	52 0 0	Do. do.
Bits	4,160 "	10 — 3 " do.	"	2d. "	34 13 4	Do. do.
Leather (new cuttings from coach-builders)	58,136 lbs.	24 — 22 cwt. yearly	"	4d. "	985 12 0	Do. to Jews and also to gunsmiths.
Ditto (morocco cuttings from do.)	960 "	20 — 48 " do.	"	1s. 6d. "	72 0 0	Do. to tailors' trimming-sellers.
Old leather (waste from ditto)	53,760 "	12 — 20 " do.	"	2¼d. "	560 0 0	Do. to Jews.
					13,560 2 8	
REFUSE LINEN, COTTON, &c.						
Rags (woollen, consisting of tailors' shreds, old flannel drugget, carpet, and moreen)	4,659,200 lbs.	do. 4 " weekly	1-1000th	½d. per lb.	9,706 13 4	Sold for manure and to nail up fruit-trees.
Ditto (coloured cotton)	2,912,000 "	do. 2½ " do.	1-500th	2d. "	6,066 13 4	Do. to paper-makers and for quilts.
Ditto (white)	1,164,800 "	do. 1 " do.	1-1000th	2d. "	9,706 13 4	Do. to paper-makers.
Canvas	44,800 "	do. 2 " yearly	none	1d. "	186 13 4	Do. to chance customers.
Rope and sacking	291,200 "	do. 4 " weekly	1-500th	½d. "	606 13 4	Do. for oakum and sacking to mend old sacks.
					36,898 13 4	
PAPER.						
Waste paper	1,397,760 "	60 colls. each disposing of 4 cwt. weekly	all	18s. per cwt.	11,232 0 0	Do. to shopkeepers.
GLASS AND CROCKERYWARE.						
Bottles (common and doctors')	62,400 doz.	200 buyers, 24 weekly	1-100th	2d. per doz.	520 0 0	Do. to doctors and chemists.
Ditto (wine)	31,200 "	200 — 12 do.	1-200th	6d. "	780 0 0	Do. to Brit. wine merchants & ale stores.
Ditto (porter and stout)	4,800 "	200 — 24 dozen yearly	none	6d. "	120 0 0	Do. to ale and porter stores.
Flint glass	15,600 lbs.	200 — 1½ lbs. weekly	1-1000th	⅓d. per lb.	16 5 0	Do. to glass manufacturers.
Pickling jars	7,200 "	200 — 36 yearly	none	½d. each	22 10 0	Do. to Italian warehouses, &c.
Gallipots	20,800 doz.	200 — 24 weekly	"	2d. per doz.	173 6 8	Do. do.
					1,632 1 8	

Article	Quantity	No. & rate of collection	Bought of	Price	Value (£ s. d.)	Disposal
Trousers	312,000 pairs	300 … 4 pr. trousers do.	"	3s. 8d. per pr.	—	Do. do.
Waistcoats	46,800	300 do. 3 waistcoats do.	"	7d. each	9,100 0 0	Do. do.
Under-waistcoats	15,600 pairs	300 do. 3 weekly	"	2d. "	390 0 0	Do. to wholesale and wardrobe dealers.
Breeches and gaiters	3,000	300 do. 1 pair weekly	"	2s. per pair	1,560 0 0	Do. to old clo' men and wholesale dealers.
Dressing-gowns	1,000	100 do. 30 yearly	"	4s. 2d. each	625 0 0	Do. to wholesale and wardrobe dealers.
Cloaks (men's)		100 do. 10 cloaks yearly	"	10s. "		Do. to wholesale dealers.
Boots and shoes	1,560,000 pairs	100 do. 60 pairs daily	none	7d. per pair	45,500 0 0	Do. to wardrobe dealers and second-hand boot and shoe makers.
Boot and shoe soles	648,000 dz. pr.	100 do. each collecting 30 dz. pr. daily	none	1s. per dz. pr.	32,400 0 0	Do. to Jews and gunsmiths to temper gun-barrels.
Boot legs	520,000 "	200 do. do. 50 weekly	bt. of old clo'men	5s. each	130,000 0 0	Do. to translators.
Hats	1,879,000	300 colls. each purchasing 24 hats daily	"	4d. each	31,200 0 0	Do. to dealers and master hatters.
Boys' suits	3,600	300 do. 12 suits yearly	"	3s. a suit	540 0 0	Do. Jew dealers.
Shirts and chemises	626,400	300 do. 8 daily	"	4d. each	10,400 0 0	Do. to old cl.' men and wholesale dealers.
Stockings of all kinds	783,000 pairs	100 do. 30 pair daily	"	1d. per pair	3,272 10 0	Do. to wholesale and wardrobe dealers.
Drawers (men's and women's)	93,600	300 do. 6 weekly	"	3d. "	1,170 0 0	Do. do.
Women's dresses of all kinds	496,800	300 do. 6 dresses daily	"	1s. 9d. each	41,107 10 0	Do. do.
Petticoats	939,600	300 do. 12 daily	"	7d. "	27,405 0 0	Do. do.
Women's stays	261,000 pairs	100 do. 10 pair do.	"	5d. per pair	5,437 10 0	Do. do.
Children's shirts	187,920	60 do. 12 daily	"	3d. a doz.	1,955 15 0	Do. do.
Ditto petticoats	261,000	200 do. 12 daily	"	1½d. each	1,639 11 8	Do. do.
Ditto frocks	522,000	200 do. 10 do.	"	4d. "	8,700 0 0	Do. do.
Cloaks(women's),capes,visites,&c	5,200	20 do. 5 cloaks weekly	"	4s. "	1,040 0 0	Do. to wholesale dealers.
Bonnets	1,409,400	150 do. 3 doz. daily	"	6d. "	35,235 0 0	Do. do.
Shawls of all kinds	469,800	300 do. 10 do.	"	1s. 2d. "	27,405 0 0	Do. to wholesale and wardrobe dealers.
Fur boas and victorines	261,000	100 do. 10 do.	"	1s. 2d. "	15,220 0 0	Do. do.
Fur tippets and muffs	130,500	100 do. 5 do.	"	5d. "	7,612 10 0	Do. do.
Umbrella and parasol frames	518,400	200 do., each collecting 12 daily	all	5d. "	10,300 0 0	Do. to Jews and old umbrella menders.
					675,555 6 8	
HOUSEHOLD REFUSE.						
Tea-leaves	78,000 lbs.	25 …	costers and fishmongers	2½d. per lb.	812 10 0	Do. to merchants to re-make into tea.
Fish-skins	3,900 "	do. 2 lbs. weekly for 6 months.		1d. "	16 5 0	Do. to brewers to fine their ale.
Hare-skins	80,000	50 do. 50 weekly	all	1s. a doz.	333 6 8	Do. to Jews, hatters, and furriers.
Kitchen-stuff	62,400 lbs	200 do. 6 lbs. weekly	none	1½d. per lb.	390 0 0	Do. at marine stores.
Dripping	52,000 "	200 do. 5 " do.	1-1000th	3d. "	650 0 0	Do. do.
Bones	3,494,400	200 buyers 3 cwt. weekly	all	¾d. "	105,625 0 0	Do. for manure, knife-handles, &c.
Hogwash	2,504,000 gals.	200 do., each purchasing 40 gal. daily	none	1d. per gallon	10,433 6 8	Do. to pig-dealers.
Dust (from houses)	900,000 loads	800 colls. each collectg. 19 bush. weekly	"	2s. 6d. per ld.	112,500 0 0	Do. for manure and to brickmakers.
Soot (from cesspools)	800,000 bush.		"	5d. per bushel	16,666 13 4	Do. to farmers, graziers, and gardeners.
Soil (from cesspools)	750,000 loads			10s. per load	375,000 0 0	Do. for manure.
					622,427 1 8	
STREET REFUSE.						
Street sweepings (scavengers')	140,983 "	444 do. the whole " 452 lds. daily	"	3s. "	21,147 9 6	Do. do.
Ditto (street orderlies')	2,817	546 do. do.	"	2s. 6d. "	2,352 2 6	Do. do.
Coal and coke (mudlarks')	64,656 cwt.	550 do., each collecting 42 lbs. do.	"	8d. per cwt.	2,151 17 4	Do. to the poor.
"Pure"	52,000 pails	do. 5 pails weekly	"	1s. per pail	2,600 0 0	Do. to tanners and leather-dressers.
Cigar ends	2,240 lbs.	50 do. 8½ lbs. do.	street-finders	8d. per lb.	74 13 4	Do. to Jews in Rosemary-lane.
					28,326 2 2	
				Gross Total …	**1,406,592 1 6**	

Figure 2.1. "A Table Showing the Quantity of Refuse Bought, Collected, or Found, in the Streets of London" from Volume II, *London Streetfolk* of Henry Mayhew's *London Labour and the London Poor* (1865). Courtesy of Stanford University Libraries.

not paying the same regard to his interests as to those of the capitalist class."[28]

With Volume 4 Mayhew intended to complete his survey of the poor with "Those That Will Not Work," but he got only so far as to reclassify his new political economy in such a manner as to obliterate all previous class distinctions and elevate physical labor. As he put it, he was then "to enunciate, for the first time, the natural history of the industry and idleness of Great Britain in the nineteenth century" (IV, 4). (There are many common misperceptions about the extent of Mayhew's input in Volume 4. It should be noted that he only wrote the first thirty-seven pages. For example, he did not write either the historical survey of prostitution or the section on London prostitutes, which should be contrasted with his meeting with prostitute/needlewomen as recounted in the *Morning Chronicle* letters.) Rejecting previous "scientific" taxonomies of the working population (such as Costaz's, Payon's, and Dupin's in France, and Prince Albert's for the Great Exhibition, the Census's, Babbage's, and Ure's in Britain), he divides the population between the autobious (seeking their own living) and allobious (living by the labor of others), energetic and anergetic, hardworking and nonworking, industrious and indolent. He then considers John Stuart Mill's classification of labor according to the "utilities" it produced in *Principles of Policical Economy* (1848). The utilitarian philosopher had classified utilities according to whether they were (1) fixed and embodied in outward objects, (2) fixed and embodied in human beings, or (3) not fixed or embodied in any object but consisting in a mere service rendered. He had duly divided labor between the (1) producers of material objects, (2) educators, broadly conceived as those who confer on human beings qualities that render them serviceable to themselves and others, and (3) servitors, or those who give pleasure or avert pain without leaving a permanent acquisition.

To Mill's three categories Mayhew proposed an additional class, subdividing Mill's category of producers of material objects into producers and those who helped the producers, called the *Auxiliaries,* "engaged in assisting those who are so occupied in fitting things to be useful. This class consists of such as are engaged in aiding the producers of permanent material utilities either *before* or during production, and such as are engaged in aiding them *after* production" (IV, 9). Mayhew includes among the Auxiliaries "capitalists, or those who supply the materials and tools for the work, superintendents and managers, or those who direct the work, and labourers, or those who perform some minor office connected with the work, as in turning the large wheel for a turner, carrying bricks to a bricklayer, and the like" (IV, 9). The Auxiliary class also includes those who assist the producers after production: "carriers, or those who remove the produce to the market, and dealers and shopmen, or those who obtain purchasers for it" (IV, 9).

With this final occlusion of all traditional class distinctions, Mayhew alters Mill's classification to include Enrichers ("those who are employed ... in producing exchangeable commodities or riches"), Auxiliaries ("those who are employed in aiding the production of exchangeable commodities"), Benefactors ("those who confer some permanent benefit by promoting the physical, intellectual, or spiritual well-being of others"), and Servitors ("those who render some *temporary* service or pleasure to others") (IV, 9, and see the complete table referred to above of "The Classification of the Workers and NonWorkers of Great Britain," pp. 12–27). In addition to identifying capitalists with brick carriers as Auxiliaries, he includes among the Servitors "Amusers" such as actors and exhibitors of monstrosities, "Servants" such as butlers, lady's maids, scavengers, and crossing sweeps, and "Protectors" such as the Sovereign, members of Parliament, and Secretaries of State for Home, Foreign, and Colonial Affairs. Having begun his *Morning Chronicle* study with the government's categories and classifications, he concludes *London Labour and the London Poor* with the taxonomic subversion of the status quo. Mayhew concludes his part in this literary monument to the producers of the material world in agreement with the utopian socialist Saint-Simon, that "economically speaking, the most important and directly valuable of all classes are those whom I have here denominated *Enrichers*" (IV, 10). As in the case of the women cooperativists, Mayhew began with the ignorant, naked, hungry, and isolated, but concluded with the source of value as human interdependence and the abolition of traditional hierarchies. The reactions to his journalism in literature, labor reform, and, unfortunately, emigration policy indicate what anthropologists and sociologists today are only beginning to recognize: "social science," even in its earliest manifestations, not only interpreted the world, it also changed it.[29]

This is not the first time such a story, one that would feed back via the lore of labor unions and cooperatives into workers' conceptions of themselves, had been told. In Engels's chapter on "Working-Class Movements" in *The Condition,* he portrayed the progress of working men from brutes to literate men in pursuit of their political destiny (see Chapter 3). What writers like Mayhew and Engels sympathetic to the subjective experiences of the working population had to counter was, of course, institutional tendencies toward the opposite effects of distancing and objectification. From the naming of the discipline of sociology by Auguste Comte in the early 1840s, the new sociologists (the later Comte notwithstanding) preferred quantitative (i.e., statistical) analysis. Far from exploring the world of the poor in terms of moral philosophy, Charles Booth would work with intermediaries (school attendance counters, clergy, police, etc.) and equate qualitative evidence with sensationalism, insisting that he would "make use of no fact to which I cannot give a quantitative value."[30] (For the range of such sociological literature see Chapter 3.)

On the other hand, in emphasizing Mayhew's distinctiveness among social scientists of his time, it is equally important to stress his affinity with the imaginative writers who borrowed from his work. By focusing upon the great variety, proliferation, and differentiation of occupations and social types and forms, especially by his presentation in *London Labour and the London Poor* of the streetfolk as idiosyncratic "characters," Mayhew occluded the very class divisions, consciousness of which, Marx and Engels were insisting, was the basis of revolutionary radicalism. Mayhew was deeply humanistic—humanly grounded—in his critique of the social system, with the humanism at the heart of the best British reformism. But, as with the industrial novelists, that very humanism precluded the kind of systematic understanding that would later come to the English socialists like Morris.[31]

In England, of course, both the socialists and the humanists lost the economic field to the scientists. In economics, after the "ethnography" of Mayhew and the shift in focus from the "laws" of production to the "customs" of distribution in Mill, came the psychic mathematicians, academic economists like Francis Edgeworth (*Mathematical Psychics* [1881]), Alfred Marshall, Stanley Jevons, John Bates Clark, and Le'on Walras, who added mathematical precision to Jeremy Bentham's proposition that humans were pleasure machines, each busily arranging his or her life to maximize the pleasure of his or her psychic adding machine.[32] Differential calculus showed that a world of perfect competition would maximize the total amount of pleasure that could be generated by the society, a principle that, even modified according to the *im*perfect competition of the real world, both advocated the demise of associations like trade unions and justified the gender and class status quo. The equations of the psychic mathematicians, like Booth's "no fact to which I cannot give a quantitative value" eventually led to the complete divorce between politics and economics. As "political" was dropped from political economy, the great proponent of scientific economics, Stanley Jevons, admitted, "About politics I confess myself in a fog."[33]

One of the few to protest against the complacency of official economics, Henry George in the United States echoed Mayhew's "I know that in science the love of theorizing warps the mind" in his *Progress and Poverty* of 1883, a work much loved and cited by working-class autobiographers in Britain: "Economics as currently taught *is* hopeless and despairing. But this [is] because she has been degraded and shackled; her truths dislocated; her harmonies ignored; the word she would utter gagged in her mouth, and her protest against wrong turned into an indorsement of injustice."[34] Like Mayhew's, there was nothing abstract or distant about George's approach to economics. He had worked as a gold prospector, sailor, compositor, journalist, government bureaucrat, lecturer, typesetter, weigher in a rice mill, and tramp.

Florence Nightingale's Violent World of Leisure

In the first section of this chapter I have argued that working women isolated within their bodies learned through intersubjective experience to use their bodies to change their culture. In the second, that in the arc of reciprocity the world made by the metropolitan workers returned to remake their consciousness and, through Mayhew, to affect the consciousness of novelists and legislators. I want to conclude this chapter on subjectivity, the body, and material culture with the case of one especially interesting woman who straddled the boundaries between woman as maternal caretaker (an image of embodied femininity that kept upper-class women in the home) and public administrator, a border crossing that is additionally complicated by the opportunities for publicity that were opening up for women in the second half of the nineteenth century. These opportunities for publicity exposed middle-class women to the public as never before, but they also masked the real exclusion of women from public positions of power. As Veblen argued in his great satire upon the leisure class of the late Victorian United States, and as our contemporary Veblen, Pierre Bourdieu, argues in *Distinction,* an equally satirical critique of bourgeois taste in France, the effects of new practices of consumption and publicity cannot be overestimated in the making of middle-class subjectivity.

Because I shall discuss upper-class women (including Nightingale) at length in Chapter 5, I shall use only one example here to indicate how their containment within the maternal image of their embodiment and confinement within the Victorian domus radically altered their perspectives on the material culture of their world. In Florence Nightingale's "Cassandra" (contemporaneous with *London Labor and the London Poor*), comforting, tasteful books and music reveal themselves as weapons of violence against women.[35]

The most significant attempt to defend a profession for women, Florence Nightingale's, foundered on the cultural identification of female with body, male with mind. At seventeen, Nightingale transgressed the conventions of her gender and class when she was called by God to abandon her very wealthy family to work in a hospital—at a time when the reputation of nursing was at its lowest, associated with immoral conduct and insobriety (repellently portrayed by Dickens in *Martin Chuzzlewit's* Sarah Gamp [1843]). Nightingale attempted to transform nursing into a profession, but her publicity only succeeded in domesticating it, making it middle-class, gendering it. In a sequence of transitional, if not transgressional, steps she first worked in a charitable nursing home in Harley Street and then moved into the male world of military medicine and media fame with the disastrous collapse of medical facilities at Scutari. As she exploited this administrative collapse to make space for a woman's profession, the *Times* correspondent supplied home readers with images of nursing ultimately in terms of the female body. These were the containing images of the Nurse—the ideal representation of ideal woman, the angel of mercy, the bedside madonna, the lady of the lamp.

Nightingale received her call to nursing as the British Medical Association received its to political power.[36] Due to overcrowding and sanitation problems at home, and the appalling medical conditions in the Crimea, the government's strategies seemed inadequate for health care, and the medical community was forced to mediate between social problems and the State. The surgeon George Dawson was quoted in 1855 in the *Lancet* with revolutionary accents: "Now we demand that the whole system of England should be altered. Not the Army only, not the Navy only, but all the Government affairs, all the Government offices."[37] The medical profession thus presumed to represent the people's interests against corrupt and inefficient government, but it also represented ideological capital and therefore status.

Unceasingly critical of the military–political complex, Nightingale wanted to seize this capital for women. Riding upon her popular image as bedside madonna, she, like the British Medical Association, proposed herself as a mediator between the people and an inept state. Yet here the obligatory, or historical, connotations of gender intervened. Reformed nursing in the nineteenth century meant the establishment of separate spheres of control between male doctors, who prescribed treatment, and female nurses, who provided care. This division between what we see today as mental and manual labor—in this case, women giving material body to male prescriptions—was typically described in terms of the nurse's "maternal instincts";[38] the Nurse was represented as Mother—a description that allowed middle-class women to preserve class status, to be manual laborers without being workers. Yet just as Mother in Western ideology is always more body, closer to the earth, than Man, so the Nurse, the manual caretaker of bodies who attempts to seize administrative, mental power from men, is doomed to failure.

To be sure, in her attempt to elevate women to professional status, Nightingale reinscribed the mental/manual distinction in the roles of Head Nurse, who gave the orders, and her staff, who cared for patients. Yet in practice the authority of the Head Nurse was continually undermined by the relationship of doctor to nurse. The professional distinction between mental doctor and somatic patient was not salient for women, who were ideologically somatic too, merely the mediators of men's words. Nightingale made her public debut under the guise of maternal body and proceeded, in a series of popular causes, to mediate between the people's interests and professional care. This liminal positioning gave rise to two images: first, the unique woman of action and, second, the threatening invert in the battle of the sexes. The latter was Lytton Strachey's view of Nightingale in *Eminent Victorians* (1918): the demonic slavedriver of cabinet ministers who, barred from the cabinet herself, attacked in immodest language the impotence of men—from the sickbed to which she had (hysterically) retired. The sickbed image relished by male historians predictably contains the threatening body. A third image is of course the commercial image that has come down to us through history: the ultrafeminine Florence Nightingale stories for girls. Yet despite the accumulation of discourse around her, Nightingale had no professional status, so the ideological capital she earned quickly reverted to the scientific community of men.

The publicity of their simulacra masked the embodied/embeddedness that inhibited middle-class women—for whom the cult of domesticity still overshadowed the burgeoning cult of personality. Witness Victoria herself. From the midnineteenth century through the 1870s the sovereign exercised significant political power despite her near total withdrawal from public view from 1861 through 1886. Yet as her political power waned, Victoria's image waxed, exchanging power for popularity in the spectacles of the Golden and Diamond Jubilees, at the heights of which she was carted through the streets. From the 1880s the middle-class provincial papers were superseded by the great national dailies, which were distributed to a greater electorate. The press favored Victoria by elevating her above politics, in that great twist of irony familiar to women, as Mother of the Nation. (The cooperativists who seized upon the phrase *needed* to proclaim their status as gendered, to be given time off from work to perform the demands of their sex; but once the material requirements of motherhood are fulfilled, gender dichotomies typically function to disable women.) Thus the Victoria of brilliant image and pageant signified not a revival of the theater of sovereign power, but rather an "invented tradition" of great cultural purchase—for the State and the consumerism of the extravagant Jubilees (heydays for advertisers)—but not for her.[39] In some sense, Mayhew had been right about the Sovereign: she *had* come to provide the same utility—"temporary amusement"— as a street performer.

This confinement of upper-class women to the home simultaneously with a cultural explosion of femininity and domesticity in the media led to reversals in women's subjective accounts of homelife and material culture that have received little attention: their frequent expressions of distaste for the hearth.

One of the most powerful of these expressions is Nightingale's "Cassandra" of 1859, a description of Victorian homelife that makes the Crimean War seem a better alternative. "Cassandra" has three topoi—Literary plots, music, and orphans—that surface in much upper-class women's writings. Music was the foremost topic of study in women's boarding schools, and for that reason many women hated it. (Due to its similar position in their curriculum, many schoolboys responded equally to Latin.) Nightingale, like Frances Power Cobbe and many others, says that music, especially playing the piano—emblem as it is of the trivialization of women's abilities—drives women mad. Thus the piano, icon of Victorian domesticity, is reversed as a weapon that drives women mad.

Nightingale also perceives the limitations of literature for the Victorian lady. Managing a large house and consequently having no time to herself, she could not (in our contemporary terms) "produce the text" autonomously—imaginatively engage with it—but was "read aloud to," what Nightingale calls "the most miserable exercise of the human intellect" (34). In an image prophetic of the forced feedings of the suffragettes (and, of course, of the passive mouthpiece of the Gods), Cassandra curses being read to: "It is like lying on one's back, with one's hands tied and having liquid poured down one's throat. Worse than that, because suffocation would immediately ensue and put a stop to this operation. But no suffocation would stop [our being read to]" (34). Here, again, the goods made to enhhance one's privacy within the home become weapons against women, who are trapped and tortured within that privacy. Furthermore, women's experiences of pain within that private sphere are precisely that—private—so that, like the women cooperativists' experiences of childbirth, they go long unacknowledged by a liberal state that recognizes its domain as the public sphere.

Nightingale finally analyzes the age's fascination with fiction and orphans as imaginative centers of women's lives. Why were Victorian ladies drawn to novels and orphans, and novels about orphans? Novels posited an imaginary space of freedom, one in which the protagonists could develop interests and affection without the social constraints of the age—without, especially, a family. "The heroine," Nightingale explains, "has *generally* no family ties (almost *invariably* no mother), or, if she has, these do not interfere with her entire independence" (28). She describes the romance of orphans: "parental neglect or the accident of having no parents at all, which is generally the case in novels . . . such alternatives as these give food and space for the development of character and mutual sympathies" (48).[40] The great philanthropic ladies seized upon orphans as an image of hope and a means of escape from the private pain of their homes—at least until a state bureaucracy of professional "social workers" took over their function and women were forced back into the home.

Ultimately Nightingale objects to leisure itself: the world of goods and practices (at-homes, teas, dinner parties, etc.) that simulate substance for thinking women who want to work outside the home, to traverse more ground—the streets of East London, the fields of Crimea—and make something other than children. In their attacks upon gender conventions, John Stuart Mill and Florence Nightingale deplored the same conditions and demanded similar reforms; but Nightingale's demands for economic reform before the franchise are of a piece with the urgent and indeed *visceral* tone of her critique, a tone that is absent in Mill's devastatingly reasoned attack. Nightingale is writing from the confined woman's body, suffocated by the drawingroom and tortured by mindcrushing ennui, while Mill is writing from the head. Throughout *Cassandra*, Nightingale refers to the physical suffering induced by women's frustration: "What these suffer—even physically—from the want of such work no one can tell. The accumulation of nervous energy, which has had nothing to do during the day, makes them feel every night, when they go to bed, as if they were going mad; and they are obliged to lie long in bed in the morning to let it evaporate and keep it down" (43). Ultimately this physical suffering is preferable to the social conditions that induced it, and it comes to serve as an excuse, a liberation from social life. "[For a woman] to be absent from dinner is [socially] equivalent to being ill. . . . Bodily incapacity is the only apology valid" (30); "a married woman was heard to wish that she could break a limb that she might have a little time to herself. Many take advantage of the fear of 'infection' to do the same" (34). "And so," Nightingale concludes, finally with some of Mill's *cui bono* reasoning, "is the world put back by the death of every one who has to sacrifice the development of his or her peculiar gifts (which were meant, not for selfish gratification, but for the improvement of that world) to conventionality" (55).

Andrea Dworkin has written about the sinister world of pornography, in which common household objects are used as sexual weapons against women: telephones and hair dryers are used as dildoes, telephone wires as instruments of bondage, "pliers are for loosening bolts until one sees them cutting into women's breasts; Saran Wrap is for preserving food until one sees a person mummified in it."[41] She concludes that the mundane world in which men live is full of doorways and light fixtures from which to hang women and telephones with which to batter them, observing that the most pervasive violent abuse of women takes place in their homes and by means of the most common domestic artifacts. This perversion or betrayal of everyday objects is what Elaine Scarry, with respect to the torturer's "art," calls the unmaking of the world of the victim of torture and what Mayhew called the perversion of the laborers' craft, when their tools were used as weapons against them. These are extreme examples, but my point in this chapter has been that goods—including knowledge—were valued differently and played different parts (including harm) in subjective experience depending upon one's material/biological position on the social spectrum and that dualistic theories of mind and liberal projects for freedom have taken too little notice of the differences.

3.

Representations of the Working Classes by Nonworking-Class Writers: Subjectivity and Solidarity

> Detailed descriptions of the life and labour of the people in all its various aspects, sensational or scientific, derived from personal observation or statistical calculation, become a characteristic feature of the publications of the [the 1880s], whether newspapers or magazines, plays or novels, the reports of philanthropic organisations or the proceedings of learned societies. It may be said that this novel concentration of attention on the social condition of the people was due neither to intellectual curiosity nor to the spirit of philanthropy, but rather to a panic fear of the newly enfranchised democracy.
>
> BEATRICE WEBB, *My Apprenticeship* (1926)[1]

The collaboration of Engels and Marx that we identify as Victorian Marxism was the most systematic and self-conscious theory of subjectivity in the period, first in the discovery of its contingency upon social arrangements and then in the analysis of the atomization that had come to be characteristic of individualism under modern conditions. When Engels writes in the Historical Introduction to *The Condition of the Working Class in England* (1845) that the industrial revolution had been as important for England as the political revolution for France and the philosophical revolution for Germany, he means that with it came the creation of the English proletariat, a class of people whose identity would not transcend their class ("Today he who is born a worker must remain a worker for the rest of his life. This is why it is only now possible for an

organised working-class movement to spring up") and who, locked in
conflict with their Hegelian antithesis, the bourgeoisie, would dialectically transform the nature of human nature.[2] That nature had been transformed already by the bourgeoisie as cited earlier in Engel's "We know
well enough that this isolation of the individual—this narrow-minded
egotism—is everywhere the fundamental principle of modern society"
(31).

In the chapter "Working-Class Movements" Engels constructs a delicate and complex narrative of working-class subjectivity that takes the
worker from the status of "inanimate object" (the property of the middle
classes to appropriate and use as they will), through "hot-blodded . . . animal . . . passions" (from his fury against their tyranny), to the rational,
articulate "working men . . . the real power of the nation and the hope of
its future progress."Having been "degraded to the level of animals" (240),
workers become "manly, noble, and attractive" with their first confrontations with the masters; Engels reads their history of conflict in light of
this virile heroism, with each activity—Luddism, Peterloo, repeal of the
Combination Laws in 1824, trades unions, or strikes—as a lesson in progressive self-assertion and self-consciousness. He lauds the "courage" of
the workers for beating up police, the repressive apparatus of the State
(257–58), and counterposes the workers' own Law, the Charter, to the
reified "sanctity of law" that masks bourgeois domination ("The middle
classes certainly are all in favour of the sanctity of the law . . . They have
made the law; they approve of it; they are protected by it, and they gain
advantages from it" [257]). Furthermore, the workers' legal literacy constitutes only a part of their consciousness, and Engels conflates the political and the literary avant-garde: "No better evidence of the extent to
which the English workers have succeeded in educating themselves can
be brought forward than the fact that the most important modern works
in philosophy, poetry, and politics are in practice read only by the proletariat" (272). He mentions Diderot, Strauss, and Proudhon as well as
the revolutionary and antiestablishment poetry of Shelley and Byron:
"The middle classes, on the other hand, have on their shelves only ruth-
lessly expurgated 'family' editions of these writers" (273). He concludes
the chapter with the image of fully self-conscious "working men" artic-
ulately "addressing" themselves at Chartist meetings (273).

Engels's subsequent chapter on the "Attitude of the Bourgeoisie"
reverses the story of subjectivity for the middle classes, tracing the devo-
lution of human beings into subhuman ghouls. Including the aristocracy
within his scope, he now begins with a legislature of educated men who

use their education and law as weapons to attack the workers: he mentions the Corn Laws, Enclosure Acts, and Poor Laws. These masters are not simply bellicose; they also bear malign intent, their will more malignant than even the letter of their law: "On paper the new poor law makes certain provisions for the humane treatment of paupers in workhouses. But these provisions are entirely at variance with the true spirit of the Poor Law of 1834. That law was firmly based on the idea that since paupers were criminals it followed that workhouses must be prisons. It followed that the inmates of workhouses were people beyond the pale of the law—even beyond the pale of humanity" (325). Engels continues that it was this "idea" about the poor, even more than the brutal conditions, that was the most damaging to the impoverished: "Workhouse paupers were regarded as objects of horror and disgust. No pious instructions to the contrary from the Poor Law Commissioners can avail against the spirit of the law itself. Workhouse paupers have discovered that in practice it is the *spirit* of the law—and not the *letter* of the law—that counts" (ibid.).

By the end of the chapter Engels has entirely reversed the narrative of the workers, now reducing the middle classes to "a social class so degraded by selfishness and moral depravity as to be quite incapable of salvation" (310). He provides the concluding image of ghoulish capitalists obliterating for their own profit all bonds of kinship and sacred rights, defiling the bodies and resting place of the dead, and emphasizes that the "idea" of the poor as "superfluous" population literally prevents the capitalists from seeing their disinterred corpses:

> In Manchester there is a pauper burial ground in the Old Town on the other side of the Irk. This, too, is a desolate piece of waste ground. Two years ago a new railway line was built which ran through the burial ground. Had it been a churchyard in which "respectable" people were interred the middle classes and the clergy would have protested loudly against the desecration of the burial ground. But since it was only a pauper burial ground—the last resting place of "superfluous" paupers—they did not show the slightest concern. No one bothered to give a decent burial on the other side of the churchyard to the half-decayed corpses which were dug up to let the railway go through. The navvies dug holes where they pleased and great stakes were knocked into fresh graves. Since the men were working in marshy land, water containing putrefying matter from these graves was forced up to the surface and the whole district suffered from the nauseating and dangerous gases which filled the air. I cannot give the more revolting details about the consequences of this callous and disgusting act. (329–30)

In this stage of Engels's dialectic, master and slave have changed places. Masters are reduced to brutes and slaves elevated to rational, self-conscious humanity.

Needless to say, Engels's and Mayhew's depictions were unusual among middle-class cultural production. Self-consciousness and self-determination were more typically class-, and often gender-, specific, the lower classes seldom portrayed with the same subtlety or discrimination as their "masters." In this chapter I shall examine the narrative possibilities for representing the lives of the poor and working classes in the classic realist novel (the first section); nonfictional or sociological writings (the second section); and late Victorian fiction, especially short stories (the third section).

I have come to these conclusions, as Engels came to his, dialectically: having had long familiarity with Victorian fiction, I immersed myself in working-class people's representations of themselves for several years. When I returned to the classic authors I could not help but compare their representations of "the lower classes" with those classes' own diverse self-representation.

I have been advised against including a brief section on "the classic Victorian novel" because, of course, it cannot do justice to a topic on which so many have written with scope and depth. I have decided to include my conclusions nonetheless because of my pragmatic approach: I am by no means attempting to tell the definitive story about Victorian fiction but rather to describe the tensions between working-class and middle-class self-representation and the ways they were interdependent. To my knowledge, no other literary or cultural critic has studied this contrast.

My second reason for including a brief section on the classic Victorian novel has little to do with professional literary critics or Victorianists. There has been a recent tendency for nonliterary critics to romanticize imaginative literature, whether scientists defending "Western Culture" courses in university curricula or "postanalytic" philosophers weary of Anglo-American metaphysics. In *Contingency, Irony, and Solidarity* (1989), Richard Rorty argues for the position of the "liberal ironist," one who believes that "cruelty is the worst thing we do" and also acccepts the contingency of this belief.[3] He claims that solidarity is created by imagination rather than reason (xvi); that the vocabulary of metaphor and self-creation, of poetic "geniuses," is a more useful tool for democratic progress than that of truth, rationality, or moral obligation (44); that great literature gives us moral data (82), whereas philosophy only gives us theory (94); and that great literature gives us the *only* voice of the oppressed that we can have (94). I shall return at the conclusion of this chapter to whether solidarity is created by imagination rather than reason; however, with Chapter 4, which includes some voices of the oppressed whose existence Rorty overlooks, I hope that the section on classic Victorian fiction will suggest some problems with such an uncritical approach to imaginative literature. My ultimate goal is, again, not primarily canon-reformation but rather a critical examination of how subjectivities and values are perpetuated through time.

My thesis is that the great proliferation of sociological writing about poverty, roughly intervening between the proper realist novel and the late Victorian short fiction discussed in section three, is the source of the contrast between the Christian-romantic optimism of Condition of England novelists at midcentury and the pessimistic but more radical critique of the social system by late Victorian writers of short fiction. I also argue that the contrast between the reformist sociologists, with their obsession with numbers, and the canonical literary writers, with their obsession with individual character that led to stereotyping, is most instructive concerning the limits of the Victorian literary imagination. I intend these narrative analyses of middle-class writing, adding to a long tradition in scholarship on value in British fiction and one just beginning on value in Victorian social science, to serve as prelude to the writing of workers themselves in Chapter 4: to indicate the fields of discourse in which workers' self-representations were embedded and to indicate why those self-representations are worth our consideration.

The Classic Victorian Novel: Solidarity for Whom?[4]

> Certainly we render our social duties uncommonly easy by mentally substituting for the *actual* man who demands our help, the *ideal* man who could probably help himself.
> SCHILLER, *On the Aesthetic Education of Man* (1795)[5]

Until the last two decades of the nineteenth century, middle-class fiction was largely of a piece in its representations of the poor and working classes, which is to say that for readers interested specifically in these representations the similarities finally outweigh the differences. As I indicate in Chapter 4, these representations worked dialectically with working-class identities, but the influence can be, and I believe has been, overstated. In the worst cases, working people serve as mere sensational (threatening) or picturesque (nonthreatening) Others, or, alternatively, as comic relief, in the staging of middle-class plots and protagonists—usually in Dickens, Thackeray, and Trollope, and often in George Eliot and the Brontës. Although Dickens was the most popular writer among the working classes themselves, his representation of them was basically deductive, deriving from his own moral principles. His description of the industrial Coketown, for example, in *Hard Times* (1854) crystallizes into so rich and creative a gestalt image of his moral outrage that it precludes the kind of differentiated activity that Engels found behind the facade of Manchester's mainstreets, and that Steven Marcus's reading of Engels has rendered so memorably.[6] Dickens, to quote his own narrator, "saw nothing in Coketown but what was severely workful": that is, he saw a very partial view. Similarly, *Oliver Twist* was published immediately after the new Poor Law Amendment and formulated the benign case of lower-class appeal in Oliver's "Please sir, I want some more." The plot is generated through Dickens's devices of the good (middle-class property owners), the bad (unemployed thieves in the East End), and the contemptible (civil servants); yet in the end the source of evil is revealed to be sibling rivalry for inheritance. When working people loved to read Dickens— and their autobiographies are testimony that many of them did—it was what Bourdieu would call his "moral agreeableness" that they admired, rather than his representations of themselves.

More interesting for my purposes are the novels that attempt to place the lower classes centrally. The aesthetic problem here, of course, was how to make the life of a working person sufficiently dramatic for middle-class readers, remembering that, if realism were to prevail, work, rather than marraige, death, and property transmission (the basic repertoire of middle-class fiction), would have a significant role in motivating the plot. (In middle-class *life,* clearly, work played an equally large part, yet the conventions of middle-class fiction suppressed this part. Characters who were "dominated" or "obsessed" by their work were typically caricatured, as in Dickens.) In Harriet Martineau's collection *Poor Laws and Paupers Illustrated* (1832), which greatly influenced Elizabeth Gaskell, work *is* central. Yet printed under the auspices of the Society for the Diffusion of Useful Knowledge, the rhetorical force of the fiction is to encourage "the" working class to accept its condition with dignity and fortitude. Authors who wrote for the middle-class press did not sustain this focus.

The "Condition of England" fiction of Disraeli, Gaskell, and Kingsley avoided the formal problem of the tediousness of working-class life by substituting the very dramatic focus of class conflict, responding to the threats of Chartism and trade unionism with alternative conciliatory solutions.[7] Engels himself—urbane, gentlemanly, witty—praised the courage and good intentions of Benjamin Disraeli's "Young England" (Tory Radical) plan to revive "Merry England" with its colorful romantic feudalism and its assault upon Whig reform, and had nothing more negative to say about it than that it was obviously unattainable and a ridiculous—if unintended—satire on the normal process of historical development. In *Sybil, or The Two Nations* (1845), more influenced by Walter Scott than Chartists, humourous pseudodialect is reserved for Chartist rabble ("Hell-Cats") but not for the "Daughter of the People" protagonist, who turns out to be an aristocrat by birth anyway. The Chartist leaders themselves are unmasked (they did it for love of Sybil) and politics are recuperated for Great Souls animated by Great Ideas. This last is emblematized by the enlightened aristocrat Egremont's chivalric defense (with sword) of the chaste Sybil in Mowbray castle at the novels' climax.

Elizabeth Gaskell presents the working classes with considerably more sympathy and subtlety. *Mary Barton: A Tale of Manchester Family Life* (1848) begins with the "acuteness and intelligence" of Manchester factory girls in complex working-class communities, and the book senstively portrays independent working women, only one of whom is a prostitute (she dies). But because Gaskell attributed most social evil to the destruction of family life under the factory system, and simultaneously rejected early working-class alternatives to family life in cooperatives and unions, like Disraeli she also structurally conjoins working-class consciousness with violence, whose only alternative is emigration to the Americas. Gaskell's first title was "John Barton": the substitution of daughter for father reflects her shift from the dangerous (political) to the humane (domestic) aspects of the workers she lived among. Her workers give up unionism/violence for reading and butterfly-collecting, and the callous industrialist undergoes a change of heart, acknowledging "the spirit of Christ as the regulating law" between capital and labor. Charles Kingsley's *Alton Locke* (1850), drawing upon Mayhew to represent conditions in London slums, also concludes with the deportation of the dying Chartist-poet to America and the depositing of England's future hope in a self-sacrificing aristocratic woman's Christian association, again showing the mediation that, long before the Charity Organization Society, was expected of upper-class women in class reconciliation. As I indicated earlier in a different context with the case of Florence Nightingale, middle-class women could mediate between masters and men.

By the publication of Gaskell's *North and South* (1854), the various communities of the poor are peripheral to the plans of the bourgeoisie for their salvation. Margaret Hale, the most humane of southern agriculturists, interposes her body between the irate operatives and the most virile of the self-made factory owners, and the marriage of Margaret and John Thornton reunites benevolence and profit. (In other words, when class conflict becomes unresolvable without extreme violence, the plot turns into a love story.) Indeed the second half of the text is dedicated not to probing the subjective viewpoints of the poor but rather to revealing the subjective mollification of the factory owner (her presentation of the mill-owner Mr. Carson in *Mary Barton* had alienated some middle-class readers): through Thornton's love for Margaret the reader comes to empathize with him and consequently with his general enterprise. It is certainly the case that with *Mary Barton* one of Gaskell's most courageous tasks was to encourage sympathy for a militant working-class radical. Part of the book's sensational response was due to John Barton's lack of formal punishment for the murder and his deathbed forgivenenss by the father of the victim. Yet by *North and South* the focus has shifted from the lower classes, and the narrative trajectory reverts to more traditional domestic romance.[8] Gaskell's critics, then and now, have called *Mary Barton* and *North and South* politically naïve and aesthetically confused.

George Eliot, whose sensitivity to the fine negotiations of self and society is partially expressed in her thought in *Felix Holt, The Radical* (1866) that there is no private life that has not been determined by a wider public life, typically represented the working classes anachronistically. In *Silas Marner* (1861) a handloom weaver already "looked like the remnants of a disinherited race," and the village still remained a place for working-class boys and girls to marry. In *Adam Bede* (1859), preindustrial peasant artisans have no class aspirations; those on Hetty Sorrel's part to be a lady are represented by Eliot as a moral failure (vanity, frivolity, etc.), thus mystifying the rigid roles of social class. Through the plot of Hetty Sorrel and Arthur Donnithorne, class conflict is reinterpreted as an ethic of egotism (sensual and luxurious) against an ethic of work (busy and asexual: Adam and Dinah). Maids and gentry pay for transgressing class boundaries, and gender roles are recuperated: like Mary Barton and Alton Locke, Hetty is transported (see the sociological theme of transportation in the next section), and Arthur enlists in the Army; Dinah is forced by the Methodist Conference to give up preaching, and her new lord and husband Adam (literally) says it is good.

Felix Holt, the Radical, set during the first Reform Bill and published just before the second, is more concerned with inheritance, patrimony, and demagoguery than working people per se—Eliot's earliest conception was of the tragedy of Mrs. Transome. Not conceived of by the author as a "Condition of England" novel, its vague politics were precisely articulated by Eliot's own "Address to Working Men" in the persona of her protagonist on the passage of the second Reform Bill in 1867. At the request of John Blackwood, Eliot extrapolated the novel's conservative politics. She disingenuously informs Working Men that their deprivation of middle-class culture—the property, incidentally, of her two "working-class" protagonists Esther and Felix—"the common estate of society," signifies no more than her own class's deprivation of "sunlight and the air, of the sky and the fields, of parks and holiday games."[9] (The middle class has Culture and the poor their holiday games.) Unlike Mayhew and echoing the Arnold of *Culture and Anarchy*—also composed during this period of the franchise and Education Acts—she values this Culture, "that treasure of knowledge, science, poetry, refinement of thought, feeling, and manners . . . over and above buildings, machinery, produce, shipping" (621), and urges that it not be threatened "by any attempt to do away directly with the actually existing class distinctions and advantages, as if everybody could have the same sort of work, or lead the same sort of life" (616). She further urges, at the moment when almost half the working class had won the franchise, that they substitute their class "interests" for more enobling "duties"; and with remarkable insensitivity to the exigencies of her fictive dramaturgy, describes "Holt's " less fortunate brethren as "the multiplying brood begotten by parents who have been left without all teaching save that of a too craving body, without all well being save the fading delusions of drugged beer and gin. They are the hideous margin of society." She also exhorts Working Men "to see to it that we do not help to rouse what I may call the savage beast in the breasts of our generation—that we do not help to poison the national blood, and make richer provision for bestiality to come" (618–19). Sharing her contempt for the Working Men addressed, Blackwood returned the proofs with the approving remark that he wished "the poor fellows were capable of appreciating it. If they were we should be all right" (607). In her later work, like *Middlemarch* (1871–1872), Eliot turned to describing the psychic life of her own class, the processes by which the upper classes themselves were subjected into "duty" and failed in their individual projects to "alter the world a little." "Nothing in the world," she writes of the Lydgates, Trawleys, Ladislaws, and Casaubons, "is more subtle than the process of their gradual change." Here, in representing the subjectivities of the defeated and resigned bearers of Culture, lay her genius.

Although early in his career Thomas Hardy was taken as an imitator of Eliot in his representations of provincial life, he was soon called the historian of rural Dorsetshire.[10] With Gissing, he probably comes closest to the voice of much working-class writing. To take only his best-known works, once one has gotten past the melodrama of Tess's seduction to the tragedy of her life (*Tess of the d'Urbervilles* [1891]), the passivity of some southern agrarian working people and the long process of learning to communicate in writing (in Tess's case, first through her letters) are perhaps best evoked by Hardy. From the beginning critics have ridiculed Hardy's "pessimism," interpreting his representations of class and gender determinism in terms of universal or existential crises or destiny; yet working-class texts are often marked by the same determinism. In *Jude the Obscure* (1895) the stonecutter's desire to raise himself (a combination of Hardy's stonecutter father's desire for prosperity and Hardy's desire for a proper education) as well as the harried feeling of needing work and forever being told to "move on" also reflect the thematic concerns of much working-class autobiography. Hardy also adds another dimension overlooked by writers less intimate with the class they wrote about: romance is a disaster to the upwardly mobile—Sue, Jude, Tess, and Angel. Only the Gissing of *The Nether World* (1889) comes closer to capturing the feeling of systematic overdeterminism in working-class life, and he, like Hardy, has often been mystified by critics as describing an existential condition rather than, as Raymond Williams and Terry Eagleton have ceaselessly pointed out, social injustice. In *The Nether World,* there are no upper-class characters and—perhaps consequently—no hero, so the form is entirely different from that of the typical middle-class novel. No individual will or action, nothing short of total economic restructuring, can raise the poor above the status of "hands."

At the other extreme, the fairy tale components and sensational atmospheric quality of James's *Princess Casamassima* (1886) can be traced to James's representation of the social problem as between aristocrats and plebs (as opposed to capital and labor) and a British public generally mystified (as we can see in the *Times* for the period) by anarchist activity in the 1880s. Even among such a short list of middle-class represenations of the poor, one cannot delete this, the most improbable view of working-class life. But here, as in the text itself, James's *Princess* requires a preface (by way of a contrast with Joseph Conrad). The years 1880 through 1914

were the height of anarchism in Europe. In England anarchists repudiated state control and authority as increasingly embodied in the social
welfare system. With partisans representing the full range of opinion
from Stirner's (Johann Caspar Schmidt's [1805–1856]) uncompromisng
individualism to anarchosyndicalism (trade unionism), England also had
followers of Mikhail Bakunin (1814–1876), who had called for a spontaneous revolution of all underprivileged—from peasants and proletarians to unemployed intellectuals and students; the printer Pierre Proudhon (1809–1865), author of *What is Property?,* who wanted economically
independent craft guilds; and Peter Kropotkin (1842–1921), the Russian
prince who resided in London from 1886 until 1917 and called not for
conflict but co-operation and "a permanent revolt by word."[11] In popular
anarchist mythology, the 1890s were to be the "heroic" decade. The fin
de siècle would represent the end of the Century of the Bourgeois Order.

In 1907, while tailors and artisans in the East End were reading the
anarchist teachings of Rudolf Rocker, Joseph Conrad published *The
Secret Agent,* "a simple tale" of a double agent spying upon European
anarchists in London, and inspired by the explosion of Martial Bourdin
near the Royal Observatory in 1894. Conrad's novel is best described as
ironic, but it captured the mystified aura surrounding anarchism in the
London press from the 1880s, a press saturated with gory accounts of
bombings and stabbings but without specifics of the organizations reputedly sponsoring them.[12] Amid the corruption of uniformly fatuous anarchists, all financially supported by their women, and the equal corruption
of the forces of law and order (from assistant commissioners to the Prime
Minister), Conrad entrusts the story's moral value to a wife, Winnie Ver-
loc, whose "supreme illusion" had been that her mentally disabled
brother would be loved by her husband, and to the fragile and unpro-
tected Stevie himself, a boy who had been abused by his father and had
mutely grown to hate oppression with an impotent fury. "It's a bad world
for poor people," Stevie says before being blasted "to pieces" carrying the
bomb for his sister's husband.

Although it is psychagogically exploitative for Conrad to wrench readers' sentiments with a case so desperately pathetic as Stevie's, or worse,
to invoke it in a work so wickedly ironical that one feels embarrassed to
be moved by it at all, the novelist did distinguish between the world of
the poor of Winnie and Stevie and that of political violence, a distinction
that the earlier novelists—with their tendency to sensationalize the
poor—had not often recognized. (Yet even in Conrad the demagogue
remains a threat, here in the person of foreigners.)

In *The Princess Casamassima* James does not make such fine distinctions, but objectifies the world of the poor as the laboratory of the expert writer. As he says in his preface, the fiction proceeded "quite directly from his habit and interest of walking the streets."[13] The bourgeois artist par excellence continues, "One walked of course with one's eyes greatly open, and I hasten to declare that such a practice, carried on for a long time and over a considerable space, positively provokes, all round, a mystic solicitation, the urgent appeal, on the part of everything, to be interpreted and, so far as may be, reproduced." Tossing off the Stevies of the world with one breezy wave—"We care, our curiosity and our sympathy care, comparatively little for what happens to the stupid, the coarse and the blind" (9)—James offers us the spectacle of Hyacinth Robinson, "some individual sensitive nature of fine mind, some small obscure intelligent creature . . . sprung out of the London pavement," for whom "every door of approach" to "freedom and ease, knowledge and power, money, opportunity and satiety . . . [had been] shut in his face" (8). Tracing Hyacinth Robinson's lineage in James's other characters of discerning sensibility on the one hand (16–17), and his fictive implication in "his small cluster of dingy London" (17), "shady underworld of militant socialism" (18), indeed his entire "life of a dingy little London bookbinder" (19) in "the sinister anarchic underworld, heaving in its pain, its power and its hate" (21), on the other, James goes on to write of his own qualifications for writing.

Mayhew's metropolis exists for James to "penetrate, imaginatively, in as many places as possible—*that* was to be informed, *that* was to pull wires, *that* was to open doors, *that* positively was to groan at times under the weight of one's accumulations" (22). Like the social explorers to be discussed shortly, James invokes the "rich principle of the Note" and the accuracy of his "reporting": "If one was to undertake to tell tales and to report with truth on the human scene, it could be but because 'notes' had been from the cradle the ineluctable consequence of one's greatest inward energy: to take them was as natural as to look, to think, to feel, to recognize, to remember, as to perform any act of understanding" (21). Thus, as we have seen in Chapter 1, James was one of the "natural" authors, a sensibility formed "from the cradle" to take notes, distinct from others, whose lives are there to be reported by him. "If you are so armed," he vigorously concludes the preface, "You are not really helpless, not without your resource, even before mysteries abysmal" (23)—"mysteries abysmal" referring, again, to the people of London outside the social circles of Henry James (we have come a long way from Henry Mayhew).

The phrase will resonate in the next section in the discussion of the social explorers and sociologists' response to "the abyss."

After such testimony to the quality and discernment of his perception—the typical sublimation of his (and his reader's) literary sensibility that informs most of James's prefaces—one may be surprised when one turns to the novel: what James apparently "saw" in 1886 was the metropolitan poor in the form of an illegitimate son of a French revolutionary and an English aristocrat. Hyacinth Robinson is educated by a dressmaker, a violinist, a former Communard, and a German anarchist, and is victimized in love by an Italian-American Princess and a Lancastrian chemist—a working person's life, a skeptical Lady Bracknell might say, unusually crowded with incident. "I like to know all sorts of people," the Princess, née Christina Light, confides to Hy "very gently and kindly" on their first meeting—at the theater (158), with what can only be called Jamesian distance from "the huge, swarming, smoky, *human* city" (166, my italics). Moreover, with the plot centered upon the conflict between Hyacinth's love for the Princess (including the world of ease and culture that she represents—"the beauty of the world, *actual order* and all" [18, my italics]) and the "famous iniquity of social arrangements" (18), the antagonists face off as aristocrats and plebians, James apparently not wanting to touch capital and labor.

Hyacinth's sensibility, like Disraeli's Sybil and Dickens's Oliver, and most notoriously James's own Maisie's later, appears to have been innate, with him from the cradle, like James's ability to take notes; nor is he ever to be found in any such unliterary haunt as a workplace (James preferring the theater). Torn between the revolutionary dreams of "a terribly light Frenchwoman" (i.e., his mother) and the power of "a nobleman altogether wanting in nobleness" (his father), Hyacinth suffers from the bourgeois psychodrama and inhabits a world essentially bourgeois. Nor do his fellow revolutionists indulge in physical labor or activism: like the novelist and the Princess, they converse, which conversation alone bears the weight of defining character. An actionless world of psychic pain expressed in conversation, a world rocked by continuous postering and masquerading, is the bourgeois world—an unlikely scene of a novel about "a dingy little London bookbinder."

In *The Princess Casamassima* what James "saw" was mediated by his class, and even gender, perspective. Yet elsewhere he wrote about politics in less fantastic fashion. Roderick Hudson had killed himself when Christina Light married the Italian Prince: as others have pointed out, James is most political in representing the American colonization—usually via young women—of Europe.[14] (Gertrude Stein called him a General.) And he is not unperceptive of the politics of gender. Hyacinth resists acting for the anarchists out of loathing of "repeating" his mother's work. When he shoots himself instead, the Princess resolves to return to her husband, who had cut her off financially, at which point her anarchist lover agrees that she is useless without her money. But with respect to representing the lower classes, *Princess Casamassima* is but a reductio ad absurdum of earlier tendencies among middle-class British fiction. Patrick Brantlinger has observed in *Rule of Darkness: British Literature and Imperialism 1830–1914* that whereas the rationalists and utilitarians like Macaulay and James Mill believed Indians capable of enlightenment and therefore avoided the more extreme forms of racism, fiction writers' focus on detail, particularity, and individual character led to racial stereotyping and individualistic moralizing about the Other.[15] The point is a crucial one. Without Mayhew's sheer multiplicity and diversity of working-class "characters," the middle-class focus upon particular, individual character when incorporating working people into middle-class plots tended to grotesque stereotyping like James's. By not presuming to *represent* the working classes' own viewpoints but rather by taking their side, Engels resisted the appropriative tendencies of the novelists, never eliding himself as author speaking to a German audience with the English workers speaking to themselves and their employers.

In a study focusing upon middle-class fiction, one could also map middle-class representations of the lower classes according to their portrayals of violence. Clearly—that is, with a frankness that is, for readers today, surprisingly unmediated—the middle classes feared the possibility of working-class violence (rickburning, riot, assault on person and property, etc.), and much of the fiction, like Disraeli's and Eliot's, portrays it. The deeper fear in England, however, was of psychological violence, of "abjection" or the loss of self and status in a society that had always differentiated elite from commoners. Both Gaskell and Kingsley explicitly employ images of the lower classes as Frankenstein's monster, to them a subhuman predator of domestic and social life. Additionally, demagogues were represented as the Frankensteins of the age, creating they knew not what horror in mating humankind with the beast. In the great scenes of horror—technically the effect of loss of boundaries—in Victorian fiction the working class forfeits its human status and brutalizes *itself*: Sikes's unspeakable bludgeoning of Nancy in *Oliver Twist;* Hetty Sorrel's live burial of her baby in *Adam Bede;* Grace Rudd's disfiguring the face of Clara (with vitriol—that working-class weapon in lieu of something more expensive) before her own body is mutilated beyond recognition beneath the rush of the locomotive in *The Nether World;* Stevie's witless self-immolation in *The Secret Agent* ("Blown to small bits: limbs, gravel, clothing, bones, splinters—all mixed up together. . . . [T]hey had to fetch a shovel to gather him up with."); and Father Time's execution of his infant siblings and subsequent suicide as an underclass's premonition of "the coming universal wish not to live" in *Jude the Obscure.* The authors of such scenes objectified the poor doing violence to themselves and recoiled in horror that humanity could be, or in Hardy's and Gissing's case, could be driven to, *this* (Eliot's "savage beasts in the breast of our generation"). Engels did not opt for the psychological defense, refusing to project the violence back onto the workers. In perhaps the greatest scene of horror of the century, the castration of Maigrat the company storekeeper by the miners' wives in *Germinal* (1885), Zola reinvokes the class conflict that had been occluded by representations of a class's self-immolation.

Now whether claims like Rorty's are borne out, that is, whether fiction is a more useful tool for democratic progress than that of truth, rationality, or moral obligation, depends upon how fiction is received by its readers. To summarize what I have argued about high Victorian "social problem" fiction, I shall consider this dynamic, borrowing some of the technical terms of structuralism and narratology. In middle-class fiction, when a crisis of irreconcilability occurs between the two classes (e.g., "masters and men" find their interests irreconcilable), and the plot logically threatens violent conflict, it is redirected from class conflict to romantic love and Christian charity. This plot redirection is concomitant with a narratological event called *suture*—when the viewpoints of the implied author, the characters, and the intended readership gradually converge at the point of closure. (My own readers familiar with narrative theory will recognize here the subject of the enunciation [implied author], the subjects of the énoncé [characters], and "interpellated" readers.)

The implied author's views are sutured with (or become "seamlessly" indistinguishable from) model characters', and that identification sutures with the interpellated reader's, to create an ideological view of "reality." In the fiction I have been discussing, the convergent viewpoints of author, character, and reader hold that social conflict can be resolved by acceptance of hierarchy and philanthropy rather than economic restructuring, or that the human spirit can survive any amount of material deprivation.

To say that these texts interpellated readers is to say that they addressed themselves to readers who came to occupy the position from which the text was most intelligible. As I have argued, this was not the position of the different working-class people they purported to represent. When the suture or interpellation failed, the failure was attributed to readers not having the education (Eliot) or sensibility (James) to make the identification with the implied author's and characters' perspectives; and without the identification, the ideological power of the fiction was diminished. In these terms, Eliot's masquerading as Felix Holt (a middle-class woman masquerading as a man masquerading as a worker) addressing Working Men was something of a crisis of interpellation: it is unlikely that most working men having just received the vote after a century of struggle—even those in the position to read Blackwood's *Maga*—would find themselves in the position from which Eliot's text would be most intelligible.

All this simply supports the fact that the Condition of England fiction or James's *Princess* was not primarily intended to interpellate working-class readers who were the *subjects* of class conflict but rather readers of the writers' own class, who were to learn thereby the lessons of Christian charity and liberal reform. This objectification of working-class people for the novelists' own ends of liberal reform explains the lack of plausible depictions of working people's subjectivity in middle-class fiction. For those who have read working people's own writing, it is merely ironic that liberals like Rorty—who read only "geniuses" and believe that literature can give us the *only* voice of the oppressed that we can have—remain committed to the same "democratic progress" by way of the same undemocratic methods as their nineteenth-century predecessors: a method that excludes the subjects of the allegedly desired emancipation. I shall return to Rorty's further claims for literature and solidarity at the conclusion of this chapter.

Nonfictional Representations

> I have no shipwrecks, no battles, no moving adventures by flood and field, to record. Such perils as I and my fellow-traveller have encountered on our journey are not of the order which lend themselves to stirring narrative.
>
> GEORGE SIMS, *How the Poor Live* (1883)[16]

James and Conrad may serve as transitions to late Victorian middle-class representations of the working classes. With respect to these, the late

period evokes a return to the metropolis from the northern industrial cities as well as inroads into more "sociological" fiction. When the middle
class looked at itself it saw individual case histories, and the high Victorian writers tried to psychologize their working-class protagonists in kind,
generally at the cost of making them psychologically middle-class; by the
later period, when it looked at the lower classes it tended to see a social
stratum. In this section I shall consider some of the nonfictional representations that contributed to this shift. In the final section of this chapter
I shall return to the kinds of fiction most strongly influenced by the social
sciences.

In his preface to the English edition (1892) of *The Condition of the
Working Class in England,* written three years before his death, Engels
concludes, "the revival of the East End of London remains one of the
greatest and most fruitful facts of this *fin de siècle,* and glad and proud I
am to have lived to see it" (371). He has just described the autonomy of
East End new unionists from bourgeois hegemony and the revival's projected consequences for Socialism:

> That immense haunt of misery is no longer the stagnant pool it was six
> years ago. It has shaken off its torpid despair, has returned to life, and has
> become the home of what is called the "New Unionism," that is to say,
> of the organisation of the great mass of "unskilled" workers. . . . The new
> Unions were founded at a time when the faith in the eternity of the wages
> system was severely shaken; their founders and promoters were Socialists
> either consciously or by feeling; the masses, whose adhesion gave them
> strength, were rough, neglected, looked down upon by the working-class
> aristocracy; but they had this immense advantage, *their minds were virgin
> soil,* entirely free from the inherited "respectable" bourgeois prejudices
> which hampered the brains of the better situated "old" Unionists. And
> thus we see now these new Unions taking the lead of the working-class
> movement generally, and more and more taking in tow the rich and
> proud "old" Unions. (370–71)

Engels's view was again atypical in its central vision of organized labor
in the East End. Contemporary nonSocialists, often called *sociologists,*
saw rather a mysterious "abyss," a stagnant pool, as we shall see, of
another kind. For them, when this pool could be rationalized by nothing
so intelligible as unionisms it could at least be recorded by statistics.

With the development of British sociology in the last three quarters
of the century, the poor began to be accounted for by statistics only occa-

sionally accompanied by Mayhew's personal interviewing practices.[17] In the "exploration literature" that thrived from the 1830s, from the Royal Commission Reports through the more journalistic essays into the urban home of the underclass on the parts of James Greenwood (*A Night in a Workhouse* [1866] and *The Wilds of London* [1874]), George Sims (*How the Poor Live* [1883]), Andrew Mearns (*The Bitter Cry of Outcast London: An Enquiry into the Condition of the Abject Poor* [1883]), and Margaret Harkness ("John Law") (*In Darkest London: Captain Lobo, Salvation Army* [1889])—to name only a few—the poor were represented to the middle-class reading public as a dark continent within the patria. By 1882, Walter Besant described the East End as a wilderness thoroughly inhospitable to guests or visitors, offering no hotels, harboring no tourists.[18]

Except in Engels, the East End was characterized not by an identifiable "proletariat" like Chartists or factory workers, or even immigrants from the provinces who, like Hardy's laborers, were common in earlier middle-class fiction, but rather by extensive small-scale production in seasonal flux causing seasonal unemployment. Consequently, the effect of bad winters could be to alter dramatically workers' status on a large scale. The frozen river could put builders out of work and force their wives to glut the market, causing extensive dovetailing: a pianomaker could be demoted to cabinetmaking, to streetselling, and finally to the docks, where it was crowded at the bottom.[19]

In 1879, one of the infamous cycles of capitalism induced a severe depression that, combined with the growing housing crisis in the East End, made heavy demands upon the previous middle-class solution, the Charity Organizations Society (C.O.S.). Distributing cocoa and blankets, the C.O.S. had treated the poor as demoralized and themselves as cultural missionaries—hence their term "settlement," evoking colonizers bringing the benefits of civilization to alien populations.[20] With a staff of lecturers and undergraduates, Samuel Barnett, rector of St. Jude's, Whitechapel, opened Toynbee Hall (1884), and the People's Palace followed in 1887. Parish- and individually- based, they were intended to provide models of virility. Henrietta Barnett described her husband and Octavia Hill's philosophy in the early days of the C.O.S.: "Counting that the only method of improving social conditions was by raising individuals, [Hill] held that it was impertinent to the poor and injurious to their characters to offer them doles. They should be lifted out of pauperism by being expected to be self-dependent and ... be offered work instead of doles."[21]

Interpreting "the problem of the East End" as demoralization, the

C.O.S. denied economic aid to the poor and unemployed, but, having peaked in the 1870s, the Society declined as the economic crisis escalated. Under the strain of the depression, the settlement movements were challenged by calls for government intervention on a national scale, and by 1886 Burnett himself had parted with the C.O.S. and declared that State intervention was necessary. The influential Webbs and J. A. Hobson advocated a network of agencies and institutions on behalf of "national efficiency" that was virtually co-extensive with the nation-state. From the mid-1880s, socialists like H. M. Hyndman's Democratic Federation and Morris's Socialist League tried to organize workers.[22] After the riots and threats of riots in the West End in 1886–1887, Charles Booth and social scientists superceded the C.O.S. and opted for governmental policy rather than philanthropic community. In passing, the new social reformers offered some highly publicized Draconian temporary solutions, such as the physical removal of the "residuum" (Booth's "Class B," casual earners, the very poor) to State-supported or socialized farms in the country so that individualism could be permitted to thrive in the city: Booth called this "the dual system of Socialism in the arms of Individualism." (The superiority of immigrants from the country to urban-born workers was a middle-class myth of some duration.) Consequently, rather than the C.O.S.'s interpretation of demoralization for lack of proper role models, with the housing crises of the 1880s arose a new myth of urban degeneration, that of an infection at the heart of the city. The poor were not merely victims of the plague: they were the plague itself.

The bearers of this infection were seen as essentially different from other laborers. The Great Dock Strike of 1889, appearing as a relief after the earlier riots and threats of riots, was supported by many influential members of the upper classes. The upper classes also supported the organization of unskilled workers insofar as unionism would separate respectable workers from Booth's residuum. In the literature discussed later, Arthur Morrison deals with the residuum, Nevinson with union workers. This perceived distinction led to debates in parliament on the utility of forced technical training and transportation of the residuum—all of them now, not merely Mayhew's fallen needlewomen—to the colonies beyond England. In fact, the Workhouse Union was currently transporting nine-year-old orphans and deserted children to Canada as thoughtlessly as Dickens, Eliot, Gaskell, and Kingsley had transported their characters in fiction.[23] Institutional discussion frequently compared the unhealthy, undernourished bodies of the residuum with those of colonial subjects, reinforcing a correlation between English nationalism and physical health (see middle-class athleticism in Chapter 5).

In 1891 Henry Stanley had published his travels in "the dark continent" for the home audience under the title, *In Darkest Africa.* Immediately General William Booth published his plan for the Salvation Army, an "army" of the urban poor that would be trained in the provinces and then reintegrated into the urban centers or, failing that, shipped to the colonies overseas. Exploiting imperial metaphor, Booth titled his book *In Darkest England and the Way Out* (1891) and argued that there was a way out of urban poverty. The metaphor of the East End as Africa, wilderness waiting to be colonized, was well established: in 1883 Mearns had compared the homes of the poor to "the middle passages of slave ships."[24] With such metaphors of horror—like Robert Sherard's *The White Slaves of England* (1897) and *The Child Slaves of Britain* (1905)— came the representations of the East End as abyss: Jack London's *The People of the Abyss* (1903), C.F.G. Masterman's *From the Abyss* (1902), Mary Higgs's *Glimpses into the Abyss* (1906). Clearly by the turn of the century the fear that the middle classes themselves were in danger of being engulfed found its corollary in the fear that the nightmares of the empire had come home (Conrad's theme in *Heart of Darkness* [1899]).[25] Although the fear of engulfment goes back at least to Malthus, and was exacerbated by Chartism (e.g., see the reactions to the movement in Dickens's *Barnaby Rudge* [1840–1841]), its representations in sociology and sociological journalism had undergone a significant shift in the course of the century: as Peter Keating points out, one may observe a workhouse, but one falls into and is swallowed by an abyss.

It is important to reiterate that this descriptive sociological work was published in the middle-class press. James Greenwood's *A Night in a Workhouse* (1866) appeared in his brother Frederick's newly founded *Pall Mall Gazette.* Greenwood's notorious description of a brutal sporting event in which a man fought a pitbull in Hanley—which raised angry protests from working people—was first published in the *Daily Telegraph* (July 6, 1874). Other "exploration" literature circulated in Dickens's *Household Words, The Pictorial World, Pearson's Magazine, The London Magazine,* and the *Daily Express.*

It is also noteworthy that although the explorers were themselves traditionally educated middle-class women and men, all except Greenwood, one of the earliest, rejected Church, philanthropy, and "self-help" as possible solutions, repeatedly and explicitly calling for state action. In this, social exploring had led them to conclusions contrary to those of their middle-class peers writing fiction, who, with notable exceptions like

Hardy and Gissing, reassured their audiences with optimistic Christian-romantic solutions at the level of tokensim, or individual characters.

In 1889, Charles Booth published the first volume, entitled *East London,* of his seventeen-volume survey *The Life and Labour of the People of London* (1902–1903): his statistics showed 30.7 percent of London in poverty and 35.2 percent of the East End. Of the 4.5 million workers in London, 1.5 million worked half time; 1.5 full time; and 1.5 were unemployed. Casual labor, defined as short temporary engagements, described ten percent of the population, or 400,000. Booth's study called up again the speculative measures introduced by Malthus's Essay on the *Principle of Population* (1798) a century earlier. Wells and Shaw, among the Fabian socialists, advocated forced sterilization to prevent the spread of the social disease of poverty, and anarchists began to react to the threat of centralized political authority. The Reverend A. Osborne Jay, Vicar in Shoreditch (according to Charles Booth, the highest poverty level in the East End) and the model for Father Sturt in Morrison's *Child of the Jago,* recommended penal settlements in isolated parts of the country, where the inmates would be well treated under life sentences, "and will not under any circumstances be allowed to propagate their species and so perpetuate their type."[26] And even Morrison himself, who resolved in creating Dicky Perrott "To tell the story of a boy who, but for his environment, would have become a good citizen"—that is, who laid stress upon the environmental causes of crime—exhibited irrational moments of fear of contagion after the neighborhood had been torn down: "The Jago [the Old Nichol in Shoreditch] as mere bricks and mortar is gone. But the Jago in flesh and blood still lives, is crowding into neighbourhoods already densely over-populated."

This fear of contagion from the residuum grew into fear of general contagion from the democratic multitude that had been brewing since the earliest demands for the franchise. By the end of the century Charles Frederick Gurney Masterman presented them almost as T. S. Eliot would in his hordes rushing over the city in *The Wasteland* (1922). Educated at Cambridge, Masterman became involved in the settlement movement and social work and moved to a tenement block in Camberwell, South London to better understand the lives of the urban poor. What he learned was collected in *From the Abyss: Of the Inhabitants by One of Them* (1902) and *The Condition of England* (1909). He was a member of a group of Young Liberals who published in 1901 a collection entitled *The Heart of the Empire* examining the social problems of the modern city, a Liberal Member of Parliament from 1906–1914, and a government official under Asquith. Sensing early the feel of a mass society whose affective desolation Eliot would memorialize in *The Wasteland* and Orwell in *1984,* Masterman represents it in *From the Abyss* with the sheer shock—the *sublime* shock, in the Kantian mathematical sense—of statistics:

> This, then, is the first thing to note of us, not our virtue or vices, beauty, apathy, or knowledge; but our overwhelming, inconceivable, number— number continually increasing, multiplying without a pause, coming not with observation, choking up the streets of the great city, and silently flowing over the dismal wastes beyond. . . . Our streets have suddenly become congested with a weird and uncanny people. They have poured in as dense black masses from the eastern railways; they have streamed across the bridges from the marshes and desolate places beyond the river; they have been hurried up in incredible number through tubes sunk in the bowels of the earth, emerging like rats from a drain, blinking in the sunshine.[27]

Masterman notes outmoded cultural practices insufficient to represent the startling growth of democracy:

> The Newspapers stir uneasily, talk in a shamefaced manner about natural ebullitions of patriotism, police inefficiency, and other irrelevent topics; deprecate the too frequent repetition of the ceremony, and praise the humour of a modern crowd. But within there is a cloud on men's minds, and a half-stifled recognition of the presence of a new force hitherto unreckoned; the creeping into conscious existence of the quaint and innumerable populations bred in the Abyss.

He writes, with increasing agoraphobia, of political power unleashed if yet unrealized:

> We had thought that a city of four millions of people was merely a collection of one hundred cities of forty thousand. We find it differing not only in degree, but in kind, producing a mammoth of gigantic and unknown possibility. Hitherto . . . it has been hedged within isolated districts, each separate, apart, ignorant of the other. . . . Through the action of a benevolent autocratic Government it has now been invited to contemplate its strength. It has crept out into the daylight. At first it has moved painfully in the unaccustomed glare, as a cave bear emerging from his dark den. Now it is straightening itself and learning to gambol with heavy and grotesque antics in the sunshine. It finds the exercise pleasant; it uproots a

small tree, displaces a rock, laughing with pleased good-humour. How long before, in a fit of ill-temper, it suddenly realizes its tremendous unconquerable might?

This image of a genial infant Pantagruel, with its polymorphous, immature pleasures, or of Frankenstein's monster awakening to the light, gives way to that of total abjection—all loss of boundary and distinction—in a South American rain forest, whose noble trees are overwhelmed by lush, infinitely varied parasites:

> Whither is this tending, and what is to be the end of it all? That is the one unanswerable question. Remember, again, the South American forest. Tall trees insolently rise to heaven; surrounding them is the mass of tangled, choking vegetation; gorgeous colours of unequalled beauty; easeless, silent strife. Below are all forms of life driven under, forced to adapt themselves to unnatural surroundings, distorted into repulsive, twisted, grotesque forms of existence; each seemingly prepared for any monstrous change if only it can preserve its life and propagate its kind. Some, as parasites, cling to the tall trees in order that they, too, may see the sun, finally throttling their protectors in their deadly embrace. Others take fresh root on the ledges of boughs, or support themselves by slimy suckers or clinging thorns. Everywhere exuberant, many-featured life, struggling under the tropical sun; a struggle continued ardently year after year, through innumerable succeeding generations.

Despite this strikingly Darwinian picture, Masterman did not share Mayhew's joy in the infinite variety of the masses. Ultimately the struggle among life forms is suicidal, and in Masterman's metaphor of tropical forest a literal wasteland prevails:

> Only always at length the end. Some inexplicable change; slowly, imperceptibly, the torrent of life has overreached itself; the struggle has become too terrific; the vitality is gradually dying. And then, as the whole mass festers in all the gorgeous, wonderful beauty of decay, comes the mangrove—dark-leafed, dank, slippery, unlovely, sign and symbol of the inevitable end. And with the mangrove the black-marsh and the reeking, pestilential mud. Until at length all the glory and life and struggle of the tropical forest has passed away for ever; and in its place stretch the wide spaces of sullen swamp, and dull, gnarled, fruitless trees, and the silence of stagnant, scum-coated pools, and the salt, interminable, tideless sea.

Such descriptions were contemporaneous with the aesthete Arthur Symons's impressionistic assessment of the common people of London. (Symons, the author of *The Symbolist Movement in Literature* [1909] profoundly influenced the young T. S. Eliot.) In *London: A Book of Aspects* (1909), Symons incorporated his earlier essay "Edgware Road: A Study in Living" (1902):

> As I walk to and fro in Edgware Road, I cannot help sometimes wondering why these people exist. Watch their faces, and you will see in them a listlessness, a hard unconcern, a failure to be interested. . . . In all these faces you will see no beauty, and you will see no beauty in the clothes they wear, or in their attitudes in rest or movement, or in their voices when they speak. They are human beings to whom nature has given no grace or charm, who life has made vulgar.[28]

During the first world war, the residuum, the people of the abyss, the "unemployable," were revealed as myths of Victorian–Edwardian social science. What had impoverished them was neither innate nor infectious, but rather scarcity—poor housing, inadequate wages, and irregular work. With the war came employment, and the crisis, or at least that particular crisis, ended.

Despite such evocative responses as Masterman's, in general after Booth's survey the poor came to be represented as statistical tables, poverty cycles, and subsistence levels; and from the status of social explorer, a personal act of heroism allied with earlier individualistic models of self in relation to others, the observer of the mass was increasingly allied with the sociologist, the "disinterested" observer of abstract data. Also after Booth, parasociology in the form of exploration literature turned its attention to areas outside the metropolis. In *Poverty: A Study of Town Life* (1901), Benjamin Seebohm Rowntree found similar statistics in York (27.8% in poverty to London's 30.7%). In 1902 Rider Haggard, commissioned by the *Daily Express,* turned from his fictive exotica *(King Solomon's Mines, She)* to his native Norfolk in *Rural England,* in which, however, due to the laborers' "shyness" and "suspicion" (i.e., of Haggard), his descriptions were largely culled from the landowners and employers. But the rise of sociology had permanently transformed the way middle-class fiction writers represented the poor. Henceforth the "solution" to the "problem" of poverty would increasingly be not Christian-romantic but secular-political.

Late Victorian Short Fiction

As in the Chartist period or the so-called Hungry Forties, the establishment's concern in the 1880s and 1890s was both allayed and exacerbated by attention to the lower classes: its discourses on poverty were both a form of control and an obsession that threatened a loss of control. Class as well as gender tensions were expressed in the panic caused by the "Ripper" murders of at least five poor women in Whitechapel in 1888, a panic heightened by the speculation that the murderer was himself upper-class, perhaps a surgeon or a member of one of the elite clubs. But unlike the sustained organic worlds of earlier Victorian novels, in which the lower classes were peripheral to upper-class protagonists, the late Victorian representations of the poor were typically short tales ostensibly from their own point of view. Or, if not from their own point of view, at least deliberately not presuming to speak for them, as in Kipling's explicit refusal to speak for Badalia in his "in what manner these thoughts wrought upon her mind will not be known."[29]

In Clarence Rook's stories, modeled upon his own sociological exploration, Rook self-consciously mixes his language with Hooligan slang, consciously experimenting with new language-forms. The novels themselves—such as George Gissing's working-class novels published during the 1880s and culminating in *The Nether World* (1889), Maugham's *Liza of Lambeth* (1897), Arthur Morrison's *Child of the Jago* (1896), and George Moore's *Esther Waters* (1894)—were, like their (geographically) provincial counterpart *Jude the Obscure* by Thomas Hardy (1895), explicit social critiques, and it is noteworthy that they were as concerned with the oppressive consequences of the sex–gender system for working-class people as with class. Maugham based *Liza of Lambeth* on his experiences as a medical student in obstetrics in Lambeth, where he saw sixty-three confinements in three weeks.[30] *Liza* begins with a group of children and pregnant women in the street, for whose amusement a free-spirited Liza dances. The text reveals Liza's increasing humiliation and abuse, with that of other female characters, at the hands of men: "It was a Saturday night, the time when women in Vere Street weep" (156). Driven to alcoholism, Liza dies of a miscarriage. Gissing, whose representations of working women (including middle-class working women in *The Odd Women* [1893]) have reaped both praise and blame from feminist scholars, was born into the middle class, but had been expelled from Owen's College, married an alcoholic prostitute, and lived in the slums. In Kipling's "Badalia," having a husband amounts to being beaten on a regular basis.

The great novels and novelists notwithstanding, it seems likely that the rise of, and high demand for, the modern short story in the 1880s had something to do with the failure of the organic, panoramic view of the "realist" novel to incorporate a world disintegrating into class and gender perspectives. Indeed the apocalyptic conclusion to *Jude the Obscure,* amounting almost to parody of the form's organic closure (i.e., the triple execution and suicide of Sue and Jude's children because they have become a burden to their parents—emblem of the futurelessness of working-class children), may be seen as Hardy's rejection of the conventional novel as a realistic form in modern society. (He turned to the relative isolation of romantic lyric poetry after *Jude.*) In addition, Gissing's *Nether World* made it clear that, contrary to the optimism of the earlier fiction of Dickens, Eliot, Gaskell, et al., the only solution to the problem of poverty was economic restructuring.

The authors of the new short fiction, more suited to the fractured perspectives of class and gendered social relations, were typically middle-class or upwardly mobile like Arthur Morrison, who had been born in the East End in 1863. Many of them, like Maugham, wrote as hopeful social reformers. Morrison worked as a clerk for the "Palace of Delight"—Walter Besant's term in *All Sorts and Conditions of Men* (1882) for the project that became the People's Palace—for literature and the arts for the poor until its transformation into what he considered a "polytechnic" under the Draper's Company in 1890. Morrison was also engaged in polemics in the press about the possibilities of social amelioration, answering his critics in his preface to the third edition of *A Child of the Jago* (1897), "But chiefly this book of mine disturbed those who had done nothing, and preferred to do nothing, by way of discharging their responsiblity toward the Jago and the people in it."[31] The question, consequently, was, how most productively to represent the poor to the middle classes? In the following analyses of some representative collections of short stories, each published in the 1890s, I indicate the late Victorian narrative possibilities for representing the lives of the poor.[32]

In the 1970s, Nadine Gordimer has written, black writers in South Africa arrived out of their own situation at Brecht's discovery: that their audience needed to be educated to be *astonished at the circumstances under which they functioned.* The writers began to show a black audience that their living conditions were their story. Faced with their stories or plays, Gordimer says, whites often experience boredom, for "nothing happens"; they do not see the development of actions, but merely the presentation of conditions.[33]

Setting his characters in the class into which he was born, Arthur

Morrison's descriptive introduction to *Tales of Mean Streets* (1894), entitled "A Street," indicates by a sequence of negations that the inhabitants
are going nowhere and therefore will form the basis of no dramatic plot.
The description of a street in the East End ("any street"—the lack of
particularization is thematic) unfolds monotonously: "It is not pretty to
look at"; "it is not a pleasing object"; "And this is the record of a day in
this street; and every day is hopelessly the same"; "Thus goes Sunday in
this street, and every Sunday is the same as every other Sunday, so that
one monotony is broken with another"; "No event in the outer world
makes any impression in this street. . . . Nothing disturbs this street—
nothing but a strike"; "Nobody laughs here"; "There is no exchange of
promises, no troth-plight, no engagement, no love-talk"; "Nobody from
this street goes to the theatre"; "For ignorance is the inevitable portion
of dwellers here: seeing nothing, reading nothing and considering nothing"; and the last sentence: "That [the East End] is planned in short
lengths is true, but there is no other way in the world that can more properly be called a single street, because of its dismal lack of accent, its sordid
uniformity, its utter remoteness from delight" (pp. 1–7).

Morrison problematizes literary devices like plot, character, setting,
and dialogue according to the material constraints upon casual labor.
The setting is the claustrophobic monotony of the East End that denies
novelistic panoramic space. Story after story begins in the street, in the
crowd, and ends there, denying private space for internal character development and denying progressive plot, confirming the "plotlessness" of
casual labor. With one exception to be discussed below, there are no
structural conflicts. With no self-consciousness, the characters have no
internal psychological struggles; rarely do they possess internality at all.
With no human characteristics but ignorance and apathy, there are no
conflicts between good and evil. Transcribed from dialects Morrison
knew well, the dialogue is incoherent—short, often profane epithets, or
pleas from victims, rather than shared communication. To middle-class
readers, Morrison drained the category of human, with its contemporary
liberal associations of human spirit overcoming its trials. He further signifies this dehumanization with the insignificance of the personal names
of his nonheroes: "Somewhere in the register was written the name Elizabeth Hunt; but seventeen years after the entry the spoken name was
Lizerunt" ("Lizerunt"). "His first name was properly James, but that had
been long forgotten. 'Scuddy' meant nothing in particular, was derived
from nothing, and was not, apparently, the invention of any distinct person. Still, it was commonly his only name, and most of his acquaintances
had also nicknames of similarly vague origin" ("A Conversion"). Mor-

rison's are a casual people, without lineage on the earth, and without future.

The insignificance of personal individuation is a constant throughout late Victorian fictional presentations of the working classes, finding its analogue in the "social atom" phenomenon in the autobiographies I shall discuss in Chapter 4. Some names are elided with employment: in "Billy the Snide" (i.e., the counterfeiter) in *The Hooligan Nights* (1899), Clarence Rook writes, "Bill Day was 'is name . . . but we never called 'im nuffink but Billy, or Billy the Snide." Others are reconstructed with identifiable real-world reference: "Pennyloaf's legal name was Penelope," writes Gissing in *The Nether World,* "which being pronounced as a trisyllable, transformed itself by further corruption into a sound at all events conveying some meaning." All names are abbreviated, and some are generic. In one of Henry Nevinson's interracial romances, the husband's (only) name is Sissero. Nevinson's child-narrator introduces Sissero's wife, "Same as all red-'aired people 'er name was Ginger. But after she got married 'er proper name was Mrs. Sissero, but she wasn't never called that. . . . The rest on us used to call 'er Mrs. Kentucky, or Tennessee, or Timbuctoo, or Old Folks at 'Ome, or anythink else 'andy as 'ad connection with niggers. For the thing as made 'er famous was she'd married a nigger and couldn't never get over it" (62). Other names are occasional or associational and ad hoc. In "The St. George of Rochester," a waterman narrates the christening of a child, "And if it 'ad been a female, we'd 'ave called it Deborah Jane [the name of his barge], but through it bein' a boy, there didn't seem nothing necessary to call it. So we called it all manner" (51).

The one constant structural conflict—the exception alluded to earlier—in *Mean Streets* is gender. In "Lizerunt" the parasite Billy Chope lives off his sick mother, who mangles at home, and, after her death, his wife, whom he finally forces into prostitution. In presenting this scene of domestic violence Morrison answers the question "who were the working classes" with charwomen and pieceworkers who mangled at home in cold rooms and were beaten by men who had been irrevocably brutalized by unrelenting conditions of scarcity. Scarcity constituted the condition of nature, the "habitus" of *Mean Streets,* and survival differentiated its inhabitants one from another. The only way to contain the threat of their contamination—Billy as a welfare case and Lizer as a prostitute—was to change the conditions in which they were born and reproduced. Morrison presented, that is, a material analysis of the poor that confronted readers with the limitations of middle-class philanthropy.

On the other hand, in the lyrical prose of *Neighbours of Ours* (1894), Henry Nevinson presents a liberal world in which workers transcend the scarcity and violence to participate in richer, more emotionally satisfying interpersonal relationships than were generally represented among the bourgeoisie. Thus Nevinson humanized the poor for the middle-class reading public, attempting to reconcile the classes under one common humanity, a "we the people of Britain." The narrator of the stories is a son of respectable working parents pointedly named "Britton," whose naïve depictions of interracial and interclass couples give the illusion of human plenitude and freedom, a world in which class and race are not the determinant social factors in characters' identities: a liberal world. In "Sissero's Return," an Irish woman supports her children by being mistress to a Jew when her husband, a black sailor, fails to return from a voyage. (While waiting for passage home, it turns out, he has been sheltered by a Chinese girl.) The last lines, when Sissero returns, are an image of sexual pleasure (they make love upstairs) and social *jouissance,* as he is incorporated within the community and Ginger is implicitly forgiven by her respectable (racist and antisemitic) neighbors.

In "The St. George of Rochester," in which Britton's narration embeds the words of a dying waterman, a barge on the Thames is the site of an extraordinary love between the bargeman and a lady who has mysteriously come aboard to bear an illegitimate child. The waterman contrasts this love of plenitude and freedom with his three subsequent marriages to practical women of his own class: "And I wasn't talkin o' none o' my three wives neither, for all I've no word agen them, and they wasn't none of 'em bad-lookin' to start with. But it's a different kind o' woman as I'm speakin' on'" (44). The barge itself becomes a moist utopia removed from the vicissitudes of land and urban crowding:

> Yer see, livin' on a barge ain't at all the same thing as livin' on shore and goin' out to work. Yer've mostly always got time on a barge, and there ain't no call to 'urry about sayin' anythink, more especial when the two of yer's livin' together on it, and tomorrer goes by much the same as today, only for the matter of the wind blowin' or not blowin'. . . . I've mostly been 'appy enough all my time. . . . but that night when I 'eard the flood commin' in, and felt the old barge startin' to move through the water, shovin' away the blocks of ice same as me shovin' through a crowd, and I knowed as she was . . . layin' still and thinkin' o' me, that time was worth all the rest o' my good times put together (52–53).

Just as the bargeman doesn't mind "losin' money" while Erith (the lady takes the name of a port on the river) stays on the boat, she too transcends her class. On her "difference," her uniqueness among upper-class women, Timmo remarks, "I used to think it was praps only through 'er bein' a lady born, but I've set eyes on a deal o'ladies since that time, and 'ave quite give up that notion" (53). She conforms to life on the barge, "and afore the year was out, the river was fair mad in love with 'er" (55).

As some of these quotations indicate, Nevinson uses figurative language as "naïvely" or unselfconsciously as the ancient poets (i.e., to represent a mutable world, a world of metamorphoses), a usage banished from Morrison's metaphorless, determinist economy. Timmo's lady is like a Spinnaker (47); with the birth of her baby she took "such care as if it was goin' to be the only one baby in the world, and people was to take a fresh start from it, same as from Adam" (52). Keeping company with Sissero, Ginger dressed "all in white, and nothink on 'er 'ead but 'er orange 'air, so as, if seen from the top winders, the women said she looked like a poached egg" (65). Waiting and watching for Sissero's return, Ginger "Some'ow got to 'ave the look of a curly Newfoundland bitch as I once seen with stones and things tied to 'er, and they was just goin' to 'eave 'er over the dock-bridge, and she kep' lookin' round to see if 'er old master wasn't comin' along" (72). While Ginger sews flags in the streets at night by the light of streetlamps and her children sleep in the empty room, Britton ironically sees, "the two little darkies curled up together under a Union Jack" and thinks "on what our teacher 'ad used to tell us about the flag o' the Empire standin' for a sign o' purtection to all the different kinds a' people round the world, for all that a good blanket would no doubt 'ave been warmer" (76).

That Morrison uses character to show the overwhelming determinism of environment and Nevinson uses environment to test the virtue of characters is one way of distinguishing their relatively pure forms of environmental determinism and optimistic liberal autonomy, the beliefs that one is a product of one's environment or that one can rise above one's material conditions. Morrison is interested in poverty—its causes and consequences, Nevinson in an apparently autonomous and universal human spirit.

In the novel *A Child of the Jago,* the causes of unemployment, the most significant problem of Morrison's world, are beyond the control of the Jago people. Even the mere opportunity for Dicky to work (the narrator aptly calls this an "experiment") is only possible through Father Sturt's intervention: he must promise to cover the employer's losses, "should the experiment end in theft" (130). The experiment fails, but again due to events beyond Dicky's control. Morrison never explains Dicky's father's aversion to work—when Father Sturt offers him a job, Perrott feels that "he would gladly have risked another lagging ... [rather] than take Father Sturt's advice" (181)—but given the uniformity of experience in the Jago, readers assume a similar history. Morrison's refusal to explain it, indeed, corroborates that history as the ordinary way of life. Referring to Dicky's employment experience, Father Sturt says, "Dicky was but one among thousands, and the disappointment was but one of many hundred" (143).

In Nevinson's fiction, on the other hand, material conditions function either to enhance individual character or to provide metaphors for the character's individuality. Sissero is a stoker on a steamship—the man who regulates the fire and steam, a job so arduous that even Mayhew's virile enginemen held it in awe.[34] Yet Nevinson avoids the facts of Sissero's labor, showing only how he rises above it with an innate and stereotypical "laugh": "You'd only got to look at Sissero and 'e'd start laughin'. 'E seemed to 'ave a kind of 'appiness always brewin' and workin' inside of 'im" (64). The image of blackness and fire is transferred into his home, where Ginger decorates the wall with a sole picture of a volcano (probably Krakatoa, which had violently erupted in 1883), a metaphor, presumably, of Sissero's equally stereotypical sexuality, which goes unremarked but not unnoticed in the community: "And all the women was wild [when Sissero and Ginger started keeping company], for all they didn't exactly want the nigger neither. But likin' to 'ave him about, they aimed at keepin' of him unmarried ... on a kind of off-chance of goodness knows what" (65). The toughest job in the world cannot prevent Sissero's laughing and loving; in Morrison's world of "A Street," on the other hand, "nobody laughs—life is too serious a thing, nobody sings. There was once a woman who sang" (4).

In Nevinson, as in much of the earlier Condition of England fiction, poverty is essential as an obstacle that can be overcome, not merely by patience, faith, and love, but almost by a "positive outlook" (according to Norman Tebbit, by a bicycle). "Now, don't yer be troublin' yer sunny 'ead about the money, darlin,'" Sissero tells Ginger, "I'll make the double on it as easy as kiss yer', and then I'll love yer twice as much—cos why, yer'll be twice as expensive" (68). When poverty forces Sissero away for longer and longer periods, Ginger is troubled by his absence and preoccupied with finding food and shelter for her children, but she persistently maintains that her husband will return, and her faith is ultimately repaid.

Moreover, Nevinson formally constructs his narratives as luxurious

reflective reveries. The boy Britton's stories are flashbacks leisurely
unfolding during moments of pause in laboring life. "Sissero's Return"
begins, "Just before that there Chris'mus time, when Mrs. Simon was
kind of gettin' used to 'avin' a baby same as other mothers, and the
women was turnin' up chippin' 'er about it, and was lookin' round for
somethink fresh, we 'ad a rare set-out in our street by reason of somebody
else turnin' up unexpected" (62). Morrison's Jago, on the other hand,
brooks no time for storytelling. Though Dicky imagines the fruits of the
"straight game" (i.e., his own shop, Em on the piano [13]) when he is
working, the daydream is abruptly shattered when he loses his job.
Reflection, or pausing to think, is time-wasting, "daydreaming," for
Morrison.

One of the few occasions that Morrison gives his characters the luxury
of internality is near the end of the *Jago,* when the narration shifts from
the nonintrusive, descriptive and detached (often ironic) style of the narrator to the reverie of Josh Perrott, Dicky's father, during his trial for
murder. Perrott considers evidence for his defense one of the oppressive
trivialities with which he would rather not bother: "He felt some interest
in what was coming—in the sentence, and the black cap, and so on—
never having seen a murder trial before" (194), but "the evidence was a
nuisance. What was the good of it all?" (193). Daydreaming during his
defense, he is "oppressed by a plague of galloping thought" (193), a rush
"of crowded trivialities" (195): of the freshly gilt Lion and Unicorn, the
big sword on the wall, a strong smell of stale pickles, a four-legged linnet
in Club Row, the price of pigeons, a show in Bethnal Green Road with a
two-headed sheep; "they were small things, and had nothing to do with
his own business" (193). When he hears the verdict "Guilty," he feels no
bitterness, no contrition, and no hope: "Yes, that was right; this was the
real business. His head was clear and ready now"—not in the sense of a
renewed ability to think clearly, but cleared of this oppressing "plague of
galloping thought." He no longer needs to think—after five years in
prison thought is foreign to him in any case—but to be ready to respond
to whatever stimuli his environment offers. The reflective process of the
judicial system is irrelevant to his life of action: it will only be used to
crush him, and his response is to take it like a man.

When his sentence is pronounced, Perrott thinks, "Well, well, that
was over. The gaoler touched his arm. Right" (196). He thanks the gaol-
ers for his grub and for being "kind and wot not" and is curious about
the straps binding him at the hanging ("This was how they did it,
then.... This way?"). The narrator writes that "nobody sympathised

with him, nor got up a petition for pardon, nor wrote tearful letters to the newspapers" (199). His son Dicky, now "doubly sealed of the outcasts: a Jago with a hanged father" (200), tries one last time to dream, "How good for [him, his mother, and siblings to die] together, and wake in some pleasant place, say a place like Father Sturt's sitting-room, and perhaps find—but there, what foolishness!" (201). Then he dies in a street fight. The lyrical language and metaphorical transformations of Nevinson may best be contrasted with the utter futility of thought in Morrison.

Perhaps one last representational mode need be mentioned here, for like Morrison's radical enviromental determinism and Nevinson's liberal humanism, sensationalism also influened working-class self-representation. In the *Hooligan Nights* (1899) Clarence Rook eroticizes the voices of the poor, transforming a street urchin into a Scheherazade, a transformation appropriated by actresses and circus performers in their own autobiographies:

> "They took you for a split," said young Alf, as we met at the end of the court. "I know'd they would. 'Ello, Alice!"
> A girl stood in the deep shadow of the corner house. Her head was covered by a shawl, and I could not see her face, but her figure showed youth and a certain grace. "'Ello!" she said, without moving.
> "When you goin' to get married?" asked young Alf.
> "When it comes," replied the girl softly.
> The voice that falls like velvet on your ear and lingers in your memory is rare. Wendell Holmes says somewhere that he had heard but two perfect speaking voices, and one of them belonged to a German chambermaid, The softest and most thrilling voice I ever heard I encountered at the corner of one of the lowest slums in London. (130–31)

In Edwin Pugh's *King's Circumstance* (1898), the prose distances the reader and objectifies the poor ("Unmentionable things happened in these houses, and untranslatable language was sometimes used" ([107]), going so far as to have his unfortunate protagonist Moll, an alcoholic widow, refer to herself (for the reader's benefit) as "too orrible an vile" to touch a child. Pugh's fictional community again objectifies Moll for the reader as a "beast" (111); and reverting to the earlier mode of Dickens, Pugh objectifies the community itself as comic and foolish. The story concludes with a sensational running down of the child by a lorry—it was noted by Jack London in *The People of the Abyss* that when he posed as a seaman vehicles obviously took less care to avoid him in the street, "My life had cheapened in direct ratio with my clothes"[35]—and an even more sensational image of Moll entering death's arms—whether morally or physically is not clear—in the arms of another woman in the catacombs of the Thames.

It is possible, however, to do an "anarchist" reading of "The Inevitable Thing" that locates the subjective isolation of the poor vis-à-vis a coercive, "objective," and objectifying State.[36] With an analytic shift from plot to imagery, the scene of "The Inevitable Thing" appears as that of Masterman's hordes, precariously patrolled by the Law. When Moll fails to conform to respectable life in the suburban slums, she is driven into Tottenham Court Road, like Symon's Edgware Road, the heart of the metropolis. The parents of the child she has kidnapped immediately set the "tecs" upon her (117) and she is sensible of pursuit by "the strong, long arm of the law" and "suspicion" on the part of every passerby. The police "lay a heavy hand on her shoulder" before the child Bet again "becomes lost in the crowd" (120). When the policeman and Moll rush toward the scene of the accident, "The crowd was fifty humans deep, and she could not reach its centre, though she fought and struggled towards it with the strength of madness. For ten horrible minutes she stood with her arms pressed hard to her sides and her face flattened against a bricklayer's fustian coat, unable to do aught but moan despairingly" (120). Fixed in the crowd, "it was as hard to retreat as go forward. . . . Even as she stood panting in that writhing phalanx, she could see herself arraigned behind the spikes of a prisoner's dock before a buzzing court, and heard the voice of Bet's mother rising in shrill denunciation of her" (121).

Driven through "the hurrying throng and ceaseless tumult," enjoined by the "omnipresent policeman" to "move on" (121), Moll "staggered across the widest road in the world and wandered on through a maze of kerbs till she found herself under the dripping trees of the Embankment" (122). Asleep, "a bull's-eye flashed in her face and awoke her. 'Come,' said a voice from the blackness behind the bull's-eye; 'you can't sleep 'ere you know.' She knew it and rose wearily" (122). The madwoman who offers her a stone bed beneath the bridge anticipates Moll's unspoken fears, "no policeman's bull's-eye ever shines down here," and queries musingly "why the laws of England have ordained that no one shall sleep in the streets by night, whilst everyone is at liberty to sleep in the streets by day" (123).

This representation of the poor as a surging dangerous crowd barely controllable by ever-vigilant police is ancient, reaching back through Dickens *(Barnaby Rudge)* to Hogarth, and is visually represented in General Booth's map of the redemption of the Salvation Army, in which the

Army's Rescued reach out to their brethren in the Sea of Starvation, Homelessness, Criminality, and Despair (see Figure 3.1). However, in Dickens's representation of the death of Sikes in *Oliver Twist* the crowd is equally able to be an instrument of justice. In Pugh's story, as in the hunting down of Josh Perrott in the Jago, the crowd is irrational as well as anonymous—Masterman's "numbers." Caught between a crowd irrationally "moving on" and an objectified Law whose purpose is to crush them, Moll and Perrott represent subjects objectified by the reader and subjugated by the system, the peers of Hardy's hunted Tess (prefigured by the rabbits cut down by the reaping-machine in Chapter XIV) and Sue and Jude hounded with their children from every town and lodging in Oxford, that "home of lost causes and impossible ideals" (Mathew Arnold, quoted by Jude). While Nevinson aestheticized the poor for middle-class readers as autonomous, even progressive, social agents transcending the objective conditions of their existence, Morrison and Pugh, like Hardy and Gissing, also objectified the Law that brought them down.

Figure 3.1. *(Overleaf)* "Social Campaign of the Salvation Army" from General William Booth's *In Darkest England and the Way Out* (1891).

The Chart is intended to give a birdseye-view of the Scheme described in this book, and the results expected from its realization.

The figures on the pillars represent the appalling extent of the misery and ruin existing in Great Britain, as given in Government and other returns.

In the raging Sea, surrounding the Salvation Lighthouse, are to be seen the victims of vice and poverty who are sinking to ruin, but whom the Officers appointed to carry out the Scheme are struggling to save.

On the left, a procession of the rescued may be seen on their way to the various REFUGES, WORKSHOPS, and other Establishments for Industrial Labor in the CITY COLONY, many of which are already in existence.

From the CITY COLONY in the center, another procession can be seen, of those who, having proved themselves worthy of further assistance, are on their way to the FARM COLONY, which, with its Villages, Co-operative Farms, Mills, and Factories, is to be created, far away from the neighborhood of the public-house.

From the FARM COLONY are to be seen Steamers hurrying across the seas, crowded with Emigrants of all sorts, proceeding either to the existing Colonies of the British and other Empires, or to the COLONY-OVER-SEA, yet to be established; whilst the sturdy baker on the left and the laundress on the right suggest, on the one hand, plenty of work, and on the other, abudance of food.

The more the Chart is examined the more will be seen of the great blessings the Scheme is intended to convey, and the horrible destruction hourly going on amongst at least Three Millions of our fellow-creatures, which we are anxious to bring to an end. And the more the Scheme contained in this book is studied and assisted, the more will the beautiful prospect held out on the Chart be likely to be brought into reality.

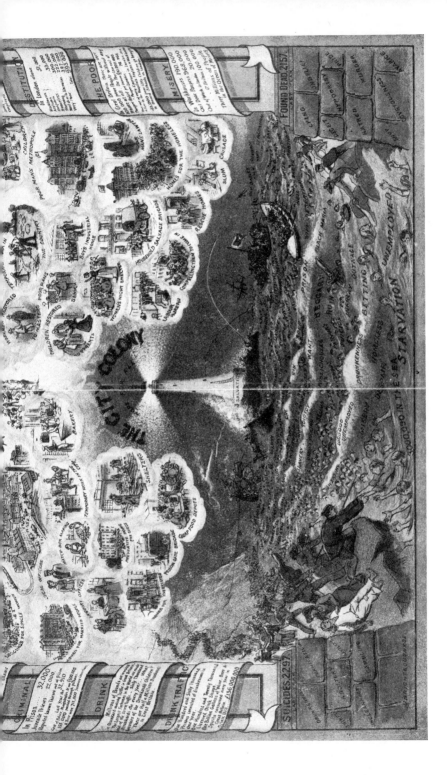

These are imaginative writers as concerned as Rorty about cruelty and as committed to solidarity. Now we can return to Rorty's claim that solidarity is created by imagination rather than reason, by the language of literature rather than that of truth, rationality or moral obligation. His liberal perspective is very like Nevinson's: assuming that solidarity is dependent upon a notion that "we" are alike in some underlying sense, we can sympathize with others as long as we see them as "one of us"; and the liberal project is to expand the "we" to a more inclusive acceptance of others. In its sympathetic portrayals of others, literature prepares us for this expanded "we".[37] The difficulties with this position are as follows. First, as I suggested earlier, what we call great literature (by Rorty's "geniuses" like Dickens, Eliot, or James) does not give us the "voice of the oppressed," but rather objectifies the oppressed for its own (often liberal) ends. Therefore, what "we" get from literature is not an expanded "we" but more of the same old "us."

I can illustrate this by the reception of the works discussed in this chapter, which as far as I can ascertain has changed surprisingly little since the nineteenth century. I have taught Victorian fiction, canonical and obscure, for some years. With the exception of Marxists and cultural critics (i.e., readers whose primary interest in literature is not aesthetic but social), middle-class students today respond to writers like Hardy, Nevinson, Gissing, and Morrison like Victorian middle-class readers responded to them. They want to "identify" with characters, and the only characters they can identify with are those with subjectivities (introspective, self-conscious, self-interested subjectivities) like their own. Thus they feel solidarity with Jude, the stonecutter with a highly literate sensibility and self-consciousness, or the ironic child Britton, rather than Morrison's or Gissing's undramatic drudges. Indeed, like Victorian reviewers of Morrison, they almost always find his fiction "overwhelming" and "offputting." Similarly, for years Gissing has been relegated to the status of a minor writer, largely because he fails to develop characters with the rich subjectivity of Hardy's. If literature does not give "us"—the status quo—ourselves, we do not identify with it and it is not canonical.

The problem this causes for authors against cruelty and for solidarity is obvious, and very like the notorious problem of Victorian "reticence" in writers like Dickens and Engels.[38] Both acute social observers, Dickens and Engels were frequently perplexed about how to represent social conditions so appalling that the conventions of middle-class decorum in writing made no provision for their expression. Acceptable language simply had no way to represent the conditions whose amelioration the reformers demanded. If one maintained linguistic decorum, one cooperated in the occlusion of the conditions of immiseration. Sacrificing convention, on the other hand, was personally revolting for the authors and threatened to jeopardize their readerships. Now whereas Nevinson and Hardy maintained the illusion of "us" united by a human spirit not entirely determined by its context, writers like Morrison and Gissing sacrificed the illusion that people living in conditions appalling to "us" could be "like us," or part of some "we." Thus Nevinson and Hardy cultivated the complacent response of Victorian and modern readers alike: since Jude, Sissero, and Ginger are so much like "us," the effects of poverty must not be determinant. The more radical critiques of Morrison and Gissing, on the other hand, have simply been marginalized, and the real differences of the poor from "ourselves"—the differences caused by poverty—have been muted. It is precisely because Rorty's great "literature" has heretofore worked only by allowing "us" to identify with subjectivities like "our" own that it has not in practice been a more useful tool for democratic progress than that of truth, rationality, or moral obligation. The students who are receptive to rational argument, on the other hand—students who analyze rather than identify—tend to see in Jude, Sissero, and Ginger implausible instances of dualism (bourgeois heads on laboring bodies) and in Morrison and Gissing the case for outrage and social intervention.

In teaching imaginative literature, what has come to interest me most about narrative is how the suture—the convergence of author's, characters', and readers' viewpoints—occurs; and I believe with Rorty that this process of identification will tell us something about our own cruelty and our capacities for solidarity. What the study of literature and other narratives and their reception show, however, is that as long as we need to see the other as "one of us" we will not approach solidarity. Rather we need to sympathize with others precisely in their differences from ourselves, not hiding those differences under a wash of human spirit that transcends context, but rather understanding those differences precisely as products of contingencies over which we have much control. The point is perhaps all the more urgent today because differences in late twentieth-century life go even deeper while they are more dramatically juxtaposed: today the poorest inhabitants of the East End of London are likely to be Bangladeshi. Whatever the merits of Rorty's rejection of the role of Reason in ending cruelty and announcing solidarity, to the extent that this is a task for the Imagination, alongside great literature we should also read the "voices of the oppressed" and respect their differences, as in the next chapter.

4.

Working-Class Autobiography, Subjectivity, and Value

> I have found it an interesting life to live, but I do not know whether it will be interesting to read.
>
> Foreword to MARIANNE FARNINGHAM,
> *A Working Woman's Life: An Autobiography* (1907)

> It may perhaps, appear ridiculous to fill so much paper with babbling's of one's self; but when a person who has never known any one interest themselves in him, who has existed as a *cipher* in society, is kindly asked to tell his own story, how he will gossip!
>
> JOHN NICHOLLS, quoted by John James Bezer in
> *The Autobiography of One of the Chartist Rebels of 1848* (1851)

A study of nineteenth-century British working-class autobiography is at last possible for cultural critics because of the labors of John Burnett, David Mayall, and David Vincent, compilers of *The Autobiography of the Working Class*.[1] This chapter is based upon the reading of several hundred of the 804 autobiographies included in the bibliography. Their authors were born before 1895 and were designated "working-class" by themselves as well as by the compilers of that bibliography. Their works are called autobiographies despite their differences from traditional autobiography as the literary community has defined it, and despite their formal and rhetorical variety, because these are the responses that workers produced when asked or compelled, for whatever reasons, to record their lives. The bibliography represents a wealth of work experiences—1400 separate occupations and a variety of individual occupational histories.

Although there is concentration on London and the northern industrial centers, and in general Scotland is represented more strongly than Wales, the geographical spread of the bibliography is virtually comprehensive. The only obvious underrepresentation is, predictably, by gender: only one-tenth of the autobiographies having been written by women. The conditions under which these texts were written, published, or preserved will be discussed in the upcoming analyses.

It is a commonplace of literary criticism that in their writings workers often appear to lack what Jerome Buckley calls the "significant selfhood" (typically in conjunction with "Significant Others") that organizes traditional autobiography: they do not exhibit flair and "personality." I previously cited Virginia Woolf's observation when Hogarth Press published the papers of the Women's Co-Operative Guild, that their "writing lacks detachment and imaginative breadth, even as the women themselves lack variety and play of feature."[2] Such class-bound notions of the self have resulted in working-class autobiographies being relegated to illustrating the psychological effects of social deprivation on rhetorical self-expression. The goals of this chapter are both positive, to indicate the variety of forms and rhetorical functions of working-class autobiography, and critical, to indicate the ways in which working-class autobiography alters the genre of autobiography as it has been conceived in literary studies. I shall frame the analyses of working-class autobiography between discussions of literary value as represented by literary history and the implications of working-class self-representation for our notions of subjectivity.

Working-Class Subjectivity and Aesthetics

Working-class autobiographies, often by people about whom little is known but the one work, have been declared lacking in the self-revelation and concomitant literary indices of literary autobiography.[3] In his collection of five politically motivated autobiographies from the period of the birth of working-class radicalism in the 1790s to the passing of the third reform bill (universal male suffrage) in 1885, Vincent claims that despite their value in showing the foundations of the modern labor movement, "the moment [the autobiographers'] focus shifts from [their personal experiences] to a general history of the period, their autobiography suffers."[4] Nan Hackett explains literary critics' lack of interest in working-class autobiographies by claiming that the works are not coherent artworks with literary devices: they are not revelations of self, but of class.

The three distinct periods, therefore, in which Hackett has discerned common elements are congruent with the three shifts in working-class politics in nineteenth-century Britain: 1800–1848, 1848–1880, and 1880–1900. The first attempt of the working class to define itself as a class, ending with the Chartist failure, translated in the autobiographical writings into minimal self-representation, extensive documentation of the movements, and little introspection. In the second period, character-ized by an improving economy and the formation of a labor aristocracy, Hackett's autobiographers were primarily artisans. They emphasized mutual aid over Smilesian self-help and extolled moral welfare. The third period, 1880–1900, includes political activists and outcasts who were no longer concerned with impressing middle-class morality upon readers, whose viewpoints projected either mass agitation or apathy. In both cases the autobiographers had replaced the topos of self-made agent with that of class determinism.[5] Clearly although Vincent, a social historian, and Hackett, a literary critic, are deeply sympathetic toward their authors, both have accepted the view of autobiography as the revelation of a cen-tered, unified subject or self—at the very least one that, as in postmodern writers, is undone by her or his own self-consciousness. Such views have led Roy Pascal to call autobiography a middle-class form of narrative and Vincent to wonder whether working-class writers sacrificed their inde-pendence when they adopted the autobiographical form.[6]

Consider autobiography as it is treated in literary studies. Traditional theorists of autobiography have remarked upon the rise of self-portraiture and subjectivity from the self-contemplation made possible by the inven-tion of Venetian mirrors. The height of this self-contemplative model is probably Wordsworth as Hazlitt estimated him: "He is the greatest, that is, the most original writer of the present day, only because he is the great-est egotist. . . . He does not waste a thought on others. Whatever does not relate exclusively and wholly to himself is foreign to his views."[7] How-ever, this mirror metaphor of self-absorption is a misplaced model for writers whose impediments to literacy included lack of time, space, and adequate light. In *The Autobiography of a Working Man* (1848), Alex-ander Somerville, the son of itinerant farm laborers in the Borders, describes the conditions under which his family learned to read in the first quarter of the century: "My father and mother had a window (the house had none) consisting of one small pane of glass, and when they moved from one house to another in different parts of Berwickshire in different years, they carried this window with them, and had it fixed in each hovel into which they went as tenants."[8]

Whatever epistemological and compositional problems the canonical autobiographers of nineteenth-century Britain, predominantly men of property and leisure, may have had—and theorists of "self-writing" and "self-representation" like Avrom Fleishman and Paul Jay suggest that they had many[9]—the roles of "Wordsworth the dedicated poet," "Darwin the scientific observer," "Ruskin the critical spectator," "Newman the religious leader," and "Mill the defender of intellectual liberty" were as real to their audiences as to the authors. The epithets themselves— which are Buckley's—suggest the authors' critical distance from their objects of reflection and from their audiences. The poet and leader are as distant from the majority of their readers as science, criticism, and defense are distant from unreflective practice. For working-class autobiographers, on the other hand, subjectivity—being a significant agent worthy of the regard of others, a human subject, as well as an individuated "ego" for onself—was not a given. In conditions of long work hours, crowded housing, and inadequate light, it was difficult enough for them to contemplate themselves, but they also had to justify themselves as writers worthy of the attention of others.

As already observed, most working-class autobiographies do not begin with a family lineage or a birthdate, but rather with an apology for their authors' ordinariness, encoded in titles like *One of the Multitude* (1911) by George Acorn. Their authors lacked differentiation, were, as radical journalist William Adams put it, the "social atoms" making up the undifferentiated "masses": "I call myself a Social Atom—a small speck on the surface of society. The term indicates my insignificance. . . . I am just an ordinary person."[10] Similarly, Robert Blatchford, another radical journalist, opens his autobiography: "On St. Patrick's Day of 1852 the eternal Saki, engaged at his own good pleasure pouring out millions of bubbles like us, poured out me."[11] Chester Armstrong, an East Cumberland lead miner, emphasizes the ordinariness of his own life story: "We may place [my father] in the category of the ordinary. He was . . . a representative of that vast mass of human material that was laid upon the altar of the gods of work and wealth in the nineteenth century. . . . Of my courtship little need be said. It coincides with too much of common human experience to bear extensive comment."[12] Likewise, East London dressmaker Kathleen Woodward writes of her mother (in a psychological, if not literal, autobiography): "The circumstances of my mother's life in no matter differ from the circumstances of the lives of those inarticulate people without number who compose the "lower classes.'"[13] Mrs. Layton, a member of the Women's Co-Operative Guild, began: "I was my mother's seventh child, and seven more were born after me—fourteen in all—which made my mother a perfect slave" *(Life as*

We Have Known It, 1).I have already noted the Hanley potter Charles Shaw's bitter, "We were a part of Malthus's 'superfluous population.'"[14] Such examples can be multiplied indefinitely, and their affective range extends from defensive self-effacement through defiant irony.

Part of the problem in presenting subjectivity lay in obvious material conditions: workers, as Engels pointed out in 1844, were not "heads" but "hands," not *Homo cogitans* but *Homo laborans;* the conditions of their labor often mitigated against self-perception as an integrated, autonomous agent (see Chapter 2). One of the most self-conscious illustrations of, and protests against, the absorption of individuality into an undifferentiated and unhuman mass is *A Narrative of the Experience and Sufferings of William Dodd, A Factory Cripple* (1841), a key factor, along with Dodd's 1842 letters to Lord Ashley, in the passing of the Factories Bill of 1844. From the age of six, Dodd worked as a piecer in the woolen mills of Kendal. Due to his physical position while working, first one and then both of his knees collapse, his fingers bleed continually, his hands grow swollen from cold, and he suffers serious blood clots resulting in permanently distorted and disfigured limbs. When he can afford it he tries to marry—first young women, then, after repeated rejections, old ones, all of whom reject him on the basis of his deformity. He refuses to marry within the factory population out of fear that both husband and wife will eventually be immobilized. And finally he loses his job because of his inability to work. The entire text is Dodd's personal battle with the factory's literal machinery. In the exchange, part by part, he loses.

Dodd analyzes the absorption of his body and life into the factory by contrasting its relentless mechanization with the organic, humanistic life of agricultural laborers in the South—a literary contrast that would later be taken up by Gaskell in *North and South* (1855). Agricultural laborers are subjects, situated in the gaze of a benevolent God; Dodd is a piece of machinery, dehumanized and disregarded:

> In their daily toil they meet with so many instances of the wisdom and power of an all-wise being, that a love for his handiworks is sure to be impressed upon their mind;—the cheering influence of the sun, the refreshing breeze, the singing of birds, etc., all inspire this feeling. The manufacturing labourer knows nothing of these blessings by experience. He is placed in a mill or factory as a machine, for the performance of a quantity of labour—he hears nothing but the rumbling noise of the machinery, or the harsh voice of the overlooker—sees nothing but an endless variety of shafts, drums, straps, and wheels in motion; and though

these may at first inspire him with a feeling of respect for, and admiration of, the inventive powers of his fellow-creatures, yet this feeling will vanish, when he reflects on their power to destroy or render useless for life that exalted piece of mechanism formed by and after the image of God.[15]

Dodd's text terminates abruptly and grotesquely with the most recent of his injuries and amputations in his ongoing physical exchange with the machine, the amputation of his arm, without which, presumably, he cannot continue to write. He has "systematically" been denied childhood, paternity, livelihood, and, finally, authorship.

Yet Dodd's agonized subjection to machinery has given him a political identity; as Engels wrote within three years of the publication of *A Factory Cripple,* the self-conscious industrial proletariat was as much a product of the factory as the goods produced. Workers themselves articulated this, again through the contrast between North and South. Charles Shaw, who grew up in the southern Potteries in Dodd's "Hungry 40s," saw mechanization, seeing onself as one cog in a large machine, as psychologically useful in producing activism, and contrasts the politicized North with his slower-paced, unorganized South:

Now, if there had been a governing power like machinery, and if a steam-engine had started every Monday morning at six o'clock, the workers would have been disciplined to the habit of regular and continuous industry.... Machinery seems to lead to habits of calculation. [The Northern Counties'] great co-operative societies would never have risen to such immense and fruitful development but for the calculating induced by the use of machinery.... Yes, any true inner history of the Pottery working-people will account for the absence of a beneficient co-operative movement and an effective trades-union. There was a want of economical discipline in their work and life.[16]

Here, by "calculation" Shaw seems to mean something like Engels's "self-consciousness."

Of course the problem of subjectivity was not limited to the destruction of the human body under the conditions of industrialization. Most of the autobiographers were more concerned with their image and status as atoms of the masses. Many writers self-consciously distinguished themselves from others in order to establish themselves as subjects. One third of the way through *Pilgrimage from Nenthead,* Chester Armstrong distinguishes himself from the "vast mass of human material that was laid upon the altar of the gods of work and wealth" by distancing himself from co-workers in the mines: "Whatever compromises were required in seeking a harmonious relationship with my fellow workers, I managed to preserve my own identity, or, in other words, I held out against the evil effects of a gross environment" (76). He writes a book, *Social Freedom, or the Terms of a Progressive Order,* and his autobiography thus takes him from the dark, indistinct life in the mines into the world of the author, an enlightened world of science, philosophy, and history.

A similar process of differentiation occurs in *Jipping Street.* In Chapter 6, Kathleen Woodward rejects her assimilation into the factory matrix. Hearing "the mysteries of sex" from women in the factory, she feels disgust, fear, and curiosity: "Imperceptibly the novel experience of taking my place, a woman among women, began to lose its bloom. I found myself for ever dwelling on the sufferings of the women about me. I was oppressed, suffocated by them" (93–99). Margaret Bondfield's early experiences among married women in Yorkshire textile factories also deflect her from motherhood: "I just lived for the Trade Union Movement. I concentrated on my job. This concentration was undisturbed by love affairs. I had seen too much—too early—to have the least desire to join in the pitiful scramble of my workmates."[17] Elizabeth Bryson's *Look Back in Wonder* (1966) begins with a chapter entitled "One Among the Many" and thematizes a struggle to distinguish herself from family members, friends, and classmates in the 1880s.[18] She went on to "distinguish" herself as a successful physician—inverting the fate of the Angry Young Man clinging to working-class identity in John Osborne's *Look Back in Anger* (1956).

Yet once they did distinguish themselves from other workers, and establish themselves as individual agents unlike other miners or other women in the factory, they did not quite undergo embourgeoisement. Rather, they frequently worried about their "egotism"—not in the sense in which middle-class protagonists of Victorian fiction worried (i.e., about the effects of their actions upon others, or George Eliot's "duty"), but rather in questioning the rightness of individualism or social distinction generally. In his preface to his *Memoir* (1832), Thomas Hardy explains that he uses third-person narrative "to obviate the necessity of calling the great I so repeatedly to my assistance."[19] Marianne Fainingham (also known as Hearn), who published thirty-four books and wrote extensively for the *Christian World, Sunday School Times,* and *Christian World Magazine* for fifty years, begins *A Working Woman's Life* (1907) with a foreword: "I have had frequent misgivings while writing this autobiography, for I know of no particular reason why it should have been written; and it has appeared very egotistic to do it."[20]

The problem of the subject was doubly compounded by the view that the working classes were competing with more imaginative and compelling pictures of themselves in fiction. Due to the climate of political unrest and fear extending from the French Revolution through the housing crises of the 1880s, middle-class fiction increasingly included representations of the lower classes within the structure of a compelling and conflict-ridden narrative. See, for example, the so-called Condition of England novels of the 1840s–1860s by Dickens, Gaskell, Disraeli, Kingsley, and Eliot, among others, and the "naturalist" fiction of fin de siècle writers like Thomas Hardy, George Gissing, Arthur Morrison, Henry Nevinson, Edwin Pugh, and Clarence Rook (discussed in Chapter 3). "Books of recollections constitute what may be called a favourite class of literature. Though they cannot of course compete with novels," Adams writes in defense of his *Memoirs of a Social Atom* (Adams, p. xv). In his dedication to *One of the Multitude,* Acorn begs that "the public will recognize that experiences LIVED, and written down however poorly are of more real value and interest than imaginary fictions beautifully disguised."[21] Blatchford insists, "I have never written a book as a novelist writes a novel or a historian a history. I have always been a journalist; not an author" (Blatchford, 215).

Although the pioneer of popular journalism, Peter Paterson, dedicated his *Behind the Scenes* (1859) to Dickens, "the Creator of Mr. Vincent Crummles and the Infant Phenomenon,"[22] and Blatchford partially credited Dickens's "democratic sentiments and passionate sympathy with the poor" in his chapter on "How and Why I Became a Socialist" (Chapter VII), many writers found middle-class fiction both unflattering and disturbingly untrue to their experience. With *The Life and Adventures of a Cheap Jack* (1876), the hawker William Green wished to disabuse the public of the notion that his "fraternity" was represented by Dickens's Dr. Marigold.[23] Armstrong writes with bitter irony that at the age of twenty-five he married on a very limited income to "toe the line with that enforced integrity and humility which is much extolled in fiction" (Armstrong, 76). In *Jipping Street,* a childhood friend of Woodard is read romantic "novelettes" by her mother, forced by her mother to marry, and then beaten by her husband (Chapter 2). It is significant in the context of working-class responses to representations of themselves that Thomas Cooper published his *Life* in 1872, twenty-two years after Kingsley presented it fictively in *Alton Locke.*[24] John James Bezer specifically published his *Autobiography of One of the Chartist Rebels of 1848* (1851) in the *Christian Socialist* to counter Kingsley's disparaging representation in *Alton Locke* of April 10, 1848 (the third Chartist petition—made by the government, and Kingsley, into a spectacular confrontation between the forces of law/order/property and those of anarchy and violence).[25] Even as late as *The Classic Slum: Salford Life in the First Quarter of the Century* (1971), Robert Roberts was compelled to repudiate D. H. Lawrence's romantic memories of working-class virility: the peers of Roberts's childhood were as prudish in language as in love.[26] The autobiographers insisted upon their own histories, however difficult it was to write them.

By the turn of the century, the Women's Co-Operative Guild collectively rejected fiction—or at least relegated it to the realm of applied art (*Life As We Have Known It,* 92–93, 114–129)—for reasons that Pierre Bourdieu has theorized in differentiating popular culture from bourgeois "taste":

> Working-class people expect every image to explicitly perform a function, if only that of a sign, and their judgements make reference, often explicitly, to the norms of morality or agreeableness. . . . Intellectuals could be said to believe in the representation—literature, theatre, painting—more than in the things represented, whereas the people chiefly expect representations and the conventions which govern them to allow them to believe "naïvely" in the things represented. The pure aesthetic is rooted in an ethic, or rather, an ethos of elective distance from the necessities of the natural and social world, which may take the form of moral agnosticism. . . . The detachment of the pure gaze cannot be dissociated from a general disposition towards the world which is the paradoxical product of conditioning by negative economic necessities—a life of ease—that tends to induce an active distance from necessity.[27]

Mrs. Hood, J.P., president of the Guild and Poor Law Guardian, only reads novels set in places where she must travel; Mrs. Wrigley reads only co-operative literature and newspapers; Mrs. Scott, J.P., prefers Wells and Bellamy, utopian literature; and Mrs. Burman reads atlases (*Life as We Have Known It,* 66, 92–95, 115, 120). Annie Kenney's *Memories of a Militant* (1924) shows Kenney rejecting fiction for European and American political writers like Voltaire, Emerson, and Whitman.[28]

When working-class readers did read fiction they, again, expected representations and the conventions governing them to allow them to believe in the things represented, and they judged them according to what Bourdieu calls "the norms of morality or agreeableness." The felt-hat worker Mrs. Scott explains why *Peter Pan* moves her—"That sense of longing and stretching out after dreams and ideals is so vivid"—and why she admires Wells: "I can sympathise with him in some of his situations when one is not used to hotels . . . how he hits off the class we belong to, the small shopkeepers . . . and the conversations carried on at funeral parties by some of the older women" (*Life as We Have Known It,* 92–93). Of *Robert Falconer* she writes, "That is a splendid book, the grandmother is such a fine character, just like some of our old chapel people. My mother and my grandfather were of that type." Earlier in the century, Dickens's *Pickwick Papers* (1836–1837) had been more plagiarized in cheap popular editions than any work of its time, largely due to the public's enthusiasm for Sam Weller. Unlike upper-class readers, Louis James points out in *Fiction for the Working Man,* the working classes enjoyed prolonged cycles of adventures of the beloved character, independently of the vehicle promoting it.[29] In her survey of 200 ironworkers in Middlesborough, Florence Bell found that half read newspapers only (primarily evening papers and secondarily weekly papers on Sunday, when many stayed in bed reading and smoking, recuperating from the weekly toil), and one quarter read books as well as newspapers. Of this quarter, the most popular novelist was Mrs. Henry Wood, author of *East Lynne* (1861). Bell bases Wood's popularity upon her "admirable compound of the goody and the sensations," meaning by *goody* moralism and by *sensations* something like class envy, "just enough above their usual standard of possibilities to give an agreeable sense of stimulus."[30]

In *A Poor Man's House* (1909), Stephen Reynolds also distinguishes between the realism of his comrade Tony's art and the conventionalism, what Reynolds calls "repetition," of bourgeois art: "Tony sees, *lives* what he is singing. Between this sort of song and most, there is much the same difference as between going abroad and reading a book of travels. . . . His art is perpetual creation, not repetition of a thing created once and for all. The art that is *lived,* howsoever imperfect, has an advantage over the most finished art that is merely repeated."[31] Sounding even more like Bourdieu characterizing the bourgeois aesthetic as "an ethos of elective distance from the necessities of the natural and social world . . . a product of conditioning by negative economic necessities," Reynolds writes, "The taste of the educated consists of beautifully developed wrongness, an exquisite secession from reality. As Nietzsche pointed out, degenerates love narcotics; something to make them forget life, not face it . . . they hate, they are afraid of, the greatest things in life—the common place." Lawrence imitated this kind of bourgeois-bashing on behalf of the proletariat in *Sons and Lovers* (1913):

"Do you like singing? Miriam asked [Clara].

"If it is good," she said. Paul, of course, coloured.

"You mean if it is high-class and trained?" he said.

"I think a voice needs training before the singing is anything," she said.

"You might as well insist on having people's voices trained before you allowed them to talk," he replied, "Really, people sing for their own pleasure, as a rule."

"And it may be for other people's discomfort."

"Then the other people should have flaps to their ears," he replied.[32]

Paul Morel would go on, in *Sons and Lovers,* to develop an "applied art" opposed to an aesthetics of distance (see Chapter 6).

To return now from working-class aesthetic values to subjectivity, it is probably most useful to see the problem of the masses' subjectivity with respect to upper-class audiences as a dialectic, much as Dependency theory sees First–Third world relations as interrelations. Thus Jean Franco's summary of international Dependency theory can easily be translated into terms of class relations or the construction of subjecthood: "Dependency theory is based on the assumption that underdevelopment is structurally linked to development in the dominant nation. . . . Thus the theory cuts across the concepts of development and underdevelopment. . . . It is no longer possible to treat the two terms as if they were separable. At the very least, the dependency model suggests the possibility of regarding [the dominant and subordinate, developed and underdeveloped, full and partial subject] as 'intertextuality' of a very special kind."[33] In other words, working-class writers were by no means dominated by the bourgeois form, but neither were they independent of it. Some of them, especially the commemorative and political writers discussed later, resisted bourgeois individualism; others accepted it and represented themselves as weak subjects; others wavered between the two extremes in confusion. The point is that Cartesian subjectivity was not assumed by most working-class writers and as a consequence autobiography often meant something different from emplotted self-sufficiency.

One must also say that bourgeois subjects were constituted within the same dialectic: they became individuated subjects because others did not. One acute example is Robert Graves's account of his first awareness of social class in the 1890s. (For others see Chapters 5 and 6.) In a public fever hospital at the age of four and a half, Graves does not distinguish himself from the twenty-odd little proletarians who are his fellow patients, but he notices that his double, a clergyman's child, is treated with extravagant deference. At home, rebuked for his adopted accent ("vulgar"), he learns the difference—and the upper-class province of the "self": "In hospital, we had all worn the same institutional night-gowns, and I did not know that we came off such different shelves. But I suddently realized with my first shudder of gentility that two sorts of Christians existed—ourselves, and the lower classes. . . . The servants were the lower classes, and we were 'our-selves.'"[34] In this view, bourgeois subjectivity as autonomous self-knowledge and self-pride is not natural but a form of power-knowledge in Foucault's sense; conversely, the lack of bourgeois subjectivity may be an indication of powerlessness or it may be a competing form of power-knowledge, as in the upcoming political autobiographies. As the commemorative autobiographies will also illustrate, there were other forms of being; however, what is commonly called bourgeois subjectivity was the dominant ideology in nineteenth-century Britain, and working-class writers could not help but confront it.

Taking self-conscious individual autonomy, the "I" or "Ourselves" to oneself and others, as one possible pole of social relations, and anonymous disappearance into the "mass" as another, one could map similar discursive strategies of other groups in stratified societies. In a paper on the functional aesthetic of black antebellum writers in the United States, Frances Smith Foster discussed the problem that slaves and ex-slaves confronted in writing, not only needing to establish themselves as worthy of an audience, but further needing to establish themselves as human, capable of rational thought, at all.[35] In another paper, presenting her own autobiographical memoir *A Bridge Through Time* (1985), Egyptian feminist Laila Said addressed the problem of an Egyptian woman's autobiography, which as she described it amounts to stages in the development of individual subjectivity in relation to a nonindividualist—but for women nonetheless oppressive—cultural ethos.[36] In Islam, *woman* emerges as a primarily biological—rather than rational or spiritual— entity, rather like the slave under slavery. Said, a woman, is educated in the United States. She returns to Egypt with what she calls an acquired "identity" as a Ph.D., filmaker, and so forth, but finds herself henceforth isolated within her culture. Most interestingly to the student of subjectivity, Said says that she has begun to experiment in the theater with different roles and, still deeply conscious of her isolation within Egyptian society, sees her future as one of indeterminate role-playing. Two things were very clear in Said's presentation: her extreme self-consciousness throughout the writing process of her developing individual "identity," and her perception of this individuation and "identity" as a personal achievement, a triumphant assertion of female rationality against the biological reduction of women under Islam. Said's case is not a simple one of a Third-World woman assuming the values of a First-World individualist identity, but rather one that shows the role of writing in a particular construction of self and the role of gender and race—or religion—in qualifying bourgeois and Cartesian notions of subjectivity.

The Variety of Working-Class Autobiography

Beyond the problematic relationship of author to audience, the second way that working-class autobiographies differ from classic spiritual autobiographies is in form. The classic realist, nonprogressive (that is, unselfconscious of its epistemology and production) autobiography includes such elements as remembered details of childhood, a confrontation with parents, a reassessement of the subject's education, a crisis, and a recovery or a discovery of a new self.[37] The covergence of most of these elements identifies the spiritual autobiography that began with Augustine's subjectivity through the grace of God and developed with the secularized, self-interested perspective that seems to have arisen concurrently with European capitalism. Except for those that are derived from specifically religious models, most workers' autobiographies do not fit the narrative pattern of the spiritual autobiography for the reasons discussed in Chapter 1: absence of "childhood," discontinuous and/or prolonged educational practices, lack of dramatic structure according to differences in gender roles, economic instability, etc. By contrast, as will be seen in Chapter 5, the autobiographies and memoirs of nineteenth- and early twentieth-century English public school boys map the developmental narrative of upper-middle-class European men. They, too, were removed from their homes at the age of eight years, not for labor, but for all-male preparatory schools that funneled them into public schools like Eton, Winchester, and Harrow with the attendant socialized and oedipal transferences of power. In school they learned to be boys without women, then to be the superiors of other boys, then to be leaders of empire. This ordered progress differs in significant ways from the experience of workers who left home at eight for labor rather than boyhood, had no distinct time for childhood, and had no especially climactic time for duty, leisure, or romance, and the forms of public school memoirs differ from workers' autobiographies correspondingly.

The following analyses survey the formal varieties of working-class autobiography. An explained in the Introduction, I provide this not to lay down rigid generic taxa, but rather to indicate the diversity of working-class autobiography, its different rhetorical functions, and their appurtenances with respect to labor, status, and geography. Given that many working-class examples provide alternative models for autobiography, there is no reason (except perhaps Bourdieu's "taste," which amounts to class hegemony) to take middle-class autobiography as constitutive of autobiography as such. Given that many working-class examples provide what also appear, at least in writing, as alternative models of subjectivity, there is considerable reason not to take middle-class subjectivity as constitutive of subjectivity as such.

Of the major group of 804 autobiographies, one-third, including the more sensational works for London audiences, were published by London publishers and one-quarter by local businesses and printers, large and small. Publishers probably thus exerted varying degrees of control over the content of just over one-half of the autobiographies. The authors of the remainder retained more control over their material: one-tenth were published by occupational journals and newspapers representing the self-identified interests of the writer; one-twentieth were published by the author, sometimes by subscription but more often at his or her own risk; and one-fifth (or half of the uncontrolled half) remained intact in manuscript or typescript at the time of the author's death.[38] These conditions of publication may be correlated to six rhetorical genres of the autobiographies: two exemplary modes of conversion and gallows narratives, vestigial religious forms found most often in the provinces by the nineteenth century; commemorative stories, largely by southern agrarian, domestic, and itinerant workers, and including soldiers' and sailors' reminiscences after the Napoleonic and Crimean wars; political or polemical narratives by authors with organized political bases, largely from the industrial North; confessions—in the popular sense of "true confessions"—more often by women, sensational, and usually for London audiences; and therapeutically motivated self-examinations, which have no obvious occupational or geographical correlations but are characterized by an unusual degree of introspection and self-criticism. This last category, illustrating the effect of middle-class hegemony upon some working-class writers, was the subject of the second section of Chapter 1 and will not be discussed here.

CONVERSION AND GALLOWS TALES

By the nineteenth century the true conversion narrative, with its Biblical epiphanies, was relatively rare, but its continued appearance illuminates the source of working-class autobiography in the Puritan's responsibility for personal salvation.[39] The gallows confessions reached a peak of popularity during the second and third decades of the century; many of these were wholly fictional, while others, including George Allen's, which follows, bear the influence of prison chaplains or broadside publishers. The two exemplary modes of conversion and gallows narrative constitute formal antitheses at the most highly structured pole of working-class autobiography.

Mary Saxby's *Memoirs of a Female Vagrant* (1806) is a true conversion narrative. Saxby is all bad until her conversion, then she is all good: events—even the most dramatic—have no effect upon the narrative of her salvation. Her mother dies when Saxby is very young. Until her father's discharge from the army, she lives with relatives. She eventually runs away and lives with a male gypsy, goes to prison, is released, and bears three illegitimate children. John Saxby fights the gypsy for her and they marry. Her first child dies in bed, the second in a fire that destroys all their belongings. She has a breakdown and returns to a life of "obscene jests, filthy ribaldry, and profane swearing."[40] When she is converted (under the influence of "An Alarm to Unconverted Sinners" [1673] by Joseph Alleine) her husband persecutes, but God protects, her. She gives birth to twins, one of whom dies. She begins to preach. Her oldest son dies. She works to convert her husband and does so on his deathbed. Her favorite son drowns. Of her ten children, four daughters remain, all either abducted or pregnant out of wedlock. She ends the tale in praise of God. Saxby is the Puritan subject who is granted subjectivity (self-importance and the attention of readers) through personal salvation in conversion.

By the nineteenth century, conversion narrative worked in two contradictory ways. First, it reproduced the official ideology of the middle-class religious societies that published—and occasionally forged—such tracts: hardship in this life was necessary for redemption in the next. Second, it permitted the dream of a pilgrim's progress to people whose life-events were doomed to hopeless repetition—a dream that empowered the religious radicals, typically Methodist, whose ideology generated working-class movements. The personal salvation narrative that was primarily a religious form in the sixteenth century was inherited by the nineteenth century in conjuction with other elements of English religion—such as dissidence and nonconformism—and secularized by radical working-class writers. Later "conversion" narratives would testify to the efficacy of conversion for material success, as in the Methodist David Barr's *Climbing the Ladder: The Struggles and Successes of a Village Lad* (1910), in which the ladder is both religious (i.e., Jacob's ladder to God) and secular (i.e., the ladder of status from shepherd in boyhood, to shoemaker's apprentice, to clerk, salesman, estate agent, and public official).[41] Similarly, the "social atom" phenomenon discussed earlier probably had its sources in Puritan self-denial before an all-transcendent God prior to its transformation into materialist anti-individualism.

Despite their formulaic structure, conversion narratives can be surprisingly varied, especially when they record ambivalence about conversion. In Josiah Basset's *Life of a Vagrant, or the Testimony of an Outcast to the Value and Truth of the Gospel* (1850)—notice that again it is the vagrant who must be converted, the mobile who must be stabilized—there is a tension between the freedom of the vagrant and outcast (with his habitual practice of "lying," or telling tales for his livelihood) and the alleged conversion to the value and truth of the Gospel (with its accompanying formal constraints upon his *vita*). The first (preconversion) half of the autobiography has Basset at his storytelling best, interrupted occasionally by moralism that was probably interjected by an editor. The second half represents his life after conversion.

Basset was born in London in 1812, the son of an impoverished baker. His earliest memories are of his elder brother's drowning and his mother's paralysis and death. As a child he was thought to be an idiot because he stammered and looked stupid. Leaving his family in the workhouse, he resists work (even when it is available), neglects Scripture, and exploits a talent for "inventing the most shameful falsehoods to excite pity," thereby receiving drink, food, and money.[42] Moving his contemporaries with his tales of destitution, and charming his reader with his descriptions of the Scots Highlands, herring salting, and peat stacking—with incongruous religious admonitions interjected—he thematizes the problem of his tale by literally juxtaposing his father's "spiritual instruction and advice" from the workhouse with his own "practice of telling lies."

As cholera forces the Scots poor to migrate to London, Basset returns to his father, brother, and sister, who succumb to the epidemic in St. George's Workhouse. Basset continues hawking around London, at which time "lying was my habitual practice. . . . My life was one of continual uncertainty and often did I promise myself to become religious at some future time, if I should ever become settled, and so not exposed to temptation as when travelling" (48). In 1838 he is converted in Beverley

Gaol, but he worries about his ability "to keep from lying"—that is, to maintain a proper job rather than tell tales for money—upon release (82).

The second half of the text turns to sermonizing, but Basset interjects a few adventures concerning helpful women, his being robbed by a collier, his carrying advertising boards, and his teaching the alphabet twice weekly in a ragged school. Although his conversion has led him to renouce his errant ways, it also amounts to his getting less for honest employment than for begging. He is finally received into a Church in London, prospers materially through continuous employment, is educated and devout, yet suffers several severe lapses during which he is drawn to storytelling. The text concludes abruptly with some appended moralizing by another hand on vagrants as "the vampires of society" (130).

Thus Basset thematizes the struggle between storytelling (his irrepressible lying) and the constraints of conversion narrative. In a leveling amounting to comic genius, his euphoric outbursts of religious belief come more and more to have the status of the stories he tells to receive his living, just as his admonition that he must lie to make a living is ever present in the reader's mind as she reads the probable lies of both his life and conversion. I have not been able to find how *The Life of A Vagrant* was received by nineteenth-century readers, but of the two Remarks and Supplementary Remarks appended to the text, one is skeptical of Basset's conversion and the other is not. Throughout, there is contradictory testimony to the value and truth of the Gospel according to Josiah Basset. As in James Burn's *Autobiography of a Beggar Boy* discussed in Chapter 1 and some of the writing of gangrels, cheap jacks, and poachers discussed later, the tension between the secular ideology of freedom of some of the itinerant beggars on the Borders and the Christian work ethic is never resolved, but show two incompatible discourses confronting one another in one life. In one the lost sheep is incorporated within the legitimate fold of Church life and cultivates relationships conducive to social mobility; in the other his status as an outcast allows an unhampered geographical mobility and freedom in unstructured relations with others.

The narrative of the gallows tale, intended to warn and thus pacify the poor, works in the opposite direction from the conversion narrative, but is equally formulaic: rather than the bad becoming good and being saved, the good become bad and are punished. In *The Machine Breaker: Or the Heart–Rending Confessions of George Allen* (c. 1831), Allen is fired from honest employment, breaks the hearts of his parents, and abandons his family to the workhouse when an agitator from London introduces him to public houses and "malcontent politicians"—that is, active Luddites, or workers who raised their hands against the machines they perceived to be supplanting them. (In general, in Victorian working-class writing, *politican* means politicized, or activist, worker.) With a gesture that would remain symbolic for working-class autobiographers through the time of the Labour Church of the 1880s, Allen ceases to observe the Sabbath, opting to play cricket on that day. Meanwhile, the remaining workers in the factory are "discharged for their irregularity, and machinery substituted" (here a footnote recommends "a most excellent treatise" by the Society for the Diffusion of Useful Knowledge [SDUK] extolling "The Results of Machinery").[43] The evil agitator incites him to destroy the factory at the next Sabbath cricket match. He and the discharged workers do so and he is condemned to death for instigating the riot. He writes from the gaol to warn others. The chaplain had edited his "confession," presumably to delete extraneous information that would detract from the moral.

Gallows narratives were clearly ways that the SDUK and similar organizatons admonished against violence among the working classes; on the other hand, as I shall elaborate later in connection with the commemorative storytellers and as Foucault has suggested in *Discipline and Punish,*[44] the sacred status of the speaker at the moment of death, about to impart whatever wisdom he or she has to bestow in this life, gave the form (as well as the commemorative form discussed later) a haunting force that could easily arouse sympathy among readers rather than admonish them.

The gallows and conversion narratives mark the most formulaic pole of working-class autobiography. These forms were transformed or died out as the influence of organizations like the SDUK over the lower classes diminished and religion, especially Methodism, was politically radicalized. Conversion became less important to organized workers than politicization, and a surprising number of the texts bear out the working-class deconstruction of religion for political purposes.[45] For more conservative writers, including some Methodists like Barr, the personal salvation of conversion became the ideological linchpin of individual secular success.

STORYTELLERS AND POLITICIANS

For workers unaffiliated with Church or organized labor, and among the commemorative (or conservatively reminiscent) genre, the picaresque remained a natural form for adventurous transients like Peter Paterson, the strolling player of *Behind the Scenes,* the poacher turned gamekeeper

in John Holcombe's *The Autobiography of a Poacher* (1901), the vagrant
of William Cameron's *Hawkie: The Autobiography of a Gangrel* (1888),
or the heroes of Alec Alexander's *A Wayfarer's Log* (1919) and William
Green's *Life and Adventures of a Cheap Jack*.[46] Although the authors are
usually itinerant and reenact the time-honored oral tradition of inconsequential anecdote, the narrative disjunctiveness is exactly the same as
that in Frederick Willis's *Peace and Dripping Toast* (1950) or Ernest
Ambrose's *Melford Memories* (1972), in which the nonagenarian narrator describes himself as a "spectator of the great game of life which we all
play" in the village, chronicling the itinerant travellers passing through
the village green.[47] Such texts read like travelogs by tourists in their own
land—typically transients, southerners, or, as mentioned earlier, soldiers
returning from the wars.[48] With minimal self-consciousness, they preserve memories of a way of life that is changing or has already ceased
to be, the social exotic, or sociohistorical heterogeneity of their own
country.

These commemorative storytellers can be seen as disorganized and
reactionary in the negative view, or deeply rooted in history and wisdom
in the positive view. They present the unstructured, thematically arbitrary, disconnected anecdotes and events of a world in which nothing
changes. There are no distinctive autobiographical subjects apart from
the continuous life of the village, farm, or crafts-mystery, and no Other
but the future that will end this way of life.

These autobiographies can be understood in terms of the two archaic
representatives of storytelling theorized by Walter Benjamin: the resident
tiller of the soil (the farmers, craftspeople, and domestic workers below)
and the merchant sailor (the soldiers, hawkers, vagrants, wayfarers, and
gangrels).[49] These archetypes correspond to Mikhail Bakhtin's chrono-
topes—temporal and spatial principles of organization—of folkloric time
and the road, which are associated with nonclass agricultural societies.
From the bourgeois point of view, with its emphasis on protagonist and
plot, or the self in society, such texts look anarchic and confused: "Individual life-sequences have not been made distinct, the private sphere does
not exist, there are no private lives. . . . Food, drink, copulation, birth and
death are not aspects of a personal life but a common affair. . . . On the
road the spatial and temporal series defining human fates and lives com-
bine with one another in distinctive ways, even as they become more
complex and more concrete by the collapse of *social distances*."[50] The
storytellers give counsel from their own experience and that of others;
they do not have explanatory narratives, so they can include superstition
and supernaturalism. They write from a place where time is not corre-

lated to money so much as to the entire rhythm of cyclical life, and they speak with the authority of someone who at the point of death must communicate experience to a knowable community in which hierarchies share common space and understanding. Consequently they are always nostalgic. The later among these autobiographies typically end with the first world war and they are often called "Memories." Their authors alone among the autobiographers are happy with the status quo and consequently "write up." In short, their nonprogressive structure reveals a static subject.

Ambrose's *Melford Memories,* for example, is significantly centered in village life. A chapter entitled "Roads: Travellers, Itinerant Traders, and Entertainers" amounts to stories about the storytellers who have passed through the village and describes a masked promenade through the downs that reads as if it were medieval. Ambrose describes home remedies, courtship rituals, and how the classes mixed at fairs in top hats, bowlers, and cloth caps. He describes the Great War in relation to the village organ and laments the passing of good pubs (with the church "the chief meeting place of the people") and respect for the "Law of Church [meaning less belief than courtship and marriage rituals], Green, and School" ("the law at that time was harsh and unforgiving. . . . Our fear of punishment kept us in the straight and narrow way" [33]). He is thoroughly reactionary, disturbed by technology, and he writes through the last page with no doubt about his ability to embody the wisdom of the past, "just in case some future generation may care to learn what life was like when I was young, 94 years ago" (121).

In *Peace and Dripping Toast* Willis also writes of a society in which hierarchies (top hats, bowlers, cloth caps) shared a common space and lifeworld. The masquerade/harlequinade image thus paradoxically represents a thoroughly knowable community that only plays at mystery and deception: the Lyceum when the proletariat mixed with Society; shopping in the 1890s as everyone's psychological tonic; the fire at the Crystal Palace, "the centre of wholesome pleasure in a world of sanity and peace" (46); and Willis directs his jeremiads against these "documented times" (105), longing for the time before the State took over and Britain lost its confidence and hope. Both of these storytellers as figurative tillers of the soil romanticize the carnival image of a past that seemed timeless—just as Holcombe, self-proclaimed descendant of Robin Hood and Shakespeare, recalls in *The Autobiography of a Poacher* a forgotten phase of West Country life when a poacher was only a gamekeeper turned inside out.

Within this group of storytellers and memoirs are the majority of domestic servants' autobiographies. Between the wars the occupation of domestic service declined both socially and numerically. Before the first world war, servants were typically regarded as dependents, rather like children or livestock, and typically regarded themselves as ideologically loyal to their employers. In 1900, William Clarke wrote, in an article entitled "The Social Future of England," "There is no class less open to democratic ideas than a contented servant class. Compared with them, their titled and wealthy employers are revolutionists. They cannot bear change, their minds are saturated with the idea of social grades and distinctions, they will not even live with one another on terms of social equality."[51] Servants' autobiographies are filled with differential regard for houskeepers, cooks, ladies' maids, upper and under maids, and (according to the division of labor) French man-cooks, butlers, coachmen, grooms, gamekeepers, gardeners, and laborers. As an eleven-year-old page-boy at Almacks Bridge Club in London in 1904, Edward Humphries minutely noted degrees of status in artifacts such as Egyptian, Turkish, and Virginian tobacco, and felt himself drifting socially from his less discerning Devonshire parents.[52] In 1837 the London footman William Tayler maintained that despite their low status in comparison with factory operatives, servants were the most sophisticated and respectable of the working classes: "Being so much in the company of the gentry, from the private gentleman to the Highest Duke in the land allways traveling about with their masters, learning and seeing hundreds of things which mechanics or tradespeople never knew there was in the country. . . . I think servants are the most respectable in consequence of their characters and actions being so thoroughly investigated by their superiors."[53] The thirty-year-old Tayler himself starkly juxtaposed the dilemma of young people considering service—knowledge of the full range of social behavior at the cost of loss of liberty: "If a person wish to see life. I would advise them to be a gentleman's servant. They will see high life and low life, above stairs as well as life below. They will see and know more than any other class of people in the world," (185) yet, "The life of a gentleman's servant is something like that of a bird shut up in a cage. The bird is well housed and well fed but is deprived of liberty, and liberty is the dearest and sweetes object of all Englishmen. Therefore I would rather be like the sparrows or lark, have less houseing and feeding and rather more liberty" (ibid.). Yet the gilded-cage life of service ended with the war. "The Great War undoubtedly upset service," wrote William Lanceley (b. 1854), who had worked his way from footman and butler to house-steward and called his autobiography *From Hall-Boy to House-Steward* (1925): "The War called for hands to help, and many servants responded to the call. The work they were asked to do was a novelty to them, the pay was big and they had short hours, hundreds being spoilt for future service through it. It made those who returned to service unsettled."[54] Loyal to the end, Lanceley derides parliamentary commissions of inquiry and newfangled schools for training servants that would raise the taxes of his employers, and he opts for the traditional apprenticeship: "it is to be hoped that the country, with its crushing taxation, will not go to a big expense over servant training. It is doomed to failure. Teach the girls in the schools to be clean and tidy in their habits and appearance. The head house-maid or kitchen-maid will soon put them wise to their duties" (ibid.).

The storytellers possess the wisdom of the past; they do not have crises of self or doubts about their ability to speak, although they may be melancholy when they realize that their way of life will cease to be, and they may be relieved not to have to participate in the new ways of the future. In his preface, Paterson says that the railroad ended the adventures of the strolling players, the itinerant family-companies breaking up as their audiences rode into the great towns (also 138). After the first world war, Ambrose "returned to England and found a great change in the country. There was a spirit of discontent and disillusionment. Even in our own much loved village life was never the same again" (113). Willis concludes his reminiscences: "Thus it remained to thousands of Londoners who were young and hopeful in 1914" (188). And Robert Blatchford, half storyteller and half political journalist, tells of one moment Christmas shopping in 1917 when crowds rushed past on the pavement and he "felt like the man in *News from Nowhere* when he realized that he had become invisible and inaudible to his fellow-guests in the festal hall" (252). When storytellers enter Time, their stories end.

The opposite form to the storyteller's is the political narrative, and "narrative" often appears in the title. It is highly structured and politically radical, meant to rival bourgeois histories and the bourgeois novel, and is typically from the industrial and organized North, with its accelerated upheavals and mechanization. If the storytellers represent a reactionary lifeworld in which world and self stay the same, the political autobiographies assert the world changing and the worker's adequacy to change. Whereas the storyteller does not explain or organize but offers random counsel and wisdom from the past, there is no past that retains its wisdom for the northern factory workers. Thus the political narrative is the self-conscious working-class answer to the bourgeois novel. Especially in its form of *Bildungsroman,* the novel channels all experience into one great conflict, the integration of social process and personal development in time. Like the novel, the political autobiography is dedicated to one hero, one odyssey, and one battle. Time is the frame in which the hero is the working class, the odyssey is the quest for political power, and the battle is class warfare. In the five autobiographies included in Vincent's collection *Testaments of Radicalism,* for example, the dramatic moments, or structural turning points in the plot, are typically class confrontations with the law, in which the law appears as the repressive, rather than—as in middle-class autobiography—the ideological, state apparatus (e.g., it appears as the police or militia). These politically conscious autobiographers—called by themselves "politicians"—assume the authority to write their own working-class history in order to ensure the subjecthood of working-class writers in the future. In general their private selves cannot be divorced from their political projects. In fact, these texts are not typically called autobiographies at all because they include so little of the self separate from political activity and documentation. In some cases there are a few pages of pre-activist life, but these are generally undirected and considered unimportant. For working-class writers, however, these autobiographies hold the same position as Wordsworth's *Prelude* (1850) for upper-class writers: they establish the authors as epic protagonists.

The general form of these political autobiographies was established with Thomas Hardy's *Memoir.* Hardy, a shoemaker and bricklayer, was a founder of the London Corresponding Society, a seminal organization for parliamentary reform and working-class representation. He considered his life insignificant before he became politically active and therefore awarded only a few pages of his memoir to his first thirty-nine years. His lengthy documentation concerning the Society, on the other hand, sought to counteract a press often hostile to working people's activities and ensured the preservation of the Society's history.

The second feature of Hardy's autobiography to which I want to draw attention is the correspondence between the documentary and reportorial style of the political argument, and Hardy's anger, expressed in a personal narrative of desire. This and other political autobiographies show the meeting of personal desire in narrative and political purpose in argument primarily because—as in the case of the Factory Cripple's desire for companionship and children—personal desire could not be satisfied without political change. Such autobiographies have been denied status as autobiography precisely because personal desire in narrative is satisfiable without political change for bourgeois readers. The bourgeois subject is liberal, autonomous; in denying the status of autobiography to writers for whom the political is personal, literary historians reject alternative conceptions of identity. Even Vincent implicitly subscribes to this view when he concedes that whenever personal experience gives way to a general history of the period the autobiography suffers.

One might see this dialectic of personal and political in the context of our contemporary theoretical expansion of the scope of subjectivity. Fredric Jameson has argued that the ratio in "First-World" literature of private to public, libidinal Unconscious to politics (or poetics to politics), is inverted in so-called Third-World literature, in which subjectivity is politicized as dramatically as politics are subjectivized in the "First World."[55] His analysis has been subjected to devastating criticism, but a generous reading would recognize the source of its errors in Jameson's own "First-World" longing for a nonisolated subjectivity: the longing of the self-confessedly postmodern U.S. intellectual man for a less disembodied, fragmented, identity.[56] If Jameson had considered the writing of women and workers in Western Europe at the height of bourgeois realist fiction, he would have found that it often shared the politicization of the personal—even the communitarianism—that he hoped to attribute to the entire Third World.

The greatest part of Hardy's autobiography is taken up by his arrest and trial for treason in 1794 as secretary for the Society. Shortly after his arrest, a reactionary "King and Church" mob attacked his home. His wife, pregnant with her sixth child, attempted to escape through a window and was seriously injured. She died giving birth to a stillborn child. Hardy blamed the government for their deaths while he was in prison, and he includes a poem to Mrs. Hardy with his transcripts of the trials. A similar example of the lack of distinction between personal and political interests in working-class life is from Lewis Lyons, a Jewish tailors' trade union leader in the East End in the 1880s and 1890s: Lyons met his wife Fanny at a Trafalgar Square protest meeting in 1887 when they held hands to meet the onslaught of the police.[57]

Hardy's is probably the most dramatic example of how personal narrative and political argument could not be separated for these autobiographers, but there are similar illustrations and formal turning points in all of them: when the desire to learn, bear children, love, or sell labor is frustrated, the autobiography turns to argument. The politicization of the "social atom" is thus the equivalent in working-class autobiography of the discovery of a new self in the traditional spiritual autobiography. For Robert Blatchford this turning point happens in Chapter 39 of *My Eighty Years*. The early chapters unfold in typical undifferentiated storytelling fashion: descriptions of the girls the young Blatchford played with while other boys stoned frogs; his brief career in acting; his hatred of schoolmasters; his first male friend, an artist; his dreaminess throughout childhood and youth; his worship of women and hatred of his regiment; six chapters (27–32) on particular friends, old women, thieves, mad colliers, girlfriends, and sergeants; and his marriage to a wife whom he cannot overpraise. In Chapter 39, however, he says that his private and public lives converged when he wrote a story on the housing crisis in Manchester and (like many political autobiographers) became a journalist for the poor. He abandons his previous avuncular tone and storytelling structure for a history of his relationships with various socialist programs, only noting in passing his consciousness of his dual personality:

> Things have to be said and I say them. Having said them I retire from the dust and noise and am once more "me." That is to say I am the little wondering child, the clinging husband and father, the grateful happy friend; the brush-maker's apprentice, the carefree young sergeant of the Fusiliers. Fame and money and power have no attraction for that "me." Nature filled me up with love and forgot the ambition. . . . I was happy at home with my wife and children, or out with a few good pals. Great political issues did not interest me, unless they threatened our own people. I am, in fact, an ordinary domestic animal with an inbred hatred of injustice and a kind of fierce pity for all unfortunate and unhappy creatures, especially women and children. As for Robert Blatchford, he is a fighting dog; but he is not "me." (222)

Most of the political autobiographies work by means of such narrative transformations of the personal into political, or desire and narrative into argument. *The Life and Struggles of William Lovett in his Pursuit of Bread, Knowledge and Freedom* (1876) is divided into three parts: Lovett's life as a cabinet maker, as a radical publisher, and as an activist in the London Working Men's Association and People's Charter. Thus it replicates the West's three master narratives: the quest for material well-being, or freedom from Nature; the quest for Truth, or freedom from ignorance; and the quest for justice, or freedom from political tyranny and economic exploitation. Lovett's early life is a disorganized string of anecdotes, with most paragraphs wandering aimlessly for pages. Then he moves to London and becomes an activist. At this point the text fills with manifestoes, debates, and comment, as if history is being made faster than Lovett can record it. In his preface, he explains the relationship of his life-story to the texts of the associations to which he belonged: "I think that those who desire to know anything of me, would like to know what my opinions and sentiments were—(as well as great numbers who thought with me)—regarding the great questions of human right, social progress, and political reform; and these, in fact, constitute a great part of my own history."[58]

Similarly, Samuel Bamford, the radical weaver, journalist, and poet of Lancashire, advertised his *Early Days* (1848–1849) as "as much a history of a time, and of a district of the country, as of the individual whose name it bears."[59] And Thomas Bell, the founder of the Communist Party of Great Britain (CPGB), says in his foreword to *Pioneering Days* (1941) that he writes not as an ordinary autobiographer but as a recorder of the experiences of the party for the young men and women coming to it without them.[60] Beginning with his own family of labor aristocrats, he writes the history of labor movements with which he was involved: the Independent Labour Party, the Social Democratic Federation, the Socialist Labour Party, and the CPGB. Perhaps the most acute image of how little the bourgeois notion of privatized, psychologized self—rather than a self whose desires must be expressed through public and political action— meant to these writers is in Benjamin Wilson's *Struggles of an Old Chartist* (1887), which begins five years before his birth, not with his family lineage (no aristocrats of labor here), but with Peterloo: "I was born at Skircoat Green, August 7th 1824. This village had long been noted for its Radicalism. On August 16th, 1819, a Reform meeting was held in St. Peter's Field, Manchester, (afterwards called 'Peterloo,') at which 60,000 persons were present; the magistrates ordered the calvary to charge the people, when they dashed onward, striking a great number down with their swords and trampling under their horses' feet, 6 people were killed and 640 wounded" (*Testaments of Radicalism,* 195).

The communities created in—and to some extent reproduced *by means of*—these works were oppositional, as were the forms of writing and means of producing the texts. In 1825 Thomas Hardy attacked the notion that historians were impartial and dismissed them as irrelevant to the creation of working-class history: "We learn but little from modern histories, for each historian accomodates the facts to his ideas, almost in the same manner as a cook sauces up his dishes to his palate. We must dine in the taste of the cook. We must read in the humour of the historian" (*Testaments of Radicalism,* 10). Hardy begins his *Memoir,* then, as a revisionary story, ringing with the tones of a revolutionary age: "As every man, whose actions, from whatever cause, have acquired publicity, is sure, in many things, to be misrepresented, such a man has an undoubted right, nay, it becomes his duty, to leave to posterity a true record of the real motives that influenced his conduct. The following *Memoir* requires no apology, and none is offered" (*Testaments of Radicalism,* 37). Lovett explains his extensive documentation:

> I have yet another reason for adding the documents of the Associations I have taken part in, and for giving a brief account of their proceedings; and it is this—That hitherto, little is found in history, or in our public papers, that presents a fair and accurate account of the public proceedings of the Working Classes; for if the Whig and Tory papers of the day ever condescend to notice them, it is rather to garble and distort facts, to magnify faults and follies, and to ridicule their objects and intentions. (xxxi)

And Lovett, too, will "offer no apology to the reader for the manner in which I have executed my task; as I have done it, as I best could, in those intervals of time not devoted to my labours for bread" (xxx).

Dependence upon those intervals not devoted to labours for bread resulted in an entirely different rhythm of production from that of middle-class authors, who often completed works at breakneck speed for monthly subscriptions: Lovett's autobiography took thirty years to write. In Stafford Gaol, the shoemaker, schoolmaster, preacher, and journalist Thomas Cooper confronted the luxurious opportunity to compose his *Purgatory of Suicides: A Prison-Rhyme in Ten Books,* which had been conceived years earlier but which could only be written in the relative leisure of prison.[61] Insofar as the desire that creates narrative for dominated groups must include political arguments, there would have been no subjects of the modern labor movement without the creation of sociopolitical agency that actually occurs in these texts. Hence the auracular spell—in Benjamin's sense of local and historical texture and uniqueness—of history being made in their writing.[62]

CONFESSIONS AND SELF-EXAMINATIONS

Up to this point, the sex of the author has figured significantly less with respect to style or content than in upper-class autobiography, or it has figured only in the most straightforward ways. For example, in exemplary modes like conversion and gallows narratives, the only difference between men's and women's narratives is that women refer far more frequently to their husbands or lovers and children (their personal relationships) and men refer more to their jobs or occupations (their social status). In the commemorative genres male storytellers predominate, but their works do not significantly differ from those by women who tell what it was like to be in service to the great families forty or fifty years before writing. Both, for example, are equally conservative. Among the political autobiographers there is little *structural* difference between the narratives of Annie Kenney on militancy, Margaret Bondfield on her rise in the labor movement, or Elizabeth Bryson on her struggle to be a physician, and their counterparts written by male activists, although their ways of seeing politics often vary in the manner described in Chapter 1.

In the remaining two groups, however—the confessions and the self-examinations—gender has significant structural consequences in the autobiographies. The confessions, in which women writers outnumber men, are characterized by a kind of aimless, unstructured writing that I call confessional in the vulgar sense of "true confession," like sensational slices of life from the underworld. The word "confessions" often appears in their titles. Written by the rootless and friendless for immediate profit, neither secularized religious narratives nor commemorative stories nor politicized plots, they are intended to momentarily sustain—by publishing—the life of the writer by giving readers immediately consumable sensation. The authors are politically, and often socially, apathetic.

If we see personal identity as a function of a temporal unification of past, present, and future, the writers in this category make no attempt at such identity: their pasts, especially their childhoods, are fragmentary or obliterated; their presents are arbitrary and anecdotal; their futures are unanimously uncertain. For example, in *Tiger-Woman: My Story* (1929), set in Tidal Basin, East End, Betty May's first memories are of a sailor, her mother's lover, and of a pregnant neighbor's suicide by hanging. Claiming a family lineage of "costerblood" (see Chapter 2), May writes as an intimate of the "underworld," where crime and criminal detectors mix and mate. Her father manages a brothel with his lover, the madam, until his own father, a police inspector, arrests him. As a child, May dances on barges for sailors, is taken to France by a white slave trader, and joins an Apache gang in Paris. As an adult, she is a drug addict and a member of a Thelemite cult in Sicily (a mystical association allegedly devoted to the suppression of the ego; their motto was "Do what thou wilt shall be the whole of the law; Love is the law, love under will" [Chapter 7]), where one of her serial lovers is murdered. She returns to England to marry a country gentleman whose mother she attacks out of boredom; and she ends up back in London. The text's sensational and self-exploitative perspective is that of a woman who can only see herself as an object of sensation for men. Here she describes her meeting with the sculptor Jacob Epstein at the Cafe Royal: "I was sitting, as I have described, with my chin cupped in my hands and my remarkable face framed in my black hair, alone, an intriguing object I suppose, in a way, when to my amazement and consternation I saw Epstein look at me, get up from his place, and walk towards me."[63]

When Florence Bell interviewed the poor concerning their reading habits, she found a fifty-year-old woman who was making a great attempt to learn to read. Asked what books she would prefer, she allegedly responded "something with a little love and a little murder."[64] May's is that kind of book. She excuses the brutality of her activities in Paris by her youth, presenting herself as the modern child forseen at the end of (the contemporaneous) *Jude the Obscure*—"they seem to see all [life's] terrors before they are old enough to have staying power to resist them"[65]—(70), and her seventh chapter (aptly titled "The Abbey") includes recognizably Gothic touches of self-mutilation, passion, and mysticism.

The anonymous author of *Confessions of a Dancing Girl* (1913) was born in Camden Town in 1887. Her mother died when she was a child, and her father's pub failed. She was sent to her grandparents, who beat her, and apprencticed to the circus at the age of twelve, where she was beaten by her master. She seemingly unconsciously turns from descriptions of her beatings to the circus animals' love for music, fondness for applause, and sensitive temperaments.[66] After adventures in Spain and France, she too returns to London, the great metropolis still functioning as the inevitable home of the homeless: "And very soon I began to realize how much keener the fight for a living is in this country than in Spain or France. At least, it is so for those who call themselves artistes, and who live by amusing the public. I am not clever enough to explain why this is so, for England is such a rich country, and there is no scarcity of variety halls or theatres" (156).

It is characteristic of the confessions, especially in distinguishing them from the self-examinations discussed in Chapter 1, that their authors accept and exploit their experience rather than analyze it: they self-objectify rather than self-examine. Their stories end inconclusively with the authors open to indeterminate—even random—futures. Unlike the authors of the self-examinations, those of confessions do not attempt to structure their episodic lives into familiar middle-class narratives (like domesticity) and, correspondingly, they do not expect to succeed in middle-class terms. The Dancing Girl concludes that at twenty-four she has seen more than most women her age and perhaps she will take up acting (p. 192), and she makes the sole reference to the "confessional" nature of her *Confessions* in her last sentence: "One thing I have learned from my various experiences, and that is a sort of understanding of men and women that makes one hesitate before condemning the greatest sinner" (ibid.). Kathleen Woodward moves out of Jipping Street and her last chapter is entitled "Whither?"

The male counterparts to these texts are less sensational: whereas women are objectified according to their gender in ways that lend a sexual *frisson* to the expected economic exploitation, men are more simply economically frustrated. They confess scene upon scene of hardship and humiliation, again without structuring or reflecting upon them. In *One of the Multitude,* George Acron never succeeds in rising above the multitude. His text, too, ends in medias res. A husband and father, seriously undertimed and underpaid or overtimed for underpayment, his metaphor of the future in the final sentence could hardly be more ambivalent: "a rugged path along which bloom a few rare flowers that make the path well worth treading, though the way be rough at times" (300).

The anticlimactic character of these writings is generally related to the isolation of their authors from social process: Betty May is an aging dancer, the Dancing Girl a near transient, Woodward a nonunion factory worker and lapsed socialist, and Acron a nonunion furnituremaker. Their lack of coherent, progressive narrative centered upon themselves as subjects is matched by their frequent lack of name—the anonymous Dancing Girl or pseudonymous Acron. All of them represent their early lives as rejection by parents. Yet, unlike the authors of self-examinations, who believed in progressive or domestic ideology, these never expected anything more.

With the confessions, as with the self-examinations discussed earlier, it again seems the case that working-class subjects were able to fashion functional identities in writing their lives to the degree that they shared a participatory discursive engagement with others and that they were unable to do so to the degree that they did not. This is equally borne out by the two other main "genres" of working-class autobiography whose formal structures are not predetermined (as in the conversion and gallows tales): the storytellers (participating and identifying with a traditional community in geography or ideology) and the political autobiographers (participating and identifying with other workers against the system).

Conclusions: Subjectivity and Value

In showing that "memories" often come from southern agrarian workers who hoped to preserve local history for members of the community, "narratives" from organized northern industrial workers who sought to edify other workers and compete historically with the bourgeoisie, and "confessions" from transients who hoped to gain cash by giving readers an immediately consumable sensation, I do not intend to limit or confine these works within rigid definitions of genre. Rather, I mean to indicate some uniformity in how texts are written, read, and historically assessed in terms of the social contexts of value, consensus, hegemony, domination, or appropriation. This extends what Roland Barthes called "the pleasure of the text" beyond the conventional autonomous relationship (usually psychoanalytic) between bourgeois reader (intellectual, academic) and canonical text. In moving beyond the traditional literary community, my goal is neither to justify nor smash the canon but to pursue critical theory as "the self-clarification of the wishes and struggles of the age."[67]

By finding and making accessible the autobiographies of working people, social historians have made it possible for cultural critics to situate literary history and, more importantly, the subjectivity that it values. Early in this chapter I cited examples of first sentences of workers' autobiographies in which the writers called attention to their "insignificance" and negotiated ways to serve as subjects worthy of an audience. Public school Old Boys almost invariably began their memoirs with their family lineages, in that way establishing their hereditary right as subjects in a society that valued family position. For example, the beginning of David Herbert Somerset Cranage's first chapter is merely an exaggerated form of the typical beginning of public school memoirs: "The first man to bear the name was Randle or Ranulph de Cranach who lived at the end of the twelfth century and the beginning of the thirteenth. He was the grandson of Wolfric, who married his first cousin Aldith, the widow, first of Griffin King of Wales, and second of Harold II King of England. She was the only daughter and the only surviving child of Leofric, Earl of Mercia, and Lady Godiva."[68] Cranage goes on to derive himself from Alfred the Great and William the Conqueror.

In the first paragraphs of the canonical "literary" autobiographies of the nineteenth century, however, one finds a dual emphasis on family and *literary* lineage. Ruskin's *Praeterita* (1885) begins: "I am, and my father was before me, a violent Tory of the old school;—Walter Scott's school, that is to say, and Homer's. I name these two out of the number-less great Tory writers, because they were my own two masters."[69] John Stuart Mill's *Autobiography* (1873) opens with the sentence: "I was born in London, on the 20th of May 1806, and was the eldest son of James Mill, the author of the History of British India."[70] (For discussion of the canonical literary autobiographies, see Chapter 6.)

Students of rhetoric know that bourgeois subjectivity is not the only source of literary value, but autobiographical theory and literary history from Romanticism to postmodernism have minimized the distinction. As represented by the canon, bourgeois subjectivity and literary value both consist of belief in creativity, autonomy, and individual freedom; self-reflection as problem-solving, especially in writing; and a progressive narrative of self, especially in relation to family and material well-being. This conflation of middle-class norms and "taste," for example, explains the exclusion of *My Apprenticeship* (1926) from the literary canon. Bea-trice Webb structures her autobiography by her political allegiance to a general welfare rather than her personal life and does not recount with sufficient detail her privileged childhood. Webb's narrative is thus much closer to Lovett's *Pursuit of Bread, Knowledge and Freedom* than to that of bourgeois individuation. She has consequently appeared to lack that "significant selfhood" or personality that signals spiritual autobiography, and *My Apprenticeship* has been the province of historians rather than literary critics.[71] Literary history's kinship with bourgeois subjectivity also explains the popularity of Mill's chapter, "A Crisis in My Mental History," among literary anthologists. In contrast to the self-reflexivity of the "Crisis" chapter, much of the rest of Mill's *Autobiography* is a relentless listing of "books which had any considerable effect on my early mental development" (Mill, p. 45), and thus closer to the study habits, moral-improvement style of Thomas Cooper than to Wordsworth. This is prob-ably why Carlyle reacted so strongly against it as the "autobiography of a steam-engine."[72]

We have seen that the embourgeoisement of workers, as in the self-examinations discussed in Chapter 1, produces a proliferation of indica-tors of bourgeois subjectivity. By comparing workers' autobiographies to canonical texts, readers can see the "personality" of bourgeois art and the power of bourgeois individualism even to those who were denied it or rejected it. But the storytellers and political autobiographers also show that subjectivity as the art of individualism and internality was merely one among many uses of literacy. The question is often asked whether writing did not necessarily make nineteenth-century workers culturally middle-class. The sophisticated version of this question, to be addressed at length in Chapter 6 and relating to the Cartesian dimension alluded to in the earlier parts of this chapter, was addressed by Walter Ong in *Orality and Literacy*. Ong claimed that writing (like Venetian mirrors) made possible an increasingly articulate introspectivity that henceforth divided itself from an increasingly objectified external world.[73] As Chapter 6 will show, writing did have these consequences for a very self-conscious group of literary modernists, but the division between subjective and objective, internal and external, was already established by social forces other than writing. There is no evidence that most literate workers adopted this introspective splitting off of the self any more than that all divided selves are the consequences of writing.

5.

The Making of Middle-Class Identities: School and Family

In 1844, the year of Marx's *Economic and Philosophical Manuscripts* and Engels's *Condition of the Working Class in England,* the Anglophile and scholar Barbey D'Aurevilly wrote that whereas the working classes were constrained by scarcity and necessity the upper classes of society were constrained by their own rules and conventions, hence the dandy's role to entertain a class boring itself to death within the terms of its elite status.[1] This chapter takes up the rules and conventions of upper-class life, specifically as evidenced within its elite educational system, and the possible subjects produced within that system. The first part is devoted to the male public schools; the second to women's corresponding educations and opportunities. Both parts begin with brief histories of the schools and then go on to the subjective reactions conveyed in former pupils' autobiographies, with special attention to convention, hierarchies, and the oppositional moves they fostered. Both parts ultimately consider the broader implications for subjectivity, value, and literary value. In recent debates within Critical Legal Studies, critics like Robert Gordon have suggested the importance of "decoding the vernacular," or studying how law has been imbricated in, and has helped to structure, the most routine practices of social life.[2] In studying the effects of rules and hierarchy, or social formalism, upon Victorian subjectivity in this chapter, I attempt one such decoding of the vernacular.

The Male Public Schools[3]

> Histories have previously been written with the object of exalting their authors. The object of this History is to console the

reader. *No other history does this.* History is not what you thought. *It is what you can remember.* All other history defeats itself.

This is the only Memorable History of England, because all the History that you can remember is in this book, which is the result of years of research in golf-clubs, gun-rooms, green-rooms, etc.

For instance, 2 out of the 4 Dates originally included were eliminated at the last moment, a research done at the Eton and Harrow match having revealed that they are *not memorable.* The Editors take this opportunity of acknowledging their inestimable debt to the mass of educated men and women of their race whose historical intuitions and opinions this work enshrines.

Also, to the Great British People without whose self-sacrificing determination to become top Nation there would have been no (memorable) history.

History is now at an end (see p. 115); this History is therefore final.

"Compulsory Preface," 1066 and All That[4]

America was thus clearly top nation, and History came to a .

Last chapter (p. 115), 1066 and All That

When Thomas Gray wrote "Ode on a Distant Prospect of Eton College" in 1742 (pub. 1747), the boys still possessed in their school a realm of freedom; only what they called "afterlife" (or life after school) victimized them. In contemplating the prospect of Eton's grounds, Gray feels a "momentary bliss," "a second spring." Yet stanza six begins, "Alas, regardless of their doom,/ The little victims play!" He calls on Father Thames to forewarn them of their future, "Ah, tell them, they are men." (The poem's epigraph is from Menander, "A human being: cause enough for misery.") Gray proceeds to list what boys may anticipate in afterlife: anguish, pain, destructive and frustrated ambition, cuckoldry, madness, disease, poverty, age, and death in due course. Knowing this—"All are men,/ Condemn'd alike to groan"—Gray revokes the warning, indeed the education ("Thought would destroy their paradise"), and leaves Eton to its play: "[W]here ignorance is bliss,/ 'Tis folly to be wise."

A haven from life only, Eton keeps boys from knowledge as long as possible. Gray was twenty-six when he wrote the "Ode," with a bitterness that would come to be customary of a type of school memoir. But the difference is significant: what embitters Gray is afterlife, the brutal focus of the poem, not Eton, which is merely the physical occasion for its contemplation. The autobiographies and memoirs of public school boys discussed in this chapter, however, find all the vicissitudes of afterlife—anguish, pain, destructive and frustrated ambition, cuckoldry, madness, disease, poverty, age, and death—already in place at school, which serves rather as the boy's initiation than haven.

After Gray's, the next school poem that has survived in twentieth-century anthologies is Matthew Arnold's "Rugby Chapel" (1857, pub. 1867). Yet rather than the school or afterlife, Arnold's poem is about the loss of his father Thomas Arnold's exalted mission (I hope to make Christian men of them, Arnold—the "Doctor" of *Tom Brown's Schooldays*—legendarily said of his pupils, I cannot expect to make Christian boys), and amounts to an ode to duty in a time of despair. The poem begins in Arnold's customary "Dover Beach" mood—cold, sad, wet, and withered:

> Coldly, sadly descends
> The autumn evening. The field
> strewn, with its dank yellow drifts
> of withered leaves, and the elms,
> Fade into dimness apace,
> Silent.

This is a world that needs a Father to guide it, and in Rugby Chapel the "gloom" reminds him of the absence of his own father:

> That word, *gloom,* to my mind
> Brings thee back, in the light
> Of thy radiant vigor, again.

He recalls such autumns illumined by his father's cheerfulness and imagines him in paradise, still with his earthly virtues, "zealous, beneficent, firm."

According to Arnold's customary irony, the poem develops through the contrast of poetic hero and prosaic age, the extraordinary whom we desire and the everyday who "Eat and drink,/ Chatter and love and hate . . . achieving Nothing." Without the example of the Father, even the otherwise extraordinary are mere egoists: "We bring/ Only ourselves! We lost/ Sight of the rest in the storm." The mythic heroes would not have been saved alone: "Still thou turnedst, and still/ Beckonedst the trembler, and still/ Gavest the weary thy hand."

Through his father's mediating image Arnold retains a model of the "noble and great who are gone," Promethean "helpers and friends of mankind." They are needed to save humankind, soon enough to be lost in T. S. Eliot's wasteland among Masterman's hordes. "Rugby Chapel," like *The Waste Land,* concludes as a prayer:

> Ye fill up the gaps in our files,
> Strengthen the wavering line,
> Stablish, continue our march,
> On, to the bound of the waste,
> On, to the City of God.

The poem praises a Father whose power to mobilize men is gone. It is rousing but hollow, concerning hollow men, bitterly (like *The Waste Land*) ironic and self-accusing.

In the 100 years intervening between Gray's and Arnold's poems, the public school had changed from a symbolic bastion of an aestheticized childhood—a childhood free (at least in literature) from the exigencies of everyday life—to an ideological state apparatus, an institution for the formation of national character. The specific period under consideration here is further marked by the shift in school literature from wide cultural representation, epitomized in Thomas Hughes's *Tom Brown's Schooldays* (1857), to narrow representations of Culture, epitomized in Cyril Connolly's *A Georgian Boyhood* (1938). I shall argue that this shift occurred in part as a reaction against the schools and that this reaction played a significant role in the retrospective creation of literary history and the canon formation of the modern period. In this transition from Hughes's culture in the broad sense to Connolly's literary coterie, which is marked by a shift from the "objective" conventions of realism to introspective or subjective representation, we may read two historical narratives: a literary community's divorce from the realm of political power and retreat into the subjective aesthetic discussed in the final chapter of this study, and the establishment of literary value as we have known it from Romanticism through modernism—value measured by the self-reflexivity, introspection, individuality, and putative autonomy that are challenged if not already defeated by the forces of post-modernism.

THE HISTORY[5]

> The Romans were top nation on account of their classical education.
>
> Chapter 1, *1066 and All That*

The first schools were founded in the sixth and seventh centuries to provide clerics and choristers for the cathedrals. With the dissolution of the monasteries many schools disappeared, to be revived later by the Crown, wealthy patrons, and livery companies. Until the early sixteenth century, dog Latin was the international language of commerce as well as of the schools. When the classical languages were revived (the "Renaissance"), commerce turned to the vernaculars and the classics were relegated to Grammar schools. There the curriculum remained practically fixed until the twentieth century.

During the fifteenth and sixteenth centuries, approximately 800 grammar schools were established in England. By the 1830s about 100 survived, and the nine great schools had come to the fore (i.e., Eton, Winchester, Westminster, Rugby, Charterhouse, Harrow, St. Paul's, Merchant Taylors', and Shrewsbury). *Pace* Gray's "Distant Prospect," before the 1830s the schools were most often characterized as autonomous, brutal, and anarchic. (Games, for example, were not yet instructive of "character.") Images proliferate like that of Long Chamber at Eton, where boys were locked in without supervision at night amid rats, filth, sex, torture, and alcohol, and where Shelley was horribly abused for four years and wandered sleepless through the night, cultivating his Gothic imagination. The late eighteenth century was also the period of schoolboy rebellions against the inefficiency and corruption of masters, and of the school "champions" battling it out on behalf of favored lower boys (although the greatest rebellion was at Marlborough in 1851, when bombings raged for a week).

From the 1840s through the 1870s the schools underwent reform, consolidation, and conformity. Appearing in the last quarter of the eighteenth century, the preparatory schools (for ages eight to twelve) grew in number after 1860, and thus younger boys were removed from potential bullying and moral contamination by adolescents. The Clarendon Commission of 1861 suggested reform of the great schools, and the Taunton Commission of 1864 proposed nationalized education for all, which led to the Endowed Schools Bill of 1869. To defeat this Bill the public school

Headmasters Conference was organized, and its members concentrated their forces for more efficiency and morality in the schools. In 1865 there were approximately twenty-five schools housing 7,000 pupils, and by 1902 sixty-four housed 20,000. The consolidation and standardization in the second half of the nineteenth century found its image in athletics and games, reaction against which gained force with the new century.

J. Fischer Williams prefaced his 1901 *Harrow* volume of the Handbooks to the Great Public Schools series with, "They are a national institution; no account of modern England or the British Empire would be complete, did it not give prominence to the public schools."[6] Their common conditions at that time consisted of a student body of at least eighty post-prep-school boys ages twelve to nineteen, self-government by the boys, admission by competitive exam and/or high fees, and the expectation of Oxbridge as the natural sequel to the school.[7] The two essentials of British public schools, John Corbin instructed his American audience in 1897, were that boys be in separate houses and self-governing.[8] The schools housed fee-paying commoners ("Oppidans" at Eton) as well as boys on scholarship (in a distinct college at Eton), often in great country houses by such architects as Inigo Jones.

Free of government control, individual schools retained or cultivated their own "personalities." As F. B. Malim put it in *Almae Matres* (1948), "the most potent influence in education is personality, and the fortunate pupil is he who has encountered the personality not only of great teachers but of a great school."[9] Its autonomy from State control allows the public school to "become different from other schools and to develop the individuality which alone commands devotion and wins love." The autobiographies duly include frequent characterizations of individual schools in the nineteenth century, such as an aristocratic Eton that cultivated "poise" and politicians who went to King's or Christ Church; a middle-class Rugby, the "nursing mother" of Victorian schools, that sent boys to other schools as infiltrating masters; a "mannerly" Winchester, the oldest of all the schools, founded in the fourteenth century; and a Harrow associated with missionary work (Shaftesbury was a Harrovian). Marlborough was for clergymen's sons and supplied the professions. Sedbergh ("Eton of the North") was "rugged, but a good nurse of men," like Homer's Ithaca. Haileybury supplied governors for India. Wellington, founded for sons of deceased army officers and basing admission on father's service and mother's need, provided the army. Epsom was for doctors' sons and provided the medical corps.[10]

During the nineteenth century the curriculum included Greek and

Latin—language, not literature or culture—and, later on, French, maths, and science. Yet the pedagogical "method" consisted of the translation (construing) of excerpted passages, writing-out of geometrical propositions and exercises (including parsing, or explaining each part in a sentence grammatically), and the calculation of sums. There is a world of testimony to the futility of this "method." After describing his school days in the 1820s and 1830s as "the worst period of my life," Trollope concludes "Nor did I learn anything—for I was taught nothing. When I think how little I knew of Latin or Greek on leaving Harrow at 19, I am astonished at the possibility of such waste of time."[11] Charles Darwin wrote laconically of Shrewsbury in the 1820s, "Nothing could have been worse for the development of my mind than Dr. Butler's school."[12] "The teaching was tragic" Edward Lyttleton reported of Eton in the 1880s, "the dullest boys still . . . being besotted with the rudiments of ancient grammar, without a hint of who Greeks and Romans were, what they did, and hardly when they lived."[13] In a section entitled "Education—Or What?," Esmé Wingfield-Stratford apologizes for a chapter in his autobiography on the public schools (disingenuously, since most Old Boy autobiographers included them), but he claims that it will explain how people in the 1890s came to be so "vacuum-witted": "You could have talked of the ignorance of a gentleman, the provincialism of a gentleman, the Philistinism of a gentleman, and any educated person would have known only too well what you meant, but hardly of the education of a gentleman, without your tongue in your cheek."[14]

Not only were the classics ill-taught, but maths, French, and science, when they were selectively introduced in the third and fourth quarters of the century, fared no better. "I should say that during my time at St. Paul's School our French was with the exception of our pronunciation absolutely contemptible," wrote Robert B. Gardiner of the years 1854–1861, "We knew nothing of French literature, and neither in literary nor commercial French could we produce anything: nevertheless I was twice a prize-winner."[15] Walter John Lawrence wrote of the speciousness of St. Paul's debating society at midcentury, "We were never allowed . . . to discuss any political subject which was less than twenty years old. So we were . . . divided about the Statesmanship of Pitt and Burleigh . . . and upheld Marlborough or Napoleon . . . which, however, after a short time became somewhat dull."[16] Henry Green concludes of his more recent public school education, "I was always confused and everything seemed pointless."[17]

Such views of the curriculum were shared by headmasters. "I am

quite sure that the time of most boys was elaborately wasted," wrote W.
F. Bushell, a master at eight different schools during fifty years.[18] S.P.B.
Mais, a master at Rossall and Sherborne, wrote "I resented intensely having to correct exercises. It dulled my brain and was of no value to the
boy."[19] In addition, Guy Kendall, a headmaster at Thresham, Charterhouse, and University College School in London, assessed education as
"boredom for all."[20] Yet the curriculum, as Lyttleton wrote, could not be
changed because no one knew what to put in its place.[21]

HIERARCHY, FORMALISM, AND RESISTANCE

In fact, the implicit assumption of masters as well as boys was—as stated
by themselves—that it did not matter what a boy was taught provided
that he hated it enough.[22] This soi-disant theory of education suggests
what one might call a "vulgar" Foucauldian (after "Vulgar Marxist")
reading of Victorian public school education: that what boys learned was
discipline not knowledge, surveillance not learning, *pouvoir* not *savoir.*
In this view, if *savoir* has content, *pouvoir,* power, is the hierarchical
structuring of relationships. Through the autobiographies one can trace
the development of upper-middle-class European men. They were
extruded from their homes at the age of eight for all-male prep schools
that funneled them into public schools and the socialized and oedipal
transferences of power. They learned in school to be boys without
women, then to be masters of other boys, and then to be guardians of
state and empire. (Kipling's school story *Stalky and Co.* (1899) begins
"Western wind and open surge/ Tore us from our mothers,/ Flung us on
a naked shore ... / 'Mid two hundred brothers.")[23] Through new-boy
status and fagging they learned what it was like to be on the bottom. Then
they learned what it took to climb the ladder and stay there. For some
this was academic performance, but for most it was athleticism; and as
the century progressed the Christianity seemed to melt away from the
athletic project, leaving only the muscle.[24] Each school had its own hier-
atic vocabulary to distinguish the boys from outsiders, and, within
schools, houses distinguished themselves from other houses. The majority of autobiographies and memoirs thus concern themselves with such
compartmentalized divisions and hierarchies, with discrete chapters on
the physical plant of the school, the masters, the boys, sport (cricket or
rowing), and miscellany depending upon the Old Boy's pursuits in
afterlife.

What should be emphasized about this characteristic of the typical school autobiography is its formalism, its games aspect. These texts lack plot. Old Boys mix past and present anecdotes and prescribe for the future with the full expectation that schoolboydom will last forever. The typical schoolboy served a team, and the typical autobiography provides discrete chapters in praise of the players, all of whom were equally familiar to all others. The same anecdotes of the great flogging masters like Keate of Eton or charming boy rebels like O'Brien of Charterhouse are repeated with equal enthusiasm in memoirs fifty years apart. The ostensible timelessness of the community renders plot, or progressive narrative, unnecessary. The same tales are told and retold, same matches at Lords played and replayed, in a sort of collective memory.

Robert Graves, an atypical schoolboy, describes his and a friend's feelings upon having made it to the top of the hierarchy, only to anticipate with dread repeating the whole endeavor in perpetuity:

> Finally, our only regret at leaving the place was that for the last year we had been in a position, as members of the sixth form, to do more or less what we pleased. Now we were both going on to St John's College, Oxford, which promised to be merely a more boisterous repetition of Charterhouse. We should be freshmen there . . . and hurt somebody and get hurt ourselves. There would be no peace probably until we reached our third year, when we should be back again in the same sort of position as now, and in the same sort of position as in our last year at our preparatoy school . . . We'[d] get our degrees, and then have to start as new boys again in some dreadful profession.[25]

This sense that as a schoolboy one had no content but rather only relative value in the hierarchy until one finally assumed one's privileged position in society or the empire distinguishes the two genres of public school autobiography: the game or "comic" autobiography of typical boys, which includes the majority of memoirs written before 1901 and many written later, versus those of dissenting or critical boys, which—although there are some striking early examples—primarily came into fashion around the first world war. Structurally, these latter are narratives. They have plots, beginning generally with an idealized preschool childhood ("Home seemed a heaven and we were cast out," wrote Green),[26] proceeding through an agony of education, and then concluding very often with an image of school-end as a literary closure, indeed as a death. In many cases the first world war is merely an objective correlative for the phantasmatic end of the public school system that is a microcosm of the corrupt and self-immolating larger world. When Cyril Connolly dramatically concludes *A Georgian Boyhood* in 1938 "when Europe trembles and dictators thunder" with the schoolboy's promise as "guilt—promise is the capacity for letting people down," he has accepted adult responsibility, finitude, and death, and has rejected the comic view that the game will continue, with generations of place-holding boys, indefinitely.[27]

These critical texts thematize frustrated idealism and alienation, the authors insisting that they write in loneliness and despair of the school and Western society. (In analyzing the mass suicide in Jonestown, Guyana, in 1978, the anthropologist Gordon K. Lewis compared Jim Jones's heroic aspirations and rebelliousness to a public school dissenter's.)[28] They are less concerned to rehearse the structures of power than to dissent from them, and their dissent typically takes the form of appeals to the imagination or literature. Henry Green published his autobiography *Pack My Bag* in 1940 because he thought that he would be killed in the war,[29] and, unlike typical school memoirs, his includes no friends, only a Society of Arts of which he is the only evident member. At school Green is so isolated that he begins to write, not for others on the team but for the aestheticized, introspective, monadic self, emphatically unshareable and asocial: "Prose is not to be read aloud but to oneself alone at night . . . Prose should be a long intimacy between strangers with no direct appeal to what both may have known."[30] In opting for power rather than prose, a character in Arnold Lunn's *The Harrovians* (1913) had posed the opposition: "Culture has its place, and I would be the last to deny it; but our success as a nation is not a little due to the sturdy common sense that has saved us again and again from the decadent disciples of 'Art for Art's Sake'."[31]

Although technically written as fiction, Lunn's *The Harrovians* was reviewed by contemporaries (other Old Boys) as an authentic description of public school life. It is an anatomy of cruelty. In the climax of the book the protagonist, after a long struggle to the top, seizes absolute power as Head of the House, abolishes the "privs" of other school elites, and enjoys being hated by the socially powerful athletes: "Power was very sweet. . . . He had learned the grammar of handling men."[32] Lunn explicitly connects gameplaying and power as the highest goals of the system: "The Public Schools aim at something higher than mere Culture. They build up character and turn out the manly, clean-living men that are the rock of empire. . . . They teach boys something which is more important than the classics. They teach them to play the game."[33]

These formal differences between the two kinds of autobiographies have ontological corollaries. For the typical autobiographers or memoirists, relatedness precedes autonomy. They present little of themselves and many anecdotes of others: unselfconscious and other-regarding, they subsume themselves to the team and write on its behalf. For example, the familiar masters who appear in their anecdotes provide continuity for the generations of readers-boys who passed under a single master's purview. In the critical texts, on the other hand, autonomy precedes relatedness. These writers are self-consciously self-regarding; as in the nineteenth-century realist novel, the plot is provided by the individual's encounter with the social process, but in this case he chooses to say no to the partnership. These texts emphasize one's most private feelings and sensations—indeed the most intense feelings the men were ever to have were at school—and they end with personal tragedy.

The two formal categories with their respective banners of Power (hierarchy) and Literature (resistance to hierarchy) can help explain the ideological failure of socialism among the British upper-middle class, and I shall return to this. Here, however, I want to pursue the tragedy and comedy of public school education through some common topoi of the texts, for these became positive conventions of the genre and they reflect the antagonistic political and aesthetic dimensions I have been exploring. The basic antagonism may be pursued through the topoi of rules, success, outlawed emotions, and school relationships.

Rules, understood to be for the ruling class and enforced by ferrules, could mean two distinct things to boys: either the signals of one's inevitable inadequacy or the formal structures defining the game and reassuring the players that they were in it. Because he was beaten for wetting the bed at his prep school, Orwell learned that he lived in "a world of good and evil where the rules were such that it was actually not possible for me to keep them."[34] "Call no man happy till he's dead. Next time [the beating] may be mine" was Connolly's way of putting his "Gospel of the Jealous God," that no matter how one tried, one would inevitably break the rules and be punished: "Everything in life has to be paid for. . . . When we are enjoying ourselves most, when we feel secure of our strength and beloved by our friends, . . . our punishment—a beating for generality, a yellow ticket, a blackball or a summons from the Headmaster, is in preparation."[35] This view of inevitable tragedy derived, of course, from Orwell and Connolly's status as scholars, that is, as social unequals of fee-paying Oppidans. Orwell's recognition of inevitable inequality and vulnerability—despite any amount of personal desire and effort—would ultimately move him toward substantive equality under socialism.

Yet for the majority of boys, who see the system as an interminable and comic cycle of newboy to God (a technical status term) through prep school, school, university, and "afterlife" (the pun on Gods in afterlife is intended in this divine comedy)—for those, that is, who play by the rules—the game continues indefinitely through comforting formal structures. For example, granting the vestigial predatory nature of boys, headmaster Lyttleton proposes the silent substitution of Kodak for guns in boys' confrontations with small animals,[36] or Gerald Priestland describes the war "games" at Charterhouse during wartime as resulting in a comfortable familiarity: "It was impossible for any of us to take the outside War seriously. Perhaps the fact was that we took it without reluctance or moralising, first as a welcome adventure, then as our normal background."[37] Personality or individualism, of course, can only disrupt this smoothly operating formal system. In Alec Waugh's *Loom of Youth* (1917) the deposed Head of House accuses Gordon Caruthers of the cultivation of personality, which destroys the comedy:

> *Après moi le deluge;* that's your philosophy. . . . [W]hat sort of future have you left the House? Order was kept all right when you were here; you are strong. But when you have left, who is going to take your place? . . . The new prefects will be too weak. At the best they would have had a hard time. But probably the prefectorial dignity would have been sufficient, if you hadn't smashed it up. You say 'personality' must rule, but there is not so much personality flying about. We weak men have got to shelter ourselves behind the strength of a system, and you have smashed that . . . [Y]our success has meant the ruin of the House for at least a year.[38]

As Tom Brown says approvingly of cricket, "It is such an unselfish game. It merges the individual in the eleven; he doesn't play that he may win, but that his side may."[39]

The topos of success operated similarly: success was either rigidly defined and unattainable in the tragic view, or merely a matter of playing the game—frustrated individualism or self-abnegating teamwork. For Orwell, the determinants of success were unjust and overdetermined: "There were the strong, who deserved to win and always did win, and there were the weak, who deserved to lose and always did lose, everlastingly."[40] Yet for the majority of schoolboys, success was tantamount to playing the game, whether one won or lost, for these internalized and naturalized the hierarchy. (See the discussion of *Tom Brown's School Days* in Chapter 6.) The dogged Alfred Lubbock, a midcentury cricketer, contentedly asserts that a boy who has been long at Eton learns "to find his own level, and become the agreeable and sensible being he ought to be."[41] In *Rambles Round Eton and Harrow* (1882), Alfred Rimmer agrees that "At a public school . . . every youth finds his proper level."[42] Schoolboy *character*—a significant term in all these texts—amounts to conformity and as Connolly says "is more important than Intellect . . . and desirable because it makes for success at school, prepares boys for the university, and is the foundation of success in business, politics, the army, the navy, the Indian and Egyptian civil services, and the African Police."[43] In countless memoirs one reads the usual progression from school, to university, to the Bar, to the House of Commons. Character, for the schoolboy, is playing the game and consequent success; to be "schoolproof" is to be morally centered: another step toward tragedy.[44] As other scholars of the public schools have pointed out, it is this goal of character formation that appears unique to British education among all other Western systems.

In this context one can assess Cotton Minchin's observation in *Old Harrow Days* (1898)—and expressed by many—that the public schools "produced few men of imagination but many of action" and the autobiographies' corresponding long lists of successful MPs and colonial governors.[45] Wingfield-Stratford laments abandoning the State to Eton's Oppidans, or fee-paying "non-intellectuals." He cites one Major Christopher Stone: "[W]hile the Collegers [scholarship boys] were condemned to do the world's intellectual drudgery, the majority of the future statesmen, soldiers and landowners were recruited from the Oppidans. Which as a commentary on the military, political, and diplomatic history of our time, may be left to speak for itself."[46] On their part, the critics rejected public life for the life of literature or imagination. In Waugh, Graves, and Green, the school taught conformity and mediocrity, and athletics created "the national satisfactory type," to which each opposed literature, or, what amounted to the same thing, individualism, as escape.[47] Walter Le Strange put it in the schoolboy's terms of team versus self: "If we live for others we spoil ourselves. If we live for ourselves we harm others. The only course is to give ourselves up to art or literature or such."[48]

The game pervaded every aspect of the boy's thought and emotion. If it succeeded, the boy was preadjusted to British society; if it failed, the boy grappled with outlawed emotions, in the sense that feminists use the term to indicate perceptions that will not conform to the ideological norm or rules of the system.[49] (Others may prefer the term *hysteria*.) Years of outlawed emotions conditioned the boy to the tragic mood. In Orwell's terms, the child overtly accepted adult nonsense, but its senses told it otherwise.[50] Despite his Headmaster and mistress's continuous humiliation of him as a scholarship boy who should be grateful for their attention, Orwell did not *feel* gratitude: "whatever one did, one's only true feeling was hatred."[51] "The schoolmaster who imagines that he is loved and trusted by his boys is in fact mimicked and laughed at behind his back."[52] Outlawed emotions pervade the critical memoirs, and—as we know from *The God that Failed*—often shifted into the rhetoric of larger resistance and liberation. Walter Le Strange dreams of emancipation from public school oppression in a wilderness of tropes drawn from several stages of political development: "Whipt like a mere slave—that is, an oppressed fag, or lower boy . . . O may everyone be free! Let not the wretched new boy be oppressed and mishandled just for the convenience of the idle . . . priests of Athleticism and Public School Spirit of Imperialism."[53]

The enormous issue of sex versus sentimental friendships, or in the period's terms eroticism versus amorousness, was often analyzed in terms of outlawed emotions. What we now call puberty was then an outlawed emotion, a prohibition that served to heighten and prolong sexual awakening. At the age of fifteen in 1887, when Bertrand Russell "was sitting at work, endeavoring to concentrate, I would be continually distracted by erections, and I fell into the practice of masturbating . . . I was much ashamed of this practice, and endeavored to discontinue it. I persisted in it, nevertheless."[54] "So many things were forbidden me," wrote Russell, "that I acquired the habit of deceit. . . . It became second nature to me to think that whatever I was doing had better be kept to myself." And, again, reading is one of the targeted practices: "I still have an impulse," Russell confides sixty-five years later, "to hide what I am reading when anybody comes into the room."[55] Like Connolly's recollection that "poetry was something to be ashamed of, like sex," such associations further dislocated a private life of reading and writing from the public life of school.[56]

On the other hand, to adjust one's emotions to the school was to accept the status quo absolutely, as in Harold Nicolson's expressed sentiment in *Some People* (1927): "I hate the lower classes. . . . People who have not endured the restrictive shaping of an English School are apt in After life to be egocentric, formless and inconsiderate."[57] "We [at Eton] rode on the backs of the workers with the insouciance of the man who sat on the back of a whale," L. E. Jones wrote in *A Victorian Boyhood.*[58] Derek Hudson's last editorial in *The Salopian* (March 1, 1930) confirmed without apology that the social system was mapped within the schools: "Yet, when we [boys] consider the earnestness with which we struggle against each other, it might well be the battle of life itself. . . . In the jealousies between our social orders moves . . . all the latent snobbishness of high society, and the swollen heads of this funny little world of ours find their counterpart in the greater world beyond."[59]

Thus the two views to be contrasted are Orwell's tragic description of a boy's life at St. Cyprian's as "walking the tightrope over a cesspool" versus the many comic accounts, as in Rimmer's *Rambles* or Malim's *Almae Matres,* of the nurturing beauty of the Great Schools' architecture and grounds;[60] or Connolly's Nietzschean contrast between Oppidan friendship—"a luxury—a touch of failure, inequality, absence, [and] it perished"—and that of the collegers stigmatized by their poverty, for whom friendship was "a religion invented by sensitive boys under hard conditions and which existed to combat them."[61]

HOMOSOCIALITY AND THE STATE

> The editors' thanks are also due to their wife, for not preparing the index wrong. There is no index.
>
> Acknowledgments, *1066 and All That*

After 1875, the schools acquired loyalties and affection rivalling those for home and family. The network and intensity of school relationships must be seen in this context. Called the *barbaric epoch,* this period was dominated by athletics. The bigger boys' ethos of house autonomy distanced them from masters, poor material conditions were ameliorated, the curriculum came under criticism for its lack of rational interest (i.e., Culture alone was perceived as insufficient training for a gentleman in a competitive market), and the first public acknowledgments of immorality (boyhood erotic activity) were made at the Headmasters' Conference founded in 1869. During this period, women acquired increasing employment opportunites, property and divorce rights, admission to the universities and professions, and the vote.

The critical writers responded by romanticizing the home at the school's expense, and the rest transferred their affections to, and rallied around, the School. The two poles here include Orwell and L. E. Jones.

Despite Orwell's indifference toward his father—"One ought to love one's father, but I knew very well that I merely disliked my own father, whom I had barely seen before I was eight and who appeared to me simply as a gruff-voiced man forever saying 'Don't'"—Orwell contrasted the school with the home, ruled by love rather than fear, where the boy was not continuously on guard against the people around him.[62] The idealization or sublimation of a pre-lapsarian homelife before one entered the masculine world of fear, distrust, and competition contributes significantly to the tragic narratives: the school, however detested, replaces the home and then repeats its inevitable rejections. For Jones, on the other hand, homelife was so oppressive, familial duties and compulsory allegiances so stifling, that Eton with its boy realm seemed free:

> I was happier, because more free, when [my parents] were not there. Freer
> . . . from the continual demands for the outward expression of affection,
> and for absolute conformity with my parents', which meant my mother's,
> views on all questions, big and small. We were each allowed a favourite
> flower and a favourite pudding, but, beyond that, there could only be a
> wearisome conflict, certain to end in surrender, if we differed from my
> mother in opinions, tastes, or values. To avoid this conflict, as I had said,
> we became "yes-children" and outwardly conformed; but with the result
> that, for my own part, I did not want to hear her step upon the stairs.[63]

But whether the image of home is Edenic or oppressive, as Graves says, "School life becomes the reality, and home life the illusion. In England, parents of the governing classes virtually lose all intimate touch with children from about the age of eight, and any attempts on their parts to insinuate home feeling into school life are resented."[64]

In *The Public School Phenomenon,* Jonathan Gathorne-Hardy argues that this extrusion, or removal of boys from their families from the ages of eight to eighteen for all but four to six weeks of the year, and segregation in a one-sexed environment is the single most important social factor distinguishing the British upper classes from the lower and indeed distinguishing Britain's *national* male-bonding for power, or homosociality, from that of other Western societies.[65] (He also argues persuasively in *The Rise and Fall of the British Nanny* that middle-class boys' early preschool life with working-class nannies was equally significant in the maintenance of class stability.)[66] This extrusion refocuses the boys' loyalty onto the State, resulting in the upper classes' so-called sociological interdependence. The family being withdrawn, the boy imprints, as it were, on the community, from school to army, business, Parliament, or Civil Service. "Take the City," wrote Gathorne-Hardy in 1977, "This— the Stock Exchange, the Bank of England, the accepting houses, the merchant and clearing banks—is really a giant public school in which, even today, the Eton group is particularly strong."[67] In *Marxism and Domination* Isaac Balbus has argued that if we take the intensity of the infant's initial identity with its caretaker as one cultural variable, and the severity of the infant's separation from the caretaker as another cultural variable, object relations theory can account for differing forms of the State.[68] Without arguing for such a theory's universal scope, we can use public school memoirs in support of the thesis that the core of the Victorian middle-class and gendered "self" was influenced by opportunities to identify with paternal authority that replaced initial female authority, henceforth retroactively romanticized as refuge. In *Memories and Hopes* Lyttleton wrote of the nervousness of celibate housemasters around women at Eton, where fifty out of sixty-six masters were bachelors, some of whom had had no contact with women since they had been taken from their mothers.[69]

The autobiographies reflect the intensity of male bonding among boys at school to an astonishing degree. Probably most Americans cannot remember more than a handful of their childhood experiences at state-supported schools with any vividness. Yet in the public school memoirs—and their great number and volume support my point—men from twenty-two to eighty ("four-score years") endlessly evoke trivial incidents from their childhoods, Connolly's boyhood obsessions being only the most notorious. Remarking upon the total rationalization of boys' time and surveillance of behavior—especially surveillance by other boys, Henry Green concludes, "And so it was only to be expected that in circumstances such as these we lived at a higher pitch and reacted more strangely than we do now in a less competitive world where we just try to keep alive."[70]

Green writes of the pettiness and self-consciousness of this male theater as its effemination. His school diary "gives exactly that sensation of being watched and of oneself keeping track of even simple actions for the reactions these might bring on the part of house opinion . . . [W]e watched the effect produced on others in the way women do."[71] In *Sinister Street*'s (1913) brilliant parodies of literary pastoral, decadence, realism, chivalry, sentimentality, and melodrama, Compton Mackenzie, enthralled by the details of school life and puerile friendships, takes self-consciousness to the point of total narcissism. On his first bicycle ride with a girl, Michael Fane watches the image of his interaction "in the shop-windows, as they rode past, to observe the effect"—of himself.[72] He engages in conversation with his mother "as if by doing so she would give him an opportunity of regarding himself and his behavior objectively."[73] Mackenzie was so concerned to regard himself objectively that he is forced in his dedication to apologize for writing about his school days to the length of 1,000 pages in two volumes. It is this obsessiveness and intensity of school life that, for its critics, made university such a relief: Oxford and Cambridge were free and even-tenored; the boy's time was his own; the pressure for athletics was off; and a boy's pursuits were of little interest to others.[74] Even Oxford, however, was not different enough for Green: he came to love his father's factory, where the exigencies of labor defeated the boy's intense self-absorption.[75]

Predictably, the intense emotional investment in school resulted in the paradoxically nostalgic tone of the great critical memoirs. The school was bad, but it was also the most vivid experience of the man's life, tragically irrecoverable. His imaginative investment in recreating its details was indistinguishable from the introspection, specificity, and individuality of literature itself. I shall return to this point.

Theoretically, the boys' own institutions of self-government made it possible for masters to be neither disciplinarians nor enemies, yet the relationships between masters and boys are described in the familiar devices of tragedy or comedy. If one took the master's authority seriously—as in the case of scholarship boys who did not have the support of the community and were dependent upon scholarships to the university in afterlife—one was doomed. Trollope was in this tragic category: "It was by their ferules that I always knew [the masters], and they me. I feel convinced in my mind that I have been flogged oftener than any human being alive," he writes in *An Autobiography,* and one may read that queer, bleak textbook of success as therapy for Trollope's humiliation at the hands of masters: "I had been looked upon always as an evil, an encumbrance, a useless thing,—as a creature of whom those connected with him had to be ashamed," he concluded of his public school education.[76] (To further illustrate the point about the timelessness of the memoirs, in a section on "Old Harrovians" written seventy years after Trollope was at school, Cotton Minchin avers that Trollope was right: he *was* a dirty boy.)[77]

Yet if one perceived the boy's realm as an autonomous, and indeed the significant, realm of public school life—and if one played the game—life was a Tom Brown comedy. This opposite view to the tyranny of masters was the view of autonomous spheres, a view shared by many masters as well as boys. W. F. Bushell gleefully records the masters' clandestine competitions for the most scathing epigrams at a boy's or parent's expense.[78] Among boys, G. D. Martineau, at Charterhouse just before the war, argued that after "t'other'un's" (the prep school's) rule by masters, the public school was the domain of boys, and all memoirs confirm that lying to a master was encouraged by the school code but lying to a boy was interdicted.[79] The best illustrations of the separate spheres view are the great comic scenes in Waugh's *The Loom of Youth,* in which Caruthers and the Headmaster confront one another with total incomprehension of each other's values, making communication impossible.[80] (Fundamentally, of course, such incomprehension is an institutional expectation—all part of the game.) Similarly, *The Harrovians* begins with an innocent Vicar lecturing on Debrett to a contemptuous Cricket Eleven.[81] From the boy's point of view, as Orwell wrote, "an adult who does not seem dangerous nearly always seems ridiculous."[82] Tragedy (domination) or farce (contempt) were apparently the only legitimate alternatives for boys' relationships with their teachers.

CONCLUSIONS: LITERARY SUBJECTIVITY AND POLITICS

> Within five minutes I went through some such reflections as the following: the loneliness of the human soul is unendurable; nothing can penetrate it except the highest intensity of the sort of love that religious teachers have preached; whatever does not spring from this motive is harmful, or at best useless; it follows that war is wrong, that the use of force is to be deprecated, that a public school education is abominable.
>
> BERTRAND RUSSELL, *Autobiography*

> I write books but I am not proud of this any more than anyone is of their nails growing. . . . Moneyed people have invented interests to pass their long hours of leisure and whatever their inclinations, that is whether they are interested or not they read, they look at pictures and listen to music. They become constipated with things they cannot grasp. In the ironfoundry we had a close discussion each day in the lunch hour nearly always about some nonpolitical event in the news . . . [T]he conversation was more like that of intellectuals than the half-baked talk about novels people who fancy themselves put over.
>
> HENRY GREEN, *Pack My Bag*

So if it did not teach classics, or French, or maths, or science, then what did this institution—that for many and with great consequences replaced the bourgeois family—teach the children? The answer is more complex than Eton's impassive response to Connolly's indictment that its education was of no use in afterlife. Eton responds, "No education is. We are not an employment agency."[83] The public schools taught negatively and formally. They taught their critics values by default. In lieu of providing him admirable companions in pursuit of worthy goals, Fernherst (Sherborne) taught Gordon Caruthers (Alec Waugh) self-reliance.[84] Because masters failed to dispense it, Lyttleton learned that what boys looked to elders for was justice.[85] Perhaps the most noteworthy values that the restrictive, goal-oriented system taught its critics were, again, oppositional: aesthetics and imagination. The game players, on the other hand, learned their place in the game and, with a failure of imagination, assumed that the game would go on forever. "A knowledge of boys when in England is much the same as a knowledge of men," wrote Jones in 1955—just as Tom Brown had said in 1857, "I suppose soldiers are very like boys."[86] Ex-schoolboy C. A. Vlieland wrote (unimaginatively) from Malaysia, "Naturally we believed wholeheartedly in . . . the permanence of the British Empire."[87]

In this eternal childhood of the schoolboy it is clear that their comic vision precluded the players' seeing history sneaking up on them and their empire. I want to conclude this section on the male public schools, however, with the critics and literature's relationship to politics. In rejecting "the national satisfactory type" of their schooling, the critics also rejected totalitarianism. (The analogy school/totalitarianism is explicit in countless early twentieth-century memoirs and autobiographies.) But they had always fought totalitarianism with art, creativity, and individualism in isolation; therefore, they could not quite trust socialism, either. Consider the melancholy end of the schoolboys of *The God that Failed* (1949).[88] They preferred tragedy—with its fetishized personality, internality, individuality, and imagination—to the Soviet bureaucracy and the party line. Richard Crossman concluded that the Protestant God was the tragic Prometheus and that communism destroyed half his soul. Arthur Koestler detailed the paradoxical blend of comradeship and mutual distrust in the Apparat nets that transformed human relationships and annihilated language. Stephen Spender rejected communism because it did not cultivate art and imagination.

In martyring literature and individualism, the standardized public school had left the boys only two alternatives: tragic individualism or whole-hearted acceptance of the game. In turn, they treated socialism not as a project to be perfected but in the way that they had learned to treat their schools: as an ideal that, if less than perfect, was a tragedy. The confining of ideals to the arena of art, the decoupling of the extraordinary from the everyday, proved to be the death of ideals. With their hearts broken, the former schoolboys wrote *The God that Failed* and a lot of lyric poetry. The critical schoolboy autobiographies were written by the same men who dominated English literature in the first half of the twentieth century—and who did not run the country.

Orwell, on the other hand, wrote a fable for the multitude, thus—and miraculously, given his background—opting out of the tragic vision, preferring the common language to the fetishized, decontextualized purple patches of poetry, using art to criticize, not escape from, politics.[89] With the fable of *Animal Farm* (1945), Orwell turned from bourgeois art (introspective, self-conscious, preoccupied with "private life," "autonomous") to a popular art intended to counter the "literature of totalitarianism" he saw developing in mass society: "Every line of serious work that I have written since 1936 has been written, directly or indirectly, *against* totalitarianism and *for* democratic Socialism, as I understand it."[90] Unlike other public school-educated writers who could not make the transition, Orwell saw the sensitive, rebellious writer as "merely an anachronism, a hangover from the bourgeois age, as surely doomed as the hippopotamus."[91]

Yet the nightmare elements of the public school haunted the ex-schoolboy Eric Blair's last book, composed while he was writing "Such, Such Were the Joys." I am not the first reader to have been puzzled by the seemingly gratuitous sadism of *Nineteen Eighty-Four,* nor the first to see the novel's similarities to "Such, Such Were the Joys." In Oceania loneliness is palpable; privacy in Newspeak is "ownlife . . . meaning individualism and eccentricity";[92] outlawed emotions are fatal; art and imagination are rewritten or wiped out; the preservation of the hierarchy is the final goal; and the society, like the school house, is so isolated that even its wars are "purely internal affairs."[93] Like *The Harrovians, Nineteen Eighty-Four* is a study in sadism, and it threatens aestheticism by aestheticizing "power entirely for its own sake."[94] As curtailed evidence of the novel's similarity to the memoir, I cite the Inner Party Old Boy O'Brien's initiation speech to the new boy Winston Smith and a passage alluded to earlier:

Power is in inflicting pain and humiliation. Power is in tearing human minds to pieces and putting them together again in new shapes of your own choosing. Do you begin to see, then, what kind of world we are creating? . . . A world of trampling and being trampled upon. . . . We have cut the links between child and parent, and between man and man, and between man and woman. No one dares trust a wife or a child or a friend any longer. But in the future there will be no wives and no friends. Children will be taken from their mothers at birth, as one takes eggs from a hen. . . . There will be no loyalty, except toward the Party. There will be no love, except the love of Big Brother. . . . but always do not forget this, Winston—always there will be the intoxication of power, constantly increasing and constantly growing subtler. Always, at every moment, there will be the thrill of victory, the sensation of trampling on an enemy who is helpless. If you want a picture of the future, imagine a boot stamping on a human face—forever.[95]

And here are the lines from "Such, Such Were the Joys":

The pattern of school life was the continuous triumph of the strong over the weak. Virtue consisted . . . in dominating them, bullying them, making them suffer pain, making them look foolish, getting the better of them in every way. Life was hierarchical and whatever happened was right. There were the strong, who deserved to win and always did win, and there were the weak, who deserved to lose and always did lose, everlastingly.[96]

Now if we place this discussion of the schools' particular sociopolitical function and effect in a more abstract arena, we can see certain illuminating aspects of subjectivity in the public school texts. In *Knowledge and Politics* Unger specifies three bases of conscious individuality: (1) consciousness itself, or the experience of separation and limitation, awareness of difference from others, (2) the body as the natural frontier of the boundaries of the self, and (3) the peculiar relationship between members of the species and the species as a whole, when the self who can only make use in one lifetime of a tiny fraction of the species' talents can be seen to participate potentially in the forms of life of the species.[97] The self never fully overcomes the gaps between humanity and nature, individuality and sociability, partiality and universality (or concrete and abstract self), nor does it entirely reconcile itself with the world. Yet we may say that the typical schoolboys, with their interminable and comic cycles of newboy to god, overcame the problem of partiality and universality by subsuming themselves to a team, in which each was no more than an anecdote in school memoirs writing themselves, as they imagined, in perpetuity. They partook, in Unger's terms, of universality. Success was tantamount to playing the game, whether they won or lost, so the ultimate loss, personal finitude, was nothing so long as the game went on. They had, so to speak, no personalities of their own. On the continuum of the passions, they are contained within fixed hierarchical relations in a condition of stable, if uncreative, social relations.

To represent the critical schoolboys I draw upon Unger's moral idyll of the relation of the self to others in *Passion: An Essay on Personality* (1984). Unger sees the generative polarities of the passions, the source of "personality," as the longing for, and fear of, others. Thus human personality can be mapped upon a continuum in which fear and antagonism on one pole are contained by fixed hierarchical relations (playing the game), leading to a condition of stable, if uncreative, social relations. Trust and participation, on the other pole, represent the vulnerability and risk of nonhierarchical social relations. The life of the passions, or personality, may be seen in the way women and men participate in or reject Unger's "moral idyll," which rejects the pole of fixed relations for the pole of risk and vulnerability, for a world of encounters in countless combinations of longing and fear. In the moral idyll, one learns to experience oneself as never wholly contained by a character and growing to greater self-knowledge and self-possession by willed acts of vulnerability or accepted accidents of fortune that put a character under pressure. "What with all this danger," Unger muses, "it is natural that most people should play for low risks. Through a suitable combination of work and domesticity they retreat into the most secure material haven they can find. They make neither their livelihoods nor their characters hostage to fortune."[98]

It is fitting that Unger opposes the moral idyll to "character." The schoolboys who dissented against the "national satisfactory type" and British character appealed to literature and imagination and they developed a moral idyll—but relegated it to aesthetics, to the realm of the extraordinary. In both their prose and poetry, they endlessly rang the changes of personal relationships, of deeper exposure to other people in countless combinations of longing and fear, finally epitomized in risk and vulnerability opposed to hierarchy in the story of Winston and Julia in *Nineteen Eighty-Four*. Personality so defined was raised to horrific proportions in the Etonian Ian Fleming's James Bond series: brief, intense personal encounters in a terrifying, dangerous world—007's world of desire and fear. Only having a character, a fixed self, was the failure. It is no surprise that Unger's and the public school idyll sound so much like

Walter Pater's "success in life," defined by Pater as the failure to form habits and the habit of burning with a hard gemlike flame.[99] Pater called this *aestheticism* and relegated it to art and song. The antagonistic schoolboys raised it to a literary ideal, with the consequence that through the mid-twentieth century England's most articulate class would be endlessly fascinated with the details of psychic distress in personal relations, and the possibility that society might be deeply transformed through collective action would be made to look like a revolutionary reverie.

Women on Schools and Rules

> [Florence Nightingale and Margaret Bondfield] were nevertheless endowed with so much force of character that they were almost certain to push through to the light they needed . . . they insisted on making their way in spite of obstacles that might well have seemed insurmountable, in the face of an environment whose hostility must have daunted any ordinary person, must have persuaded her into supposing that there was no way out.
>
> I belonged to none of these categories. I doubt, I very much doubt, whether if I had been born say twenty years earlier, or had a less understanding family or less amazingly modern-minded father, I should ever have done anything outside the home at all. Or even so much as known that it was possible to get out of the prison in which I found myself. I know that I should have been unhappy, but I doubt if I should have known why I was unhappy. These people had to get out or perish. I should not have perished. I should merely have lived uncomfortably—uncomfortably for myself and notably uncomfortably for other people.
>
> My autobiography is the autobiography of a normal person.
>
> MARGARET HAIG, VISCOUNTESS RHONDDA,
> *This Was My World* (1933)

BOARDING SCHOOLS

Before the founding of Queen's College in London in 1848, which would provide a cadre of women teachers licensed in both curriculum and pedagogy, there was nothing for women comparable to the generally recognized elite male public schools. Middle-class girls were taught privately by governesses and visiting masters or sent to small privately owned boarding schools. Home education depended upon the personal preferences of parents and governesses, but the curriculum of the boarding schools usually included Scripture, verse, letterwriting, French, history, science, "general knowledge," arithmetic, handwriting, needlework, drawing and painting, and piano. Physical education was represented by dancing and the study of deportment (a graceful manner and the proper way to behave in society). While teaching was still the only paid employment available to respectable middle-class women, it tended to draw many women whose need to work outweighed their preparation to teach. As there were no accepted standards of qualification, pedagogical abilities varied greatly, and many women autobiographers joined their brothers in lamenting the uselessness of their education. From the teacher's perspective, Amy Barlow admitted that as late as the 1890s "one taught or did nothing" and called her chapter on her first post "The Agony of Teaching," in which her colleagues confessed that their pupils often knew as much as they.[100]

The tardiness of the establishment of a standardized education for middle-class girls was of course attributable to the conventions of middle-class domesticity. As Cecily Steadman writes in her first-hand history of Cheltenham Ladies College (founded 1853):

> In early and mid-Victorian days, every girl looked forward to marriage, so that the well-educated woman was she who could govern her household, decorate her home, and entertain her guests. Consequently, while acquiring household lore through practice at home, girls gave much time to the piano, harp, violin and singing, to drawing, sketching, painting on various materials such as china, satin and American cloth, to plain sewing, different kinds of embroidery, and to such forms of lace-making as crochet, tatting, and netting. They began as many as possible of these in the schoolroom and continued them with private teachers when, in the language of the day, their education was finished.[101]

Such "finishing school" curricula continued to be provided for the most affluent until the end of the nineteenth century, but beginning in the 1870s girls' schools, like boys', began to undergo reform including more academic and regularized standards, the streaming of classes according to age, examinations, standardized fees (earlier fees varied greatly from pupil to pupil), more strenuous regimes of physical education (reformers adopted the tag *mens sana in sano corpore*), and certified teachers. As Martha Vicinus writes in *Independent Women: Work and Community for Single Women 1850–1920,* "Reformers at first had to fight an uphill battle to convince parents to invest in their daughters' education. Many could not afford even low fees (all secondary education was fee paying) after they had paid for their sons; others feared that the new-style schools would make their daughters discontented or argued that they needed their help at home. The elite boys' schools always had far larger enrollments and endowments."[102] By 1898 some 80,000 girls were in secondary schools of varying quality, seventy percent in private schools, and one-seventh of these in private boarding schools.[103] These reformed schools were intended to meet the needs of a rapidly industrializing society. Typically supervised by graduates of women's colleges, they produced, in addition to their great majority of better-educated wives, the New Woman, made for something more than marriage, who scandalized late Victorian fiction, as well as the suffragettes of the early twentieth century. The standardized, reformed schools were thus paradoxically liberating for women. Unlike boys' schools, which were intended to train independent men, girls' schools officially trained girls to be dependent upon teachers and headmistresses so that they could later be dependent upon husbands and, if necessary, employers. Yet repeatedly in their accounts of school, girls learned to elude the constraints of convention.

WOMEN AND CONVENTION

Certain similarities prevail in a comparison of male public school writing and that of middle-class women who attended comparable boarding schools. The women also emphasize family status and provide detailed accounts of school friendships, revealing deep intimacy with, and affection for, school associates that often continued throughout afterlife. Due to the fact that, unlike boys, girls were not self-governing but subjected to the intimate supervision of the staff, their bonding extended to their relationships—often very intense—with their teachers and principals. The most striking difference, however, between upper-class men's and women's autobiography is in the relaxed attitude women exhibit toward convention. Whereas the men either seamlessly adjusted to convention and unquestioningly assimilated in the social structure in afterlife or individually rebelled against the system at considerable psychological cost, women did not duplicate this tragic dichotomy. They are preoccupied with the conventions of school and family, to be sure, yet whether they ultimately rebelled against feminine convention, like the suffragettes, or whether they settled into conventional domestic life, women express both less propriety and less anxiety about their ability to conform to the status quo. The one exception to this tendency, the self-identified female literary artist negotiating the demands of literary domesticity, will be introduced in the next section and further developed in Chapter 6.

Women, for example, caricature their teachers as often as they admire or reject them. May Sinclair's self-confessed "autobiographical description of my inner life," *Mary Olivier: A Life* (1919), is laced with caricatures of authority figures in her life in the second half of the nineteenth century, and Winifred Mercier's biographer Lynda Grier, incorporating extensive correspondence between Mercier and her intimates, nevertheless had to censor the greatest part of her surviving correspondence. Grier particularly targeted Mercier's letters from Somerville College at the turn of the century, "for they are unusually concerned with personalities. She gives vivid and detailed descriptions of dons and undergraduates . . . and of her tutors and lecturers. Appearance, manner of teaching, personal idiosyncrasies, her own liking for or detestation of them, are recorded. . . . As most of them are still living these cannot be given, for, whether flattering or unflattering, they are so strongly expressed that they would embarrass their subjects."[104]

Elsewhere I have used humor theory to analyze this anarchic tendency in middle-class women's writing.[105] (If one needs a theory of tragedy to account for boys' attitudes to rules, one needs a theory of comedy to account for girls'.) According to Aristotle, Henri Bergson, Umberto Eco, and Hélène Cixous, humor occurs when one sympathizes with a breaker of a rule or convention because one sees the contradiction between her and the frame she cannot comply with. One may even think that the frame of convention is wrong. In this sense humor is metasemiotic, casting in doubt cultural convention. In Eco's terms, humor reminds us of the presence of a law that we no longer have reason to obey. Unlike both their male counterparts and working-class women, middle-class women typically found that the education appropriate to their gender and class could only be treated, in literary retrospect, with considerable, if often bitter, humor.

In working-class women's writing humor is relatively rare. Working women find humor in crossclass transgressions, as when their soi-distant superiors enter their world of necessity to make ludicrous trivial gestures or when they try to imagine themselves in middle-class situations. In general, however, the rules or convention that concerned working women—

at least the majority of working women who had not begun to undergo embourgeoisement—were the rules of survival and necessity, not polite society, and writers seldom break or see others break the rules of survival without providing pathos rather than humor. Working-class women were aware of their relative lack of humor. In *Jipping Street* (1928) Kathleen Woodward confesses that in her reading for self-improvement she was acutely conscious of losing much of the sense of middle-class authors, especially, she imagined, in her inability to detect when they were being humorous, or breaking middle-class rules or codes that remained largely mysterious for her.[106] In her interviews on reading practices collated in *At the Works* (1907), Florence Bell found that the wives of ironworkers preferred "some relief to the greyness of their lives, some suggestion of other possibilities, but for many of them anything that excites laughter goes too far in the other direction. . . . [T]hey generally prefer something emotional and not laughable."[107] With respect to their (limited) formal education, the great target of middle-class women's humor, working people of both genders reacted with bitterness generally devoid of humor.[108] In contrast to middle-class women's ridicule discussed later, Kathleen Betterton could only feel desolate and bewildered (i.e., like public-school boys on scholarship) confronting "the multiplicity and apparent irrationality of the rules" at the boarding school to which she, the daughter of an Underground liftman, had won a scholarship.[109]

The significantly greater number of rules to be broken, and the inconsequence of breaking them, relative to the few—and iron—rules of a worker's life, however, makes middle-class women's writing rather more humorous than that of working women. In autobiographies of educated middle-class women, humor is very often exclusively directed toward one thing: the rules of the school, or the education that would make them ladies. Faced with codes that were incongruous with women's perceived powers, women launched sustained and anarchic attacks upon those codes.

In her *Life* (1894) Frances Power Cobbe describes the more than 100 ladies' schools in Brighton in the 1830s with their hundreds of rows of identical girls in full evening dress, facing the wall for breaking the rules. After a curriculum of—in descending order of importance—music, dancing, deportment, drawing, Continental languages, English, and Religion ("fasting will be good for our souls *and* our figures"), the young Cobbe left school secure in a position that the older philanthropist, suffragette, and antivivisectionist could only record with considerable humor. Upon leaving school, Cobbe recalls, she thought: "I know as much as any girl in our school, and since it is the best school in England, I *must* know all that it can ever be necessary to know. I will not trouble my head ever again with learning anything; but read novels and amuse myself for the rest of my life."[110] Cobbe's humor, of course, turns to disparagement of what she calls "feminine futility" by the second volume, as illustrated by the ludicrous description of a lady attempting to uncork a bottle for three pages (II, 229–32). Ladies and labor—even such labor as uncorking champagne—were incongruous, but the humor for Cobbe consists in the disparity between this image of febrile femininity and what she knows of women's capabilities.

In *A Little Learning; or a Victorian Childhood* (1952), the educationist Winifred Peck (née Winifred Knox) recalls the 250 rules that could not be broken at Miss Quill's Day School for Christian Ladies in the 1870s. Peck recalls the rule to "Assume your underwear as modestly as possible under the covering of your night gown" and grows riotous trying to envision some flagrant disregard of the rule.[111] Peck also mocks her childhood education from standard texts like *Near Home and Far Off* for their ludicrous and incongruous formulae of national stereotypes to be learned by rote by British schoolchildren, such as "The Irish are a merry people and fond of pigs," or "The Italians are a dark, revengeful race where [sic] the stiletto is in frequent use" (22). She also grows hilarious at the specious rules of English grammar after the Romans, as in "Castle: noun, accusative; third person, neuter gender, etc."

In Mary Vivian Hughes's *A London Family 1870–1900: A Trilogy* (1934–1937), the educator Hughes also finds humor the only way to describe her own education. Her twenty-sixth edition of Brewer's *Guide to Science* (1869) presented itself in the form of a catechism: "Q. What is heat? A. That which produces the sensation of warmth. Q. What is light? A. The unknown cause of visibility. Q. What should a fearful person do to be secure in a storm? A. Draw his bedstead into the middle of his room, commit himself to the care of God, and go to bed."[112] Surrounded by strictly enforced rules at North London Collegiate in the 1880s, Hughes philosophically laughs at the impossibility of not breaking them: "We were forbidden to get wet on the way to school, . . . to drop a pencil-box, leave a book at home, hang a boot-bag by only one loop. . . . One felt that if a girl were to knock over the blackboard by mistake there would be a rule against it the next day" (165).

In her partially autobiographical *In the Days of Miss Beale*, Steadman ridiculed her own early catechismal training at the hands of a slightly prepared governess. *The Child's Guide to Knowledge* had "the same fascination as a dictionary":

> Question. What is rice?
> Answer. A kind of grain.
> Question. What is sago?
> Answer. The pith of a palm tree.
> Question. What is tapioca?
> Answer. The grated root of the manihoc.
> Question. Of what is paper made?
> Answer. Rags and clay.
> Question. What is used for tanning?
> Answer. Oak bark and water.
> Question. From what is ink made?
> Answer. Oak galls and water. (2)

Having learned answers by rote, Steadman recalls, when the teacher reordered the questions, girls were likely to rejoin "What is tapioca?" with "Rags and Clay." "Nobody concerned," she writes, "was quite sure what manihocs or oak galls were."

Perhaps the most eloquent humor at the expense of school rules for young ladies appears in Antonia White's *Frost in May* (1933), which is only nominally fictive. In the Convent of the Five Wounds, Fernanda Grey (Antonia White) rebels against the master narratives of Roman Catholicism that frame every aspect of the girls' lives. Nothing can be apprehended "for its own sake," for things are freighted with a density of religious signification that organizes and interprets the girl's experience:

> To Our Lady and the Holy Child and the saints [Nanda] spoke as naturally as to her friends. She learnt to smooth a place on her pillow for her Guardian Angel to sit during the night . . . to jump out of bed at the first beat of the bell to help the Holy Souls in purgatory. . . . The donkey in the paddock reminded her that all donkeys have crosses on their backs since the day Our Lord rode into Jerusalem; the robin's breast was red because one of his ancestors had splashed his feathers with the Precious Blood trying to peck away the crown of thorns. The clover and the shamrock were a symbol of the Blessed Trinity, the sunflower was a saint turning always towards God, the speedwell had been white till Our Lady's blue mantle brushed it as she walked in the fields of Nazareth. When Nanda heard a cock crow, it cried "Christus natus est"; the cows lowed "Ubi?

Ubi?" and the lambs down at the community farm bleated "Be-e-thlehem."[113]

Trained upon the inconsequential trivialities of the catechismal mode and such simple-minded deontologies, these elite women learned early on to be irreverent toward authority. In some cases, their ridicule of convention did not stop with curriculum, but extended to other formal constraints upon women's activity. Florence Nightingale's critique of a mid-century middle-class woman's lack of opportunity outside the home in her spiritual autobiography *Suggestions for Thought to Searchers after Religious Truth* is probably the most bitter. Here Nightingale acknowledged that whatever the formal opportunities for education, for most upper-class women destined to be homemakers nothing followed from their schooling. In the section called "Cassandra" (discussed in Chapter 2) the rules imaginatively broken, the boundaries imaginatively crossed, are the rules and boundaries of gender itself. Nightingale's text is the mad babble of Cassandra, representing "that perpetual day-dreaming [of women's emancipation], which is so dangerous" (397): Cassandra knows the possibilities for women in the future, but due to the historical connotations of Victorian gender she is powerless to enact the changes that she knows will come. The text is of women babbling their transgressions by violating gender convention and exchanging roles with men. On the restrictions on ladies' activities Nightingale writes, "But suppose we were to see a number of men in the morning sitting round a table in the drawing-room, looking at prints, doing worsted work, and reading little books, how we should laugh!"[114] Of the eternal waste of women's time in morning calls, she asks, "If you offer a morning visit to a professional man, and say 'I will just stay an hour with you, if you will allow me, till so and so comes back to fetch me'; it costs him the earnings of an hour, and therefore he has a right to complain. But women have no right, because it is '*only* their time'" (402). In her most daring assault on the boundaries between the male and female spheres, Nightingale, a deeply religious woman, does a feminist parody of the Gospel, claiming that if Christ had been a woman, "He might have been nothing but a great complainer" negligent of his duties to home and family (416). "For instance," she writes:

> Christ was saying something to [the multitude] one day, which interested Him very much, and interested them very much; and Mary and His brothers came in the middle of it, and wanted to interrupt Him, and take

Him home to dinner, very likely . . . and He, instead of being angry with
their interruption of Him in such an important work for some trifling
thing, answers, "Who is my mother? and who are my brethren? Whoso-
ever shall do the will of my Father which is in heaven, the same is my
brother and sister and mother." But if *we* [women] were to say that, we
should be accused of "destroying the family tie, of diminishing the obligation of the home duties." (417)

Such humor challenged the law that women like Nightingale no longer
had reason to obey.

Typical in many ways of autobiographies by women who attended
boarding schools, Margaret Haig, Viscountess Rhondda's autobiography
This Was My World (1933) illustrates how the ridicule for school rules
expanded for some women into a life-long resistance to convention, or
to the established role relations confining women. Describing her departure from St. Leonard's Boarding School in 1902, Rhondda cited Nightingale on how the school, unintentionally as it were, had educated her
"for something more than a young lady's life."[115] She went on to attack
the formalism of Coming Out and Seasons, which, again, was intended
to facilitate debutantes' marriages but in fact often fostered resistance in
girls:

The Seasons only lasted for three years; they came to a natural end when
I went up to Oxford, and when, after a comparatively short interval, I
came down again, I firmly refused to resume them. By that time I was
quite clear about their misery. Yet I do not remember that even then I
consciously criticised a system which was responsible for persuading a
particularly affectionate and conscientious mother . . . that she could best
do her duty by martyrising herself into dragging a bored and not even
socially successful daughter through a series of aimless and useless functions. A system which hypnotised a perfectly intelligent, though perhaps
rather naïve young woman, already anxious to investigate most accepted
notions impersonally and dispassionately, into acceding without question
to indulgence in this odd form of occupation, which in fact she was hating
so much. One knows now that the idea at the back of the system is marriage. But although I was then much preoccupied with the whole question
of love and marriage, I do not remember being particularly conscious of
the connection at the time. And I rather doubt whether my mother was.
She would have thought it, I suspect, a little indecent. Her sole concern
was to do for her daughter what had been done for her, and what other
mothers did for theirs. (93–94)

Rhondda begins her postschool chapter on "Home, College and Marriage" with a quote from *Cassandra:* "Women dream till they have no longer the strength to dream. . . . Later in life they neither desire nor dream, neither of activity, nor of love, nor of intellect" (95). The upperclass young woman's irrational regime of tea, bridge, hunting, and philanthropy was, according to Rhondda, merely "ways of using up surplus energy" (101). She writes of the substitution of her childhood dream to be Prime Minister for that of matrimony, "in the eyes of everyone around me that was the one path of self-fulfillment" (103). "Since college was to lead to nothing more than coming back home and continuing with exactly the same purposeless life that I had left behind me" (106), Rhonda leaves Somerville after a year to marry a man she will ultimately divorce.

Within four years of her marriage, she has taken up militant suffragism, "a draft of fresh air into our stiff, padded lives" (120). Surviving the struggles (literally, in the streets) of the movement, she goes on to critique the conventions of big business (shipping), a legacy bequeathed to her by her father. Writing with a sophistication impressive even to a late twentieth-century feminist, she advises her women readers on how to handle the disadvantages under which women operate on executive committees and boards of directors: male jealousy and punitive resentment, exclusion from the locales of professional gossip (men's rooms, clubs, sports, etc.), and women's inculcated inferiority and deferral to others. While resisting these conventional effects of male homosociality, she also resists the conventions of middle-class femininity: to make men feel comfortable with her at board meetings, she speaks only when she has something important to say, thus avoiding the imputation of feminine triviality, and she smokes heavily. The latter tactics had proven equally salutary for the socialist Beatrice Webb.

Rhondda was beaten and imprisoned as a militant suffragette, managed a shipping business, survived the sinking of the Lusitania, toured the Canadian wilderness unaccompanied on barge and foot, and edited *Time and Tide.* She insists throughout *This Was My World,* however, that she is an "ordinary person," with the views of an ordinary person, and that "the exceptional woman" is a myth occluding women's unequal opportunity. She is able to insist upon her ordinariness because of her strategical identification with the emancipatory discourse of the suffrage movement. "Certainly it was during those years of fused enthusiasm rather than during the ordinary years of school and college," she writes, "that, reading, studying, thinking, puzzling, I got the best of what edu-

cation I have had. And, as I have said, I suspect that that is true of many
another militant of my generation" (130). The militant movement forced
Rhondda "to educate myself and to learn to speak; it also made me take
to writing" (ibid.). The Women's Social and Political Union (WSPU)
wrote to papers, printed circulars, posted bills, and rented columns
according to Annie Kenney's instructions to "Tell them what you want,
why you want it, and how you mean to get it." They read the feminist
works available to them—J. S. Mill's *Subjection of Women* (1869), Bernard Shaw's *Quintessence of Ibsenism* (1891), Cecily Hamilton's *Marriage As a Trade* (1909), and Olive Schreiner's *Woman and Labour*
(1911)—and sought out relevant parts of others. In the course of the
movement, Rhondda was driven to study history, political science, economics, psychology, sociology, and anthropology. As with the Chartist
writers, politics preceded the women's education and writing, which in
turn intensified and broadened with the urgency of the movement. *Political consciousness preceded "self" consciousness.*

The participatory discourse of the movement for the franchise gives
way in Rhondda's autobiography, as it gave way for most feminists of her
time, to another participatory discourse—that of national unity—with
the outbreak of the Great War. Rhondda sounds like any of the working-
class storytellers in Chapter 4 when she writes of Time and the war:
"[W]e who had gone into the war young came out, as it seemed, middle-
aged. Time had not stood still, it had galloped, and in that gallop had
robbed us of the last years of our youth" (294). Unlike the storytellers, or
the schoolboys who grieved for the golden youths who had fallen, however, Rhondda is not nostalgic. What she sees is not the apocalyptic
breaking up of the civilized world (the typical male literary response to
"World" War I) but rather a less grand—for women equally significant—
breaking down of "barriers and customs and conventions": "Across the
gulf of chaos whose memory we needed above all else to wash away, the
frontiers of 1914 were already dimmed and half forgotten. We could not,
even had we wished, join this new comparatively sane world on to the
jagged edges of the one that had broken off five years before—this new
one was quite a different place. The way had broken down barriers and
customs and conventions. It had left us curiously free" (294). (It should
be noted that, however much they grieved, women autobiographers typically remarked upon this liberating aspect of the war years. Sandra Gilbert and Susan Gubar have studied this response in women's literature
in "Soldier's Heart: Literary Men, Literary Women, and the Great
War.")[116] After the war, Rhondda divorces her husband and, middle-aged

and armed with the memories that would constitute *This Was My World,* breaks out of convention into a new role for women: "I was free, free as never yet in my life had I been before. . . . I had a profession. I was rich. Owing to being my father's daughter I had, almost by accident and much to my own surprise, made a name. A name is a platform. Life was before me to do what I chose with. Already it had been good, but I knew that the best was yet to come" (295).

What might be mistaken from this description as the crowing of an individualist with recently won autonomy satiating her subjective desire in the pursuit of self-interest is not, however, the way Rhondda concludes her narrative. She is neither a storyteller nor a protagonist in a bourgeois novel, but rather a politician in the Chartist sense: a militant feminist turned social critic who identifies her "self" with a movement positively as an affirmation rather than negatively as resistance, intersubjectively rather than subjectively (i.e., unlike the negative identification of the critical schoolboy). Her father had quoted Napoleon with approbation, reinstating the second clause allegedly suppressed by history, "The British are a nation of shopkeepers, *and the odd thing is that they are ashamed of it"* (180). Rhondda concludes that she is "a merchant and the daughter of a merchant" (305) and invests her energy and entrepreneurial resources in the founding (with others) of a weekly paper, thus preparing an intervention on the ground itself of cultural convention:

> I could see that the old ideas had failed us, but what exactly were the new ones that were to save us? How could they be ventilated? . . . I wanted to find, to test, and to spread the customs and the ideas that could be health-giving and life-saving. . . . That way I could find the people who were worth hearing, and see that they were heard. . . . It was enthralling work thinking it out, finding the people one believed in, getting hold of them to write for one's paper, gradually, slowly, making the thing come alive. (301, 304–5)

As for Orwell, also a politically committed media-worker, for Rhondda "One does not write simply for the sake of writing" (302). Discussing her earliest initiations into commerce, she contrasted "big business" with Bloomsbury, with which she was familiar through her capacity as an editor. With more than a little of Orwell's virile contempt for the self-consciousness of the literati, she observes, "I must say that I like business men, especially the big ones. . . . they have as a rule straightforwardness, friendliness, lack of much touchiness or jealousy—at least, as compared with artists—and the big ones almost all have vitality. And besides that they are efficient, they get things done. I like people who can get things done" (267). Entirely opposed to the individualist mystique of the artist—she is, as it were, a corporate-feminist, a company woman— Rhondda concludes her autobiography in praise of the little praised and much deserving *communal* function of editors: "I could put before the public that mattered the things that I wanted them to hear. To the born publicist—and I am that—it had all the advantages of writing without the worry of writing" (304). By "worry" here, of course, Rhondda means the egotism and isolation of the writer.

Whether treated with humor or, as in Dorothea Beale's case, with tolerance toward changes she was personally opposed to, these women's irreverence and flexibility with respect to convention were probably a consequence of women's secondary status.[117] A boy either accepted and played by the rules, in which case he assumed his place in the power structure, or despaired of them, in which case he retreated into isolation (literature) or obscurity. Perhaps because women's status was lower, permitting them a lesser investment in the rules, women did not perceive this tragic dichotomy. They experienced the distance, even indifference, of a spectator rather than the urgent engagement, vulnerability, or risk of a player. Facing the rules, they tended toward anarchy rather than insecurity. Previously barred from the intellectual tradition, personal freedom, and independent status among the benefits of "Western culture," women like Rhondda could interpret the Great War, which for many irrevocably problematized the status of these very phenomena, as a beginning rather than an end. The corollary, of course, is that the greater the status, the more the rules are for one's benefit and the more one's relationship to them is reverent, or potentially tragic.

There are other frames through which one might understand these women's irreverence toward convention. Psychoanalysis would say that without the threat of castration, or threatened loss of power (since they have no penis/power to lose), women develop inferior superegos, or unwillingness to submit to law. Pointing to women's historical oppression, Hélène Cixous allies women with the Unconscious, that place where there are no rules and where boundaries break down, and where the repressed have managed to survive. Medusa's laughter, or "women's writing" in Cixous's sense, opposes itself to undesirable ("mechanical") rules and laws. "It will be conceived of only by subjects who are breakers of automatisms," writes Cixous reflecting Henri Bergson's terminology, "by peripheral figures that no authority can ever subjugate.... What woman hasn't felt, dreamt, performed the gesture that jams sociality? Who hasn't held up to ridicule the bar of separation? . . . Who, by some act of transgression, hasn't overthrown successiveness, connection, the wall of circumfusion?"[118] Here some would go on to employ an analysis after the sociological and revisionary psychoanalytic work of Carol Gilligan on women's resistance to rules, Nancy Chodorow on women's fluid boundaries, or Judith Kegan Gardiner on fluid characterization in women's writing.[119] Currently, my own view is that there is nothing essentially feminine about the autobiographers' reaction to rules and convention, but that it rather reflects a relationship of convention and status, in this case gender status. To say that these women were denied economic, political, and social agency means that for most of them breaking the rules that constrained them was an action deprived of any consequence. Like naughty children of their class, they could break the rules and life would continue in its customary fashion. As Peck put it, what was the use of an Oxford education to one who was bound to limit her life to conventional domesticity (167)? Compulsory femininity, to adapt a phrase from Adrienne Rich, was a concept well-known to middle-class women.[120] It was the hegemonic pattern of the majority of their lives.

On the other hand, for some of these women, to be deprived of agency, their obvious disenfranchisement and confinement within the *domus*, conflicted with other "stories" of enfranchisement that bore considerable hegemonic force of their own in British culture (e.g., working-class enfranchisement, the antivivisection movement, the entry of women into higher education, "radical chastity," and the Married Woman's Property Bill [1891]). Such discourses provided alternative models for women's lives and thus encouraged prolonged and ultimately successful assaults on convention. As in the critical boys' rhetoric of antifascism, the hegemony of liberal political emancipation (workers, women, people of color, and so on toward a pluralist society) slowly challenged traditional concepts of hierarchy and subordination. There was, however, another kind of narrative that supplied a third alternative to domesticity or liberation: the story of the woman literary artist.

SUBJECTIVITY AND THE LITERARY ARTIST

The "self-consciousness" that Rhondda associated with the London literary scene was cultivated by the women writers who were the spiritual counterparts of the tragic schoolboys. In nominally fictive autobiographies they wrote what May Sinclair called autobiographical descriptions of their inner lives, the inner life being the place from which to resist the constraints of school, family, and church. Because middle-class girls were socialized predominantly for domesticity, family in these works may be a more prominent factor in women's oppression than school; however, if the forces of constraint change from text to text, the opposition of introspection and subjectivity to the objective or external conditions of the authors' lives is constant. Although they are compromised in ways that will be discussed, these are narratives of resistance. In *Mary Olivier: A Life* (1919), Sinclair, who attended Cheltenham under Dorothea Beale in the 1880s and participated in the suffrage movement from 1908, wrote of her psychological development as a writer in opposition to family, church, and the lures of domesticity. Mary's father appears as a forbidding if mildly ironic patriarch in her childhood—"Papa walked in the garden in the cool of the evening, like the Lord God. And he was always alone. When you thought of him you thought of Jehovah"—and as an embarrassing alcoholic as she grows older.[121] He is less significant, however, in her development than Mary's mother, who dominates the family of four children through her own intellectual timidity and emotional dependency. After Mary's father's death, her oldest brother flees to India (where he dies) to escape his mother's dependency; her youngest brother dies of congenital heart failure exacerbated by his mother's selfishness; and her middle brother succumbs to what is also presented as hereditary alcoholism. Mary remains to attend her mother, as Sinclair did until her mother's death in 1901, at which point she went to London and joined the literary circles of Dorothy Richardson, Hilda Doolittle, Henry James, Ezra Pound, et al.

The subjectivity of many of these modernists is the subject of Chapter 6, but relevant here is the way that their obsessively self-conscious narratives of middle-class familialism and genderization, with their liberal pursuit of autonomy, may be contrasted with the more typical autobiographies of women who made no claims for themselves as *artists.* Sinclair's memoirs of school, like Dorothy Richardson's multivolume *Pilgrimage* (1915–1938) and Antonia White's *Frost in May,* are intended to be works of art. They make constant reference to literary and aesthetic tradition—the Brontës as well as Kant, Hegel, and Spinoza—versus the suffragettes' reference to feminist and political works. Despite its breadth of learning, however, *Mary Olivier* is claustrophobic in its thematic obsession with the constraints upon women—the sort that made Mary/ Sinclair's mother simultaneously intellectually timid and emotionally domineering—and its corresponding formal confinement to one obsessive perspective: the text opens with two-year-old Mary's impressions of her cot in her parents' bedroom and is confined to Mary's consciousness throughout.

Mary develops as a self-conscious artist in an agonistic relationship with others who would make her conform to their conventions and role expectations. When a village matron attempts to assimilate her into family patterns, inquiring whom she is "like," Mary responds with assertive independence that she is "most of all like myself" (167). When her mother reprimands her for her self-consciousness, Mary reacts:

> Your self? Your self? Why should you forget it? You had to remember. They would kill it if you let them. What had it done? What *was* it that they should hate it so? It had been happy and excited about *them,* wondering what they would be like. And quiet, looking on and listening, in the strange, green-lighted, green-dark room, crushed by the gentle, hostile voices. Would it always have to stoop and cringe before people, hushing its own voice, hiding its own gesture? It crouched now, stung and beaten, hiding in her body that walked beside her mother with proud feet, and small lifted head. (168)

Although opposition to convention is commonplace in middle-class women's writing, opposition deriving from this internalized, reified self appears with women's claim for artistic status. Within their texts, this fragile oppositional "self" is threatened by forces of immense power, from *within* as well as from external sources. The family that attacked one from without also attacked one from within in the form of heredity. Because this internalization of external constraints (e.g., the internalization of family) was essential to the period under consideration (e.g., Freudianism, an interest of Sinclair's), and will be significant in the discussion to come, I quote the passage at length. It shows Mary's great desire for autonomous individuality being undermined by inevitable interdependency. In other terms, it is the deconstruction of autonomous "genius":

> You had been wrong all the time. You had thought of your family, Papa and Mamma, perhaps Grandpapa and Grandmamma, as powerful, but independent and separate entities, in themselves sacred and inviolable, working against you from the outside: either with open or secret and inscrutable hostility, hindering, thwarting, crushing you down. But always from the outside. You had thought of yourself as a somewhat less powerful, but still independent and separate entity, a sacred inviolable self,

struggling against them for complete freedom and detachment. Crushed down, but always getting up and going on again; fighting a more and more successful battle for your own; beating them in the end. But it was not so. There were no independent, separate entities, no sacred, inviolable selves. They were one immense organism and you were part of it; you were nothing that they had not been before you. It was no good struggling. You were caught in the net; you couldn't get out.

And so were they. Mamma and Papa were no more independent and separate than you were. . . . Papa couldn't help drinking any more than Mamma could help being sweet and gentle; they hadn't had a choice or a chance. (290)

Heredity had come, as psychoanalysis would come, to be the figure of total familial control, the great refutation of liberal dreams of autonomy. Yet it was precisely against this familial control, this great denial, that the self grew up, feebly resisting.

In her biographical account *The Three Brontës* (1912), Sinclair tried to claim a literary genius independent of external influence for the three sisters, especially for Emily.[122] Yet the very reason she was able to write so empathetically of the Brontës—one very clear in her remarkable half-biographical, half-autobiographical *Three Sisters* (1914)—was the similarity between their and her own oppressive environments: family histories of alcoholism, fatal hereditary illnesses, parental domination, frustrated romance, in all their cases productive of obsessive individualism and literary creativity.[123]

In 1918, Sinclair adapted William James's phrase "stream of consciousness" in *The Principles of Psychology* (1890) to the technique she found in the early chapters/books of Dorothy Richardson's *Pilgrimage*. Also autobiographical fiction, the thirteen-volume novel represents a self-divided heroine with both domestic and literary aspirations. The first two (novel-length) chapters in Volume 1, *Pointed Roofs* (1915) and *Backwater* (1916), are concerned with Richardson/Miriam's experiences as pupil and teacher in English and German boarding schools from 1895.[124] Constrained by the conventions and prohibitions of her class and gender—Richardson's mother had committed suicide by cutting her own throat with a kitchen knife—the protagonist Miriam turns inward. Drawing parallels with earlier female literary traditions like Charlotte Brontë's, rather than moving outside of literature into a suffrage movement, Richardson came to treat writing as a form of self-analysis in the dialectic of autonomy and relatedness. Unlike her contemporary modernists Woolf and Joyce, however, who employed so-called stream of consciousness techniques only intermittently within definite narrative structures, Richardson/Miriam's is the *only* perspective of the novel, which is entirely written in "unmediated" interior monologue.

In confining herself to the art of internality Richardson provided a feminist alternative to the hierarchical writing of her class. Discrete chapters on schools, pupils, teachers, and progressive narratives give way in *Pilgrimage* to a nonlinear, noncoercive, nondevelopmental collage of open-ended human relations by no means culminating in a marriage. Richardson believed that a reader should be able to read the pages of a novel in any order; and, as Gillian Hanscombe writes, although the thematic conflicts of literary domesticity are always implicit, they are given no explicit support from the conventional devices of narration, characterization, chronology, or the delineation of milieux.[125] Miriam does not develop, all her impressions and experiences are given equal weight, and conflicts and relationships are not resolved or finalized. Richardson employs no apparent principles of selection of characters, thoughts, or events that impinge upon Miriam's consciousness, nor any such coercive structuring device as a plot. (When Richardson died in 1957, a thirteenth volume was still in preparation.) In the schools, girls and teachers interact in changing relationships of dominance or trust: Miriam's relationships with men unravel and are reconstituted with a sort of Proustian tentativeness. I take Richardson's *Pilgrimage* to be the formal and thematic repudiation of convention and hierarchy, a sort of Ungerian dream of the restless, uncontainable "self." The problem is that while the self has rejected oppressive social roles and structures—including what Richardson called "male" coercive narrative—with complete integrity (Richardson even rejected standard punctuation), it has done so at the cost of its total isolation. Many readers find Richardson's writing to verge upon a "private language."

Although Richardson contended that both "the romantic and the realist novel alike—left out certain essentials and dramatized life misleadingly. Horizontally—Always—one was aware of the author applauding, or deploring, his manipulations,"[126] the violation of literary conventions in her own work paradoxically contributed to its overwhelming authorial "presence," for convention at least implies community—while its absence implies isolation or alterity. The paradox of Richardson—a painful one for women "artists," or women who fashion themselves according to the male tradition of the "artist"—is that, despite her commitment to a gestalt feminine consciousness, in opting for the identity of the "artist" she left herself only a dichotomous alternative reminiscent of the tragic schoolboys: to reject one traditional role—in this case, a middle-class woman's—for another, that of the artist. In the last volumes of *Pilgrimage,* it is revealed that whereas other women have lovers and children Miriam has *Pilgrimage,* or a literary profession; and it is clear now that—from the perspective of "the artist"—Richardson herself was able to reject social relatedness to an impressive degree. Rebuking a friend the relationship with whom had received considerable attention in her fiction (Veronica Grad or *Pilgrimage*'s "Amabel") for requesting some of her "real" time, Richardson lashed out against all her friends' "lack of imagination" in failing to recognize her needs as "an artist":

> You sound reproachful. Imagine. All my time and strength *needed*—it used to be *given*—for my own special work. Almost *none* of it available for that work. Imagine the wear & tear of that one devastating *fact.* Again, all my time and strength *needed* for the mere business of making enough to live on, & making it, because I *can't take a regular journalistic job,* on heart-straining uncertainties, free-lancing, anything I can get and *all* of it against the grain.
>
> Imagine the drain of something, (mutual & moral drain—for domesticity is a *state of mind*—) all the detail of it & the perpetual to & fro, between homes & the business of tenants, a whole practical life which is a *third* whole-time job. Has it ever been asked of an artist before? I doubt it. I am not complaining. But my strength is not what it was & now that London has become an increasing chorus of *claims* I begin to feel I must either cut out London or cut out visiting! It could so easily be a fourth whole-time job!
>
> Anyway there *are* the four. With the complication that everybody, nearly enough, is apt to be reproachful. It staggers me. The absence in almost everybody of the imaginative faculty.[127]

The friend to whom such a letter was written, like many of Richardson's friends inside and outside her fiction, could only respond, after her death, that the novels of *Pilgrimage* were "as damming [sic] a picture of personality as were ever written":

> I loved her but Dorothy never for one moment 'loved' anyone but herself. . . . She took an avid interest in other people their lives, their misfortunes, their successes, but she never—looking back I see—gave either sympathy or help—or let herself become in any way involved. . . . Maybe it was all worth it as a sacrifice to her 'Art' I can't judge of that . . . but first everyone was 'copy' material not only for books but for stimulation

for Dorothy—You know she was rather like a vivisectionist in her attitude to us all—but, I can't see myself that the handful of pioneer books makes it any less ugly—.[128]

The paradoxes of Richardson are instructive. While rejecting literary convention, she wholeheartedly assumed the conventional male/romantic role of the artist. While rejecting the conventional domesticity of her class, she married at the age of forty-four a man of surpassing delicacy sixteen years her junior with whom her relationship was more than commonly maternal. While rejecting coercive narrative and hierarchical relations in her fiction, she displayed massive insensitivity to, and shocking manipulation of, the people who cared for her. While rejecting masculine authorial presence, she created a vision that is often judged, as her most sensitive critic to date has said, as an eccentric exercise in the annals of egotism.[129] Like her male literary counterparts, she rejected convention. Unlike the suffragettes, she also rejected a common language of solidarity, opting rather for the individualistic post of the artist with its historical connotations of genius, privacy, autonomy, and freedom from necessity (her outrage that her time should be spent on "the mere business of making enough to live on"—even if that included only "the business of tenants"). Such a choice—although its status as a "choice" is deeply problematic—could only lead to such disquieting contradictions.

As with working-class writers whose "resistance" was unconnected with larger social or collective efforts, resistance from the perspective of individualism typically came to serve the ideology it opposed; in Richardson's case, it was masculine authoritative ideology. The lesson of Richardson for feminists is social rather than individual: the only way to overcome authority without (ironically) becoming it is to overcome it with others.

It is from the knowledge of such paradoxes that Nancy Armstrong has come to claim a profound *political* significance for women writers of the last two centuries that challenges the conventional wisdom of much feminist literary criticism. Tracing the history of private desire through domestic fiction, Armstrong claims the paradigmatic position of modern subjectivity for women.[130] Thus the coercive privatizing of female experience became the very type of modern privatized experience per se. The "creative imaginations" of fictional Pamelas and Emmas, authorial Brontës, Sinclairs, and Richardsons, converged with and reinforced the meritocratic individualism of their bourgeois brothers.

CONCLUSIONS: INTERSUBJECTIVITY AND THE LITERARY ARTIST

The reformed boarding schools were often viewed by women themselves as a national response to the empire's demands upon the male population. Vicinus's *Independent Women* begins with the national debate in the press in the 1860s concerning "redundant women" and the views of the influential journalist W. R. Greg:

> There is an enormous and increasing number of single women in the nation, a number quite disproportionate and quite abnormal . . . proportionally most numerous in the middle and upper classes[,] who have to earn their own living, instead of spending and husbanding the earnings of men; who, not having the natural duties and labours of wives and mothers, have to carve out artificial and painfully-sought occupations for themselves; who, in place of completing, sweetening, and embellishing the existence of others, are compelled to lead an independent and incomplete existence of their own.[131]

In fact, in most cases the elite boarding schools continued to educate women to complete, sweeten, and embellish the existence of others, only making them, in Peck's terms, more skeptical of the universal consequence of Home Sunbeams and philanthropy and more aware of new social movements and the Welfare State in the great world outside.[132] Yet in providing a minority of women with new social roles, primarily as educators of other women, the schools slowly eroded the convention and constraints upon which women had founded their identity throughout the century. Ultimately the opportunities for self-representation for middle-class women parallel those for middle-class men—community-oriented pragmatism (school spirit, antifascism, suffragism, etc.) or literary individualism, participation in a common discourse or isolated antagonism to the status quo.

Writing the self on behalf of the community, which culminated in the autobiographies of the suffragettes like Annie Kenney or Rhondda (notably a working-class woman and an aristocrat), had precedents in both religious and secular women's literary traditions. Martha Mary Sherwood (1775–1851), Charlotte Tonna (1790–1846), Mary Anne Schimmelpenninck (1778–1856), and Mary Sewell (1797–1846) wrote spiritual autobiographies for "the spiritual good of the people" and never wavered in their belief that it was the duty of the pious woman writer to disseminate Christian truth publicly in print as privately in her own home and personal relations.[133] These women authorized their self-representation by way of a liturgical role peculiarly allotted to their sex. Confined to print and the privacy of writing by Victorian domesticity, in contrast to the relative freedom of eighteenth-century women preachers, Schimmelpenninck, for example, in an elision both practical and inspired, seizes for women participation in writing in the service of social redemption:

> The great increase of literary taste amongst women has wrought a wonderful change, not only in collections of books, but in their composition. Books were then written only for men; now they are written so that women can participate in them: and no man would think of forming a library in his house, without a thought that its volumes must be the companions of his wife and daughters in many a lonely hour, when their influence must sink into the heart, and tend to modify the taste and character. Thus, in literature, as in other things, and especially in domestic life, has the mercy of God bestowed on women the especial and distinguishing blessing of upholding the moral and religious influence, that spirit of truth and love by which man can alone be redeemed from the fall she brought upon him.[134]

Later secular women writers also authorized their autobiographies within broad cultural narratives. Many, like the working-class storytellers, believed that posterity would appreciate "the recollections of *any* truth-loving, truth-telling individual who has passed the allotted threescore years and ten of life" in a rapidly modernizing society and, like Camilla Crosland in *Landmarks of a Literary Life 1820–1892* (1892), represented histories in which the authors themselves were unobtrusive.[135] Others recorded in autobiographical form but entirely unselfconsciously the histories of the great bourgeois families. About Anne Thackeray Ritchie's *Chapters from Some Unwritten Memoirs* (1895), Mary Jean Corbett writes:

> Ritchie does not narrate her story by making herself the central character who stands out against the background provided by her family and her era but rather establishes her presence in the text as the observer who holds its different pieces together and makes them cohere. Relying on the justifiable assumption that her reading audience is familiar with the main outline of her father's life, for by 1895 at least three biographies of Thackeray had already been published, she contributes a vision of his private self, as son, father, and friend. . . . Ritchie's autobiographical strategy, then, posits the subject as knowable only through its interactions with others, as part of a larger familial and historical framework. (70–71)

Like the texts of more self-conscious and introspective authors, Ritchie's *Chapters* and Mary (Mrs. Humphry) Ward's *A Writer's Recollections* (1918) situate their authors within a literary tradition, in these cases the paternal ones of Thackeray and the Arnolds, yet the tradition here is not the romantic one of individual genius, but that of the productive bourgeois family, and such writers certainly contributed to the hegemony of that social form. If public school memoirs provided a strong communal function that shaped boys' identities in afterlife, for many women, especially of the earlier period with fewer alternatives with which to identify, the family provided that structuring role. Corbett continues on Ward:

> Ward shapes her recollections as a documentary account of an era, and places her own work—she includes, for example, a whole chapter on the origins of *Robert Elsmere* (1888)—in a context that stretches from her grandfather's age to the time of writing, in the midst of the Great War. It is thus not an "inner drama" that Ward stages, but an external, historical, public one in which she plays a part; while she is able from her privileged position to convey an intimate view of important personages, she always remains, as it were, "in role," as daughter, niece, and wife. (72)

Within a broader historical frame, the everyday lives of male celebrities like Thackeray and the Arnolds as represented by women writers may stand as the meeting of the extraordinary and the everyday, the colonization of the public arena by (private) women writers by means of commodified private individuals (celebrities). Such a meeting marks the transition, by the end of the century, from a private bourgeois to a public mass society.

Let there be no mistake about the argument I am advancing about these women's subjectivity. The agonized history of Victorian middle-class women writers attempting to negotiate the demands of literary domesticity—as writer and homemaker—and the related history of middle-class women, officially confined to the private sphere, bringing their private lives into public discourse have been portrayed by feminist revisionists during the past two decades.[136] The material difficulties attending literary domesticity—a room, or as in Margaret Oliphant's *Autobiography* (1899), even a desk, of one's own—were nearly insurmountable.[137] Oliphant reluctantly conceded that bringing up fine boys and writing a fine novel were mutually exclusive (6–7, 125). Mary Howitt's *Autobiography* (1889) shows that for the woman compelled by economic necessity, writing was not a solace but an impediment to daily life and affections. Howitt writes guiltily of the death of her son: "How often did he beg and pray of me to put aside my translation just for that one day, that I might sit by him and talk or read to him! I, never thinking how near his end was, said, 'Oh no, I must go on yet a page or two.' How little did I think that in a short time I should have leisure enough and to spare!"[138]

My point is that women's anxiety concerning self-representation decreases in proportion to women's participation in other discourse, such as that of religion, family, or human rights, and increases in proportion to women's desire to participate in the male romantic tradition of autonomous genius. This is the case in part because women were *not* autonomous but were culturally and biologically at least as other-regarding as self-regarding, and in part because, male or female, the autonomous self continuously needs to be reconstituted in opposition to others lest it realize its nonexistence outside the realms of art. That this is the case is due to the nature of human intersubjectivity, perhaps especially due to the intersubjective nature of language (see the introduction section on *Subjectivity,* especially Scheman).

Now given its prevalent valorizing of the "creative imagination" or autonomous artistic self (the aesthetic counterpart of liberalism's abstract individual), feminist critics of literary domesticity have unsurprisingly but uncritically represented "female subjectivity" not by the text of a Christian moralist, a dutiful daughter of the bourgeoisie, or a militant suffragette, but rather by Elizabeth Barrett Browning's *Aurora Leigh* (1857), an epic lyric (i.e., a novel-length expression in verse of subjective desire) impossibly reconciling—or at least violently yoking—the romantic tradition of individual genius and Victorian femininity, the former, to adapt a phrase from Corbett, determinedly a- (or even pre-) social, and the latter socially determined. Other key texts of "female subjectivity" have been Charlotte Brontë's autobiographical *Villette* (1853) and *Jane Eyre: An Autobiography* (1847).

Similarly, the most recent *arriviste* in the autobiographical canon is Harriet Martineau, who determinedly remained unmarried pursuing her male-identified literary career in the Lake District, traditional enclave of romantic genius. Sanctioned in literature early in life by her brothers, Martineau never assumed the romantic opposition between literary inspiration and other kinds of labor, but she nonetheless, unlike Rhondda, balked at taking on the social responsibilities of an editorship, choosing to remain the individual author. To spell out these steps as recounted in Martineau's *Autobiography* (1877), first her oldest brother bestows upon her his imprimatur—one that distinguishes her from others of her sex who "darn stockings": "He then laid his hand on my shoulder, and said gravely (calling me 'dear' for the first time) 'Now, dear, leave it to other women to make shirts and darn stockings; and do you devote yourself to this.' I went home in a sort of dream, so that the squares of the pavement seemed to float before my eyes. That evening made me an authoress."[139] Second, as the most popular female literary practitioner since Frances Burney, Martineau repudiates the romantic myth of inspiration stimulated either by natural or artificial causes and, like Rhondda on corporate savoir faire, assures women readers that they can achieve literary productivity without the "stimulants and peculiar habits" associated with an aesthetic—especially a Romantic aesthetic—calling:

> I can speak, after long experience, without any doubt on this matter. I have suffered, like other writers, from indolence, irresolution, distaste to my work, absence of 'inspiration,' and all that: but I have also found that sitting down, however reluctantly, with the pen in my hand, I have never worked for one quarter of an hour without finding myself in full train.... When once experience had taught me that I could work when I chose, and within a quarter of an hour of my determining to do so, I was relieved, in a great measure, from those embarrassments and depressions which I see afflicting many an author who waits for a mood instead of summoning it, and is the sport, instead of the master, of his own impressions and ideas.... I have, without particular advantages of health and strength, done an unusual amount of work without fatal, perhaps without injurious consequences, and without the need of pernicious stimulants and peculiar habits. (I, 189–91)

Yet despite her strong sense of personal competence, Martineau declines the public responsibility entailed in an offer to edit "an Economical Magazine." She quotes from her diary entries during her deliberations:

> "It is an awful choice before me! Such facilities for usefulness and activity of knowledge; such certain toil and bondage; such risk of failure and descent from my position! The realities of life press upon me now. If I do this, I must brace myself up to do and suffer like a man. No more waywardness, precipitation, and reliance on allowance from others! Undertaking a man's duty, I must brave a man's fate. I must be prudent, independent, serene, good-humoured; earnest with cheerfulness. The possibility is open before me of showing what a periodical with a perfect temper may be:—also, of setting women forward at once into the rank of

men of business. But the hazards are great, I wonder how it will end." (II, 110)[140]

Contrary to the unanimous advice of three of her "intimate friends," Martineau's brother James advises her against the project and she returns to her fiction-writing. The differences between her afterthought "also, of setting women forward at once into the rank of men of business" and Rhondda's enthusiastic "I wanted to find, to test, and to spread the customs and the ideas that could be health-giving and life-saving" is not merely the progress of women's liberation from the mid-nineteenth to early twentieth centuries, but is also the difference between writing, and the self, conceived as a subjective desideratum (Aurora Leigh's, the romantic "genius's") and as an intersubjective project or commitment. These two possibilities are the subject of the final chapter.

6.

Literary Subjectivity
and Other Possibilities
in Some Classic Texts

> Some continuity of resistance being naturally of the essence of
> the subject.
>
> HENRY JAMES, *What Maisie Knew* (1907)

> Mrs. Webb's Life makes me compare it with mine. The dif-
> ference is that she is trying to relate all her experiences to
> history.
>
> VIRGINIA WOOLF, *Diary*, Vol. 3

> I am not of a subjective disposition.
>
> T. H. HUXLEY, diary of the voyage of the Rattlesnake

Literary Subjectivity

Between 1848 and 1860 many of the major Victorian novelists experi-
mented with autobiographical fiction. In Thackeray's *Pendennis* (1848–
1850), Dickens's *David Copperfield* (1849–1850) and later, revisionary,
Great Expectations (1860–1861), Brontë's *Villette* (1853), Trollope's *The
Three Clerks* (1858), Meredith's *Ordeal of Richard Feverel* (1859), and
Eliot's *The Mill on the Floss* (1860), the protagonists' identities unfold in
antagonistic relations with family, religion, and social role (often called
"duty" by the Victorians): this is to say no more than that the individual's
relation to society, or more specifically the relation of individual development to social institutions, was the great problem of Victorian realism,
as it was of Victorian social science. Scholars are only now beginning to

understand how the obsessive scientific pretension of Victorian realists (from the panoramic detail of a Balzac or Flaubert to the "psychological realism" of a Henry James) converged with the observational and statistical projects of sociologists in the modern attempt to comprehend the relation of self to society.[1]

A work of autobiographical fiction like *David Copperfield,* probably the most influential of those named (it was Freud's favorite novel), has certain similarities with the social exploration literature discussed in Chapter 3: it reveals a middle-class world in which the protagonist is under siege from hostile Others; the self is threatened and in danger of abjection. Little David is abused by the sadist Creakle at Salem House, his trunk is stolen on the way to his aunt's house, and his jacket is stolen by a demented pawnbroker. When he is a bachelor, his landlady steals from his cupboard. When he is a married man, his cook and page swindle and cheat his wife. David goes through youth in perpetual fear of humiliation at the hands of schoolboys and coachmen and with irrepressible disgust at others who are not the sons of gentlemen. What he calls his "attraction by repulsion" to Uriah Heep reflects this horror of the abyss of propertyless anonymity into which he should slip without his authorial genius, which is consolation, sinecure, and, above all, defense. His first exposure to literature is his father's books that "kept alive his fancy" during his brutal confinements by stepfather Murdstone. He uses his storytelling abilities to gain status (the attention of Steerforth and the boys at school), and his fortune and position as an author secure his domestic life with a woman (Agnes) "suitable in mind and purpose."

By the end of the epoch, the endangered subject in its antagonistic relations could be epitomized in D. H. Lawrence's autobiographical *Sons and Lovers* (1913). Yet the subjectivity that was in Dickens threatened by the positive loss of property or social status is elevated in Lawrence to a metaphysical struggle between "I" and "Thou." The identity of Paul Morel is continuously in the balance between self-assertion and autonomy, on the one hand, and an equal longing for dependency and union on the other—for merging with cultured mother, with earthy and elemental father and Baxter Dawes, with intellectual Miriam, and with sensual Clara. Paul is fascinated by the otherness of workers and women, who are never threatened by their environment, but he equally fears that they, like his own mother, may threaten to engulf him. We have seen similar fears in working-class autobiography: fears of submerging and losing the self in the mass (see chapter 4). The only place that Lawrence deviates from his compulsive and passionate fear of, and longing for, others is in the utopian role Paul envisions for his art, which is, surprisingly, an *applied* art of human interconnectedness, diversity, and democracy—the antithesis of Lawrencian fears of engulfment. In Chapter 12, entitled "Passion," Paul suppresses his fears concerning his mother's desire for him to be an artist, reconciles the bifurcation between mental and manual labor that divides his parents, reconciles his "work" as an artist with the "labor" of economic survival, and cultivates social inclusivity.[2]

Only James fully transforms the subject of resistance into the subject of transcendence. In antagonistic relation with a thoroughly nasty and overwhelmingly familial world, Maisie resists "the strain of observation and the assault of experience" with an apparently uncontingent and inalienable self—a self that can live with the impassivity of the work of art, a subjectivity that is inherent rather than developed. James calls it the "wonder" of the autonomous self:

> This was the quite different question of the particular kind of truth of resistance I might be able to impute to my central figure—*some* intensity, some continuity of resistance being naturally of the essence of the subject. Successfully to resist (to resist, that is, the strain of observation and the assault of experience) what would that be, on the part of so young a persona, but to remain fresh, and still fresh, and to have even a freshness to communicate?—the case being with Maisie to the end that she treats her friends to the rich little spectacle of objects embalmed in her wonder.[3]

In *What Maisie Knew* (1907), what the implied author and the reader "know" converges ironically with Maisie's less sophisticated knowledge so that the convergence of author, reader, and protagonist reproduces the type of the self-congratulatory subject resistant to the corrupt society that has irrationally, or perhaps dialectically, given it birth. The solitary and contemplative nature of bourgeois writing practices reproduced such a practice of reading—of authorial and readerly identification and self-reflection. The social role of "the artist," as well as her subjective identity, that reached its culmination in literary modernism was typified by this particular economy of the resistant self, its privacy, internality, and dream of autonomy from circumstance—in brief, the objectification in literature of a self that displaced a hitherto religious soul.

In the previous chapter I cited May Sinclair's musings upon this antagonistic internalized self in *Mary Olivier:*

> Your self? Your self? Why should you forget it? You had to remember. They would kill it if you let them. What had it done? What *was* it that

they should hate it so? . . . Would it always have to stoop and cringe before
people, hushing its own voice, hiding its own gesture? It crouched now,
stung and beaten, hiding in her body that walked beside her mother with
proud feet, and small lifted head.

Whereas theorists of literacy like Walter Ong have posited a literate "consciousness" that separates the knower from the known (recorded knowledge, history, etc.), and the self from others, I am arguing that this objectifying of otherness and internalizing of the self are not necessary
concomitants of literacy per se but rather of the kinds of literacy that we
have come to value according to the epistemological, psychological, and
institutional systems that gave it rise.[4] Following Jack Goody and Ian
Watt, Ong believes that writing makes possible increasingly articulate
introspection that opens the psyche not only to the external objective
world, the world of recorded time, distinct from the self, but also to an
interior world of the self. This introspective aspect of literacy is not evident in most of the works discussed in this study, but it appears in the
works discussed in this chapter. My two-part contention, presented
through a sequence of examples, is that whereas most of these authors
have experienced the effects of literacy that Ong describes, some (the first
part) have made the resistant introspective self central to their practice of
writing and others (the second part) have resisted that resisting self for
more cooperative, or even collaborative, subjectivities. Although introspection and its concomitant objectification of Others against oneself,
key components of literary subjectivity, may be treated as an inheritance
from philosophical Cartesianism, literary Romanticism, or Protestant
individualism, I shall instead focus upon the institutional apparatuses of
Church, family, and school or State against which in the Victorian period
"the self" formed and opposed itself. Thus I will propose an idyll of the
bourgeois literary "I," from its place in grammar to its place in society.
More broadly, I will explore the modern literary personality, what Marcuse called the *sublimated artist,* who in magnificent alienation says no
to society, and then contextualize it with other possible relations of self
to society.[5]

Throughout my discussion of these texts, my focus will be, as is customary in this study, on how each author represents the "I" of the life,
whether in fictional form as in Butler or White, or self-consciously unself-
conscious as in Darwin, Ruskin, or Webb. The significance of the analyses is less the individual readings of the authors, on most of whom there

exists large bodies of criticism, than their comparative juxtaposition. This juxtaposition sheds light upon the participatory and antagonistic values of scientific, humanistic, and literary discourse; the deployment of these discourses with respect to differentials in class and gender status; and the significance of both public discourse and authorial status to the subjectivities of the classic autobiographers.

As Victorianists know, the so-called private lives of these Victorian celebrities deviate liberally from any rigid norm of the middle-class sex-gender system. John Mill and Harriet Taylor write, converse, and even travel together for twenty years under the patient gaze of Harriet's Unitarian husband John. The most filial of sons, Ruskin, and his wife Euphemia never consummate their marriage and reside mostly with their respective parents, yet Ruskin offers to give evidence of potency in the court of annulment and goes on to write *Sesame and Lilies* (1865), which establishes him as an authority on women. George Eliot's ample income supports George Henry Lewes's wife and children by another man. Samuel Butler writes the least magnanimous exposé of his parents in family history, then offers himself for merciless exploitation at the hands of young men. These lives, profoundly fascinating in their diversity, have been narrated by great biographers and critics. My subject here is not those narratives but rather the writers' own articulations, which may not include such "facts," or which may transform them.[6]

One final caveat. I have tried to be sympathetic to the subjective demands of these authors while remaining conscious of the critical frame imposed by the comparative nature of this study. Perry Anderson has written of the legacy of the Webbs, "No more poisoned legacy could have been left the working-class movement. Complacent confusion of influence with power, bovine admiration for bureaucracy, ill-concealed contempt for equality, bottomless philistinism—all the characteristic narrowness of the Webbs and their associates became imprinted on the dominant ideology of the Labour Party thereafter."[7] Although I am inclined to agree with Anderson on the negativity of Webb's influence vis-à-vis labor politics, I am equally inclined to understand her articulation in her autobiography not so much as for the working class as against her own, the capitalist class and—something that Anderson did not sufficiently register when he wrote the preceding lines—its gender roles. Similarly, Ruskin and Huxley make the kind of claims for "Objective" knowledge that feminist critics like Teresa de Lauretis and Nancy K. Miller have marked as possible only for strong male subjects, who, despite their protests to the contrary, could not help but enjoy the privileges of their gender and class.[8] That is, such arguments go, communitarianism comes cheaply to those who already have a strong, authoritative self and do not need to struggle to assert it; or, as Miller says, explaining the consequences for women of the Foucauldian banishing of the authorial signature, only those who have the signature can play with not having it. These critiques are legitimate. Surely for anyone who has the slightest familiarity with the history of modern science and political theory in Britain, there is no question but that the authors of works with such titles as *The Wealth of Nations, Principles of Political Economy,* or *The Origin of Species* little doubted their own centrality in world history. My own readers may judge the relative values of communitarianism versus individualism in the autobiographies that follow. These texts and judgments of them are not written in stone but produced, reproduced, and differently interpreted through history. Here I try to situate them in relation to the field of tensions, "private" and "public," they have invoked.

FROM HUGHES TO CONNOLLY, ORWELL, SINCLAIR, AND WHITE

Because the literary "I" was constructed in opposition to its external roles, I shall begin with an early role against which it was articulated. *Tom Brown's Schooldays* (1857) begins in a nonstructured, relatively democratic, "storytelling" Home environment in the Vale of the White Horse in Berkshire, where the "I" is centered, loved, and fed ("To Penshurst" again). Despite the intermingling of classes and the assertion that boys "play without the idea of equality or inequality," Tom is "the young master" at the fair, laden with attention, love, and commodities: "And elders come up from all parts salute Benjy, and girls who have been Madam's pupils to kiss Master Tom. And they carry him off to load him with fairings; and he returns to Benjy, his hat and coat covered with ribbons, and his pockets crammed with wonderful boxes which open upon ever new boxes and boxes, and popguns and trumpets, and apples, and gilt gingerbread from the stall of Angel Heavens."[9] In this world of plenitude and wealth ("There was more gold on Angel's cakes than there is ginger in those of this degenerate age" [41]), Tom's nurse is Charity Lamb and his favorite mates in childhood (as he is weaned from women) are seventy- and ninety-years old, respectively.

Tom sees the last of this imaginary, undifferentiated self his first morning at Rugby, where he must abandon the submerged preconscious state for his role within a social hierarchy, in which the "I" is essentially public and the poor no longer have delectable and gracious names like Angel Heavens and Charity Lamb but rather the "generic names" of servants facilitating their accommodation to "Master Tom": "Everybody, I suppose, knows the dreamy delicious state in which one lies half asleep, half awake, while consciousness begins to return. . . . After which time, the stupid, obtrusive, wakeful entity which we call 'I,' as impatient as he is stiff-necked, spite of our teeth will force himself back again, and take possession of us down to our very toes" (120). At this point a worker enters to recall Tom to consciousness of his social role: "It was in this state that Master Tom lay at half-past seven on the morning following the day of his arrival, and from his clean little white bed watched the movements of Bogle (the generic name by which the successive shoe-blacks of the School-house were known), as he marched round from bed to bed" (120).

Tom Brown learns his place in the hierarchy of school under the manipulative eye of the Doctor and through a sequence of experiences with didactic friends evidently enrolled to teach him lessons: effeminate little Arthur teaches him to nurture; East represents a struggle with his undisciplined alter ego; Flashman represents unscrupulous rivalry and competition; Slogger Williams represents healthy fair play; and Martin the scientist teaches him discipline and discrimination, patience, and tolerance. The Doctor himself additionally ensures Tom's place in Eternity.

Continually surveilled by the Doctor—"They began to come under his notice . . . his eye, which was everywhere, was upon them" (168)—Tom and East conform to his expectations. Like God's, the Doctor's expectations for the boys—the reformation, in fact, of the British public schools—fills the self, leaving no room for an antagonistic alterity. Hughes represents it as a totalitarian takeover: "The Doctor's victory was complete from that moment . . . [Tom] gave way at all points, and the enemy marched right over him, cavalry, infantry, and artillery, the land transport corps, and the camp followers. It had taken eight long years to do it, but now it was done thoroughly, and there wasn't a corner of him left which didn't believe in the Doctor. . . . He marched down to the School-house, a hero-worshipper, who would have satisfied the soul of Thomas Carlyle himself" (298).

When the Doctor dies, Hughes, with a spirited transition—"well, well!"—renders his function explicit: that Tom had to learn to submit to the Doctor so he could learn to submit to God. There is little Arnoldian longing for father here. Hughes briskly installs manly Christian faith:

It was the first great wrench of his life, the first gap which the angel Death had made in his circle, and he felt numbed, and beaten down, and spiritless. Well, well! I believe it was good for him and for many others in like case; who had to learn by that loss, that the soul of man cannot stand or lean upon any human prop, however strong, and wise, and good; but that He upon whom alone it can stand and lean will knock away all such props in His own wise and merciful way, until there is no ground or stay left but Himself, the Rock of Ages, upon whom alone a sure foundation for every soul of man is laid. . . . Such stages have to be gone through, I believe, by all young and brave souls, who must win their way through hero-worship to the worship of Him who is the King and Lord of heroes. (301, 306)

Tom Brown assumes his identity without antagonism. One cannot say that he suppresses his subjectivity in order to submit to the Doctor/God, because there is no subject independent of that submission. I shall only mention here, because it will be important later, that writing does not play a prominent part in Tom Brown's schoolday. Nor does he keep a diary. For later authors in rebellion against institutional roles, writing well was the best revenge.

Tom Brown's maturation is a purely external affair, a literary potlatch of ideology and sociopolitical technique, and Thomas Hughes's fictive memoir maps the superstructure of an entire culture. Eighty years later, Connolly's *A Georgian Boyhood* (1938) deals in Culture in the limited sense, abandoning the panoramic "realism" of *Tom Brown's Schooldays* for the introspective psychodrama of a clique. Society is superceded by Connolly's subjective perception, his subjectivity. At the outset, Connolly states his intention in writing the story of his youth as his desire to "disrobe," to relinquish the "fictions" of social privilege, stature, superiority, judgment, authority, and infallibility that he has assumed as a literary critic in order to lay bare the "illusions common to our class, our race, our time" informing the judgments of his criticism.[10] The first sentence formulates the theme of Connolly's life, his struggle between a "self" and a social role: "I have always disliked myself at any given moment; the total of such moments is my life" (143). This grammatical division between subject and object, inner self as object and external identity as subject—the objectification and internalization, in Ong's terms, of a "self"—is duplicated throughout literary subjectivity. Connolly traces the bifurcation of the "I" to his desire to be an aristocrat, to be associated with relations in Ireland rather than middle-class scholarship boys like himself at Eton. Seeing his status so incommensurate with his longing— "There were evenings when I wanted to kill myself because I was not the

O'Grady of Killballyowen. Why had not my father got a title? Why was I not the heir to Castletown? It was heartless, anguishing—why be born, why live at all if I could not have one?" (158)—he internalizes and aestheticizes a space for desire, independent of status, and externally (i.e., in his public role) reduces to absurdity emotional risks with others.

In highly stratified social spaces like his prep school and Eton, the vulnerability Connolly risks in exposing himself to others is reduced to a "favour chart" like the one he keeps for the headmaster's wife: "At that time I used to keep a favour chart in which, week by week, I would graph my position at her court. I remember my joy as the upward curve continued, and as I began to make friends, win prizes, enjoy riding and succeed again at trying to be funny. The favour charts I kept for several terms; one's favour began at the top and then went downwards as term wore on and tempers" (162). Human interdependence is thus reduced to a sequence of formal exercises in the maintenance of a rigidly stratified emotional economy.

Everything follows from this parody/reduction. For Connolly identity is not a fluid process of exchange with others, a process of risk and change, but rather a fixed commodity to be jealously guarded, as rigid as the school "character" he resisted: "In a flash it came to me that my name and myself were something apart, something that none of the other boys were or could be, Cyril Vernon Connolly, a kind of divine 'I am that I am' which I should carry all through life and at last deposit on my grave, like a retriever with a bit of stick" (150). Because Connolly takes no risks with others, his passions have little to do with others' responses to him. Merely the obsessions of his own mind, they are represented, again, in figures of a dogged mechanicalism: "Love was an ideal based on the exhibitionism of the only-child. It meant a desire to lay my personality at someone's feet as a puppy deposits a slobbery ball' (190). Unlike Tom Brown's friends, who function dynamically in the developmental narrative, Connolly's are aethesticized as picturesque types: "the Faun, the Redhead, the Extreme Blonde and the Dark Friend" (169–70).

The tension between social role and desire that differentiates one's identity from one's self is also the theme of Orwell's "Such, Such Were the Joys": "I could not control my subjective feelings, and I could not conceal them from myself."[11] Orwell cultivates a subjective resistance to the external "objective" system of social roles.

> I did not question the prevailing standards, because so far as I could see there were no others. How could the rich, the strong, the elegant, the fash-

ionable, the powerful, be in the wrong? It was their world, and the rules
they made for it must be the right ones. And yet from a very early age I
was aware of the impossibility of any *subjective* conformity. Always at the
centre of my heart the inner self seemed to be awake, pointing out the
difference between the moral obligation and the psychological *fact*. It was
the same in all matters, worldly or other-worldly. Take religion, for
instance. You were supposed to love God, and I did not question this. Till
the age of about fourteen I believed in God, and believed that the accounts
given of him were true. But I was well aware that I did not love him. On
the contrary, I hated him, just as I hated Jesus and the Hebrew patriarchs.
If I had sympathetic feelings towards any character in the Old Testament,
it was towards such people as Cain, Jezebel, Haman, Agag, Sisera: in the
New Testament my friends, if any, were Ananias, Caiaphas, Judas and
Pontius Pilate. (360, Orwell's italics)

Orwell finally accepts the standards as a power game, *and* he accepts their
antagonistic counterpart as the self. Unlike Connolly, he went on to resist
the fixed hierarchical relations of the school and society in general by
taking risks with, and for, others (i.e., fighting Fascism in the Spanish
Civil War). Orwell further rejected Connolly's picturesque and static psychodrama for the participatory discourse of politics. He attributed his
success as a writer to his rejection of Connolly's fetishism of "purple
patches" and solipsism: "It is invariably where I lacked a *political* purpose [defined as "the desire to push the world in a certain direction"] that
I wrote lifeless books and was betrayed into purple passages, sentences
without meaning, decorative adjectives and humbug generally."[12] (Connolly had described his education in poetry, "The best poems have the
most beautiful lines in them ... they are purple patches. ... When you
come to a purple patch you can tell it by an alarm clock going off, you
feel a cold shiver, a lump in the throat, your eyes fill with tears and your
hair stands on end. ... Poetry is something to be ashamed of, like sex"
[167].) As Orwell's "Why I Write" bears witness, writing was for Orwell,
as for many earlier writers from Dickens to Oscar Wilde in his autobiographical *De Profundis* (1897), the space for the individual's revenge
against the system.[13] With their tendency to cultivate an increasingly
articulate introspection that objectifies the external world against the self
that opposes it, diaries are prohibited in *Nineteen Eighty-Four*.[14]

In Antonia White's *Frost in May* (1933) the institutional Other
against which the self is articulated is Roman Catholicism, which
"loomed," in one of White's most beautiful images, "in the background,
like Fuji Yama in a Japanese print, massive, terrifying, beautiful and

unescapable."[15] It is reminiscent of Tom Brown's "the enemy marched right over him, cavalry, infantry, and artillery. . . . There wasn't a corner of him left which didn't believe." Moreover, in resisting the Church, White's autobiographical protagonist Nanda also has to resist the class system at Lippington School. Catholic "character" can only be maintained by rejecting expendable girls and thus maintaining Catholic exclusivity. The seeds of Nanda's resistance are planted with the expulsion of a friend from the school: "A small core of rebelliousness which had been growing secretly for four years seemed to have hardened inside her" (156). Ultimately Nanda herself, a mere convert to Catholicism, is as expendable as her poor and deficient friend. The impoverished and converted are precisely the expendable sorts whose expulsion reinforces the selectivity of the old aristocratic Catholics whom Lippington cultivates and who in turn maintain the social value of the school. Nanda's opposition to religious and class domination expresses a failure to conform to an external identity as well as the internalized creation of an adversarial "self" henceforth to be associated with aesthetics. For it is Nanda's clandestine novel-writing, like Winston Smith's keeping of a diary—private practices antagonistic to the public codes of Lippington and Big Brother—that causes her final expulsion from the school. As Joyce showed in *Portrait of the Artist as a Young Man* (1916), and as Protestants had always claimed, Roman Catholicism, like Big Brother, forbids the cultivation of a private self. Hence the representation of Catholicism in such cultures as the totalitarian takeover of the self by the institution. Indeed, in High Church British Protestantism, Catholicism is often represented in terms that would later describe communism-as-Stalinism—as a threat to individual liberty.

Yet the private self and artistic sublimation cultivated in Nanda's novel-writing are not conducive to her reentry into the everyday world of trade. This subjective isolation precisely duplicates the lesson of the tragic schoolboys. After expulsion from Lippington Nanda is sent by her father to "a really good High School" where she, having failed to become (i.e., *be*) a Catholic, must *learn* a trade. Lippington's exclusivity revealed that one was or was not a Catholic; one could not learn it. Nanda reacts by making the sensibility of the artist as essential and inalienable as the essence of Catholicism. After Lippington, being an artist was Nanda's fixed identity, regardless of the processes of life: "The bluff, breezy air of that 'really good High School' would kill her. . . . She felt finally she could only live in [Lippington's] rare, intense element" (176). Artistic sublimation apparently took an equally great toll on the henceforth mentally "unstable" Antonia White.[16] *As Once in May* thematizes White's contempt for "dull everyday life" (Lewis Carroll's "dull reality" at the end of the *Alice* books, Virginia Woolf's "cheapness of reality" in "Mr. Bennett and Mrs. Brown"), and her agonized struggle to perfect a style as evocative of details and intensely personal as her subjective memories of school.

Connolly's "something apart . . . a kind of divine I am that I am," Orwell's "inner self," and White's "small core of rebellion" represent a refined literary subjectivity or the artistic sublimation of modernism as exemplified in autobiography. Horrified by this "alienation" of the artist, this retreat into "personality," Lawrence Durrell would proclaim that "the artist became an autist . . . a Selfist."[17] To conclude this section on subjectivity in modern literary writers, I turn to two more detailed examples of classic Victorian literary "selves" constructed in opposition to institutional roles.

SAMUEL BUTLER, 1835–1902

Written as autobiographical fiction from 1873 to 1878, while Samuel Butler devoted himself to painting, music, and writing, *The Way of All Flesh: A Story of English Domestic Life* was published posthumously in 1903.[18] Here the bifurcation of self and social role is not confined to a private "I" that scrutinizes its public role, but is instead projected into the relationship of a rebellious and vulnerable young man to an older complacent and invulnerable one. Writing from the point of view of an avuncular older Butler called Overton about the life and history of a younger "Ernest" Butler, Butler avenges his childhood and youth, allegedly wasted at the hands of family and Church, in the strongest indictment of the bourgeois family system that the Victorians produced. Ernest's, Overton's, and the implied author's voices converge in Ernest's rejection of parents, wife, and children and his consequent success as a forty-seven-year-old unattached bachelor worth £140,000 who enlists the sum in propagating his hostile views on "marriage and the family system" (357). The survivor of this system, determined by his resistance to it, has shed not only passion but social relations altogether (with the striking exception of Overton, or Butler's adult self). The obsessive self-absorption implied in the splitting of the "I" into author (Butler), narrator (Overton), and character (Ernest) was matched only by the obsessive self-analysis of Butler's diaries. In *The Way of All Flesh* the author Butler obsessively reconstructs his blighted youth, commenting on it from the sterile perspective of the narrator Overton, whom he feared he had become.

For Ernest Pontifex, the family is more oppressive than the school. At the university, Theobald Pontifex treats Ernest as his own father had treated him, forcing his ordination and manipulating his relationships with others. Ernest's mother Christina encourages his bringing friends home so they might marry his sister and "liked tearing them to pieces and flinging the bits over Ernest as soon as she had had enough of them" (197). Thus Ernest's closest bond is his schoolfriend Towneley, "to whom Fortune had taken a fancy all round: He was good at cricket and boating, very good-natured, singularly free from conceit, not clever but very sensible, and, lastly, his father and mother had been drowned by the overturning of a boat when he was only two years old" (199). *The Way of All Flesh* represents the male version of Florence Nightingale's desire to be orphaned, to be free from the determinism—in Butler's Lamarckian view, evolutionary biological determinism—of the patriarchal system.

Ernest's goal is to shed his parents. In prison for confusing a respectable woman with a prostitute (Butler's ironic comment on bourgeois respectability), Ernest is told of two visitors waiting to see him: "His heart fell, for he guessed who they were, but he screwed up his courage and hastened to the receiving room. There, sure enough, standing at the end of the table nearest the door were the two people whom he regarded as the most dangerous enemies he had in all the world—his father and mother" (279). His parents do die, and Ernest's own rebellious and disastrous marriage to a working-class alcoholic is invalidated with the help of her former husband and Overton.

The episode of Ellen, Ernest's wife and family's former servant, demonstrates Ernest's innate superiority to her class and gender—the impossibility, despite his resistance to his own class, of his ever really sinking into the lower orders. Overton's running commentary on the impetuous alliance reiterates a bachelor's homosocial condescension: "I never have heard of any young man to whom I had become attached was going to get married without hating his intended instinctively, though I had never seen her" (292); "Of course [Ellen and I] hated one another instinctively from the first moment we set eyes on one another" (294); "A man's friendships are, like his will, invalidated by marriage—but they are not less invalidated by the marriage of his friends. . . . As soon as I found that he no longer liked his wife, I forgave him at once, and was as much interested in him as ever" (310). By manipulating their domestic arrangements, Overton ensures that Ernest never actually *lives* like a working man: "If he had been left to himself he would have lived with Ellen in the shop, back parlour, and kitchen, and have let out both the upper floors according to his original programme. I did not want him, however, to cut himself adrift from music, letters, and polite life, and feared that unless he had some kind of den into which he could retire he would ere long become 'the tradesman and nothing else'" (296). Butler then manipulates the plot, as Overton manipulates the domicile, so that Ellen also reveals the innate tendencies of her class: alcoholism, vile companions, and insensibility toward her children. With these developments, Ernest seems "to sink once and for all into the small shopkeeper . . . going his daily rounds, buying second-hand clothes, and spending his evenings in cleaning and mending them" (312).

Overton also imputes to Ellen emotional shallowness and opportunism, as he considers bribing her to run away with somebody else in order to liberate her despairing husband. Ultimately she is revealed to have similarly snared an earlier husband and Ernest is magically unmarried. Ellen accepts their disalliance with equilibrium and a pound a week severance, eventually, like many of the characters discussed in Chapter 3, emigrating to America with a "butcher's man" who occasionally beats her. Her final words to Ernest and the reader confirm their moral superiority, their distinction: "What us poor girls want is not to be jumped up all of a sudden and made honest women of; this is too much for us and throws us off our perch; what we wants is a regular friend or two, who'll just keep us from starving, and force us to be good for a bit together now and again. That's about as much as we can stand. [You] may have the children" (316). The episode with Ellen thus ensures that class and gender distinctions are maintained, even in a work outspokenly critical of the status quo.

When Ernest comes into his fortune, Overton is pleased that "he'll never marry again" (338). Believing that he will doom his own children as his father had done before him, Ernest abandons his son and daughter to a good working-class couple in the country, and his son grows up "without a spark of any literary ability" (369)—literary ability being the upper-class consequence of repression of feelings of hatred of one's family.

After his emotional trauma at the hands of parents and wife, Ernest retires on a large income into economics and philosophy, never risking himself again in human relationships (i.e., becoming Overton). Samuel Butler retired on a large income (inherited from his father) into art, music, and literature, turning his attention in his last years to Shakespeare and Homer. Far from Disraeli's domestic haven for genius, Butler rebels against the family and dispenses with intimacy altogether, substituting the connoisseurship of literature on the income of a single man. In a guilt-ridden sonnet sequence written to a saintly woman who had probably loved him, but after her death, Butler displays the cost in human feeling—the callousness—that had been exacted from him:

> For she was plain and lame and fat and short,
> Forty and over-kind. Hence it befell
> That though I loved her in a certain sort,
> Yet did I love too wisely but not well.[19]

In the third sonnet in the sequence he was more honest about her deficiencies:

> Had I been some young sailor, continent
> Perforce three weeks and then well plied with wine,
> I might in time have tried to yield consent
> And almost (though I doubt it) made her mine.
>   . . . .
> Or had she only been content to crave
> A marriage of true minds, her wish was granted;
> My mind was hers, I was her willing slave
> In all things else except the one she wanted:
> And here, alas! at any rate to me
> She was an all too, too impossible she.

Although neither his companion and biographer Henry Festing Jones nor later scholars have doubted the autobiographical content of *The Way of All Flesh,* Ernest/Overton is not a complete portrait of the artist. Butler's letters, autobiographical fragments, and photography indicate that he did maintain personal relationships not only with the unrequited Miss Savage (the "too, too impossible she") and one "Madame," but also with select male friends; that he had been prepared at least to abandon his inheritance for Art (his New Zealand fortune is always presented as if he acquired it in a fit of absence of mind); and that he had a vision of Utopian (or erewhonian) artistic communities as alternative to Ernest's isolation. Butler spent his youth seeking self-expression in literature, painting, and music for a self that he felt had been alienated—in fact denied him—by Victorian familialism. In his notebooks he analyzes his *ressentiment* as a consequence of paternally inflicted wounds that left him the opposite of all he admired, so that in later life he was at the mercy of men of better looks, charm, ease of manner, good breeding, and self-confidence—all qualities he thought he lacked. Unable to express these, his dearest relationships, in his work, he minimized his human contact in the bachelor Ernest and a relentless document of antagonism. Within his understanding of evolution (inheritance of acquired characteristics), the institutions of Church and family he indicted in *The Way of All Flesh: A Story of English Domestic Life* could not be changed; they had to be endured. Ernest's disengagement at the novel's conclusion prefigured for many the alienated artists of modernism. "Samuel Butler, who had lived below stairs," wrote Virginia Woolf coolly in "Mr. Bennett and Mrs. Brown," "Came out, like an observant bootboy, with the family secrets in *The Way of All Flesh.* It appeared that . . . the social state was a mass of corruption."[20] What was particularly "modern" in his fictive autobiography was Butler's reflexivity—that he reacted to the "corruption" with a relentless self-analysis of how he had come to be himself in opposition to it.

EDMUND GOSSE, 1849–1928

Edmund Gosse published *Father and Son: A Study of Two Temperaments* anonymously in 1907, calling it "not an autobiography" as it only dealt with his childhood and youth up to his break with his father, but rather "the record of a struggle between two temperaments, two consciences and almost two epochs": from this struggle, a poet-critic emerges.[21] With his wife Emily, a well-known writer of popular religious tracts, Philip Henry Gosse "dedicated" his son at birth to God in one of the strictest Puritan sects, the Plymouth Brethren. *Father and Son* represents the tragicomic sequence of disillusionments that led to Gosse's final rupture with his father, the liberation of his "self," and his substitution of religion by imaginative literature, a language antithetical to both his father's literalist regard for the Bible and his empirical work in marine biology. "Of the two human beings here described," Gosse writes in the first paragraph, "one was born to fly backward, the other could not help being carried forward. There came a time when neither spoke the same language as the other, or encompassed the same hopes, or was fortified by the same desires" (9).

In *The Use of Pleasure* Foucault distinguishes between a classical Greek ethics, which he characterizes as an elaboration of exercises through certain objective activities, the failure to perform which is expressed as shame, and a Judeo-Christian system of self-decipherment, or internal scrutiny of the desires of one's heart in the face of one's God, in which failure is expressed as guilt.[22] *Father and Son* is an example of the latter. In the few instances in which Gosse is with others in his child-hood—his first contact with a child his own age is at the age of ten (125)—he undergoes a sort of euphoric self-submersion and subsequently cannot remember anything of the experience. The self and its distinct memories appear only in moments of desire, or lack, or in moments of total isolation: "Once more I have to record the fact, which I think is not without interest, that precisely as my life ceases to be solitary, it ceases to be distinct. I have no difficulty in recalling, with the minuteness of a pho-tograph, scenes in which my Father and I were the sole actors within the four walls of a room, but of the glorious life among wild boys on the margin of the sea I have nothing but vague and broken impressions, deli-cious and elusive" (176). For a schoolboy such scenes on the beach would be depicted and cherished for a lifetime, but for Gosse, as for Butler, the family far outweighs the social networks of the school. To be a member of a community at all, to go to school, for Gosse was an act of disobedi-ence to his father (214), and his is the self constituted by its disobedience (Foucault's Judeo-Christianity) rather than the self constituted by its community (Foucault's Hellenism). In fact, it is the self constituted by its Christian "confession"—confession, whether to priest or analyst, being, for Foucault, the master narrative of modern Western subjectivity.

Gosse's "consciousness of self" (32) (the opposite of Tom Brown's complete identification with the Doctor's expectations for him) is pro-duced through this separation from his father. It comes to him first through the recognition that his father is not omniscient, the repressed knowledge of which provides "a secret in this world and it belonged to me and to somebody who lived in the same body with me. There were two of us, and we could talk with one another" (35). Recognition of his father's lack of omniscience derives from two externally trivial events, the first of which he recounts as, "One morning in my sixth year, my Mother and I were alone in the morning-room, when my Father came in and announced some fact to us. I was standing on the rug, gazing at him, and when he made this statement, I remember turning quickly, in embar-rassment, and looking into the fire. The shock to me was as that of a thunderbolt, for what my Father had said 'was not true'" (33). For con-firmation, the boy tests his father by lying to him and is not found out (45). Through a series of such negative epiphanies, in which the world does not correspond to his father's words, the son eventually relinquishes his belief in his father's authority and then in his father's religion itself (45, 232).

This distance between the ideology and the experience is registered stylistically for the (nonfundamentalist) reader in the ironic distance between the father's fanatic behavior and the triviality of the experiences ostensibly eliciting it—a distance mediated by the child's perspective. Eating a small piece of plum-pudding on Christmas is called "accursed idolatry" (95). Reacting to the frightened child's outcry at an insect during prayers, the father instructs, "If your heart were fixed, if it panted after the Lord, it would take more than the movements of a beetle to make you disturb oral supplication at His footstool. Beware! for God is a jealous God and He consumes them in wrath who make a noise like a dog" (121). Seeing his first picture of sculpture at the age of thirteen, Gosse asks his father about Greek mythology: "He said that the so-called gods of the Greeks were the shadows cast by the vices of the heathen, and reflected their infamous lives; it was for such things as these that God poured down brimstone and fire on the cities of the Plain, and there is nothing in the legends of these gods, or rather devils, that it is not better for a Christian not to know" (198). Tucking his son in at night, the father would say "with a sparkling rapture in his eyes, 'Who knows? We may meet next in the air, with all the cohorts of God's saints!' . . . I proposed at the end of the summer holidays that I should stay at home. 'What is the use of my going to school? Let me be with you when we rise to meet the Lord in the air!'" (229–30). His father interrogates him as a young man by post to London on the security of his teachings: "Was I walking closely with God? Was my sense of the efficacy of the Atonement clear and sound? Had the Holy Scriptures still their full authority with me? My replies on this occasion were violent and hysterical" (247).

Gosse the father's religion is as potently pervasive as Sinclair's "net" of heredity ("You were caught in the net; you couldn't get out"), Orwell's "boot stamping on a human face—forever," White's Mt. Fuji of Catholicism and Hughes's cavalry, infantry, and artillery of Rugby. The son writes, "I felt like a small and solitary bird, caught and hung out hopelessly and endlessly in a great glittering cage. . . . I saw myself imprisoned for ever in the religious system which had caught me and would whirl my helpless spirit as in the concentric wheels of my nightly vision" (157). Like Orwell's consciousness of his subjective duality—"I was aware of the impossibility of any *subjective* conformity. Always at the center of my heart the inner self seemed to be awake, pointing out the difference between the moral obligation and the psychological *fact*"—Gosse recognizes his inability to identify with his role as his father's son: "I cannot recall anything but an intellectual surrender; there was never joy in the act of resignation, never the mystic's rapture at feeling his phantom self, his own threadbare soul, suffused, thrilled through, robed again in glory by a fire which burns up everything personal and individual about him" (158). Instead, he produces a "hard nut of individuality" impervious to the onslaught of experience, like Orwell's "inner self," Connolly's "something apart . . . a kind of divine I am that I am," and White's "small core of rebelliousness." He expresses this resistant and internalized self as "the existence of two in the depths who could speak to one another in inviolable secrecy":

> Through thick and thin I clung to a hard nut of individuality, deep down in my childish nature. To the pressure from without, I resigned everything else, my thoughts, my words, my anticipations, my assurances, but there was something which I never resigned, my innate and persistent self. Meek as I seemed, and gently respondent, I was always conscious of that innermost quality which I had learned to recognize in my earlier days in Islington, that existence of two in the depths who could speak to one another in inviolable secrecy. (ibid.)

"Meek as I seemed"—the objectifying of hostile Others against a defensive subjectivity preceded Orwell's more antagonistic "whatever one did, one's only true feeling was hatred."

When Gosse is forced by his father to choose between his subjective and religious role, he interprets the dilemma as "ceasing to think for himself" or "confirming his individualism" (250). In the last sentence he chooses: "It was a case of 'Everything or Nothing'; and thus desperately challenged, the young man's conscience threw off once for all the yoke of his 'dedication,' and, as respectfully as he could, without parade or remonstrance, he took a human being's privilege to fashion his inner life for himself" (ibid.). In fashioning his inner life for himself, or claiming his "privilege" of autonomy, Gosse assumed the role of spokesperson for ("critic" of) imaginative literature, writing, among his best known works, the biography of the highly imaginative, anticlerical, and antibourgeois Charles Algernon Swinburne and introducing to the English-speaking world Henrik Ibsen, the fashioner of characters whose identifying characteristic was a brooding self-knowledge that they lived only through their dreams.

Yet, as with Butler, the rebellious subject reacting against Victorian institutions of church and family does not reject *all* the institutional supports of social identity. Throughout *Father and Son* Gosse distinguishes himself not only from his father but also from the "peasants" of his father's Devonshire congregation. He not only possesses a refined literary "taste," but also an apparently innate repugnance to the persons and pursuits of the lower classes. He is "deeply affronted" when his governess (like Jane Eyre) aspires (unsuccessfully) to marry his father (173). As a child, he "dreaded and loathed" the smells of workers' cottages, "including feminine odours, masquerading as you knew not what, in which penny whiffs, vials of balm and opoponax, seemed to have become tainted vaguely, with the residue of the slop-pail" (107). At ten, he attempts to patronize an extremely poor Irish family and is "disgusted" when his charity is accepted without due gratitude, the consequences of which being that "to this day ... the springs of benevolence [are] dried up within me" (163–65). As with middle-class women writers, the literary "I" was often formed in antagonistic relation with the Fathers, but just as often it was in equally antagonistic relation with women or workers.

Other Possibilities

The preceding section described the internalized, self-reflexive subjectivity most familiar in literary history from the Romantics to postmodernism: an intense and defensive reflexivity born in opposition to social constraints of Church, family, and school or State, yet conservative with respect to the hierarchies of gender and class. This section will describe some Victorian nonworking-class alternatives to this "literary subjectivity." In his or her autobiography, each of the following authors—all social rebels in their fashion—self-consciously resisted an isolating self-absorption or retreat into a literary coterie. Ruskin opts for encomium rather than isolation in the magnificent struggle that is *Praeterita;* Mill and Webb reject dualisms of public and private, self and society, and exhibit their marriages as ideal meetings of the personal and political; and Darwin and Huxley suppress individual subjectivity on behalf of science, identifying themselves within a scientific community. Moreover, unlike their more literary counterparts, with the exception of Darwin all of these authors articulated rational critiques of gender or class inequality.

JOHN RUSKIN, 1819–1900

Ruskin's *Praeterita* was first published between 1885 and 1889. Composed of diary extracts connected within a loose, anecdotal narrative while the author suffered intermittent insanity, the goal of the autobiography was allegedly aesthetic, to please and instruct "my friends . . . and those of the public who have been pleased by my books."[23] Ruskin writes "what it gives me joy to remember at any length I like—sometimes very carefully of what I think it may be useful for others to know; and passing in total silence things which I have no pleasure in reviewing, and which the reader would find no help in the account of" (1). Thus "praeterita" refers to both the grammatical past, things that have gone before, and rhetorical *praeteritio,* a passing over or an omission, the things not said. Within, we see Ruskin's life with his parents, wealthy wine merchant father and evangelical mother, living in religious isolation from "taste" yet in perennial fear of condescension from more graceful members of the establishment. The family includes the trio only, and nowhere in the autobiography does Ruskin mention his own unsuccessful marriage; nor does he mention friends except those he elsewhere called "tutors and enchantresses," like Carlyle and the various girls he takes pleasure in describing; and he mentions only in passing the social reform to which he had dedicated his fortune and an eloquence in English second only to Shakespeare's.

Ruskin's autobiography is first and foremost the description of the things he has seen from the viewpoint of a privileged seer.[24] Like the epideictic poets, the poets of praise, Ruskin's "self" is a service to his ideal, reflecting its glory, being satisfied in its light. This is the source of Ruskin's anachronistic chivalry, for example his wanting to *serve* girls without thought of reciprocity, or even of a self to be requited: "To please her is my hope with all girls. . . . My primary thought is how to serve *them,* and make them happy, and if they could use me for a plank bridge over a stream, or set me up for a post to tie a swing to, or anything of the sort not requiring me to talk, I should be always quite happy in such promotion" (216). Ruskin's specularity, his faculty of "seeing" the other, denies his own subjectivity, leaves himself unseen. When the object of praise turns to the praiser, she sees only—in Ruskin's own phrase for himself—a *camera lucida,* a transparent medium through which others see her. An obvious comparison is Lewis Carroll, the portrait photographer and author of the *Alice* books.

I am not interested in filling in the psychodrama passed over in *Prae-*

terita, imputing to Ruskin massive repression, nor mapping the work onto the Puritan autobiography and Biblical epiphanies that his deconversions obviously invert; rather I take this epideictic, "reflecting" (rather than reflective) subject and his travelog of visions to represent Ruskin's subjective eclipse of longing and fear in his personal dialogue with his own sanity. Again, the factual accuracy of especially the early life in *Praeterita* has been successfully challenged by scholars: I refer in what follows to Ruskin's own self-representation, or, in this case, nonrepresentation, which is also a kind of representation.

According to Ruskin, throughout their long lives he was the center of his parents' universe, and they of his. As a child, he "led a very small, perky, contented, conceited Cock-Robinson-Crusoe sort of life, in the central point which it appeared to me . . . that I occupied in the universe" (27). When he went up to Oxford, his mother took rooms in the High Street. He spent every evening with her, wrote his books supported by his father's money, read his works to his parents, and financed his political projects with his patrimony. The security of his family deprived Ruskin of risk of any kind, emotional or material:

> I never had heard my father's or mother's voice raised in any question with each other; nor seen an angry, or even slightly hurt or offended, glance in the eyes of either. . . . I had never seen a moment's trouble or disorder in any household; nor anything whatever either done in a hurry, or undone in due time. I had no conception of such a feeling as anxiety. . . . I had never done any wrong that I knew of . . . and I had never seen any grief. . . . My practice in Faith was soon complete: nothing was ever promised me that was not given; nothing ever threatened me that was not inflicted, and nothing ever told me that was not true. (33–34)

Relations with others, for Ruskin, are consequently objective, touching neither longing nor fear. He himself calls this a "calamity": "I had nothing to love. My parents were—in a sort—visible powers of nature to me, no more loved than the sun and the moon: only I should have been annoyed and puzzled if either of them had gone out . . . still less did I love God . . . I had nothing to endure. Danger or pain of any kind I knew not: my strength was never exercised, my patience never tried, and my courage never fortified" (35).

From a childhood without need or demand, a boy develops through objective relations, not distinguishing inside from outside, entirely dependent upon externalities. "I could literally draw nothing, not a cat,

not a mouse, not a boat, not a bush, 'out of my head'" (65). Uncompre-
hending of Carlyle's belief that unless one is loved the world is waste,
Ruskin explains that his youth "produced in me the precisely opposite
sentiment: *My* times of happiness had always been when *nobody* was
thinking of me. . . . My entire delight was in observing without being
myself noticed,—if I could have been invisible, all the better. I was absolutely interested in men and their ways, as I was interested in marmots
and chamois, in tomtits and trout. If only they would stay still and let me
look at them, and not get into their holes and up their heights!" (155–
56). He says of his family traveling, "We did not travel for adventures,
nor for company, but to see with our eyes, and to measure with our
hearts. If you have sympathy, the aspect of humanity is more true to the
depths of it than its words; and even in my own land, the things in which
I have been least deceived are those which I have learned as their Spectator" (107).[25]

The remainder of *Praeterita* is descriptions of what Ruskin sees: from
watching the grass grow—"I used to lie down on it and draw the blades
as they grew, with the ground herbage of buttercup or hawkweed mixed
among them, until every square foot of meadow, or mossy bank, became
an infinite picture and possession to me, and the grace and adjustment
to each other of growing leaves, a subject of more curious interest to me
than the composition of any painter's master-piece" (397)—through a
series of epiphanies leading to his final apostasy from his mother's evangelicalism for a Religion of Beauty: "'He hath made everything beautiful
in his time,' became for me thenceforward the interpretation of the bond
between the human mind and all visible things" (285); "And as the perfect colour and sound gradually asserted their power on me, they seemed
finally to fasten me in the old article of Jewish faith, that things done
delightfully and rightly, were always done by the help and in the Spirit of
God" (461).

Privileged beholder of the beauty of nature, Ruskin also depicts his
relationships with others as visual, aestheticized. He recounts a young
cousin's drowning as a Turner storm at sea: "The west wind had still
blown, clearly and strong, and the day before there had been a fresh
breeze of it round the isle, at spithead, exactly the kind of breeze that
drifts the cloud, and ridges the waves, in Turner's *Gosport*" (126). "I am
amused," he writes of his Oxford days, "as I look back, in now perceiving
what an aesthetic view I had of all my tutors and companions—how consistently they took to me the aspect of pictures, and how I from the first
declined giving my attention to those which were not well painted

enough" (190). He ranks his friends in "an aesthetic choice of idols" (194). He compares unfavorably a girl's beauty at eighteen to what it had been at fifteen and insists that sentiment did not cloud his sight: "My love was much too high and fantastic to be diminished by her loss of beauty; but I perfectly well saw and admitted it, having never at any time been in the slightest degree blinded by love, as I perceive other men are, out of my critic nature" (214). And he offers a precise and unqualified description of his taste in feminine appearance: "oval face, crystalline blonde, with straightish, at the utmost wavy, (or, in length, wreathed) hair, and the form elastic, and foot firm" (217). Of his meeting with the nine-year-old Rose La Touche, the love of his life (Ruskin was thirty-nine), he writes as if she were a piece of sculpture: "Nine years old, on 3rd January, 1858, thus now rising towards ten; neither tall nor short for her age; a little stiff in her way of standing. The eyes rather deep blue at that time, and fuller and softer than afterwards. Lips perfectly lovely in profile;—a little too wide, and hard in edge, seen in front; the rest of the features what a fair, well-bred Irish girl's usually are; the hair, perhaps, more graceful in short curl round the forehead, and softer than one sees often, in the close-bound tresses above the neck" (490). And finally he preserves a photographic transcription of her childish letters, word for word for pages in his autobiography, with the note "I leave pauses [i.e., spaces] where the old pages end" (495).

This camera's eye and seer of others had no relationships that were not objective (and objectifying), and he expected none: "In blaming myself, as often I have done, and may have occasion to do again, for my want of affection to other people, I must also express continually, as I think back about it, more and more wonder that ever anybody had any affection for *me.* I thought they might as well have got fond of a camera lucida, or an ivory footrule: all my faculty was merely in showing that such and such things were so; I was no orator, no actor, no painter but in a minute and generally invisible manner: and I couldn't bear being interrupted in anything I was about" (425). Ruskin's subjectivity was an anachronism: the seer who worshipped with his eyes and declined to have the light turned upon him; but it was also extraordinary in that it did not re-cognize—in that he had never subjectively cognized—the need in *others* that represented the distance between subjective desire and objective fact, between what the Victorians at any rate treated as inner and outer.

Yet Ruskin's eclipse of the self behind the lamp of objectivity is not total. These "objective" images of himself double as tacit explanation for the life the public had, unfortunately, been privy to, the life he could not entirely pass over. His never having been blinded by love explained the impotence he experienced when confronted with the body of a woman past puberty. His impatience with interruption when at his work explained the years he had encouraged his wife to go out alone. Doubtless Ruskin's aesthetic of life—the aesthetic that kept him distant from life—was first theophanic, to be a *speculum dei,* and then, after his deconversion in 1858, to record the sublimity of nature and the picturesqueness of humankind (hence his loving attention to the pathos of Europe's architectural ruins); yet in writing a life at all he is both observer and observed, objectifying and objectified by readers who want to know more than it pleases him to say: and he, generously, says more. Attempting, as Jay Fellows has written, to annul his increasingly apparent self, Ruskin builds up the museum of *Praeterita* only to find that self given substance by its possessions, the things that it has seen.

In the introduction to the Oxford *Praeterita,* Kenneth Clark attributes Ruskin's sacralizing of sight and consequent devotion to art to the deprivations of a philistine, puritanical home: too much "taste" would have trivialized beauty for him; he could have taken it for granted (xxi). Yet it was more than the vulgarity of the *nouveau riche* that made the Ruskin of *Praeterita* reject all subjectivity except that of a guide, an observer of the responses of others. Before Ruskin wrote as a mediator of the beauty of Nature in *Praeterita,* he wrote as the prophet of industrial capitalist society. Then he made the century's strongest claim that social relations determined artistic production. He wrote in *Fors* (see later discussion) that "the teaching of Art, as I understand it, is the teaching of all things" (424), and published *The Stones of Venice* the year the Crystal Palace became the first prefabricated building in the history of the West. When architecture revealed to him the failure of social justice, he turned, in *Praeterita,* to the beauty of Nature and Brantwood, not yet entirely polluted by humankind. The self who had failed in intimate relationships wrote in exile from the society he failed to improve—from the most beautiful house in England, returning to earlier things to forget what had come to pass.

In *Fors Clavigera* (1871–1884), however, Ruskin had written lucidly of his madness and solitude. *Fors,* whose enigmatic title means interchangeably the club of Hercules, key of Patience, and iron nail of Necessity, were the letters Ruskin published to the Working Men of Great Britain upon the founding of his Guild of St. George. *Fors* revealed a Ruskin more private when at his most public, anticipating autobiography in articulating his public position of social reformer. His failure in that position, making him a social reformer without connection to society, left only the solitude of *Praeterita*. The letters were published in Kent by George Allen without advertising or mediation at 7p. per volume to pay the workers for reproducing them. They tell, like all true love letters— for these are a kind of love letter—the tale of human interdependence.

To his Guild "Companions," living on and working the land he had given them, Ruskin writes, "I am so alone now in my thoughts and ways that if I am not mad, I should soon become so, from mere solitude, but for my [manual] work [i.e., his drawing]" (406).[26] In his eighty-eighth letter (February 18, 1880), he distinguished the sources of his madness as both physical and emotional, "the state of morbid inflammation of brain which gave rise to false visions" and that "which was simply curative of the wounded nature in me" (429–30). Fearing lest his work be discredited by his sickness, he effaces himself altogether as author of an ethical system, so that, like God's creation of the world, Ruskin's work will stand whatever comes of the author. In one of the most beautiful passages in English prose, the most literal of spectators invokes the literal heavens as the unmediated teacher of humankind and then eloquently fades out of view:

Throughout every syllable of [*Fors*] hitherto written, the reader will find one consistent purpose, and perfectly conceived system . . . a system not mine, nor Kant's, nor Comte's;—but that which Heaven has taught every true man's heart, and proved by every true man's work, from the beginning of time to this day.

I use the word "Heaven" here in an absolutely literal sense, meaning the blue sky, and the light and air of it. Men who live in that light,—"in pure sunshine, not under mixed-up shade,"—and whose actions are open as the air, always arrive at certain conditions of moral and practical loyalty, which are wholly independent of religious opinion. These, it has been the first business of *Fors* to declare. Whether there be one God or three,— no God, or ten thousand,—children should have enough to eat, and their skins should be washed clean. It is not *I* who say that. Every mother's heart under the sun says that, if she has one.

Again, whether there be saints in Heaven or not, as long as its stars shine on the sea, and the thunnies swim there—every fisherman who drags a net ashore is bound to say to as many human creatures as he can, "Come and dine." And the fishmongers who destroy their fish by cart-loads that they may make the poor pay dear for what is left, ought to be flogged round Billingsgate, and out of it. It is not *I* who say that. Every man's heart on sea and shore says that—if he isn't at heart a rascal. What-

ever is dictated in *Fors* is dictated thus by common sense, common
equity, common humanity, and common sunshine—not by me. (430–31)

One of the most agonized passages in English prose concludes this
same letter, with Ruskin's explanation of his mental disintegration as the
rejection of his labor and service, echoing Mayhew's tailors and
shipbuilders:

> I went mad because nothing came of my work. People would have under-
> stood my falling crazy if they had heard that the manuscripts on which I
> had spent seven years of my old life had all been used to light the fire with,
> like Carlyle's first volume of the *French Revolution.* [Mill inadvertently
> burned it.] But they could not understand that I should be the least
> annoyed, far less fall ill in a frantic manner, because, after I had got them
> published, nobody believed a word of them. Yet the first calamity would
> only have been misfortune,—the second (the enduring calamity under
> which I toil) is humiliation,—resisted necessarily by a dangerous and
> lonely pride. . . . All alike, in whom I had most trusted for help, failed me
> in this main work: some mocked at it, some pitied, some rebuked,—all
> stopped their ears at the cry: and the solitude at last became too great to
> be endured. (433)

Throughout the length of *Praeterita,* Ruskin would not write again of his
need to be heard by others. Like Mayhew, however, he had learned that
there was no subjectivity without intersubjectivity—only the isolation of
the body in pain, "the state of morbid inflammation of the brain which
gave rise to false visions . . . with perfect knowledge of the real things in
the room, I yet saw others that were not there" (429).

In 1885, with the first publication of *Praeterita,* Ruskin completed
The Bible of Amiens, his tour guide and "reading" of the great cathedral.
In the long preface to his French translation of that work, Marcel Proust,
who also knew the value of visual things in the moments of vision that
round out a life, who would also write of things past, describes his pilgrimage "to Amiens with . . . the desire to read the Bible of Ruskin":
"Not appreciating until then the import of religious art in the Middle
Ages, I had said to myself, in my enthusiasm for Ruskin: He will teach
me, for he too, in some portion at least, is he not the truth? He will make
my spirit enter where it had no access, for he is the door. He will purify
me, for his inspiration is like the lily of the valley. He will intoxicate me
and will give me life, for he is the vine and the life."[27] Ruskin had
instructed tourists in their approach to the cathedral ("Put a sou in every

beggar's box who asks it there,—it is none of your business whether they should be there or not, nor whether they deserve to have the sou,—be sure only that you yourself deserve to have it to give" [12]), and Proust gives to the poor as "an act of piety toward Ruskin" (13). Proust loved Ruskin's detail, his eccentricity of vision, as well as the generosity that made him cast off what Proust calls "the nothingness" of human longing for humane purpose. Searching at Amiens for a tiny figurine on the Porch of the Bookseller's, he writes what Ruskin taught him to *see* of alterity and altruism:

> The artist, who died centuries ago, left there, among thousands of others, this little person who dies a little more each day, and has been dead for a really long time, forever lost in the midst of the crowd. But he had put it there. One day, a man for whom there is no death, for whom there is no material infinity, no oblivion, a man who, casting away from him that nothingness which oppresses us to follow purposes which dominate his life, purposes so numerous that he will not be able to attain them all, while we seemed to have none, this man came, and, among those waves of stone where each lacelike effervescence seemed to resemble the others, seeing there all the laws of life, all the thoughts of the soul, naming them by their names, he said, "See, it is this, it is that." (45–46)

Finally Proust says of Ruskin what Ruskin had said of Turner, "Through those eyes, now filled with dust, generations yet unborn will learn to behold the light of nature" (49).

In what is probably his most celebrated passage, Ruskin wrote in *Modern Painters III,* "The greatest thing a human soul ever does in this world is to *see* something and tell what it saw in a plain way. . . . To see clearly is poetry, prophecy, and religion,—all in one." Ruskin would have liked to represent himself as a strong subject—a camera lucida or an ivory footrule. His egotism lay in his claim that he could "see" the ethical Truth, and he attempted to maintain this "view from nowhere" against mental distintegration and the knowledge that others did not see things his way. Feminists would be correct to observe that Ruskin's was a familiar masculine tragedy, in which not to concede to his "vision" is to destroy him. Yet there is something to the art critic who saw that material conditions mattered, that the fact that children should have enough to eat was as evident as the sea and the shore. The tradition of praise (and, as in Ruskin's anger as a social critic, of its negative of invective) was always to promote on the part of its audience a virtuous emulation of the

Figure 6.1. William Holman Hunt's *The Light of the World* (1853–1856). By permission of the Warden and Fellows of Keble College, Oxford.

model it panegyrically mimed (or an allotropic or apotropaic emulation of the object it, again mimetically, blames).[28] In letter thirty-four of *Fors,* Ruskin had distinguished two kinds of language—blasphemy or "harmful speaking—not against God only, but against man and against all the good works and purposes of Nature" and "euphemy, the right of wellspeaking of God and His World." In his earlier work he had prophecied and seen come to pass a polluted earth and a world gone mad. He opted in *Praeterita* to represent himself by speaking well of God, and more importantly, of the earth and world. He made one last effort to annihilate the ego rather than submit to Connolly's "divine I am that I am," Orwell's "inner self," White's "core of rebelliousness," and Gosse's "innate and persistent self." Then he stopped speaking and writing and retired into madness and his own personal demons.

JOHN STUART MILL, 1806–1873

In different ways Ruskin, Butler, Gosse, Sinclair, and White deal in an economy of the self contingent upon religion and family. Butler, Gosse, Sinclair, and White create the "self" antagonistically, in spiritual rebellion against parents, school, and/or Church. Rejecting Evangelicalism as the colorless religion of affectless, mercantile parents, Ruskin made the beauty and morality of the created world a religion demanding a paradoxically selfless eloquence modelled upon the Bible's. John Stuart Mill was unique among major Victorian writers in that religious practice played no part in his life. Additionally, his education at home and family relations were highly unusual. I shall argue that without the usual circumstances of religious and secular development, Mill does not develop a corresponding account of the self or a corresponding distinction between the public and private. Although he provided the definitive defense of individual freedom from social control in Chapters 3 and 4 of *On Liberty* (1859), that individualism has little to do with the defensive retreat into private self that became characteristic of literary artists. Individualism for Mill is demonstrated liberty of thought predicated upon tolerance and education, not a jealously guarded property and privacy from the intrusion of others. This difference is reflected in the structure of his *Autobiography* (published posthumously in 1873), in which the more typical family–religion psychodrama is replaced by citizens and the production of civic works—James Mill, Bentham, Ricardo, "political economists," Owenites, "philosophic radicals," "Tory lawyers," and, of course, Harriet Taylor. Resuming writing in 1869 after a hiatus of seven years, Mill reiterates the social function of his *Autobiography:* "I am influenced by a desire not to leave incomplete the record, for the sake of which chiefly this biographical sketch was undertaken, of the obligations I owe to those who have either contributed essentially to my own mental development or had a direct share in my writings and in whatever else of a public nature I have done."[29] The oratorical nature of Mill's *Autobiography,* more reminiscent of Isocrates than Rousseau, represents a corresponding conception of the self as citizen.

Mill begins with his education under his father, taking up Greek at three and Latin at eight. At eight he also began to teach his siblings, establishing himself from early days within a chain of transmitted knowledge. For pleasure he read history, his radical Utilitarian father putting him on guard against possible Tory prejudices. At twelve, he commenced logic, government, and jurisprudence, beginning with the ancient authors and learning to correct the proofs of his father's *History of India.* By thirteen, he had embarked upon a complete course of political economy. In the early drafts of the autobiography edited by Harriet Taylor, Mill insisted upon the "very considerable drawbacks" (23n.) of his education, yet these refer to his father's severity, which he feels was unnecessary, rather than the content of the education itself, of which he approves. He concludes the summary of "Childhood and Early Education" with a consideration of his lack of "self" under paternal and literary demands: "My state of mind was not humility, but neither was it arrogance. I never thought of saying to myself, I am, or I can do, so and so. I neither estimated myself highly nor lowly: I did not estimate myself at all. If I thought anything about myself, it was that I was rather backward in my studies, since I always found myself so, in comparison with what my father expected from me" (21). Like Ruskin, who was also reared in an environment of total parental surveillance and control ("Nothing was ever promised me that was not given; nothing ever threatened me that was not inflicted, and nothing ever told me that was not true" [34]), Mill's earliest relationships were "objective," his desires indistinguishable from his father's desires for him. Some later scholars would claim that Mill's alleged need for domination in personal relationships (e.g., with Harriet Taylor) dated from his early relationship with his father, as his antipathy to women's—or others'—subjugation dated from his perception of his mother's subjection to her role.

In the second chapter, "Moral Influences in Early Youth. My Father's Character and Opinions," Mill writes of his education at his father's hands "not as an education of love but of fear" (33n)—rather similarly to Ruskin's "dominant calamity" of his childhood, that he had nothing to love. When Mill writes of his mother at all (in the original manuscript only), he is contemptuous: "With the very best intentions, my mother only knew how to pass her life in drudging for [her children]. Whatever she could do for them she did, and they liked her, because she was kind to them, but to make herself loved, looked up to, or even obeyed, required qualities which she unfortunately did not possess" (33n). He "thus grew up in the absence of love and in the presence of fear" (33). He attributes this (again in the original manuscript) to national character as well as the personal idiosyncrasies of his parents, emphasizing, like Ruskin, the "objective" nature of familial relations in England, "like an attachment to inanimate objects":

> I do not mean that things were worse in this respect than they are in most English families; in which genuine affection is altogether exceptional; what is usually found being more or less of an attachment of mere habit, like that to inanimate objects, and a few conventional proprieties of phrase and demonstration. I believe there is less personal affection in England than in any other country of which I know anything, and I give my father's family not as peculiar in this respect but only as a too faithful exemplification of the ordinary fact. (33)

Like his account of his education at home, Mill's account of religious training was equally extraordinary. He conveys the equanimity with which he approached issues of passionate concern to his contemporaries in his discussion of how his father taught him to estimate religion: "I grew up in a negative state with regard to it. I looked upon the modern exactly as I did upon the ancient religions, as something which in no way concerned me. It did not seem to me more strange that English people should believe what I did not, than that the men whom I read of in Herodotus should have done so" (27–28).

After 1822, Mill "began to carry on my intellectual cultivation by writing still more than by reading" (45). At the age of seventeen, he received a clerkship in the East India Company, from which he retired as Chief Examiner of Indian Correspondence in 1858. Far from circumscribing an identity for him, however, his job preparing dispatches to the Central Administration in India is described as "leisure" from "my own pursuits" (54): "I have, through life, found office duties an actual rest from the other mental occupations which I have carried on simultaneously with them. They were sufficiently intellectual not to be a distaste-

ful drudgery, without being such as to cause any strain upon the mental
powers of a person used to abstract thought, or to the labour of careful
literary composition" (51). Here Mill identifies himself not by his public
role in the workplace but by his private pursuits as a writer.

Yet if Mill downplays his work in the Company in the *Autobiography*—work that he believed consistent with his abstract views on rational
government—he credits the Company with teaching him the value of the
free exchange of ideas, the negative value of writing in isolation or having
"no one to consult but myself," a view that was the linchpin of *On
Liberty*:

> The occupation accustomed me to see and hear the difficulties of every
> course, and the means of obviating them, stated and discussed deliber-
> ately, with a view to execution; it gave me opportunities of perceiving
> when public measures, and other political facts, did not produce the
> effects which had been expected of them, and from what causes; above all
> it was valuable to me by making me, in this portion of my activity, merely
> one wheel in a machine, the whole of which had to work together. As a
> speculative writer, I should have had no one to consult but myself, and
> should have encountered in my speculations none of the obstacles which
> would have started up whenever they came to be applied to practice. But
> as a Secretary conducting political correspondence, I could not issue an
> order or express an opinion, without satisfying various persons very unlike
> myself, that the thing was fit to be done. I was thus in a good position for
> finding out by practice the mode of putting a thought which gives it easiest
> admittance into minds not prepared for it by habit. (52–53)

Yet despite Mill's insistence upon the corporate nature of intellectual
and social life, the value, as he puts it, of being "merely one wheel in a
machine," with the exception of a brief term in parliament (a public
office for which he refused to canvass publicly or commit himself to the
views of his constituency—that is, a public office in which he remained
adamantly autonomous), the majority of his engagement with society
and politics was at a distance, in fact from the privacy of his own home.
In a word, he retired to a life of politics: "I had now settled, as I believed
for the remainder of my existence, into purely literary life; if that can be
called literary which continued to be occupied in a preeminent degree
with politics, and not merely with theoretical, but practical politics,
although a great part of the year was spent at a distance of many hundred
miles [in Avignon] from the chief seat of the politics of my own country,
to which, and primarily for which, I wrote" (156). The point is that

although Mill did not display the emotional range in relationships with others that Unger calls passion, or personality, neither did he relegate the risks of encounters with others to the intimacies of private life. He does not distinguish between public and private in his life as an autonomous citizen.

His response to his "crisis" of personal happiness, up to which point his book and his life had been occupied with abstract reasoning and ideas, was to try to form a Radical party and cultivate his relationship with Harriet Taylor. His twenty-year relationship with Taylor before her husband died and they were at liberty to marry (they traveled abroad together as well as visited together in the Taylors' home) violated the conventions of private life, and the encomium of Harriet Taylor in the *Autobiography* rhetorically reinforces this collapse of the public and private distinction and its concomitant gender stereotyping. Simultaneously with their "courtship," Mill joins Comte and Saint-Simon in attacking private property and the private family: "I honoured them most of all for what they have been most cried down for—the boldness and freedom from prejudice with which they treated the subject of the family, the most important of any, and needing more fundamental alterations than remain to be made in any other great social institution, but on which scarcely any reformer has the courage to touch" (101). With Harriet Taylor ("My mental progress . . . now went hand in hand with hers" [137]), he begins to question the institution of private property and "welcome[s] with the greatest pleasure and interest all socialistic experiments," eventually calling themselves Socialists (138–40).

Mill's "crisis" entailed his not being happy while self-consciously reflecting upon happiness; his recovery entailed his acquiring an intimate companion, and like Orwell, his rejecting self-consciousness for public-consciousness. During and after his crisis he defends voluntary birth control for the poor and the French Revolution (79); joins the working classes—against nearly the whole upper and middle class, "even those who passed for Liberals" (159)—against the South in the American Civil War; published cheap People's Editions of his *Principles of Political Economy, On Liberty,* and *Representative Government* for the working classes, giving up his own profits in order to offer the lowest possible price (165); proposed radical views directly influencing Irish Land reform; chaired the Jamaica Committee in 1866 for the prosecution of a colonial government's "abuses of power committed against negroes and mulattoes" (176); tirelessly supported women's suffrage (179–80 and passim); and defeated the Extradition Bill of the late 1860s in order to protect

European political refugees (177). The "liberalism" whose foundational tenet predicates individual freedom upon privacy from the intrusion of Others has nothing to do with such labors on behalf of human interaction. (He warned in *On Liberty* of "misplaced notions of liberty preventing moral obligation.")[30] The causes for which Mill wrote and spoke as well as the actors who populate his *Autobiography* exemplify the philosophy of his *On Liberty,* which he described as "a kind of philosophic textbook of a single truth . . . the importance, to man and society, of a large variety in types of character, and of giving full freedom to human nature to expand itself in innumerable and conflicting directions" (150). Ultimately Mill had learned the heterogeneity and diversity of human endeavor from his books and debating societies, and it was this diversity that free speech was to guard.

The one exception that should come to mind today is India. The attitude of "benevolent despotism" regarding the governance of India that Mill held during his thirty-five years in the Examiner's Office of the East India Company represents the blight of imperialist paternalism ("barbarism" in Rosa Luxemburg's deliberately inverted sense) upon even the most progressive thinkers of the age. Although Mill held in contempt his contemporaries' racist theories of inherent natural differences, he did believe that by historical accident the mission had fallen to Britain to ameliorate the stagnation and disorder into which the once progressive India had fallen and to place it once again on the road to progress through a reorganization of its political institutions and revitalization of its economy. Although in the *Autobiography* he passes over the 1,700 dispatches on Indian affairs he sent from the Office as "an actual rest from the other mental occupations which I have carried on simultaneously," he did consider his post, as in the long passage cited earlier, conducive to the formulation of free speech in *On Liberty.*

The typical literary judgment of Mill may be represented by his editor in the fifth edition of *The Norton Anthology of English Literature* (1986)—significant because its prejudices are sanctioned by scholarship and often taken for granted by students: "It is evident that Mill is the least literary of the important Victorian prose writers. His analytic mind, . . . self-effacing manner, and his relatively colorless style are the marks of a writer whose value lies in his generalizations from experience rather than in the rendering of particular experiences for their own sake."[31] In Chapter 3, citing Patrick Brantlinger's work on imperialism and fiction and criticizing Richard Rorty's claims for literature as a progressive social force, I indicated how the very particularity of realist literature—its detail, particularity, and preoccupation with individual characters—led to racial stereotyping, individualistic moralizing about the Other, and sentimental approaches to social problems. Here I would like to reclaim Mill's style and "self-effacing manner" for *passion,* but passion redefined as political as well as personal, as in a passion for justice. Mill's imaginative extension of sympathy to cooperativists, revolutionaries, workers, North American slaves, Irish tenants, Jamaican Blacks, women, and political refugees may be seen as the making public of passionate relations with others. I would insist upon the importance of this making public of human interdependence even while agreeing with Perry Anderson's estimation of Mill's altruistic international campaigns (i.e., that they functioned as the refuge of liberalism's avowed norms when the objective structure of empire and economy prevented their ascendancy at home).[32] Moreover, the private or personal effect of Mill's altruism entailed the literal invasion of his privacy. His "general mass of correspondence swelled into an oppressive burthen. . . . When I became a member of parliament I began to receive letters on private grievances and on every imaginable subject that related to any kind of public affairs, however remote from my knowledge or pursuits" (181).

I would also locate the persistent issue of what Mill owed Harriet Taylor Mill—persistent, that is, to critics obsessed with individual "genius," "originality," or "the anxiety of influence"—within this context of Mill's self-styled defense of the project of the Enlightenment, the foundation of which was securing the conditions for free speech and rational exchange of ideas. I personally find the scholarship that confirms Mill's own views of their joint collaboration more persuasive than that which argues that his acknowledgment of her is due to mere modesty or uxoriousness. Psychoanalytic critics have often interpreted Mill's praise of his wife as his transference from one dominant figure, his father, to another. More subtle critics in the same vein, like Phyllis Rose, put it more subtly: Harriet Taylor like the idea of equality and the feel of dominance, and Mill approved of equality but craved domination. He atoned for the subjection of women by the voluntary, even enthusiastic, subjection of one man, and portrayed the result as a marriage of equals.[33] Jack Stillinger expresses the still more common attitude of dismissal in his introduction to the *Autobiography:* "It is reasonably clear in fact that Harriet was no originator of ideas, however much she may have aided Mill by ordinary wifely discussion and debate. . . . It is unfortunate that Mill did not simply thank his wife for encouragement, perhaps also for transcribing a manuscript or making an index, and let it go at that" (xvii–xix). Similarly, Kenneth Clark writes with homosocial condescension of Ruskin's unfortunate difficulties with a crude materialist "Effie," susceptible, like her animals, to the "natural pleasures" of sex and good grounds: "He shrank, as many sensitive men have done, from the physical act of love-making. . . . Effie, from her sensible, worldly, and not very subtle, point of view, seems to have acted with patience and dignity. . . . She later married John Everett Millais . . . and enjoyed the natural pleasures of a large family, a large house in Kensington, and a deer stalk in the Highlands."[34] And the ingenious conservative Gertrude Himmelfarb fully credits the Mills's collaboration in the production of *On Liberty* so that on the basis of the high-minded and self-contained nature of their relationship she can discredit *On Liberty* itself.[35]

Yet whatever Harriet Taylor Mill's psychological effect upon her husband, her appearances in the *Autobiography* function rhetorically to represent the consistency of Mill's private desire and political project. Opposed to stereotypes, he represented his wife as a thinker greater than the men of the age; opposed to the subjection of some to others, he made her his collaborator. From the early lessons in books, through the debating societies and East India Company, through his overwhelming correspondence at home, Mill's subjectivity developed through dialogical relations with others. He called it "the liberty of thought and discussion" in *On Liberty;* I would put it, following Habermas, noncoercive communicative interaction.[36] This was the subjectivity he represented in his *Autobiography* and generalized in *On Liberty* and *The Subjection of Women* (1869). The attention that the encomium—in the classical rhetorical sense—of Harriet Taylor has received from feminists and antifeminists alike since the publication of the autobiography is sufficient proof of Mill's wisdom in employing his personal relationship in the service of his political project.

According to Mill, the male superiority that some critics reassert for him decade after decade "perverts the whole manner of existence of the man, both as an individual and as a social being."[37] His description in the public manifesto of *The Subjection of Women* of the perfectly dialogical couple, which I take as "autobiographical," derived from personal experience and represents Mill's dialogical self, interdependent with others and ceaselessly dynamic. "The couple" is a metonymic vision of a noncoercive society to come: "Two persons of cultivated faculties, identical in opinions and purposes, between whom there exists that best kind of equality, similarity of powers and capacities with reciprocal superiority in them—so that each can enjoy the luxury of looking up to the other and can have alternately the pleasure of leading and being led in the path of development" (541). Even granting some postmodern or postliberal discomfort with the apparent unanimity of this couple ("identical in opinions and purposes"), which may suggest the fitting of one to the other's mold, to see Mill's achievement we need only contrast this representation of dynamic equality with the commitment to essentialism and paternalism of a later reader. Sigmund Freud discredited the Mills's collaboration and thought "Mill's" views on gender equality "absurd," "inhuman," "prudish," and "unearthy." At the age of twenty-seven, Freud advised his fiancée, who had raised the subject of the Mills, on the right relation of wife to husband:

> I believe that all reforming activity, legislation and education, will founder on the fact that long before the age at which a profession [for women] can be established in our society, nature will have appointed woman by her beauty, charm, and goodness, to do something else.
>
> No, in this respect I adhere to the old ways, to my longing for my Martha as she is, and she herself will not want it different; legislation and custom have to grant to women many rights kept from them, but the position of woman cannot be other than what it is: to be an adored sweetheart in youth, and a beloved wife in maturity.[38]

Freud later devised a more subtle explanation of how the self was acculturated to gender. Following him, generations recommenced private excavations of family histories that resembled archaic forms of spiritual confession. Only now, a post-Freudian generation can reconsider the possibilities that Mill proposed: a respect for diversity and heterogeneity that dispenses with Freudian dualisms; a public critique of, rather than a private therapy for, "the subject of the family, the most important of any, and needing more fundamental alterations than remain to be made in any other great social institution, but on which scarcely any reformer has the courage to touch"; and passionate and diverse citizenries with longings for social justice.

CHARLES DARWIN, 1809–1882, AND
THOMAS HENRY HUXLEY, 1825–1896

> L'art, c'est moi; la science, c'est nous.
>
> CLAUDE BERNARD, *Introduction à l'étude de la médecine expérimentale* (1865)[39]

Like Mill, in their autobiographies Charles Darwin and Thomas Henry Huxley do not deal in the poetic economy of the privately resistant subject, but situate themselves within the public project of the Enlightenment. Like the public school boys, they subsume themselves to a team, in this case the scientific community. Darwin and Huxley identify themselves as objective scientists by differentiating "science" from subjective experience and explicitly rejecting literary society and literature. Darwin goes so far as to claim for himself—in a rhetorically efficacious move on behalf of the institution of science—an unsusceptibility to human feeling and personal attachment. Just as Dickens created a type of the professional writer, Darwin and Huxley created a modern institutional scientist.

For Huxley, one's personal measure of fame could be known only by consensus within the scientific community, and he duly considered a personal autobiography irrelevant, even self-indulgent. He wrote one—of nine pages in total—only in 1889 and under protest to his publisher. He is as self-conscious about his "egotistical gossip" as some of the working-class writers, but Huxley's resistance to writing derives from an altogether different sense of what constitutes authority. Rather than class-status it was "science," and science had nothing to do with subjective experience. "You put before me the alternative," he wrote to his publisher, "of issuing something that may be all wrong, unless I furnish you with something authoritative; I do not say all right, because autobiographies are essentially works of fiction, whatever biographies may be. So I yield and send you what follows, in the hope that those who find it to be mere egotistical gossip will blame you and not me."[40] He concludes his autobiography with a brief attack on the similarly fictive genre of religious belief in order to prevent his autobiographical "fiction" from diverting from his real project:

> The last thing that it would be proper for me to do would be to speak of the work of my life, or to say at the end of the day, whether I think I have earned my wages or not. . . . But if I may speak of the objects I have had more or less definitely in view since I began . . . they are briefly these: to promote the increase of natural knowledge and to forward the application of scientific methods of investigation to all the problems of life to the best of my ability, in the conviction which has grown with my growth and strengthened with my strength—that there is no alleviation for the sufferings of mankind except veracity of thought and of action, and the resolute facing of the world as it is, when the garment of makebelieve, by which pious hands have hidden its uglier features, is stripped off. (108–9)

Huxley then concludes that he has subordinated his individual status as discoverer-scientist to his role as a popularizer (Darwin's proverbial "Bulldog") in order to further this scientific and socially redemptive process:

> It is with this intent that I have subordinated any reasonable or unreasonable ambition for scientific fame, which I may have permitted myself to entertain, to other ends: to the popularisation of science; to the development and organisation of scientific education; to the endless series of battles and skirmishes over evolution; and to untiring opposition to that ecclesiastical spirit, that clericalism, which in England, as everywhere else, and to whatever denomination it may belong, is the deadly enemy of science. (ibid.)

The last sentence situates him within the scientific community, expressing the hope that he has "somewhat helped that movement of opinion which has been called the New Reformation" (ibid.). When Huxley first saw New York harbor in 1876 he was reported to have reflected, "If I were not a man I think I should like to be a tug."[41] His identification with the little boats with very powerful engines that drag big boats into harbor is evident everywhere in his autobiography, which occupies itself exclusively with "the *work* of his life" "at the end of the day," and his "earning his *wages.*"

Charles Darwin's posthumously published *Autobiography* (1887) represents the unself-conscious scientific observer par excellence. Although his stated purpose in writing is to amuse his children and grandchildren, Darwin establishes himself as the objective seer of science in the first paragraph, writing with dispassionate distance, without personal emotion to cloud him or literary style to obscure his meaning: "I have attempted to write the following account of myself, as if I were a dead man in another world looking back at my own life. Nor have I found this difficult, for life is nearly over with me. I have taken no pains about my style of writing."[42] As in Huxley, personal style, or personality, or subjectivity can only obscure objective truth. One is to write as if one were "dead," looking back disinterestedly upon life.

Darwin's early life is presented as straightforwardly ordinary, one of the boys. The son of a wealthy physician whom he professes to adore, Darwin realized that he would inherit a substantial living and suffered little anxiety or overexertion in school (46). I have already alluded to his low assessment of the value of his education at Shrewsbury; during his two terms at Edinburgh, he pursued the habits of an idle (rich) sporting man. To prevent further idleness, his father sent him to Cambridge, where he also reputedly wasted his time, but wasted it with pleasure and enthusiasm. In the *Autobiography* he names his school friends and teachers with customary old school camaraderie. After the voyage of the Beagle 1831–1836 ("by far the most important event in my life" [76]), where he "discovered . . . that the pleasure of observing and reasoning was a much higher one than that of skill and sport" (76–79) (i.e., that knowledge was more powerful than physical prowess), Darwin eschews personal for professional, or institutional, vanity—"I was ambitious to take a fair place among leading scientific men . . . though I did not care much about the general public" (81, 82). He assumes a gentlemanly attitude toward his colleagues, other distinguished men of science, while distinguishing them from more literary types: he disapproves of Spencer's penchant for deduction and generalization, for example, and finds Carlyle a narrow-minded bore (109, 112). He himself is devoted to patient observation and scientific induction.

Like Mill, at the height of his powers Darwin finds that life in Society is not conducive to the dispassionate distance necessary to clear thought, and begins to suffer the mysterious bouts of illness that plagued him for the next forty years and necessitated his retirement from London into secluded domesticity at Down.[43] At the end of the *Autobiography,* he writes of his ill-health that "though it has annihilated several years of my life, [it] has saved me from the distractions of society and amusement" (144), stressing the scientist's distance from social engagement. With his retirement into his scientific writing he begins to experience emotional distance as well—"a grievous loss of feeling" and "a loss of the power of becoming deeply attached to anyone" (115). Thus in social retirement except for his devoted wife and children, Darwin claims that nothing noteworthy happened to him during the last thirty years of his life except the publication of his work and he duly devotes the rest of the autobiography to it: "My chief enjoyment and sole employment through life has been scientific work . . . I have therefore nothing to record during the rest of my life, except the publication of my several books" (115–16).

Darwin does, however, qualify the static characterization of his life with an insistence upon his increasing rejection of lyric poetry and poetic drama—the literary forms most representing the subjective, soliloquized "self": "For many years I cannot endure to read a line of poetry: I have tried lately to read Shakespeare, and found it so intolerably dull that it nauseated me" (138). He attributes this nauseous response to literary subjectivity to his brain having been underexercised in the emotional faculties. This self-criticism, however, is but a form of praise: rhetorically, even the enfeeblement or atrophy of emotion adds to his strength as the distanced, objective, dispassionate observer. Like Ruskin, unexceptional in all else, he is remarkable only for the clarity of his vision (141) and he is fortunate in "having ample leisure [to pursue seeing] from not having to earn my own bread" (144); but his sight leads to scientific rather than Ruskin's ethical Truth.

This character of the objective scientist, whose *vita* or "life" consists of scientific *res gestae* approved by one's colleagues in science, was an emerging contemporary type. Within the cultural antagonism of Literature and Science that had become popular in debates upon school curriculum, Darwin's support for science was reinforced by his admission of a proudly philistine taste for the only "literature" he found tolerable— popular novels with happy endings (138). Sounding like any number of workers with Bourdieu's "naïve" functional aesthetic of morality or agreeableness, he writes, "A novel, according to my taste, does not come into the first class unless it contains some person whom one can thoroughly love, and if it be a pretty woman all the better" (138–39). Today eminent men—especially men—of science often affect a great reverence for Literary culture now that the cultural dominance of science is assured and Literature in mass society functions less as Marcuse's critical and antagonistic Other to society than as Bourdieu's cultural capital. It is instructive in this context to remember that in the early days of the struggle for legitimacy between "the two cultures" (C. P. Snow), Charles Darwin found it strategical on behalf of science to report his nausea at the literary culture that many scientists now profess to cherish. His loathing for literature and love for science are the most passionate aspects of the *Autobiography*.

Even from Francis Darwin's early *Life and Letters* of his father (1887), and now with the full publication of Darwin's letters and notebooks, it is clear that the view promoted in the *Autobiography* of a Baconian inductivist disengaged from society is a literary construction whose effect was to represent the "scientist" as a cultural type.[44] With Huxley's help, Darwin's representation of the scientist was successful and influential and is only now being challenged by historians and philosophers of science. For example, it is clear that Darwin was very engaged with the scientific community, especially concerning the antivivisectionist movement, and that he had a circle of intimates, including Huxley, Joseph

Hooker, Charles Lyell, and the American botanist Asa Gray, whom he determinedly manipulated to defend and represent his views within and without the scientific community. Furthermore, the letters reveal Darwin's intense concern to manage his business affairs *so that* he would have time to do his scientific research (which was by no means exclusively, or even predominantly, inductive). As James R. Moore and Robert M. Young have argued, Darwin's social position was something akin to a "squire/parson's."[45] So well ensconsed in the daily habits of the Victorian bourgeoisie and so respectable within it was he, that, unlike George Eliot, he could be buried in Westminster Abbey. Huxley, on the other hand, did not have equal time, the permanent income, nor the elite status to devote to original work.

Although Darwin's life has received, and continues to receive, more attention, Huxley's life and letters add a new dimension to our discussion of subjectivity and intersubjectivity, participation and antagonism. For Huxley, a life devoted to "science" meant living in London, organizing museums, writing textbooks, teaching and examining, giving public lectures to working men, serving on eight Royal Commissions, attending and presiding over innumerable societies from Russia to Egypt to the United States, receiving nine honorary degrees, producing original research giving rise to a plethora of articles, and serving on the school board. As a fluent student of languages, he is credited with establishing the convention of scholarly consultation of all authorities available, and thus was instrumental in building an international scientific community. Science was to Huxley what the Doctor's regime was to Tom Brown: it pervaded every aspect of the self. Far from dividing his private life from his public life as a promoter of scientific values, he insisted before their marriage that his wife be equally devoted to the project.[46] In a famous letter to the Christian Socialist Charles Kingsley, who had written on the death of Huxley's first son to console the parents with the possibility of immortality, Huxley refused to be consoled by gratifying illusions even at a moment of searing personal need.

> I have searched over the grounds of my belief, and if wife and child and name and fame were all to be lost to me one after the other as the penalty, still I will not lie. . . . The longer I live, the more obvious it is to me that the most sacred act of a man's life is to say and to feel, "I believe such and such to be true." . . . I know what I mean when I say I believe in the law of the inverse squares, and I will not rest my life and my hopes upon weaker convictions. (I, 217)

Like Darwin, Huxley inevitably drew contrasts between scientific and literary thought to science's benefit. He dismissed Wordsworth as "sensuous caterwauling," and his son reported that, "a busy man, time and patience failed him to wade through the trivial discursiveness of so much of Wordsworth's verse" (II, 419). On the other hand, he admired Tennyson for his "comprehension of the meaning of modern science" (II, 420). After Tennyson's memorial service, Huxley contrasted his own poem for the laureate with those of the bourgeois literati: "They are castings of much prettier pattern and of mainly poetico-classical educated-class sentiment. I do not think there is a line of mine one of my old working-class audience would have boggled over. I would give a penny for John Burns' thoughts about it" (II, 339). Unlike more literary writers, with more "personal" investment in their work, Huxley took no credit for the verses, merely asserting that they came to him "in the train."

In a dated but still useful joint biography of Darwin and Huxley, William Irvine contends that Huxley's ideal auditors were intelligent working-class men (like "John Burns"), and in his letters as well as his autobiography Huxley repeatedly aligns himself with them against respectable bourgeois religious and secular culture. His Lectures to Working Men began in 1855, when he contended that he was "sick of the dilettante middle class, and mean to try what I can do with these hard-handed fellows who live among facts. . . . I believe in fustian, and can talk better to it than to any amount of gauze and Saxony" (I, 138). He insisted that working people, less sheltered from the hard realities of the physical world, and less susceptible to consoling illusion, were more open to scientific truth, and he duly devoted some of his copious energies to their technical education. In 1880, he wrote, "There are two things I really care about—one is the progress of scientific thought, and the other is the bettering of the condition of the masses of the people by bettering them in the way of lifting themselves out of the misery which has hitherto been the lot of the majority of them. . . . If I am to be remembered at all, I would rather it should be as 'a man who did his best to help the people'" (I, 476). He began his four famous essays on political equality that were published in 1890 as "a Primer of Politics for the masses" (II, 245), and Leonard Huxley included in the *Life and Letters* extensive testimony from working men in appreciation of his educational efforts on their behalf.

All of Huxley and Darwin's constructed antagonisms, the community of scientific men against the solipsistic poet, science against religion and high culture, working men against an intellectually benighted, superstition-ridden bourgeoisie, are consistent with Huxley's explicit evaluation of subjectivity. In a momentary insight into the traditional literary province of "the self," Irvine wrote of Huxley's considerable talents:

> That he did not turn so fine a talent permanently to literature is not surprising. Huxley was too little attracted to the characteristic subject-matter of the writer. He became interested in man as a physical mechanism, as an anthropoid ape, as a social unit and a citizen, as a delicate machine for the discovery of scientific truth, but never to any appreciable extent in man as a personality and a human being. . . . He was not even interested in himself. Seldom has so vivid and articulate a writer had so little of importance to say, even in his most intimate letters, about himself. . . . For him, writing was an instrument, never an end.[47]

At seventeen, Huxley copied in his notebooks the phrases from Carlyle, "In the mind as in the body the sign of health is unconsciousness" and "The ages of heroism are not ages of Moral Philosophy. Virtue, when it . . . has become aware of itself, is sickly and beginning to decline" (I, 13). Upon his entry into London's scientific community, he wrote to his sister in America of his accomplishments ("a list of titles")—in the third person (I, 158–59). In the aforementioned letter to Kingsley, in which Huxley confessed to "have spoken more openly to you than I ever have to any human being except my wife," he explicitly stated his views about "the self." Kingsley had "rested in the instinct of the persistence of that [personal] existence which is so strong . . . in most men" (I, 218–20). Huxley, on the other hand, rejected the attempt to explore personality, mortal or immortal: "[I]t leads me into mere verbal subtleties . . . ontological speculation has been a folly to me." In subsequent correspondence, he wrote to Kingsley, "*Cogito, ergo sum* is to my mind a ridiculous piece of bad logic, all I can say at any time being 'Cogito.' The Latin form I hold to be preferable to the English 'I think' because the latter asserts the existence of an Ego—about which the bundle of phenomena at present addressing you knows nothing" (I, 242). Whereas Kingsley's subject or "self" is religious, autonomous, indubitable within him, Huxley's is Humean empiricist, verifiable by sense experience only. "I cannot conceive of my personality as a thing apart from the phenomena of my life. . . . My business is to teach my aspirations to conform themselves to fact, not to try and make facts harmonise with my aspirations" (I, 218–21). Pressed by Kingsley on whether he needed the hope of future reward, he adamantly responded that he did not: sinner that he was, he had been "redeemed" by (1) "a deep sense of religion compatible with the entire absence of theology," (2) scientific truth, and (3) love, which "opened up to me a view of the sanctity of human nature, and impressed me with a deep sense of responsibility." "If in the supreme moment when I looked down into my boy's grave," he concludes, "my sorrow was full of sub-mission and without bitterness, it is because these agencies have worked upon me; and not because I have ever cared whether my poor personality shall remain distinct for ever from the All from whence it came and whither it goes." "I am not of a subjective disposition," he wrote as a young man in his diary of the voyage of the Rattlesnake.[48] Like Ruskin, he was an objective recorder of Truth, and as such his "view from nowhere" is open to similar criticism from pluralists. Both men denied themselves as subjective agents in order to speak for objective Truth, which stance, in turn, gave them distinctive individual voices imbued with confidence and self-importance. More than anything, this banish-ment of the individual subject lent to science its prodigious claim to speak for "us."

BEATRICE WEBB, 1858–1943

The last sentence of Beatrice Webb's *My Apprenticeship* (1926) reads, "Here ends 'My Apprenticeship' and opens 'Our Partnership': a working comradeship founded in common faith and made perfect by marriage; perhaps the most exquisite, certainly the most enduring, of all varieties of happiness."[49] Webb's autobiography, however, is neither a utilitarian juggling of varieties of happiness nor a comedy culminating in a mar-riage. As Virginia Woolf, who disliked the workaholism of the Webbs, wrote, fascinated despite herself, "Mrs. Webb's Life makes me compare it with mine. The difference is that she is trying to relate all her experi-ences to history. . . . She has always thought about her life and the mean-ing of the world. . . . She has studied herself as a phenomenon. Thus her autobiography is part of the history of the 19th century."[50] Webb's auto-biography is a discourse on the relationship of the One to the Many, or self to society.

Webb's "apprenticeship" refers to her apprenticeship as a professional social investigator while leading a double life as a Society hostess in one of the wealthiest and most well-connected families in England: an apprenticeship that terminated in 1892 with her marriage to the Fabian Socialist Sidney Webb. From the autobiography's first pages Webb is both personally and theoretically interested in the relationship of self to society. After analyzing her privileged family and childhood and her rejection of revealed religion, she organizes her chapters on her profession ("The Choice of a Craft"), the condition of England's poor ("The Field of Controversy"), her participation in Charles Booth's survey ("A Grand Inquest into the Condition of the People of London"), her management of a housing project and study of labor in the East End ("Observation and Experiment"), and her work with the Consumers' Co-Operative and the Fabians ("Why I Became a Socialist"). When she does introduce her family lineage on the second page, it is not as a personal history ("My father was so and so of such and such a place"), but rather as a product of world-historical events: "The family in which I was born and bred was curiously typical of the industrial development of the nineteenth century" (2).

Webb says in her Introduction that her purpose in writing is to reveal her "philosophy of work or life" (she does not distinguish them), which consists in her answers to two questions. The first concerns the possibility of a science of social organization "enabling us to forecast what will happen, and perhaps to alter the event by taking appropriate action or persuading others to take it." The second asks whether science can be sufficient for the normative component of the project, "Is man's capacity for scientific discovery the only faculty required for the reorganisation of society according to an ideal?" (xliv). Professing her lack of talent and training as a philosopher, Webb justifies her answer to these questions in the form of an autobiography because "the very subject matter of my science is society; its main instrument is social intercourse; thus I can hardly leave out of the picture the experience I have gathered, not deliberately as a scientific worker, but casually as child, unmarried woman, wife and citizen" (1). For Webb, the eye of the social scientist, or of the scientific autobiographer, has already been fashioned by the circumstances of her society—her subjective experience will influence her objective science: "It is [the sociologist's] own social and economic circumstance that determines . . . the inevitable bias which ought to be known to the student of his work so that it may be adequately discounted" (2). With this assertion of the implication of the observer in the social circumstance, of the subject in the object of study, Webb instructs the reader, "if in describing my apprenticeship I tell too long and too egotistical a tale, the student can skip what appears to him irrelevant" (2).

Like Darwin's, Webb's resistance to limiting her autobiography to her private life or even to her individual life is calculated. She presents herself as writing to students of society rather than leisured consumers of personal biography. In many ways the distinction, which pervades her written life, is motivated by her peculiar position in British society. She understands this position as her subjective "controversy between an Ego that affirms and an Ego that denies" (vliii and passim). The Ego that affirms "lives 'as if' the soul of man were in communion with a superhuman force which makes for righteousness" (345) and represents "the power of self-sacrifice in the individual for the good of the community" (101). The Ego that denies exhibits the individualism that denies human interdependence.

Webb understands this "controversy" as a subjective, personal struggle related to her particular social position as well as an "objective" or general struggle between the social classes. The ego that denies is exemplified by her genial and beloved father, the industrial capitalist and financier Richard Potter, who in her estimation "tended to prefer the welfare of his family and personal friends to the interests of the companies over which he presided, the profits of these companies to the prosperity of his country, the dominance of his own race to the peace of the world" (7). She discovered early on that personal vanity was an "occupational disease" of London Society (49) and that she, as an ornamentally pretty young woman, was especially susceptible to it. While hostess of her father's household in Hyde Park and his private secretary in business affairs, she visits slums with the C.O.S. and experiences "the strain and stress of a multiple personality" (114). She participates in morning calls in the West End whose topics revolve around sales at Christie's and clandestinely reads psychology and political economy, experiencing a "doubleness of motive" between her "active" and "real" lives, respectively (121–22). She sees the controversy between egotism and altruism possessing society at large as well: "The flight of emotion away from the service of God to the service of man ... became a characteristic feature of the publications of this period [i.e., early 1880s] ... due neither to intellectual curiosity nor to the spirit of philanthropy, but rather to a panic fear of the newly enfranchised democracy" (150).

A similar duality of egoism and altruism is evident in Webb's complex attitude to literature and her own literary style. The autobiography is intended to reflect the conditions of its production: large chunks of her diary, extending sporadically from her childhood and systematically from the age of sixteen, are incorporated verbatim within the narrative of the sixty-year-old woman, so that she may comment critically upon her intellectual and emotional development, giving *My Apprenticeship* the kind of "objective" and self-conscious quality that has made it unusually agreeable (i.e., for autobiography) to historians. She intends this representation of self and society as a sociohistorical process to predominate over the relatively "closed" form of monologic narrative, in her terms, the "personal outlook and originality" of more "literary" authors (94–95). Like Darwin, and with Darwin's purchase for "science," she writes of the "mental defect" that encourages her to read everything but poetry. Like Mill, she attributes the expressiveness of internal life to poetry—"a picture of what is taking place within"—composed of a "magic of words" to which she, however, is impervious. The internality of soliloquy and individualism of authorship do not conform to her social sense: "Racine and Corneille . . . brought to me no conviction that they knew anything about the men and affairs they portrayed. . . . Tennyson's . . . sentimental imagery seemed to me incomprehensible nonsense. . . . Shakespeare's plays and poems . . . bored me" (95). "One of the unforeseen pleasures of old age," she concludes, "is the faint beginning of a liking for exquisite literature irrespective of its subject matter" (96). The subject matter that had previously attracted her was "MS. minutes, or bundles of local Acts relating to particular towns."

Webb distrusts the descriptive specificity in poetry that contributes to a psychological state of sentimental empathy rather than transformative engagement. (Later she would call Virginia Woolf's work "trivial.") In a famous passage, she answers the charge of Henry Nevinson—whose "liberal" stories about workers in the East End are discussed in Chapter 3— that her undefined and unimaginable "class" was less likely to motivate her readers than an individual case sympathetically presented. Webb replies in defense of her statistics, "To me 'a million sick' have always seemed actually more worthy of self-sacrificing devotion than the 'child sick in a fever' preferred by Mrs. Browning's *Aurora Leigh*" (258)—a response that reinforces, as in her later differences with Woolf, her rejection of gender stereotypes. In the famous agon between Aurora and Romney in Book 2 of Barrett Browning's "novel in verse," a Victorian anatomy of female subjectivity and female desire for literary authorship, Romney attacks Aurora for her feminine sentimentality, "personal and passionate," and passionately appeals to the statistical study of society and the amelioration of social conditions. I quote the passage from *Aurora Leigh* (1857) because it confirms Webb's implicit identification with the systematic Romney against the female author's appeal to the artistic detail, the "special case." It is significant that Barrett Browning, progressive in many ways for her times, had rejected socialism (repre-

sented by Romney's Fourier-styled phalanstery) because she thought it
would stifle individualism, art, and literature. Romney says to Aurora:

> ... Dear, my soul is grey
> With poring over the long sum of ill;
> So much for vice, so much for discontent,
> So much for the necessities of power,
> So much for the connivances of fear,—
> Coherent in statistical despairs
> With such a total of distracted life, ...
> To see it down in figures on a page,
> Plain, silent, clear. ... that's terrible
> For one who is not God, and cannot right
> The wrong he looks on. May I choose indeed
> But vow away my years, my means, my aims,
> Among the helpers, if there's any help
> In such a social strait? The common blood
> That swings along my veins, is strong enough
> To draw me to this duty.[51]

Webb further denied the role of the "feminine" motivations of feeling
and compassion in her choice to study the chronic destitution of whole
sections of the population, insisting rather that she had been moved by a
rational (for Barrett Browning, "male") interest in the great problem
"raging in periodicals and books" (173). That is, she entered the controversy intellectually, not emotionally.

Yet the great problem of the relationship of the One to the Many, the
self to society, continued to preoccupy Webb in the relation of personal
observation to statistical data. In this she turned for guidance to the social
novelists (later, she would recommend the very Edwardians like Bennett
and Wells whom Woolf deplored). She found in sociological fiction
"descriptive psychology," "the mental make-up of individual men and
women, and their behavior under particular conditions." She "experi-
mented" in such descriptive prose herself: "there begin to appear in my
diary, from 1882 onwards, realistic scenes from country and town life,
descriptions of manners and morals, analytic portraits of relations and
friends. ... It is, however, significant that these sketches from life nearly
always concern the relation of the individual to some particular social
organisation: to big enterprise, or to Parliament, to the profession of law,
or of medicine or of the Church" (109).

Webb's interest in the relationship of the individual to state power, "some particular social organisation," drove her from the psychology of her time with its abstraction, "yielding no more accurate information about the world around me than did the syllogisms of formal logic," toward the powers and human agency represented in fiction and narrative poetry like the Brownings'. "For any detailed description of the complexity of human nature, of the variety and mixture in human motive, of the insurgence of instinct in the garb of reason, of the multifarious play of the social environment on the individual ego and of the individual ego of the social environment, I had to turn to novelists and poets, to Fielding and Flaubert, to Balzac and Browning, to Thackeray and Goethe" (138). She cites a diary entry of 1889 in which her social planning finds release "in the vulgar wish to write a novel": "This last month or so I have been haunted by a longing to create characters and to move them to and fro among fictitious circumstances. . . . I see before me persons and scenes; I weave plots, and clothe persons, scenes and plots in my own philosophy" (398). She favorably contrasts "the comparative ease of descriptive writing" with the material of the sociologist, "movements of commodities, percentages, depreciations, averages, and all the ugly horrors of commercial facts."

Yet Webb cannot yield to creative desires that in the long run she believes to be less effective in transforming society, which is her motivating passion. Like Huxley, who had had prolonged exposure to the very poor when he was a medical student, Webb also believed that "there was no alleviation for the sufferings of mankind" except "the application of scientific methods of investigation to all the problems of life": "The whole multitude of novels I have read pass before me; the genius, the talent . . . what have the whole lot of them, from the work of genius to the penny-a-liner, accomplished for the advancement of society on the one and only basis that can bring with it virtue and happiness—the scientific method?"(399) Webb's view of imaginative literature (in the restricted form of the social novel—that which "showed the relation of the individual to some particular social organisation") was not that it was wrong, for it provided richer descriptions of psychology and social life than did the social science of her youth, but that it was no longer a credible agent or discourse for social change in the modern world. Suppressing her longings to manipulate broad social life in the personally gratifying form of a novel, she accepted her altruistic duty to speak to the Many in the current coinage of scientific authority. One of the outstanding dramas of *My Apprenticeship* remains Webb's subjective debate concerning the appropriate discursive form to influence social change.

Webb ultimately opted for collaborative writing, she interviewing and recording personal observations, while Sidney collated the voluminous statistical reports necessary to social investigation (the woman again mediating between the experience and the abstraction). The second volume of her autobiography, prepared for posthumous publication by others, was an autobiography *à deux* entitled *Our Partnership* (1948) that followed the Webbs at midcareer, showing the middle-aged couple at work. Woolf, childless herself, and still skeptical that a political project could be the foundation of personal happiness, shook her head at "the pathos of the childless couple."[52]

Webb's autobiography has been neglected by literary critics after Woolf because, as Jerome Buckley wrote apropos her exclusion from the canon, spiritual autobiography "requires the premise of interest in significant selfhood and something, too, of a poet's regard for remembered individual detail."[53] Webb has been marginalized, that is, precisely for succeeding throughout a lifetime of struggle in overcoming "the significant selfhood" (upper-class individualism and "autonomy") and "individual detail" (women's sensitivity to the special case and minutiae) that her class and gender had provided for her, to her mind, unjustly. In rejecting Buckley's generic limitations upon autobiography, I would still like to preserve for Webb some of the personality, and for her discourse some of the detail, that Buckley (and other less knowledgeable critics) have denied her. To do this I shall use the cases of Joseph Chamberlain and Sidney Webb. I do this not as a defensive retreat into Webb's so-called personal life as a way to establish her "individuality." That would be to reinstate the feminine connotations of private life that I believe have been problematized in the context of the very heterogeneous women I discuss in this study. On the contrary, I wish to stress that part of Webb's claim on our attention is, like Mill's, the consistency with which she rejected a dualism of public and private, of society and self.

Even in the public form of *My Apprenticeship,* Webb confesses that her persistent suitor won her by his "resolute, patient affection, his constant care for my welfare—helping and correcting me—[and] a growing distrust of self-absorbed life and the egotism of successful work" (411–12). To her diary she explicitly confessed her intention to marry as a means "to serve the 'commonwealth'" (cited xxxix). This extraordinarily rational—most, I imagine, would say "perverse"—decision may be contrasted with her agonized diary entries (omitted from the autobiography) from 1883 to 1888 on her passion for Joseph Chamberlain, a passion she perceived to be irreconcilable with her work.

At that time Chamberlain was mayor of Birmingham and spokesperson for the influential Radical wing of the Liberal Party. In a description of him at a political demonstration in Birmingham in 1884 in *My Apprenticeship,* Webb projects onto him the obsessive dialectic of ego- and altruism that she dissected in herself and—evidently unconsciously—projects her own fear of his power to dominate her, and her own desire to submit to him, onto his working-class audience. Some Victorians saw Chamberlain as an exceptionally charismatic demagogue— he was certainly the most controversial politician of his day; but I quote the passage at length for Webb's striking portrayal of the quintessential "object of desire" and its effect upon Webb:

> You could watch in his expression some form of feeling working itself into the mastery of his mind. Was that feeling spontaneous or intentioned? Was it created by an intense desire to dominate, to impress his own personality and his own aim on that pliable material beneath him; or did it arise from the consciousness of helpful power, from genuine sympathy with the wants and cravings of the great mass who trusted him?
>
> As he rose slowly, and stood silently before his people, his whole face and form seemed transformed. The crowd became wild with enthusiasm. Hats, handkerchiefs, even coats, were waved frantically as an outlet for feeling. The few hundreds of privileged individuals seated in the balcony rose to their feet. There was one loud uproar of applause and, in the intervals between each fresh outburst, one could distinguish the cheers of the crowd outside, sending its tribute of sympathy. Perfectly still stood the people's Tribune, till the people, exhausted and expectant, gradually subsided into fitful and murmuring cries. At the first sound of his voice they became as one man. Into the tones of his voice he threw the warmth of feeling which was lacking in his words; and every thought, every feeling, the slightest intonation of irony or contempt was reflected on the face of the crowd. It might have been a woman listening to the words of her lover. (127)

In *My Apprenticeship* Webb refers to these years of frustrated passion (not presented as such) as "the dead point," when she is self-divided between a longing for domestic love and an incompatible (i.e., incompatible with Chamberlain) career. "I saw myself as one suffering from a divided personality; the normal woman seeking personal happiness in love given and taken within the framework of a successful marriage; whilst the Other Self claimed . . . the right to the free activity of 'a clear and analytic mind'" (279). In her uncensored diary she was more explicit: "There is a glitter all around me and darkness within, the darkness of blind desire yearning for the light of love."[54] Her interpolated diary entries in *My Apprenticeship* show her constructing an internalized self she calls "the Unknown One." The Unknown One is precisely the self that is constructed antagonistically, by the insufficiency or oppressiveness of daily life. It is Orwell's "inner self," Gosse's "two in the depths who could speak to one another in inviolable secrecy," and White's "small core of rebelliousness." Webb compares her desire for Chamberlain in her diary to her lack of love in childhood (i.e., her mother's comparative lack of interest in Beatrice in relation to her nine siblings). The passage is a dense representation of defeat, first in its defensive introspection and then in its self-denial through reason and the crucible of passion. It is additionally interesting in its self-consciousness of the function of writing in the creation of an isolated subjectivity:

> It would be curious to discover *who it is* to whom one writes in a diary? Possibly to some mysterious personification of one's own identity, to the Unknown, which lies below the constant change in matter and ideas, constituting the individual at any given moment. This unknown one was once my only friend; the being to whom I went for advice and consolation in all the small troubles of a child's life. Well do I remember, as a small thing, sitting under the damp bushes, and brooding over the want of love around one (possibly I could not discern it), and turning in upon myself, and saying, "thou and I will live alone and if life be unbearable we will die".... So then I went my own little way, and noted diligently what I saw, and began on that to reason. Soon I found that there were other minds seeing and reasoning, who would in their strength carry me on my way.... But still I loved only the Unknown one, and my feeling was constantly looking inward, though my reason was straining its utmost to grasp what was outside. Then came friendship in the guise of intellectual sympathy; in later years, discovering its true nature in affection, gently putting reason, with its eternal analysis, on one side. And last of all came passion, with its burning heat; and emotion, which had for long smouldered unseen, burst into flame, and burnt down intellectual interests, personal ambition, and all other self-developing motives. (280–81)

"And now," Webb concluded the passage, putting away the privatized self, "the Unknown one is a mere phantom, seldom conjured up, and then not grasped. Reason and emotion alike have turned towards the outer world. To-day, I say humbly, 'we have learnt, poor thing, that we can neither see, think nor feel alone, much less live, without the help of others. Therefore we must live *for* others, and take what happiness comes to us by the way" (281). When John Stuart Mill was at his emotional nadir (represented in his "Crisis" chapter), a point he calls "irrepressible self-consciousness," he rejected his self-absorption with purpose similar to Webb's "we must live *for* others": "Those only are happy (I thought) who have their minds fixed on some object other than their own happiness; on the happiness of others, on the improvement of mankind, even on some art or pursuit, followed not as a means, but as itself an ideal end. Aiming thus at something else, they find happiness by the way."[55] Structurally, Mill's gesture is the same as Orwell's putting away his egoistic motives for writing ("the same instinct that makes a baby squall for attention") to insist that, "it is invariably where I lacked a *political* purpose that I wrote lifeless books . . . and humbug generally."[56] Norman Mackenzie has argued that Webb came to depend upon her diary as she got older precisely to embody that private self that was suppressed by her altruism. I would rather argue against a theory of repression and for the nonexistence of that self *outside* of the frame that had first given it life, the frame of writing, her diary. This self is not so much suppressed by her life in society as it is cultivated independently elsewhere. It is not so much primary as, literally, Other.

For even if Webb was the Unknown One to herself, *My Apprenticeship* is dedicated "To the Other One," Sidney, marriage with whom constituted "this culminating event of my life" (401) (i.e., what the voyage of the Beagle was to Darwin). As with Chamberlain (always called, with some irony, "the great man"), Webb includes a description of "the Other One" from her diary, not as an object of desire dramatically elevated above his subjects, but as an object of domestic amusement at the most sociable of events, a dinner party: "Sidney Webb, the socialist, dined here [Devonshire House Hotel] to meet the Booths. A remarkable little man with a huge head and a tiny body, a breadth of forehead quite sufficient to account for the encyclopaedic character of his knowledge. A Jewish nose, prominent eyes and mouth, black hair, somewhat unkempt, spectacles and a most bourgeois black coat shiny with wear. But I like the man" (408). In a diary entry not included in *My Apprenticeship,* she struggled against her own class prejudice, wearing away her own distaste for Sidney's alterity: "That man's tiny tadpole body, unhealthy skin, lack of manner, Cockney pronunciation, poverty are all against him."[57] She insisted that she would not marry him until she loved him, and that she did not love him yet; yet the *reasons* for loving him were in place—again insisting that reason and passion, like public and private, must not be divorced. She told him, "Dear Sidney, I will try to love you, but do not be impatient. . . . What can I do more? I am doing more than I would for any other man, simply because you are a socialist and I am a socialist. That other man I loved but did not believe in; you I believe in but do not love."[58]

At the age of ten, a precocious Beatrice Potter had estimated that novels "destroy many a young mind": "The whole of their thought is wasted on making up love scenes, or building castles in the air, where [the reader] is always the charming heroine without a fault. . . . [W]henever I get alone I always find myself building castles in the air of some kind" (62). Around Joseph Chamberlain she built such a castle in the air. With Sidney Webb, she founded the London School of Economics.

Yet there is a coda to this tale of a citizen's successful attempt to evade the egotism of her class and sentimentality of her gender. Her diary being the space she reserved for the Other life, she had little to write on the day she married "for the Commonwealth." But she did write, "Exit Beatrice Potter. Enter Beatrice Webb, or rather (Mrs.) Sidney Webb for I lose alas! both names."[59] Thus she registered her triumphant, but very self-conscious, self-suppression.

Concluding Observations through 1990

In "The Society of the Future" (1887), William Morris criticized the "hunters of introspection" and predicted that in the society of the future "you will no longer be able to have novels relating the troubles of a middle-class couple in their struggle toward social uselessness, because the material for such literary treasures will have passed away."[60] Morris's communitarian concern over introspection and the privatizing of experience, and the Church, family, and state that gave them rise, is borne out by the preceding analyses of literary subjectivity—a subjectivity that rebels against its external environment even while it conserves and defines itself by means of traditional social prejudices. This objectifying of others and internalizing of the self was either unavailable to others due to their material positions in a society stratified by gender and class or rejected by others with more communitarian (the Chartists or Suffragettes) or corporate (the scientists, public school boys, Viscountess Rhondda) values: literacy per se is not essential to the distinction. If the predominance of the self in modernist literature led to what Durrell called the "autism" of the modern artist, many critics today still claim that the alienated artist's opposition to community on the one hand was compensated by the possibility of constructing a new world on the other. There is no doubt that the sort of writers whom Harold Bloom calls "strong poets" or Richard Rorty calls "creators of new language" and "the vangard of the species" construct possible *worlds,* but it is less likely that, in their passionate individualism, they have it in them to create possible *communities.*[61] In this chapter, I have tried to show how the "strong poets" or rebellious literary writers were more conservative than we have thought and how Ruskin, Mill, Webb, perhaps even Darwin and Huxley, still have something to tell us about a commitment to community. In the preceding chapters I have hoped to show that possible communities as well as possible worlds have been eloquently articulated and even *built* by common people for whom "the anxiety of influence" and distinctions between their private lives and public duties were the last things on their minds. In general, history shows us more kinds of selves and communities than dreamt of in literature or philosophy. Rather than be mesmerized by the postmodern death of the strong, centered subject, secure in his Truth, I have hoped to release a plurality of subjectivities that have not always been valued heretofore.

Two observations seem appropriate in concluding this chapter on literary subjectivity and its alternatives in Victorian and early twentieth-century Britain. First, the very qualities that have made modern imaginative literature dear to the introverted, marginal, isolated, or rebellious—its indomitable "creative imagination," persistent individualism and concern for the "special case," and dream of autonomy from oppressive social institutions—have also prevented it (and its readers) from fully appreciating the cooperative social visions of a Thomas Hardy (the shoemaker) or William Lovett, an Annie Kenney or Annie Besant. (An alternative cooperative vision, Darwin and Huxley's corporate science, could still be said to be in antagonistic relations with literary individualism.) Second, religious and familial discourse of the sort that Gosse, Butler, Sinclair, and White rebelled against, and that working-class writers like James Burn and Emma Smith suffered under, has never been more pervasive in U.S. life, from television Evangelism to the mantralike incantation of "Family Values" since the National Conventions of both political parties during Summer 1988. One might still remark with Mill upon "the subject of the family, the most important of any, and needing more fundamental alterations than remain to be made in any other great social institution, but on which scarcely any reformer has the courage to touch." At the same time, the Chartists', Suffragettes', or Webb's passion for social justice—Ruskin's "whether there be one God or three, no God or ten thousand, children should have enough to eat"—or Mill's for tolerance of diversity, is less evident than it has been at any time during my lifetime. As we enter what many are calling the postliterate society, one wonders whether the critical perspectives of literary subjectivity will survive the decline of reading in mass media culture. If literary subjectivity does decline, one wonders whether the "other possibilities," the cultural narratives of freedom (from scarcity, from superstition and lies, and from political tyranny) will revive.

On the other hand, the traditional discourses of social justice—the communitarianism of Ruskin or the progressivism of Mill—have been criticized in the past century by feminists and non-Europeans for clothing differences in veils of identity and contributing to oppositions of civilization and barbarism. At least in the United States, the more extreme of these critiques can make communitarianism and progressivism appear as oppressive and intolerant as the New Right narratives of Family Values and Flag Allegiance are to those without families or the full rights of citizenship. Moreover, there are forces within contemporary society that erode the meaningfulness of traditional communitarian or progressive discourses in people's lives. It is too early to say with any confidence, but it appears that amid the sheer volume of "information" produced in media societies the traditional discourses of social justice—like the Labour Party's or progressivism's or traditional feminism's—are less available, are diffused and levelled among other signifying systems, and that more fluid affinities and alliances rather than the monolithic identities of traditional progressive politics seem to be the way people see their lives.

With these affinities and more "fractured" identities, a new kind of autobiography is emerging that both addresses the critique of traditional progressive politics and participates more fully in the universalizing yet multicultural nature of contemporary society. In these autobiographies, the self that cannot adjust to the status quo no longer retreats inward in the isolated aesthetic of a White or a Connolly, but, like Victorian working-class autobiographers, rather draws upon many narratives of personal and public histories, situating itself always in history and always among others, both friendly and hostile. Multicultural autobiographies like Audre Lorde's *Zami: A New Spelling of My Name* (1982), Kate Simon's *Bronx Primitive: Portraits in a Childhood* (1982), Kim Chernin's *In My Mother's House: A Daughter's Story* (1983), Sandra Cisneros's *The House on Mango Street* (1984), Carolyn Steedman's *Landscape for a*

Good Woman: A Story of Two Lives (1986), Joan Nestle's *A Restricted Country* (1987), and Gloria Anzaldúa's *Borderlands/La Frontera: The New Mestiza* (1987) are the new narratives of social justice, continuing the projects of Ruskin, Mill, and Webb without their respective myopias.[62] They—like all autobiography—show that the study of autobiography is not merely a genteel (or gentile or genital) literary exercise but a gauge of citizens' degrees of social participation and exclusion, consensus and revolt. Autobiographies can tell us the views of those who in polls "have no opinion," and they can tell us why a people do not vote. Their stories are largely overshadowed by the more familiar narratives of capitalist mass culture; but, as this study has shown, once cultural narratives (macro- and micro-) are in circulation they have a way of drawing in Others.

Notes

Introduction

1. See Chaim Perelman and L. Olbrechts-Tyteca, *The New Rhetoric: A Treatise on Argumentation* (Notre Dame: University of Notre Dame, 1969) and Perelman, *The New Rhetoric and the Humanities* (Holland: Reidel, 1979). Also see Wesley Trimpi, *Muses of One Mind: The Literary Analysis of Experience and Its Continuity* (Princeton: Princeton University Press, 1983).

2. Isocrates, *Antidosis* (13). Trans. George Norlin. Loeb Classical Library in *Isocrates* 3 vols. (London: Heinemann, 1929), p. 193.

3. Adena Rosmarin, *The Power of Genre* (Minneapolis: University of Minnesota Press, 1985), pp. 3–15.

4. *Social Text* 16 (Winter 1986–87), pp. 38–79. See especially the discussion of Johnson's diagram of the circuit, p. 47. For the project of cultural studies associated with the Birmingham Centre for Contemporary Cultural Studies, see Stuart Hall et al., "Cultural Studies and the Centre: Some Problematics and Problems" in *Culture, Media, Language,* ed. Stuart Hall, Dorothy Hobson, Andrew Lowe, and Paul Willis (London, 1980), pp. 15–47. The two classic founding texts of cultural studies in Britain are, of course, Richard Hoggart's *The Uses of Literacy* (Harmondsworth: Penguin, 1958) and E. P. Thompson's *The Making of the Working Class in England* (Penguin, 1968). Of nearly equal importance were Raymond Williams's *Culture and Society* (Harmondsworth: Penguin, 1961) and *The Long Revolution* (Penguin, 1965).

5. Thomas Henry Huxley and Charles Darwin, *Autobiographies,* ed. Gavin de Beer (London: Oxford University Press, 1974), p. 100.

6. Michel Foucault, "What is an Author?" *The Foucault Reader,* ed. Paul Rabinow (New York: Pantheon, 1984), pp. 101–20.

7. *The Foucault Reader,* pp. 362–70. See also Volumes 2 and 3 of Foucault's History of Sexuality, *The Use of Pleasure* (New York: Random House, 1985) and *Care of the Self* (New York: Random House, 1986).

8. Louis Althusser, *Lenin and Philosophy and Other Essays.* Trans. Ben Brewster (London: New Left Books, 1971).

9. *I, Pierre Rivière, Having Slaughtered My Mother, My Sister, and My Brother,* Ed. Michel Foucault (New York: Pantheon, 1975); *Herculine Barbin: Being the Recently Discovered Memoirs of a Nineteenth-Century French Hermaphrodite* Ed. Michel Foucault (New York: Pantheon, 1980).

10. Raymond Williams, *Culture and Society* (Harmondsworth: Penguin, 1961), *The Long Revolution* (Penguin, 1965), *The Country and the City* (London: Chatto and Windus, 1973), and *Marxism and Literature* (Oxford: Oxford University Press, 1977); E. P. Thompson, *The Poverty of Theory* (London: Merlin Press, 1979); Pierre Bourdieu, *Outline of a Theory of Practice* (Cambridge: Cambridge University Press, 1987); Anthony Giddens, *The Constitution of Society: Outline of the Theory of Structuration* (Berkeley: University of California Press, 1984), *A Contemporary Critique of Historical Materialism* (University of California Press, 1981), *Social Theory and Modern Sociology* (Stanford: Stanford University Press, 1987), and ed. with Jonathan H. Turner *Social Theory Today* (Stanford University Press, 1987).

11. Anthony Giddens, *The Consequences of Modernity* (Palo Alto: Stanford University Press, 1990).

12. See Mary Douglas and Baron Isherwood, *The World of Goods* (New York: Basic Books, 1979); Donna Haraway, "A Manifesto for Cyborgs: Science, Technology, and Socialist Feminism in the 1980s" (*Socialist Review* 80 [March–April, 1985]) 65–107; Elaine Scarry, *The Body in Pain: The Making and Unmaking of the World* (New York: Oxford University Press, 1985).

13. Thomas Nagel, *Mortal Questions,* especially essays 11, 12, and 14 (Cambridge: Cambridge University Press, 1979).

14. See also the work of Bernard Williams in *Problems of the Self,* especially essays 1 and 2 (Cambridge: Cambridge University Press, 1973), in which Williams argues, *contra* Locke, that (1) bodily continuity is a necessary condition of personal identity; (2) we cannot distinguish personality without reference to a body; and (3) the omission of the body deprives the idea of identity of all content.

For a major analytic work on personal identity (within the context of liberalism as discussed later) see Derek Parfit, *Reasons and Persons* (Oxford: Oxford University Press, 1986), esp. Part Three "Personal Identity," 199–347.

15. Scheman cited in Alison Jaggar, *Feminist Politics and Human Nature* (Totowa: Rowman and Allanheld, 1983), p. 43.

16. Tom Wolfe, *The Bonfire of the Vanities* (London: Picador, 1988), pp. 546–47.

17. See Jacques Lacan, *Ecrits: A Selection,* trans. Alan Sheridan (New York: Norton, 1977); Margaret Homans, *Bearing the Word: Language and Female Experience in Nineteenth-Century Women's Writing* (Chicago: University of Chicago Press, 1986); Julia Kristeva, *Desire in Language,* ed. Leon Roudiez, trans. Thomas Gora et al. (New York: Columbia University Press, 1980); Luce Irigaray, *This Sex Which Is Not One,* trans. Catherine Porter with Carolyn Burke (Ithaca: Cornell University Press, 1985) and *Speculum of the Other Woman,* trans. Gillian C. Gill (Ithaca: Cornell University Press, 1985).

18. I discuss feminist postmodernism at length in "Feminist Postmodernism: The End of Feminism or the Ends of Theory," in *Theoretical Perspectives on Sexual Difference,* ed. Deborah Rhode (New Haven: Yale University Press, 1990), 21–30. See also Jane Flax, "Postmodernism and Gender Relations in Feminist Theory," *Signs* 12(4) (Summer 1987), pp. 621–43; Donna Haraway, "A Manifesto for Cyborgs. Science, Technology, and Socialist Feminism in the 1980s," *Socialist Review* 80 (March–April 1985), 65–107; Sandra Harding, *The Science Question in Feminism* (Ithaca: Cornell University Press, 1986), esp. Chapters 6 and 7.

19. Nancy Armstrong, *Desire and Domestic Fiction: A Political History of the Novel* (New York: Oxford University Press, 1987).

20. *Borderlands: La Frontera: The New Mestiza* (San Francisco: Spinsters, 1987), p. 66.

21. Nadine Gordimer, John Dugard, Richard Smith, et al., *What Happened to Burger's Daughter, or How South African Censorship Works* (Johannesburg, SA: Taurus, 1980), p. 55. I am grateful to Alexandra Chasin for this reference. For Gordimer on the role of the writer, see also, "Living in the Interregnum," *New York Review of Books* (20 January 1983), p. 25.

22. Pierre Bourdieu, *Distinction: A Social Critique of the Judgement of Taste* (Cambridge: Harvard University Press, 1984), p. 5.

23. Immanuel Kant, *Critique of Judgment,* trans. Werner S. Pluhar (Indianapolis: Hackett, 1987), pp. 44–45.

24. Walter Pater, *The Renaissance,* "Winckelmann," (Berkeley: University of California Press, 1980), pp. 169–74.

25. *Critique of Judgment,* p. 228.

26. Pascal, *Pensées* (Middlesex: Penguin, 1966), pp. 229–30.

27. In his useful historical and philosophical survey of the uses of the concept of "individualism," Steven Lukes shows how its range of meanings extended from free competition in relation to the production and distribution of wealth to socialism (*Individualism* [Oxford: Basil Blackwell, 1985]).

28. John Rawls, *A Theory of Justice* (Cambridge: Belknap Press, 1971). Ronald Dworkin, "The Foundations of Liberal Equality: The Point of Political Theory and The Ethics of Equal Concern," Tanner Lectures in Human Values, Stanford University, May 1988.

29. Joseph Raz, *The Morality of Freedom* (Oxford: Clarendon, 1986). For this qualification concerning some of the most sympathetic defenders of liberalism, I am indebted to a sequence of correspondence with Charles Altieri.

30. *Feminist Politics and Human Nature* (Sussex: Harvester Press, 1983), pp. 28–29.

31. *An Essay Concerning Human Understanding,* ed. Peter H. Nidditch (Oxford: Oxford University Press, 1979).

32. *The Second Treatise of Government* (Oxford: Basil Blackwell, 1956). I am grateful to Kelly Mays for drawing my attention to these passages in *The Second Treatise of Government.*

33. *The Unknown Mayhew,* ed. Eileen Yeo and E. P. Thompson (New York: Pantheon, 1971), p. 348.

34. Previously the intersection of CLS and literary theory has been on common epistemological and interpretive problems. The question that CLS posed using the tools and methods of literary criticism was, do the materials of law—constitutions, statutes, judicial decisions—have determinable and objective meaning, or is what we call their "meaning" in fact created by a community of interpreters? The question has been debated in the Texas, Cardozo, Rutgers, Chicago, Stanford, and Harvard law reviews and in *Critical Inquiry:* is there an originalist or founders' authorial intention, or mere readerly invention? Legal reasoning and legal consciousness were alleged to be as indeterminate as authorial intention in literary studies. Although the legal text/literary text issues are theoretically similar, and perhaps equally divisive, such discussion usually foundered on the contention that legal interpretation issues in decisive actions. Legal interpretation has a Supreme Court, whose judgments are at least temporarily decisive. Literary interpretation, on the other hand, has many courts, from coast to

coast and internationally, and as far as we can tell it is open-ended. (Needless to say, many did not accept this distinction.) But even when theorists could agree—as it seems to me philosophically the case—that the meaning of law and literature is created by a community of interpreters, they were resistant to addressing the issue of how legal and literary interpretive communities changed. For us literary scholars who knew that although any text was a function of its interpreters, its history of interpretation was a great factor in its current reception, the debate rapidly grew tedious. Stanley Fish's altercations with legal theorists are paradigmatic of the discussion and may be taken as a starting point for readers interested in the debates. See the exchanges between Ronald Dworkin and Fish in *The Politics of Interpretation,* ed. W.J.T. Mitchell (Chicago: University of Chicago Press, 1983); between Fish and Walter A. Davis in *Critical Inquiry* (June 1984), pp. 669–718; Fish, "Interpretation and the Pluralist Vision," in *Texas Law Review* 60(3) (March 1982) pp. 495–505; Fish, "Fish v. Fiss," *Stanford Law Review* 36 (1984) pp. 1325–47 (a response to Owen Fiss, "Objectivity and Interpretation," *Stanford Law Review* 34 [1982] 739–63); Fish, "Critical Legal Studies: Unger and Milton," *Raritan* 7(2) (Fall 1987), pp. 1–20.

Such debates over intention or invention—in fact not significantly different from traditional debates in philosophy of law—have obscured for literary studies other trajectories of CLS, which was fueled in 1977 not by philosophical hermeneutics, but by the feeling that legal theory had come to justify the status quo, or, in Marxist and feminist terms, that law was in the service of the ruling class and gender. CLS's first task was to critique the so-called Law and Economics theorists and "rights" theorists for this rationalization of inequality, which it did in a form called "trashing," or "delegitimating" (deconstruction). Its second task was to propose something else, to transform the institution of the law.

The response to CLS has been voluminous. For the great collections see *Stanford Law Review* 36 (1&2) (January 1984), *Harvard Law Review* Special volume on CLS (Harvard Law Review Association, 1986); and David Kairys, *The Politics of Law: A Progressive Critique* (New York: Pantheon, 1982). See also Mark Kelman, *A Guide to CLS* (Cambridge: Harvard University Press, 1987).

35. See Robin West, "Jurisprudence and Gender," *University of Chicago Law Review,* 55(1) (Winter 1988) pp. 1–72 and "The Difference in Women's Hedonic Lives: A Phenomenological Critique of Feminist Legal Theory," *Wisconsin Women's Law Journal* 3 (1987), pp. 81–145. For the most extensive treatments of the consequences of female nurturing, see Nancy Chodorow, *The Reproduction of Mothering: Psychoanalysis and the Sociology of Gender* (Berkeley: University of California Press, 1978); Carol Gilligan, *In a Different Voice: Psychological Theory and Women's Development* (Cambridge: Harvard University Press, 1982); and Dorothy Dinnerstein, *The Mermaid and the Minotaur: Sexual Arrangement and Human Malaise* (New York: Harper and Row, 1976).

36. Roberto Mangabeira Unger, *Knowledge and Politics* (New York: Free Press, 1976); *Passion: An Essay on Personality* (New York: Free Press, 1984); *The Critical Legal Studies Movement* (Cambridge: Harvard University Press, 1986); and *Politics: A Work in Constitutive Social Theory,* 3 vols. (Cambridge: Cambridge University Press, 1987).

37. See Peter Gabel and Duncan Kennedy, "Roll Over Beethoven," *Stanford Law Review* 36 (January 1984), pp. 1–55, and Kennedy, "Legal Education As Training For Hierarchy," in Kairys (1982), pp. 40–61.

38. Drusilla Cornell, "Toward a Modern/Postmodern Reconstruction of Ethics," *University of Pennsylvania Law Review* 133(2) (January 1985), pp. 291–380 and "The Poststructuralist Challenge to the Ideal of Community," *Cardozo Law Review* 8(5) (April 1987), pp. 989–1022.

39. *Knowledge and Politics,* p. 232.

40. See Robert W. Gordon, "Critical Legal Histories," *Stanford Law Review* 36, pp. 57–125.

41. See Chapter 5; Ward Harper, "Review Essay: The Critical Legal Studies Movement," *American Philosophical Association Newsletter on Philosophy and Law* (November 1987), pp. 3–12; the two essay by Cornell in note 38; and James Boyle, "Modernist Social Theory: Roberto Unger's *Passion,*" *Harvard Law Review* 96(4) (February 1983), pp. 1066–83.

Chapter 1

1. There are many works on the history of individual professions and the crucial periods of professional consolidation, such as the nineteenth century. The one I have found most useful is Magali Sarfatti Larson, *The Rise of Professionalization: A Sociological Analysis* (Berkeley: University of California Press, 1979). See also W. J. Reader, *Professional Men: The Rise of the Professional Classes in Nineteenth-Century England* (London: Weidenfeld and Nicolson, 1966); Noel Parry and José Parry, *The Rise of the Medical Profession: A Study in Collective Social Mobility* (London: Croom Helm, 1976); Philip Elliott, *The Sociology of the Professions* (New York: Herder and Herder, 1972).

For "literary" professionalism see John Gross, *The Rise and Fall of the Man of Letters* (New York: Macmillan, 1969); Victor Bonham-Carter, *Authors by Profession,* 2 vols. (London: Society of Authors, 1978); Nigel Cross, *The Common Writer: Life in Nineteenth-Century Grub Street* (Cambridge: Cambridge University Press, 1985).

2. My edition of Disraeli is *The Literary Character of Men of Genius,* ed. B. Disraeli (New York: Crowell, 1881).

3. Mary Jean Corbett, "Producing the Professional: Wordsworth, Carlyle, and the Authorial Self" in *Representing Femininity: Middle-Class Subjectivity in Women's Autobiographies, 1805–1914* Ph.D. Dissertation, English Department, Stanford University, 1989, pp. 14–76.

4. *Annals of Labour: Autobiographies of British Working-Class People 1820–1920,* ed. John Burnett (Bloomington: Indiana University Press, 1974), p. 26.

5. Mary Poovey argued this in "'The-Man-of-Letters Hero': Literary Labor and the Representation of Women," paper presented at the "Dickens, Women, and Victorian Culture" Conference, U.C., Santa Cruz, August 6–9, 1987. The paper, in altered form, is included as Chapter 4 in Poovey's *Uneven Developments: The Ideological Work of Gender* (Chicago: University of Chicago Press, 1988).

6. Charles Dickens, *David Copperfield* (Middlesex: Penguin, 1986), pp. 279–80. See also Michael Slater, *Dickens and Women* (Stanford: Stanford University Press, 1983).

7. See Alexander Welsh, *From Copyright to Copperfield* (Cambridge: Harvard University Press, 1987), esp. p. 109.

8. Terry Lovell, *Consuming Fiction* (London: Verso, 1987), p. 42.

9. *The Autobiography of Charles Darwin 1809–1882,* ed. Nora Barlow (New York: Norton, 1969), pp. 232–34.

10. Florence Nightingale, *Cassandra* (New York: Feminist Press, 1979).

11. Florence Bell, *At the Works* (1907), in *Into Unknown England 1866–1913,* ed. Peter Keating (Manchester: Manchester University Press, 1976), p. 287.

12. See Chapter 5 for specific references. The literature on middle-class women's writing is enormous and continuing. For a solid bibliography in an accessible text, see Toril Moi, *Sexual/Textual Politics: Feminist Literary Theory* (London: Methuen, 1985).

13. However, see Lillian Robinson's wonderful essay "Working/Women/Writing," in *Sex, Class, and Culture* (New York: Methuen, 1986), pp. 223–53; Martha Vicinus, *The Industrial Muse: A Study of Nineteenth Century British Working-Class Literature* (London: Croom Helm, 1974); and Nan Hackett, *XIX Century British Working-Class Autobiographies: An Annotated Bibliography* (New York: AMS, 1985).

14. Gayatri Chakravorty Spivak, "Three Women's Texts and a Critique of Imperialism," in *"Race," Writing, and Difference,* ed. Henry Louis Gates, Jr. (Chicago: University of Chicago Press, 1986), pp. 262–80.

15. Virginia Woolf, *A Room of One's Own* (San Diego: Harcourt Brace Jovanovich, 1957), pp. 117–18.

16. *Life As We Have Known It: By Co-Operative Working Women,* ed. Margaret Llewelyn Davies (1931; New York: Norton, 1975). Further page references will be included in the text.

17. Pierre Bourdieu, *Distinction: A Social Critique of the Judgement of Taste* (Cambridge: Harvard University Press, 1984). See the section on "Aesthetic Value" in the Introduction.

18. For full discussion of the philosophical concepts normative dualism, "liberal" (classical economic) rationality, and abstract individualism, see Alison M. Jaggar, *Feminist Politics and Human Nature* (Sussex: Harvester Press, 1983), esp. II, iii "Liberal Feminism and Human Nature," pp. 27–50 and Steven Lukes, *Individualism* (Oxford: Basil Blackwell, 1973). See also the section on "Value and the Self" in the Introduction.

19. Elizabeth Roberts, "Women's Strategies, 1890–1940" in *Labour and Love: Women's Experience of Home and Family, 1850–1940,* ed. Jane Lewis (Oxford: Basil Blackwell, 1986), pp. 243–44.

20. Ibid., Diana Gittins, "Marital Status, Work and Kinship, 1850–1930," p. 265.

21. See the Introduction section on "Value and the Self."

22. William Tayler in *Annals of Labour: Autobiographies of British Working-Class People 1820–1920,* ed. John Burnett (Bloomington: Indiana University Press, 1974), p. 175.

23. Georges Gusdorf, "Conditions and Limits of Autobiography," rpt. in *Autobiography: Essays Theoretical and Critical,* ed. James Olney (Princeton: Princeton University Press, 1980); Roy Pascal, *Design and Truth in Autobiography* (Cambridge: Harvard University Press, 1960), p. 148; James Olney, *Metaphors of Self* (Princeton: Princeton University Press, 1972).

24. Paul Jay, *Being in the Text: Self-Representation from Wordsworth to Roland Barthes* (Ithaca: Cornell University Press, 1984); Avrom Fleishman, *Figures of Auto-*

biography: The Language of Self-Writing in Victorian and Modern England (Berkeley: University of California Press, 1983); Michael Sprinker "Fictions of the Self: The End of Autobiography" in *Autobiography: Essays Theoretical and Critical,* ed. James Olney (Princeton: Princeton University Press, 1980). Also on the possible end of "autobiography" as individualist project see Elizabeth Bruss, *Autobiographical Acts: The Changing Situation of a Literary Genre* (Baltimore: Johns Hopkins University Press, 1976). Although his interest remains with the canonical literary writers who write from "some imperative authorial necessity" and want "to work through something for themselves" (236), Paul John Eakin provides a balanced discussion of the cultural limits of literary autobiography. See *Fictions in Autobiography: Studies in the Act of Self-Invention* (Princeton: Princeton University Press, 1988), especially Eakin's judicious account of recent theoretical approaches to autobiography in chapter four, "Self-Invention in Autobiography: The Moment of Language," pp. 181–279.

25. Estelle C. Jelinek, ed. *Women's Autobiographies: Essays in Criticism* (Bloomington: Indiana University Press, 1980); Sidonie Smith, *A Poetics of Women's Autobiography: Marginality and the Fictions of Self-Representation* (Bloomington: Indiana University Press, 1987); Shari Benstock, ed. *The Private Self: Theory and Practice of Women's Autobiographical Writings* (Chapel Hill: University of North Carolina Press, 1988); Bella Brodzki and Celeste Schenck, *Life/Lines: Theorizing Women's Autobiography* (Ithaca: Cornell University Press, 1988); Susan Groag Bell and Marilyn Yalom, *Revealing Lives: Gender in Biography and Autobiography* (New York: State University of New York Press, 1990).

26. This formulation is a refinement of my earlier "strategic articulations in a language-power game." See "The Literary Standard, Working-Class Lifewriting, and Gender," in *Textual Practice* 3(1) (Spring 1989), pp. 36–55. Behind the earlier formulation, and thus behind this one, is the work of Ernesto Laclau and Chantal Mouffe, *Hegemony and Socialist Strategy: Towards a Radical Democratic Politics* (London: Verso, 1985); J-F Lyotard, *The Postmodern Condition* (Minneapolis: University of Minnesota, 1984); Michel Foucault, *The History of Sexuality.* 3 vols. Trans Robert Hurley (New York: Pantheon, 1980, 1985, 1986); and conversations with Miranda Joseph.

27. See Roberto Mangabeira Unger, *Knowledge and Politics* (New York: The Free Press, 1975) and *Passion: An Essay on Personality* (New York: The Free Press, 1986). See also "Value and the Self" in the Introduction.

28. See Chaim Perelman, *The New Rhetoric* (Notre Dame: University of Notre Dame, 1969) and Thomas Nagel, *The View From Nowhere* (New York: Oxford University Press, 1986).

29. For cyborg society see Donna Haraway, "A Manifesto for Cyborgs: Science, Technology, and Socialist Feminism in the 1980s," *Socialist Review* 80 (March–April, 1985), pp. 65–107. Roughly, Haraway intends "cyborg" to represent the collapse of the distinction between organic and mechanical.

30. Louise Jermy, *The Memories of a Working Woman* (Norwich: Goose and Son, 1934); Peter Paterson [James Glass Bertram], *Behind the Scenes: Being the Confessions of a Strolling Player* (London: Henry Lea, 1859); William Dodd, *Narrative of the Experience and Sufferings of William Dodd, A Factory Cripple, Written by Himself* (1841; rpt. ed. London: Cass, 1968); Rose Gibbs, *In Service: Rose Gibbs Remembers* (Cambridge: Archives for Bassingbourn and Comberton Village Colleges, 1981); Anon., *The*

Autobiography of a Private Soldier, Showing the Danger of Rashly Enlisting (Sunderland: Williams and Binns, 1838).

31. For statistics see P. Bairoch, *The Working Population and its Structure* (New York: Gordon and Breach, 1968), p. 99. For detailed descriptions of them see Burnett's introductory essays to the sections of *Annals of Labour:* The Labouring Classes, Domestic Servants, and Skilled Workers.

32. William Adams, *Memoirs of a Social Atom* (1903; rpt. ed. New York: Augustus M. Kelley, 1968), p. xiii.

33. Charles Shaw, *When I Was a Child* (1893; rpt. East Ardsley, Wakefield: SR Publishers, 1969), p. 97.

34. *Life As We Have Known It,* p. 60.

35. Emma Smith (pseud.), *A Cornish Waif's Story: An Autobiography* (London: Odhams, 1954), p. 154.

36. Carolyn Kay Steedman, *Landscape for a Good Woman: A Story of Two Lives* (New Brunswick, N.J.: Rutgers University Press, 1987).

37. For the two modes see *Life as We Have Known It* and *Testaments of Radicalism: Memoirs of Working Class Politicians 1790–1885,* ed. David Vincent (London: Europa, 1977). The fact that these primarily political and polemical documents represent a wide historical distance is less significant when it is realized that the gender difference alluded to is borne out by many "genres" of working-class autobiography throughout the period (e.g., conversion and gallows narratives as well commemorative storytelling).

38. In *Victorian Writing and Working Women: The Other Side of Silence* (Cambridge: Polity Press, 1985), Julia Swindells also analyzes some working women's autobiography in "Part 2: Working Women's Autobiographies" (115–207) in terms of what she calls "the literary." I see such "literary" effects controlling one kind of working-class writing, produced by men and women; whereas Swindells appears to find it characteristic of working women's writing exclusively and as a whole.

39. James Dawson Burn, *The Autobiography of a Beggar Boy* (1855; ed. David Vincent, London: Europa, 1978) p. 78.

40. See Vincent's introduction, p. 28.

41. John Burnett, ed., *Annals of Labour,* p. 52; Jermy (Norwich: Goose and Son, 1934).

42. Mayhew cited in John R. Gillis, *For Better or Worse: British Marriage, 1600 to the Present* (Oxford: Oxford University Press, 1985), p. 244.

43. For Herculine Barbin, see *Herculine Barbin: Being the Recently Discovered Memoirs of a Nineteenth-Century French Hermaphrodite.* ed. Michel Foucault (New York: Pantheon, 1980.)

44. For literacy figures, see Lawrence Stone, "Literacy and Education in England 1640–1900," *Past and Present* 42 (February 1969), pp. 69–139.

45. Barbey d'Aurevilly, *Of Dandyism and of George Brummell,* trans. Douglas Ainslie (London: Dent, 1897).

46. Kathleen Woodward, *Jipping Street: Childhood in a London Slum* (New York: Harper, 1928), p. 10. For a similar depiction of her own mother, see Steedman's *Landscape for a Good Woman.*

47. Ibid., p. 18.

48. Ellen Johnston, *The Autobiography, Poems, and Songs of "The Factory Girl"* (Glasgow: William Love, 1867), pp. 5, 62.

Chapter 2

1. "Science, Technology, and Socialist Feminism in the 1980s," *Socialist Review* 80 (March–April, 1985), pp. 65–107. Page numbers cited in the text.

2. "A New Romantic Reaction: The Computer as Precipitant of Anti-Mechanistic Definitions of the Human," paper presented at "Humans, Animals, Machines: Boundaries and Projections: A Conference on the Occasion of the Centennial of Stanford University," April 23–25, 1987.

3. See Julia Kristeva, *Powers of Horror: An Essay on Abjection,* Trans. Leon S. Roudiez (New York: Columbia University Press, 1982) and Kelly Hurley "The Novel of the Gothic Body: Deviance, Abjection, and Late-Victorian Gothic Fiction," Ph.D. Dissertation, Stanford University, 1988.

4. Evelyn Fox Keller, "Language and Ideology in Evolutionary Theory: Reading Cultural Norms into Natural Law," and Arnold Davidson, "The History of Horror: Abomination, Monsters and the Unnatural," papers presented at "Humans, Animals, Machines" Conference cited earlier. Roberto Mangabeira Unger, *Passion: An Essay on Personality* (New York: The Free Press, 1984) and *Knowledge and Politics* (New York: The Free Press, 1975).

5. Walter Pater, *The Renaissance: Studies in Art and Poetry,* ed. Donald L. Hill (Berkeley: University of California Press, 1980), pp. 98–99.

6. Eliot, *Adam Bede* (Boston: Riverside, 1968), p. 6.

7. My approach has been informed by such diverse writers as Carolyn Walker Bynum, Bernard Williams, Thomas Nagel, and Elaine Scarry. Bynum argues that in thirteenth and fourteenth-century Europe the body, especially the female body, became the focus for challenging the dichotomy between body and soul that would become rigid with Cartesianism. Bynum's medieval women saw their bodies as access to the divine and ultimately to a less dichotomized version of the self. In his continuing debates with physicalists, Nagel insists upon the subjectivity that implies the particularity of sensory, or somatic, modalities. Williams, in his continuing disagreement with Locke, insists that we cannot distinguish "personality" without reference to body, that the omission of the body deprives the idea of personal identity of all content. And Scarry, with reference to the archives of Amnesty International, analyzes how physical pain unmakes self and world.

See Carolyn Walker Bynum, *Holy Feast and Holy Fast: The Religious Significance of Food to Medieval Women* (Berkeley: University of California Press, 1987); Bernard Williams, *Problems of the Self: Philosophical Papers 1956–1972* (Cambridge: Cambridge University Press, 1973), esp. essays 1, 2, and 5 on personal identity and the body; Thomas Nagel, *Mortal Questions* (Cambridge: Cambridge University Press, 1979), esp. chapters 12 and 14 on subjectivity and point of view; Elaine Scarry, *The Body in Pain: The Making and Unmaking of the World* (London: Oxford University Press, 1985). Also see "Subjectivity" in the Introduction.

8. Citations in this section are from the 160 letters and other material published in The Women's Co-operative Guild, *Maternity: Letters From Working-Women,* ed. Margaret Llewelyn Davies (1915), rpt. ed. Linda Gordon (New York: Norton, 1978). For middle-class pregnancy, see Cynthia A. Huff, "Chronicles of Confinement" Reactions to Childbirth in British Women's Diaries," *Women's Studies Int. Forum* 10(1), pp. 63–68.

9. On the representativeness of the *Maternity* letters of the experience of pregnancy

among working-class women, social historian Ellen Ross writes, "The *Maternity* letters are perfectly representative of the experience of pregnancy among working-class women. The stories are found over and over again in the hospital case records, in district nursing accounts, in their journals, and of course in other autobiographies and oral histories" (personal communication). See Elizabeth Roberts, *A Woman's Place: An Oral History of Working-Class Women 1890–1940* (Oxford: Blackwell, 1984), ch. 3 on "Marriage," esp. "Pregnancy and Childbirth," 104–10; Carl Chinn, *They Worked All Their Lives: Women of the Urban Poor in England, 1880–1939* (Manchester: Manchester University Press, 1988), esp. ch. 2 "The Power of Mothers," 45–83; and F. B. Smith, *The People's Health* (London: Croom Helm, 1979).

My own interests, of course, are less in the experience itself than in the way the physical experience was shaped by cultural attitudes and then articulated for social purposes.

10. *The Unknown Mayhew*, eds. Eileen Yeo and E. P. Thompson (New York: Pantheon Books, 1971), p. 101. Further references to this edition of the *Morning Chronicle* letters and editorial matter will be in the text. For a complete edition of Mayhew's contribution to the *Morning Chronicle* survey see *The Morning Chronicle Survey of Labour and the Poor: The Metropolitan Districts*, 6 vols., ed. Peter Razzell (Sussex: Caliban Books, 1981–1982). See also Anne Humpherys's selection, *Voices of the Poor* (London: Frank Cass, 1971).

11. Whereas Marx, Engels, and Douglas will be of varying usefulness, then, in this discussion of subjectivity, material culture, and value, the Veblen of *The Theory of the Leisure Class* (1899) will be less so. Veblen was one of the first theorists of embourgeoisement as a key to social stability. His answer to the Marxist question, predicated upon its theory of social change, of why the working class had not rebelled, was that they did not seek to supplant their masters but to emulate them. Yet there was little embourgeoisement among Mayhew's informants at the end of the so-called Hungry Forties. There was hierarchy among the metropolitan poor, to be sure, but little envy, and very little capital accumulation. The stratification of nineteenth-century London society was such that workers' primary desideratum was sufficient wages to keep working, with some of them, like the streetsellers, expressing remarkable good humour and emotional elasticity even without that. Perhaps the Veblen to keep in mind with Mayhew's dense but narrow materiality is not so much the psychological as the technological Veblen, the later Veblen of *The Theory of Business Enterprise* (1904) and *The Technicians and Revolution* (1921). He fully articulated the potential of technology to, as he said, crowd out anthropomorphic habits of thought and predicted a gradual global takeover on the parts of engineers.

12. The neoconservative historian Gertrude Himmelfarb began this trend of seeing Mayhew as a media exploiter of the poor and it has been followed by others (*The Idea of Poverty: England in the Early Industrial Age* [New York: Random House, 1983]).

For Foucauldian and New Historical readings of Mayhew and others see Patrick Brantlinger's chapter on transportation in *Rule of Darkness: British Literature and Imperialism 1830–1914* (Ithaca: Cornell Univeristy Press, 1988), pp. 109–34, and Catherine Gallagher, "The Body Versus the Social Body in the Works of Thomas Malthus and Henry Mayhew," in *The Making of the Modern Body: Sexuality and Society in the Nineteenth Century*, ed. Gallagher and Thomas Laqueur (Berkeley: University of California Press, 1987), pp. 83–106.

13. For a balanced assessment of Mayhew as anthropologist in an examination of

the uses of oral history in criminology see Chapters 1 and 2 of James Bennett's *Oral History and Delinquency* (Chicago: University of Chicago Press, 1981), pp. 11–64.

14. Anne Humpherys, *Henry Mayhew* (Boston: Twayne, 1984), p. 170. All my work on Mayhew is indebted to the expertise and generosity of Anne Humpherys.

15. "A noteworthy difference between children of this standing and such as pass their years of playtime in homes unshadowed by poverty. For these, life had no illusions. Of every mouthful that they ate, the price was known to them. The roof over their heads was there by no grace of Providence, but solely because suchandsuch a sum was paid weekly in hard cash, when the collector came; let the payment fail, and they knew perfectly well what the result would be. The children of the upper world could not even by chance give a thought to the sources whence their needs are supplied; speech on such a subject in their presence would be held indecent." George Gissing, *The Nether World* (London: Dent, 1973), p. 368.

16. Henry Mayhew, *London Labour and the London Poor: The Condition and Earnings of Those That Will Work, Cannot Work, and Will Not Work* 4 vols. (London: Charles Griffin and Co., 1865). See Volume 1, pp. 535, 517, 157. Further references to this edition will be included in the text by volume and page. References to Mayhew with page numbers only are to *The Unknown Mayhew*.

17. Carolyn Steedman, *Landscape for a Good Woman* (New Brunswick: Rutgers University Press, 1987), pp. 137–38. For "Dora," see Sigmund Freud, "Fragmant of an Analysis of a Case of Hysteria," *Pelican Freud Library* Vol. 8, *Case Histories* I (Harmondsworth: Penguin, 1977), pp. 27–164.

18. *The Marx-Engels Reader*, ed. Robert C. Tucker (New York: Norton, 1972), p. 81.

19. Engels, *The Condition of the Working Class in England* (Stanford: Stanford University Press, 1968), pp. 30–31.

20. *Edinburgh News and Literary Chronicle* (3 May 1851), cited in Humpherys, *Henry Mayhew*, p. 37. Mayhew had originally criticized the Great Exhibition for not sufficiently recognizing the contribution of labour.

21. The following discussion of Mayhew's circumstances is from Thompson and Eileen Yeo's prefatory material in *The Unknown Mayhew* and Anne Humpherys's two volumes *Henry Mayhew* and *Travels into the Poor Man's Country: The Work of Henry Mayhew* (Athens: University of Georgia, 1977).

22. For other responses see Thompson's essay, in *The Unknown Mayhew*, pp. 25ff.

23. For more on Mayhew's methods, see Humpherys (1977 and 1984) and Eileen Yeo's essay in *The Unknown Mayhew*, esp. pp. 55–68.

24. For a balanced discussion of Mayhew's case against the Ragged Schools see Norris Pope, "Crime and Education: Henry Mayhew against the Ragged Schools," paper presented at the Pacific Coast Conference on British Studies (March, 1978). See also Pope's *Dickens and Charity* (New York: Columbia University Press, 1978), pp. 170–75.

25. Extracts from Parts One and Two in *The Unknown Mayhew*, pp. 463–75.

26. Humpherys, *Travels*, p. 86.

27. See Mary Douglas and Baron Isherwood, *The World of Goods* (New York: Basic Books, 1979).

28. See numbers 40 (13 September 1850) and 54 (20 December 1851); cited in Humpherys, *Henry Mayhew*, p. 141.

29. Jack Goody discusses this in the context of his continuing fieldwork in northern

Ghana (paper presented at the Stanford Humanities Center, February 1988) and Anthony Giddens argues it systematically in *The Consequences of Modernity* (Palo Alto: Stanford University Press, 1990).

30. Charles Booth, *Life and Labour of the People of London,* 17 vols. (1902–1903), *Poverty,* Vol. I (1889), p. 6.

31. I am grateful to Patrick Brantlinger for an illuminating discussion of this point. See also Brantlinger's *Spirit of Reform: British Literature and Politics, 1832–1867* (Cambridge: Harvard University Press, 1977).

32. For the mathematical psychics and late Victorian economics, see Robert L. Heilbroner, *The Worldly Philosophers* (New York: Simon and Schuster, 1967), ch. VII, pp. 154–91.

33. Cited in Heilbroner, p. 166.

34. For Mayhew see *Unknown Mayhew,* p. 105; George cited in Heilbroner, p. 166.

35. This fragment forms part of the second volume of Nightingale's unpublished (privately printed) spiritual autobiography *Suggestions for Thought to Searchers after Religious Truth* (1859). See *Cassandra: An Essay by Florence Nightingale* (New York: The Feminist Press, 1979). For Nightingale's life see also Edward Cook, *The Life of Florence Nightingale* 2 vols. (London: Macmillan, 1913); Cecil Woodham-Smith, *Florence Nightingale* (Penguin, 1955); and Lytton Strachey, *Eminent Victorians* (London: Chatto and Windus, 1918).

36. For the rise of the British Medical Association, see W. J. Reader, *Professional Men: The Rise of the Professional Classes in Nineteenth-Century England* (London: Weidenfeld and Nicolson, 1966) and Noel Parry and José Parry, *The Rise of the Medical Profession: A Study in Collective Social Mobility* (London: Croom Helm, 1976).

37. *Lancet,* I, 1855, p. 250. Cited in Julia Swindells, *Victorian Writing and Working Women: The Other Side of Silence* (Cambridge: Polity Press, 1985), p. 29.

38. See Martha Vicinus, *Independent Women: Work and Community for Single Women, 1850–1920* (Chicago: University of Chicago Press, 1985), esp. chapter three, "Reformed Hospital Nursing: Discipline and Cleanliness," and pp. 107–8.

39. For invented traditions see *The Invention of Tradition,* ed. Eric Hobsbawm and Terence Ranger (Cambridge: Cambridge University Press, 1983), esp. David Cannadine, "The Context, Performance and Meaning of Ritual: The British Monarchy and the 'Invention of Tradition,' c. 1820–1977," pp. 101–64.

40. Also on the topic of maternal absence in fiction as prerequisite for the daughter's maturation, see *The Lost Tradition: Mothers and Daughters in Literature,* eds. Cathy N. Davidson and E. M. Broner (New York: Frederick Ungar, 1980), especially Susan Peck Macdonald, "Jane Austen and the Tradition of the Absent Mother," pp. 58–69.

41. Andrea Dworkin, "A Woman Writer and Pornography," *San Francisco Review of Books* (March–April 1981), n.p. See also Dworkin's *Pornography* (New York: Putnam, 1981).

Chapter 3

1. Beatrice Webb, *My Apprenticeship* (Cambridge: Cambridge University Press, 1979).

2. Friedrich Engels, *The Condition of the Working Class in England* (Stanford: Stanford University Press, 1968), esp. pp. 24–25.

3. Richard Rorty, *Contingency, Irony, and Solidarity* (Cambridge: Cambridge University Press, 1989).

4. There is a vast amount of excellent work on Victorian class and gender ideology in the great realist fiction, generically and on individual authors, and a goodly amount on the late Victorian tradition of naturalism. The studies I have found most useful in relating literary forms to politics and ideology include: Catherine Belsey, *Critical Practice* (London: Methuen, 1980); Tony Bennett, *Formalism and Marxism* (London: Methuen, 1979); Patrick Brantlinger, *The Spirit of Reform: British Literature and Politics, 1832–1867* (Cambridge: Harvard University Press, 1977); H. J. Dyos and Michael Wolff, eds. *The Victorian City: Images and Realities* (London: Methuen, 1973); Terry Eagleton, *Criticism and Ideology: A Study in Marxist Literary Theory* (London: New Left Books, 1976) and *Myths of Power: A Marxist Study of the Brontës* (London: Macmillan, 1975); David Howard, John Lucas, and John Goode, *Tradition and Tolerance in Nineteenth Century Fiction* (London: Routledge Kegan Paul, 1966); Fredric Jameson, *Marxism and Form: Twentieth-Century Dialectical Theories of Literature* (Princeton: Princeton University Press, 1971) and *The Political Unconscious: Narrative as a Socially Symbolic Act* (Ithaca: Cornell University Press, 1981); John Lucas, ed. *Literature and Politics in the Nineteenth Century* (London: Methuen, 1971); György Lukács, *History and Class Consciousness: Studies in Marxist Dialectics,* trans. Rodney Livingston (Cambridge: MIT Press, 1971), *The Historical Novel,* trans. Hannah and Stanley Mitchell (London: Merlin Press, 1962), and *The Theory of the Novel,* trans. Anna Bostock (Cambridge: MIT Press, 1971); Pierre Macherey, *A Theory of Literary Production* (London: Routledge Kegan Paul, 1978); Masao Miyoshi, *The Divided Self: A Perspective on the Literature of the Victorians* (New York: New York University Press, 1969); Nicholas Rance, *The Historical Novel and Popular Politics in Nineteenth-Century England* (New York: Barnes and Noble, 1975); Ian Watt, *The Rise of the Novel: Studies in Defoe, Richardson, and Fielding* (Berkeley: University of California Press, 1964) and *Conrad in the Nineteenth Century* (Berkeley: University of California Press, 1979); Raymond Williams, *The Country and the City* (New York: Oxford University Press, 1973), *The English Novel from Dickens to Lawrence* (Oxford: Oxford University Press, 1979), and *Marxism and Literature* (Oxford: Oxford University Press, 1977).

Works with a special focus on gender politics and ideology include: Nancy Armstrong, *Desire and Domestic Fiction: A Political History of the Novel* (New York: Oxford, 1987); Kathleen Blake, *Love and the Woman Question in Victorian Literature* (Totowa: Barnes and Noble, 1983); Sandra Gilbert and Susan Gubar *The Madwoman in the Attic* (New Haven: Yale University Press, 1979); Ellen Moers, *Literary Women: The Great Writers* (Garden City, NY: Doubleday, 1976); Toril Moi, *Sexual/Textual Politics* (London: Methuen, 1985); Elaine Showalter, *A Literature of Their Own: British Women Novelists From Brontë to Lessing* (Princeton: Princeton University Press, 1977); Tony Tanner *Adultery in the Novel: Contract and Transgression* (Baltimore: Johns Hopkins, 1979).

Works with a focus upon representations of the working class (exclusive of those with a concentration on Condition of England fiction, for which see Note 7) include: Louis James, *Fiction for the Working Man, 1830–1850: A Study of the Literature Produced for the Working Classes in Early Victorian Urban England* (London: Oxford

University Press, 1963) and *Print and the People: 1819-1851* (London: Allen Lane, 1976); Peter Keating, *The Working Classes in Victorian Fiction* (London: Routledge and Kegan Paul, 1971); R. K. Webb, *The British Working Class Reader, 1790-1848* (London: Allen and Unwin, 1955).

5. Friedrich Schiller, *On the Aesthetic Education of Man: In a Series of Letters,* trans. Reginald Snell (New York: Frederick Ungar, 1988), p. 71.

6. See Steven Marcus, *Engels, Manchester, and the Working Class* (New York: Random House, 1974).

7. Works especially addressing politics and ideology in the Condition of England fiction include: Rosemarie Bodenheimer, *The Politics of Story in Victorian Social Fiction* (Ithaca: Cornell University Press, 1988); Louis Cazamian, *The Social Novel in England, 1830-1850: Dickens, Disraeli, Mrs. Gaskell, Kingsley,* trans. Martin Fido (London: Routledge Kegan Paul, 1973); Catherine Gallagher, *The Industrial Reformation of English Fiction* (Chicago: University of Chicago Press, 1985); Sheila M. Smith, *The Other Nation: The Poor in English Novels of the 1840s and 1850s* (Oxford: Clarendon Press, 1980); Kathleen Tillotson, *Novels of the Eighteen-Forties* (London: Clarendon Press, 1956).

8. My reading of Gaskell does not substantially differ from Raymond Williams's in *Culture and Society* and that in John Lucas's essay "Mrs. Gaskell and Brotherhood" in *Tradition and Tolerance.* For more sympathetic treatments of the Condition of England novelists, including Gaskell, and showing their occasional ethnographic bases, see Sheila Smith's *The Other Nation* and Hilary M. Schor, "Scheherazade in the Marketplace: Elizabeth Gaskell and the Fiction of Transformation," Ph.D. dissertation, Stanford University, 1986.

9. "Address to Working Men, By Felix Holt," *Blackwood's Magazine* (January 1868); Appendix A to *Felix Holt,* ed. Peter Coveney (Penguin, 1972), p. 622.

10. *Thomas Hardy: the Critical Heritage,* ed. R. G. Cox (London: Routledge and Kegan Paul, 1970); *Thomas Hardy and his Readers: A Set of Contemporary Reviews,* ed. Lerner and Holstrom (New York: Barnes and Noble, 1968).

11. See James Joll's *The Anarchists* (Boston: Little Brown, 1964); Roderick Kedward, *The Anarchists: The Men Who Shocked an Era* (New York: American Heritage Press, 1971); Leonard I. Krimerman and Lewis Perry, eds., *Patterns of Anarchy: A Collection of Writings on the Anarchist Tradition* (New York: Doubleday, 1966); Irving L. Horowitz, ed. *The Anarchists* (New York: Dell, 1964); George Woodcock, *Anarchism* (New York: Meridian, 1962).

12. See Haia Shpayer-Makov, "Anarchism in British Public Opinion 1880-1914," *Victorian Studies* 31(4) (Summer 1988), pp. 487-516. Shpayer-Makov argues that the middle-class press typically presented anarchists as stereotypical terrorists, whereas the lower-class presses (e.g., *Reynolds's,* presented a broader range of anarchist opinion and often represented it sympathetically).

13. Henry James, *The Princess Casamassima* (Penguin, 1982), p. 7.

14. See James M. Cox, "Henry James: The Politics of Internationalism," *Southern Review* 8 (1972), pp. 493-506 and W. H. Tilley, *The Background of "The Princess Casamassima"* (University of Florida Monographs, no. 5, Fall 1960)

15. See Patrick Brantlinger, *Rule of Darkness: British Literature and Imperialism, 1830-1914* (Ithaca: Cornell University Press, 1988), II 3 "Thackeray's India," pp. 73-108.

16. From *How the Poor Live* (1881), in *Into Unknown England 1866-1913: Selec-*

tions from the Social Explorers, ed. Peter Keating (Manchester: Manchester University Press, 1976), p. 66.

17. See Philip Abrams, *The Origins of British Sociology 1834–1914* (Chicago: University of Chicago Press, 1968).

18. Walter Besant, *All Sorts and Conditions of Men* (1882) (rpt. London: Chatto and Windus, 1887).

19. See Gareth Stedman Jones, *Outcast London* (New York: Pantheon, 1971).

20. See Standish Meacham, *Toynbee Hall and Social Reform 1880–1914: The Search for Community* (New Haven: Yale University Press, 1987).

21. Henrietta Barnett, *Canon Barnett, His Life, Work, and Friends by His Wife,* 2 vols. (1918) vol. I, p. 35, cited in Webb (1979), p. 197.

22. See Eric Hobsbawm, ed. *Labouring Men: Studies in the History of Labour* (London: Weidenfeld and Nicolson, 1965).

23. The records say, of course, that the children had "consented to emigrate." W. J. Fishman calls this a "forced exodus of the young." See his extraordinary *East End 1888: A Year in a London Borough Among the Labouring Poor* (London: Duckworth, 1988), pp. 56–57. I am also grateful to Dr. Fishman for drawing my attention to the photograph of one of the philanthropist Dr. Thomas J. Barnardo's destitute boys that serves as the frontispiece of this work.

24. *The Bitter Cry of Outcast London* (1883), in Keating (1976), p. 94.

25. For two excellent treatments of this theme, see Chapter 8 "Imperial Gothic: Atavism and the Occult in the British Adventure Novel, 1880–1914" in Brantlinger's *Rule of Darkness,* pp. 227–54, and Kelly Hurley, "The Novel of the Gothic Body: Deviance, Abjection, and Late-Victorian Popular Fiction," Ph.D. dissertation, Stanford University, 1988.

26. See Arthur Osborne Montgomery Jay, *Life in Darkest London: A Hint to General Booth* (London: Webster and Cable, 1891), *The Social Problem: Its Possible Solution* (London: Simpkin, Marshall and Co., 1893), and *A Story of Shoreditch: Being a Sequel to "Life in Darkest London"* (London: Simpkin, Marshall and Co., 1896); and Peter Keating's introduction to Arthur Morrison, *A Child of the Jago* (London: Macgibbon and Kee, 1969), pp. 24, 32, 42.

27. See these and other quotations from Masterman's *From the Abyss* (1902) in Keating (1976), pp. 241–48.

28. Cited in Karl Beckson, *Arthur Symons: A Life* (Oxford: Clarendon Press, 1987), p. 242.

29. Rudyard Kipling, "The Record of Badalia Herodsfoot," in *Working-class Stories of the 1890's,* ed. P. J. Keating (New York: Barnes and Noble, 1971), p. 9.

30. Somerset Maugham, *Liza of Lambeth* (London: T. Fisher Unwin, 1897), pp. vii–viii.

31. Arthur Morrison, *Child of the Jago* (1969), p. 39.

32. Unless otherwise stated, page numbers for Morrison, Nevinson, Pugh, Kipling, and Rook refer to the relatively accessible *Working-class Stories of the 1890's,* ed. P. J. Keating (New York: Barnes and Noble, 1971). The analyses themselves are based upon the original anthologies. Also cited, not in Keating, is Morrison's *Tales of Mean Streets* (New York: Modern Library, 1921).

33. Nadine Gordimer, "Living in the Interregnum," *New York Review of Books* (20 January 1983), p. 25.

34. *Unknown Mayhew,* p. 320.

35. From *People of the Abyss* (1903), in *Into Unknown England,* p. 230.

36. I am indebted to Lucio Ruotolo for the delightful notion of an "anarchist reading."

37. See Rorty, *Contingency, Irony, Solidarity,* esp. pp. xvi, 60, 64, 94.

38. On Victorian reticence, see Humphry House, *The Dickens World* (London: Oxford University Press, 1941), pp. 217–19.

Chapter 4

1. John Burnett, David Mayall, and David Vincent, *The Autobiography of the Working Class: An Annotated Critical Bibliography,* Volume 1, 1790–1900 (Brighton: Harvester, 1984).

2. Virginia Woolf, introductory letter to Margaret Llewelyn Davies, ed., *Life as We Have Known It, by Co-Operative Working Women* (1931; rpt. ed. New York: Norton, 1975), p. xxxvii. See also Jerome Buckley, *Turning Key* (Cambridge, MA: Harvard University Press, 1984), p. 45.

3. Except for the various introductions to the bibliography and several anthologies by Burnett, Mayall, and Vincent, I know of only two scholarly books dealing with these texts: David Vincent, *Bread, Knowledge and Freedom: A Study of Nineteenth-Century Working Class Autobiography* (London: Europa, 1981), a study of 142 autobiographies during a period that largely precludes texts by women and asking the questions of the social historian concerning education, family structure, and working-class relation to middle-class reform; and Nan Hackett, *XIX Century British Working-Class Autobiographies: An Annotated Bibliography* (New York: AMS, 1985).

4. David Vincent, ed., *Testaments of Radicalism* (London: Europa, 1977), p. 22.

5. See Hackett (1985), pp. 10–47.

6. Roy Pascal, *Design and Truth in Autobiography* (Cambridge, MA: Harvard University Press, 1960); Vincent, *Bread, Knowledge and Freedom,* p. 37. In her most recent work, however, Hackett has altered her view concerning the possibilities of the self in working-class writing. See "A Different Form of 'Self': Narrative Style in British Nineteenth-Century Working-Class Autobiography," *biography,* vol. 12, No. 3 (1989), pp. 208–26.

7. William Hazlitt in *Table Talk, or, Original Essays* (1821), in P. P. Howe, ed., *Complete Works of William Hazlitt,* 21 vols. (London: Dent, 1930–1934), VIII, 44; quoted in Buckley, p. 3.

8. Alexander Somerville, *The Autobiography of A Working Man, by "One who has whistled at the plough"* (1848; rpt. ed. London: Macgibbon and Kee, 1967), p. 16.

9. Avrom Fleishman, *Figures of Autobiography: The Language of Self-Writing in Victorian and Modern England* (Berkeley: University of California Press, 1983); Paul Jay, *Being in the Text: Self-Representation from Wordsworth to Roland Barthes* (Ithaca: Cornell University Press, 1984).

10. William Edwin Adams, *Memoirs of a Social Atom* (1903; rpt. ed. New York: Augustus M. Kelley, 1968), p. xiii.

11. Robert Peel Blatchford, *My Eighty Years* (London: Cassell, 1931), p. 1.

12. Chester Armstrong, *Pilgrimage from Nenthead: An Autobiography* (London: Methuen, 1938), pp. 27–29, 74–75.

13. Kathleen Woodward, *Jipping Street: Childhood in a London Slum* (New York: Harper, 1928), p. 3.

14. Charles Shaw, *When I Was A Child by "An Old Potter"* (1893; rpt. ed. East Ardsley, Wakefield: SR Publishers, 1969), p. 97.

15. William Dodd, *Narrative of the Experience and Sufferings of William Dodd, A Factory Cripple Written by Himself* (1841; rpt. ed. London: Cass, 1968), p. 311.

16. Charles Shaw, *When I Was A Child by "An Old Potter"* (1893; rpt. East Ardsley, Wakefield: SR Publishers, 1969), pp. 186, 191.

17. Margaret Grace Bondfield, *A Life's Work* (London: Hutchinson, 1949), pp. 36–37.

18. Elizabeth Bryson, *Look Back in Wonder* (Dundee, England: David Winter & Son, 1966).

19. In *Testaments of Radicalism,* p. 35.

20. Marianne Farningham [Marianne Hearn], *A Working Woman's Life: An Autobiography* (London: James Clark, 1907).

21. George Acorn [pseud.], *One of the Multitude* (London: William Heinemann, 1911).

22. Peter Paterson [James Glass Bertram], *Being the Confessions of a Strolling Player* (London: Henry Lea, 1859).

23. William Green, *The Life and Adventures of a Cheap Jack, by one of the fraternity,* ed. Charles Hindley (London: Tinsley Brothers, 1876), p. 1.

24. Thomas Cooper, *The Life of Thomas Cooper: Written by Himself* (London: Hodder & Stoughton, 1872).

25. In *Testaments of Radicalism,* see esp. p. 150.

26. Robert Roberts, *The Classic Slum: Salford Life in the First Quarter of the Century* (Manchester: Manchester University Press, 1971), p. 38.

27. Pierre Bourdieu, *Distinction: A Social Critique of the Judgement of Taste* (Cambridge, MA: Harvard University Press, 1984), p. 5.

28. Annie Kenney, *Memories of a Militant* (London: Edward Arnold, 1924), pp. 22–23.

29. Louis James, *Fiction for the Working Man 1830–1850* (London: Oxford University Press, 1963), p. 47.

30. Florence Bell, *At the Works* in *Into Unknown England,* p. 301.

31. Stephen Reynolds, *A Poor Man's House* in *Into Unknown England,* pp. 264–65.

32. D. H. Lawrence, *Sons and Lovers* (Harmondsworth: Penguin, 1977), pp. 232–33.

33. Jean Franco, "Dependency Theory and Literary History: The Case of Latin America," *Minnesota Review* n.s., 5(Fall 1975), 65–80.

34. Robert Graves, *Good-Bye to All That* (New York: Doubleday, 1957), pp. 14–15.

35. Frances Smith Foster, "Representing the Real: The Slave Literature of Octavia V. Rogers Albert," Interdisciplinary Nineteenth Century Studies (INCS) Annual Conference, Claremont College, April 1986. See also Foster's *Witnessing Slavery: The Development of Ante-Bellum Slave Narrative* (Westport, Conn.: Greenwood Press,

1979) and Robert B. Stepto, *From Behind the Veil: A Study of Afro-American Narrative* (Urbana: University of Illinois Press, 1979).

36. Laila Said, paper presented in the Jing Lyman Lecture Series, Stanford University, May 1986. See also Said's *A Bridge Through Time: A Memoir* (New York: Summit, 1985).

37. Although a few working-class autobiographers did write autobiographical fiction, like Arthur Morrison (*Child of the Jago,* 1896) and Flora Thompson (*Lark Rise to Candleford,* 1945), and many of them wrote verse (e.g., *The Shakespearean Chartist Hymnbook* of 1842), I am only dealing with texts that are intended to be realist documents. Working-class fiction, autobiographical or not, tends to be more imitative of upper-class conventions, so that the most common conclusions to be drawn about it concern cultural hegemony. (*Child of the Jago* and *Lark Rise* are arguably exceptions.) Yet even granting the intertextualities discussed in this chapter (such as Puritan conversion narrative), there were few models for working-class lives but other working-class lives. Moreover, in working-class autobiographies one does not encounter the progressive text revealing its own construction. If the canonical "literary" autobiographies partake of historical shifts in the epistemology of the subject and thus include theoretical or compositional problems arising in the subject's doubts about one's ability to write one's experience, with few—often very late—exceptions, like Elizabeth Bryson's *Look Back in Wonder* and Annie Kenney's *Memories of a Militant,* epistemological and compositional self-consciousness is absent in these texts. The writers feel compelled to justify themselves and their experience as subject matter for other readers rather than as subjects in the philosophical sense. See also Jay, *Being in the Text,* and Fleishman, *Figures of Autobiography.*

The one so-called work of "fiction" I use in this chapter is Woodward's *Jipping Street,* which, although written as a novel, appears to be, from the evidence I have been able to find, an autobiographical—or rather a psychobiographical (for Woodward made certain literal changes, such as location)—work written in third person. Furthermore, *Jipping Street* has always been received as representative of certain kinds of working-class experience.

38. For more on the conditions of publication see Burnett, Mayall, and Vincent, pp. xix–xx; *Testaments of Radicalism,* pp. 12–14; and the prefaces to John Burnett, ed., *Annals of Labour: Autobiographies of British Working-Class People 1820–1920* (Bloomington: Indiana University Press, 1974) and Burnett, ed., *Destiny Obscure: Autobiographies of Childhood, Education and Family from the 1820s to the 1920s* (Middlesex: Penguin, 1984).

39. For the sources and implications of British conversion narrative see Owen C. Watkins, *The Puritan Experience* (London: Schocken, 1972); Paul Delany, *British Autobiography in the Seventeenth Century* (London: Routledge and Kegan Paul, 1969), pp. 6–104; John C. Morris, *Versions of the Self* (New York: Basic Books, 1966), Chaps. 2, 3; Isabel Rivers, "'Strangers and Pilgrims': Sources and Patterns of Methodist Narrative" in *Augustan Worlds,* ed. J. C. Hilson and others (Leicester: Leicester University Press, 1978), pp. 189–203; Christopher Hill, "The Norman Yoke" in *Democracy and the Labour Movement,* ed. John Saville (London: Lawrence and Wishart, 1954), pp. 11–66; Deborah Valenze, "Pilgrims and Progress in Nineteenth-Century England" in *Culture, Ideology and Politics,* ed. Raphael Samuel and Gareth Stedman Jones (London: Routledge and Kegan Paul, 1983), pp. 113–125; John Walsh, "Methodism and the Common People," in *People's History and Socialist Theory,* ed. Raphael Samuel

(London: Routledge and Kegan Paul, 1981), pp. 354–62. For the relation of British conversion narrative to that in the United States, see Patricia Caudwell, *Puritan Conversion Narrative* (New York: Cambridge University Press, 1983) and Albert E. Stone, *Autobiographical Occasions and Original Acts* (Philadelphia: University of Pennsylvania Press, 1982).

40. Mary Saxby, *Memoirs of a Female Vagrant, written by herself, with Illustrations*, ed. Samuel Greatheed (Dunstable: J. W. Morris, 1806).

41. David Barr, *Climbing the Ladder: The Struggles and Successes of a Village Lad* (London: Culley, 1910).

42. Josiah Basset, *The Life of a Vagrant, or the Testimony of an Outcast to the Value and Truth of the Gospel* (London: Gilpin, 1850), p. 32. Engels discusses "a great army of beggars," at this time, "with whom the police are in perpetual conflict. . . . They perambulate the streets . . . appealing to the benevolence of the charitable by singing doleful ballads or by reciting an account of their misfortunes. It is very noticeable that such beggars are to be found only in working-class districts and that they subsist almost exclusively on the charity of the working classes . . . who know from personal experience what it is like to go hungry" (*The Condition*, p. 100).

43. George Allen, *The Machine Breaker: Or, the Heart-Rending Confession of George Allen*, ed. by "the chaplain of N———gaol" (London: J. Duncombe, 1831?).

44. Michel Foucault, "The Spectacle of the Scaffold," *Discipline and Punish* (New York: Random House, 1977), pp. 32–69.

45. Thomas Bell was disappointed in 1900 to find the ILP using religion to entice new members (*Pioneering Days*, p. 31). Chester Armstrong claimed that Methodism in Ashington was a means of promotion in the colliery: "What often appears the all-absorbing interest is but the means to other ends. This is especially the case with a religious interest" (*Pilgrimage from Nenthead*, p. 65). Charles Shaw thought that Methodism contributed to political apathy in the Potteries (*When I Was a Child*, p. 194).

46. William Cameron, *Hawkie: The Autobiography of a Gangrel*, ed. John Strathesk (Glasgow: David Robertson, 1888); John Holcombe, *The Autobiography of a Poacher*, ed. Caractacus [Frederick John Snell] (London: John MacQueen, 1901); Alex Alexander, *A Wayfarer's Log* (London: John Murray, 1919).

47. Ernest Ambrose, *Melford Memories: Recollections of 94 Years* (Lavenham, Suffolk: Long Melford Historical and Archaeological Society, 1972); Frederick Willis, *Peace and Dripping Toast* (London: Phoenix House, 1950).

48. See also *Wellington's Men: Some Soldier Autobiographies*, ed. W. H. Fitchett (1900; rpt. East Ardsley: EP Publishing, 1976). Although two out of the four soldiers' autobiographies included (in edited versions) are by officers and gentlemen, Rifleman Harris was a shepherd in Dorsetshire and then shoemaker of his company and the married Sergeant-major Anton reveals much about the experiences of wives travelling with the regiments in the Napoleonic wars.

49. Benjamin was concerned with fairy tales and legends, however, rather than working-class autobiographies. See "The Storyteller" in *Illuminations* (New York: Harcourt, Brace, 1969), pp. 83–109.

50. Mikhail Bakhtin, "Forms of Time and of the Chronotope in the Novel" in *The Dialogic Imagination* (Austin: University of Texas Press, 1981), pp. 209, 243, and more generally pp. 84–258.

51. *Contemporary Review* 78 (December 1900), p. 67. Cited in *Annals of Labour*, p. 172.

52. In *Annals of Labour,* pp. 213–14.

53. In *Annals of Labour,* p. 182.

54. In *Annals of Labour,* p. 193.

55. Fredric Jameson, "Third-World Literature in the Era of Multinational Capitalism," *Social Text* 15 (Fall 1986), pp. 65–88.

56. See especially the last three paragraphs of Jameson's essay. For the criticism see Aijaz Ahmad, "Jameson's Rhetoric of Otherness and the 'National Allegory,'" *Social Text* 16 (Winter 1987), pp. 3–25.

57. W. J. Fishman, *East End 1888* (London: Duckworth, 1988), p. 277.

58. William Lovett, *Life and Struggles of William Lovett in his Pursuit of Bread, Knowledge and Freedom,* 2 vols. (1876; rpt. ed. London: G. Bell, 1920), I, p. xxx.

59. *The Autobiography of Samuel Bamford Vol. I Early Days,* Ed. W. H. Chaloner (New York: Kelley, 1967), p. i.

60. Thomas Bell, *Pioneering Days* (London: Lawrence and Wishart, 1941), p. 10.

61. Philip Collins, *Thomas Cooper, The Chartist: Byron and the "Poets of the Poor,"* Nottingham Byron Lecture 1969 (Nottingham: University of Nottingham, 1969), p. 8.

62. For Benjamin's notion of "aura," see "The Work of Art in the Age of Mechanical Reproduction," in *Illuminations* (1969), pp. 219–59.

63. Betty May, *Tiger-Woman: My Story* (London: Duckworth, 1929), p. 47.

64. *At the Works* (1907) in *Into Unknown England,* p. 297.

65. Thomas Hardy, *Jude the Obscure,* p. 357.

66. Anon., *The Confessions of a Dancing Girl, by Herself* (London: Heath, Cranton and Ouseley [1913]), pp. 44–47.

67. Thus Marx defines critical theory in a letter to A. Ruge, September 1843, in *Karl Marx: Early Writings,* ed. L. Colletti (New York: Vintage, 1975), p. 209.

68. David Herbert Somerset Cranage, *Not Only a Dean* (London: Faith Press, 1952), p. 1.

69. John Ruskin, *Praeterita* (1885; Oxford: Oxford University Press, 1985), p. 5.

70. John Stuart Mill, *Autobiography* (1873; ed. Jack Stillinger, Boston: Houghton Mifflin, 1969), p. 4.

71. See, for example, Buckley's dismissal of Webb in *The Turning Key,* p. 45 and the section on Webb in Chapter 6.

72. Quoted in David Alec Wilson and David Wilson MacArthur, *Carlyle in Old Age* (New York: Dutton, 1934), p. 294.

73. Walter Ong, *Morality and Literacy: The Technologizing of the Word* (London: Methuen, 1982).

Chapter 5

1. J. A. Barbey D'Aurevilly, *Of Dandyism and of George Brummell,* Trans. Douglas Ainslie (London, 1897).

2. See Robert Gordon, "Critical Legal Histories," *Stanford Law Review* 36, special volume on CLS, p. 122; Duncan Kennedy, "Legal Education as Training for Hierar-

chy," *The Politics of Law: A Progressive Critique,* ed. David Kairys (New York: Pantheon, 1982), pp. 40–64; and "Value and the Self" in the Introduction.

3. I am grateful to Old Etonians John Dupré and David Millar, whose illuminating conversations augmented the pleasure of researching this chapter. As with the working-class autobiographies in Chapter 4, the works cited in this chapter are a fraction of those that were read during its composition.

4. Walter Carruthers Sellar and Robert Julian Yeatman, *1066 and All That: A Memorable History of England* (New York: Dutton, 1931).

5. There is an enormous amount of both primary and secondary work on the history, sociology, and (increasingly) anthropology of the British public schools. In the second chapter, "Dandies and Gentlemen; or, 'Dorian Gray' and the Press," of my *Idylls of the Marketplace: Oscar Wilde and the Victorian Public* (Stanford: Stanford University Press, 1986), I summarize the recurring issues and conclusions and indicate what I have found to be the most useful secondary works on the topic (see esp. pp. 90–95). These latter remain T. W. Bamford's *Rise of the Public Schools* (London: Nelson, 1967) and J. R. de S. Honey's *Tom Brown's Universe* (New York: Quadrangle, 1977). One other secondary source is less scholarly than these but more speculative and to my mind the most perceptive: Jonathan Gathorne-Hardy's *The Public School Phenomenon* (London: Hodder and Stoughton, 1977). These three books provide extensive bibliographies of secondary material.

After the history section, the contents of this chapter should not be interpreted as reflecting the objective conditions of the schools but rather the subjective reactions of the autobiographers. The critics of the schools may exaggerate their shortcomings, as in Orwell, but my interest is ideology, the imaginative investments that motivate practice, rather than historical facticity. Thus although for many Connolly is an aberration, so exceptionally "nasty" that he should not be included in a general discussion, for me he reproduces tendencies that pervade the critical texts. My interest in ideology also accounts for my inclusion here of several works of so-called "fiction" (that is, third person realist narratives like Lunn's *The Harrovians* and Mackenzie's *Sinister Street*) with first person accounts presented as "autobiography." This exception is also due to the general reception among old boys of Lunn and Mackenzie's presentations as representative of their experience.

The remaining genre of public school writing that I will not discuss—as it has little relation to personal experience, identity, or subjectivity—includes the fictional cautionary tales for children's moral edification, such as Frederick W. Farrar's immensely popular *Eric; Or, Little by Little* and Andrew Home's *From Fag to Monitor: Or, Fighting to the Front.* Farrar was master at Harrow, headmaster at Marlborough, and Archdeacon of Westminster, which is to say that he could boast extensive experience of school life; yet *Eric* is the prurient, sadistic, gloomy product of what appears to be a genuinely demented mind. (Someone has called it the kind of book that Thomas Arnold might have written had he taken to drink.)

6. J. Fischer Williams, *Harrow* (London: George Bell, 1901), p. 4.

7. Ibid, pp. 4–7.

8. John Corbin, *School Boy Life in England* (New York: Harper, 1897).

9. F. B. Malim, *Almae Matres: Recollections of Some Schools at Home and Abroad* (Cambridge: Cambridge University Press, 1948), pp. vii–viii.

10. For the most condensed stereotypes, see esp. Corbin; Malim; "Various Authors," *Great Public Schools* (London: Edward Arnold, n.d.); Fischer Williams;

Esmé Wingfield-Stratford, *Before the Lamps Went Out* (London: Hodder and Stoughton, 1945).

11. Anthony Trollope, *An Autobiography* (London: Williams and Norgate, 1946), pp. 29–35. 1st pub. 1883.

12. Charles Darwin, *Autobiography,* ed. Nora Barlow (New York: Norton, 1969), p. 27. 1st pub. 1887.

13. Edward Lyttleton, *Memories and Hopes* (London: John Murray, 1925), p. 131.

14. Wingfield-Strateford, p. 98.

15. In *Res Paulinae: The Eighth Half-Century of St. Paul's School,* eds. Robert B. Gardiner and John Lupton (West Kensington: St. Paul's School, 1911), p. 41.

16. Ibid., pp. 227–28.

17. Henry Green, *Pack My Bag: A Self-Portrait* (London: Hogarth, 1940), p. 116.

18. W. F. Bushell, *School Memories* (London: Philip Son and Nephew, 1962), p. 47.

19. S.P.B. Mais, *All the Days of My Life* (London: Hitchinson and Co., 1937), p. 43.

20. Guy Kendall, *A Headmaster Remembers* (London: Victor Gollancz, 1933), p. 304.

21. Lyttleton, p. 157.

22. See Lyttleton, pp. 32–33 and Kendall, p. 189.

23. Rudyard Kipling, *Stalky & Co.* (New York: Scribner's, 1900), p. vii. 1st pub. 1899.

24. For the decline of evangelical, or engaged "everyday," Christianity, especially as promoted in the works of Charles Kingsley and Thomas Hughes, see Norman Vance, *The Sinews of the Spirit: The ideal of Christian manliness in Victorian literature and religious thought* (Cambridge: Cambridge University Press, 1985).

25. Robert Graves, *Good-Bye to All That* (New York: Octagon, 1980), p. 36. 1st pub. 1929.

26. Green, p. 29.

27. Cyril Connolly, *A Georgian Boyhood* in *Enemies of Promise* (New York: Persea, 1983), pp. 260–61. 1st pub. 1938.

28. Gordon K. Lewis, *"Gather With the Saints at the River," the Jonestown Guyana Holocaust of 1978* (Rio Piedras: Institute of Caribbean Studies, 1979), p. 34.

29. Green, p. 5.

30. Ibid., p. 88.

31. Arnold Lunn, *The Harrovians* (London: Methuen, 1914), p. 67. 1st pub. 1913, p. 67.

32. Ibid., pp. 288, 293.

33. Ibid., p. 67.

34. George Orwell, "Such, Such Were the Joys," in *Collected Essays, Journalism, and Letters of George Orwell,* Vol. 4, eds. Sonia Orwell and Ian Angus (New York: Harcourt, Brace, Jovanovich, 1968), pp. 334, 344.

35. Connolly, pp. 255–56.

36. Lyttleton, p. 9.

37. *The Charterhouse We Knew,* ed. W. H. Holden (London: British Technical and General Press, n.d.), p. 96.

38. Alec Waugh, *The Loom of Youth* (New York: Doran, n.d.), p. 337. 1st pub. 1917.

39. Thomas Hughes, *Tom Brown's School Days* (New York: Signet, 1986), p. 289.

40. Orwell, p. 359.

41. Alfred Lubbock, *Memories of Eton and Etonians* (London: Murray, 1899), p. 200.

42. Alfred Rimmer, *Rambles Round Eton and Harrow* (London: Chatto and Windus, 1882), p. 2.

43. Connolly, p. 175.

44. Ibid., p. 192.

45. Cotton Minchin, *Old Harrow Days* (London: Methuen, 1898), p. 276.

46. Wingfield-Stratford, p. 130.

47. Waugh, pp. 147–49, 159; Graves, p. 21 and passim; Green, pp. 18–22.

48. Cited in Connolly, p. 230.

49. I first heard the term in a paper by Alison Jaggar at an annual meeting of the American Philosophical Association, Pacific Division. I believe that she coined it.

50. Orwell, p. 355.

51. Ibid., pp. 343, 351.

52. Ibid., p. 367.

53. Cited in Connolly, pp. 207–9.

54. Bertrand Russell, *An Autobiography* (London: Unwin Paperbacks, 1978), p. 34. 1st pub. 1967–1969.

55. Ibid., p. 33.

56. Connolly, p. 167.

57. Harold Nicolson, *Some People* (Boston: Houghton Mifflin, 1927); cited in Gathorne-Hardy, pp. 225–26.

58. L. E. Jones, *A Victorian Boyhood* (London: Macmillan, 1955), p. 219.

59. Cited in *A Salopian Anthology: Some Impressions of Shrewsbury School during Four Centuries* ed. Philip Cowburn (London: Macmillan, 1964), p. 225.

60. Orwell, p. 348.

61. Connolly, pp. 228–29.

62. Orwell, p. 360.

63. Jones, p. 81; see also pp. 165, 244.

64. Graves, p. 20.

65. See Gathorne-Hardy, pp. 431–39.

66. See Gathorne-Hardy, *The Rise and Fall of the British Nanny* (London: Hodder and Stoughton, 1972).

67. Gathorne-Hardy, *Public School,* p. 351.

68. Isaac Balbus, *Marxism and Domination: a Neo-Hegelian, Feminist, Psychoanalytic Theory of Sexual, Political, and Technological Liberation* (Princeton: Princeton University Press, 1982), see esp. Chapter 9.

69. Lyttleton, pp. 106, 124.

70. Green, p. 18.

71. Ibid., pp. 112–13.

72. Compton Mackenzie, *Sinister Street,* 2 vols. (London: Martin Secker, 1913), I, p. 365.

73. Ibid., p. 388.

74. See Lunn, pp. 296–301; Mackenzie, p. 482; Green, p. 199.

75. Green, pp. 236–46.

76. Trollope, pp. 35, 68.

77. Minchin, pp. 251–55.

78. Bushell, p. 98.

79. In *The Charterhouse We Knew,* p. 89.

80. Waugh, pp. 145–46, 223–24.

81. Lunn, p. 23.

82. Orwell, p. 367.

83. Connolly, p. 258.

84. Waugh, p. 346.

85. Lyttleton, p. 18.

86. Jones, p. 217; Thomas Hughes, *Tom Brown's School Days* (New York: Signet, 1986), p. 361. 1st pub. 1857.

87. Cited in Gathorne-Hardy, *Public School,* p. 122.

88. *The God That Failed,* ed. Richard Crossman (New York: Harper, 1949).

89. George Orwell, *Animal Farm* (New York: Harcourt, Brace, and Co., 1946). For another reading of Orwell's experience at St. Cyprian's, see Alaric Jacob's "Sharing Orwell's 'Joys'—But Not His Fears" (pp. 62–84) in *Inside the Myth: Orwell: Views from the Left,* ed. Christopher Norris (London: Lawrence and Wishart, 1984). The essays in Norris examine the relation between Orwell's bourgeois, humanist values and his appropriation by, and/or complicity with, mass consumerist society.

90. Orwell, "Why I Write," *Collected Essays* I, p. 5.

91. Orwell, "Inside the Whale," *Collected Essays* I, p. 525.

92. Orwell, *Nineteen Eighty-four* (New York: Harcourt, Brace, and Co., 1949), p. 82.

93. Ibid., p. 200.

94. Ibid., p. 266.

95. Ibid., pp. 270–71.

96. Orwell, "Such, Such," 359.

97. Unger, *Knowledge and Politics,* pp. 213–31.

98. Unger, *Passion,* pp. 108–9.

99. Walter Pater, *The Renaissance: Studies in Art and Poetry,* ed. Donald L. Hill (Berkeley: University of California Press, 1980). 1st pub. 1873.

100. Amy Barlow, *Seventh Child: The Autobiography of a Schoolmistress* (1969), p. 5 and Chapter 4.

101. Cecily Steadman, *In the Days of Miss Beale* (London: Burrow, 1931), p. 41.

102. *Independent Women,* p. 166, but both Chapters 4 and 5 on women's colleges and the reformed boarding schools are relevant to my discussion here.

103. Ibid., 166–67.

104. Linda Grier, *The Life of Winifred Mercier* (Oxford: Oxford University Press, 1937), p. 46.

105. See my "Between Women: A Cross-Class Analysis of Status and Anarchic Humor," in *Women's Studies* 15/1–3, pp. 135–148. Rpt. in *Last Laughs: Perspectives on Women and Comedy,* ed. Regina Barreca (London: Gordon and Breach, 1988), pp. 135–148.

106. *Jipping Street,* p. 130.

107. In *Into Unknown England,* p. 301.

108. See, for example, the autobiographical writings included in John Burnett's section on Education in *Destiny Obscure,* pp. 135–215.

109. Ibid., p. 211.

110. Frances Power Cobbe, *Life,* 2 vols. (London: Bentley, 1984), I, pp. 60–69.

111. Winifred Peck, *A Little Learning: or A Victorian Childhood* (London: Faber, 1952), p. 66.

112. Mary Vivian Hughes, *A London Family: 1870–1900: A Trilogy* (London: Oxford University Press, 1946), p. 43.

113. Antonia White, *Frost In May* (New York: Dial, 1980), pp. 169, 46–47.

114. Florence Nightingale, *Cassandra* (New York: Feminist Press, 1979).

115. Viscountess Rhondda, *This Was My World* (London: Macmillan, 1933), pp. 82–83.

116. In *Sexchanges,* Vol. 2 of Gilbert and Gubar's *No Man's Land: The Place of the Woman Writer in the Twentieth Century* (New Haven: Yale University Press, 1989), pp. 258–323. See also *Behind the Lines: Gender and the Two World Wars,* eds. Margaret Randolf Higgonet et al. (New Haven: Yale University Press, 1987).

117. Gagnier, "Between Women" (1988).

118. Hélène Cixous, "The Laugh of the Medusa," *New French Feminisms: An Anthology,* ed. Elaine Marks and Isabelle de Courtivron (New York: Schocken, 1981), pp. 253–58. And see Henri Bergson "Laughter" (1899) in *Comedy,* ed. Wylie Sypher (New York: Doubleday, 1956).

119. Carol Gilligan, *In a Different Voice: Psychological Theory and Women's Development* (Cambridge: Harvard University Press, 1982); Nancy Chodorow, *The Reproduction of Mothering* (Berkeley: University of California Press, 1978); and Judith Kegan Gardiner "On Female Identity and Writing By Women" in *Writing and Sexual Difference,* ed. Elizabeth Abel (Chicago: University of Chicago Press, 1982), pp. 177–91.

120. See Adrienne Rich, "Compulsory Heterosexuality and Lesbian Existence" in *Powers of Desire: The Politics of Sexuality,* ed. Ann Snitow, Christine Stansell, and Sharon Thompson (New York: Monthly Review Press, 1983), pp. 177–205.

121. May Sinclair, *Mary Olivier: A Life* (New York: Dial Press, 1980), p. 61.

122. May Sinclair, *The Three Brontës* (Boston: Houghton Mifflin, 1912), p. 110 and passim.

123. May Sinclair, *The Three Sisters* (New York: Dial Press, 1985).

124. Dorothy Richardson, *Pilgrimage* vol. 1 (New York: Knopf, 1938).

125. Gillian E. Hanscombe, *The Art of Life: Dorothy Richardson and the Development of Feminist Consciousness* (Athens: Ohio University Press, 1982), p. 27.

126. Ibid., p. 16.

127. Ibid., p. 140.

128. Ibid., pp. 160–61.

129. Ibid., p. 36.

130. Nancy Armstrong, *Desire and Domestic Fiction: A Political History of the Novel* (New York: Oxford University Press, 1987).

131. "Why Are Women Redundant," *National Review* 15 (1862): 436; cited in Vicinus, pp. 4–5.

132. See Peck, pp. 164–69.

133. Mary Martha Sherwood, *The Life of Mrs. Sherwood,* ed. Sophia Kelly (London: Darton and Co., 1857); Charlotte Elizabeth [Tonna], *Personal Recollections* (New York: J. S. Taylor, 1842); Mary Anne Schimmelpenninck, *Life of Mary Anne Schimmelpenninck,* 2 vols., ed. Christiana C. Hankin (London: Longman, Brown, Green, Longmans and Roberts, 1858); Mary Bayly, *The Life and Letters of Mrs. Sewell,* 5th

ed. (London: J. Nisbet, 1890): contains a 75pp. autobiography left in ms. at her death. Tonna cited in Mary Jean Corbett, "'My Authorship Self': Public and Private in Women Writers' Autobiographies," Chapter 2 in "Representing Femininity: Middle-class Subjectivity in Women's Autobiographies, 1804–1914" Ph.D. dissertation, Stanford University, 1989.

134. Cited in Corbett, ibid.

135. Ibid.

136. The classic texts are Gilbert and Gubar's *Madwoman in the Attic: The Woman Writer and the Nineteenth-Century Literary Imagination* (New Haven: Yale University Press, 1979); Ellen Moers, *Literary Women: The Great Writers* (New York: Doubleday, 1976); Elaine Showalter, *A Literature of Their Own: British Women Novelists from Brontë to Lessing* (Princeton: Princeton University Press, 1977). There is a great deal of recent work on the trials of literary domesticity. Among the most recent, one might begin with Mary Poovey, *The Proper Lady and the Woman Writer* (Chicago: University of Chicago Press, 1984); Margaret Homans, *Bearing the Word: Language and Female Experience in Nineteenth-Century Women's Writing* (Chicago: University of Chicago Press, 1986); and Armstrong's, *Desire and Domestic Fiction.* For the most recent examples of this area in feminist scholarship on women's autobiography see, in addition to Corbett and Vicinus, Sidonie Smith *A Poetics of Women's Autobiography: Marginality and the Fictions of Self-Representation* (Bloomington: Indiana University Press, 1987); *Life/Lines: Theorizing Women's Autobiography,* eds. Bella Brodzki and Celeste Schenck (Ithaca: Cornell University Press, 1988); *The Private Self: Theory and Practice of Women's Autobiographical Writings,* ed. Shari Benstock (Chapel Hill: University of North Carolina Press, 1988); *Revealing Lives: Gender in Biography and Autobiography,* eds. Susan Groag Bell and Marilyn Yalom (State University of New York Press, 1990).

137. Margaret Oliphant, *The Autobiography and Letters,* ed. Mrs. Harry Coghill (New York: Dodd, Mead and Co. 1899), p. 23.

138. Mary Howitt, *An Autobiography,* 2 vols., ed. Margaret Howitt (Boston: Houghton, Mifflin and Co., 1889), II. pp. 17–18; cited in Corbett, pp. 48–49.

139. Harriet Martineau, *Autobiography,* 3 vols. (London: Smith, Elder, and Co., 1877), I, p. 120.

140. I am grateful to Mary Jean Corbett for drawing these passages to my attention, for her wide reading in middle-class women's autobiography, and for her co-operative attitude toward research.

Chapter 6

1. See Wolf Lepenies, *Between Literature and Science: The Rise of Sociology* (Cambridge: Cambridge University Press, 1988), p. 142. In his sociology of sociology, Lepenies persuasively traces the ways in which Victorian sociology legitimized itself by distinguishing itself from the literary arts and identifying with the natural sciences. For the earlier forms of realism and presociological social theory, see John Bender, *Imagining the Penitentiary: Fiction and the Architecture of Mind in Eighteenth-Century England* (Chicago: University of Chicago Press, 1987).

2. D. H. Lawrence, *Sons and Lovers* (Middlesex: Penguin, 1977), p. 301.

3. Henry James, *What Maisie Knew* (Middlesex: Penguin, 1986), p. 28.

4. Walter Ong, *Orality and Literacy: The Technologizing of the Word* (London: Methuen, 1982). See also Jack Goody and Ian Watt, "The Consequences of Literacy," *Literacy in Traditional Societies,* ed. Jack Goody (Cambridge: Cambridge University Press, 1967), pp. 27–68.

5. Herbert Marcuse, *One Dimensional Man* (Boston: Beacon, 1964).

6. My rhetorical approach also differs from Linda Peterson's generic interests in the hermeneutics of Victorian autobiography in her fine study *Victorian Autobiography: The Tradition of Self-Intepretation* (New Haven: Yale, 1986). Claiming with other theorists of the middle-class literary "self" that all autobiography requires the act of interpretation, Peterson excludes from the genre all but authors philosophically interested in interpretation, including all women except Harriet Martineau. Those who remain are the canon of Victorian autobiography: Carlyle, with his interest in historical interpretation; Ruskin with his in art and social criticism; Newman with his in theological hermeneutics; Gosse with his in literary criticism and scientific theory.

Very exciting work on autobiography in France is being undertaken by Philippe Lejeune, drawing upon the linguistic theory of Emile Benveniste and Roman Jakobson but extending well into cultural studies of ordinary life, especially in its bourgeois familial manifestations. See Lejeune's *La Pacte Autobiographique* (Paris: Seuil, 1975) and *Je est un autre: l'autobiographie, de la littérature aux medias* (Paris: Seuil, 1980). On Lejeune, see Paul John Eakin, "Philippe Lejeune and the Study of Autobiography," *Romance Studies* (Wales) 8 (Summer 1986), pp. 1–14 and Eakin's edition of Lejeune in English, *On Autobiography* (Minneapolis: University of Minnesota Press, 1988).

In addition to works already cited in this study, see Jonathan Loesberg, "Autobiography as Genre, Act of Consciousness, Text," *Prose Studies* IV (1981), pp. 169–85; John M. Morris, *Versions of the Self: Studies in English Autobiography from John Bunyan to John Stuart Mill* (New York: Basic Books, 1966); Wayne Shumaker, *English Autobiography: Its Emergence, Materials, and Form* (Berkeley: University of California Press, 1954); William Spengemann, *The Forms of Autobiography: Episodes in the History of a Literary Genre* (New Haven: Yale University Press, 1980).

7. *Towards Socialism,* ed. Perry Anderson and Robin Blackburn (New York: Cornell University Press, 1966).

8. See Teresa de Lauretis, *Technologies of Gender: Essays on Theory, Film, and Fiction* (Bloomington: Indiana University Press, 1987) and Nancy K. Miller, *Subject to Change* (New York: Columbia University Press, 1988).

9. Thomas Hughes, *Tom Brown's School Days* (New York: Signet, 1986), pp. 41, 63.

10. Cyril Connolly, *Enemies of Promise,* pp. 142–43.

11. George Orwell, "Such, Such Were the Joys," p. 343.

12. George Orwell, "Why I Write," p. 5.

13. For my full treatment of Wilde's *De Profundis* as a work of resistance, see *Idylls of the Marketplace: Oscar Wilde and the Victorian Public* (Stanford: Stanford University Press, 1986), Ch. 5 "An Audience of Peers," pp. 177–95.

14. Paul John Eakin records a fascinating conversation with Frank Conroy on (in my terms) literary subjectivity. Conroy says, "Listen. When a man is writing—and I'm talking about a serious writer—when a man is writing, he is living in a different world.

He is free. That is what writing is all about. It is a way to freedom" (*Fictions in Auto-biography* [1985], p. 233).

15. In addition to the passages cited in Chapter 5, see Antonia White, *Frost in May* (New York: Dial Press, 1980), pp. 137, 119, 169, and passim. I have also found useful White's *As Once in May,* ed. Susan Chitty (London: Virago, 1983) and Susan Chitty, *Now to My Mother: A Very Personal Memoir of Antonia White* (London: Weidenfeld and Nicolson, 1985).

16. *As Once in May,* p. 247.

17. *The Key to Modern Poetry* (London: Peter Nevill, 1952), p. 87. Cited in Richard Pine, *The Dandy and the Herald: Manners, Mind, and Morals from Brummell to Durrell* (New York: St. Martins, 1988), p. 46. See also p. 62.

18. For more biographical data, see Butler's *Butleriana,* ed. A. T. Bartholomew (London: Nonesuch, 1932); Daniel F. Howard's introduction to *Ernest Pontifex or The Way of All Flesh* (Boston: Houghton Mifflin, 1964); Malcolm Muggeridge, *The Earnest Atheist: A Study of Samuel Butler* (London: Eyre and Spottiswoode, 1936). Quotations are from Samuel Butler, *The Way of All Flesh* (New York: New American Library, 1960).

19. "Miss Savage" I–III, *Butleriana* (1932), pp. 151–53.

20. "Mr. Bennett and Mrs. Brown" was published in several different versions and finally included in Virginia Woolf, *The Captain's Death-Bed and Other Essays* (London: Hogarth Press, 1950). This quotation is from *The Nation and The Athenaeum* (Dec. 1923), p. 342.

21. Edmund Gosse, *Father and Son: A Study of Two Temperaments* (New York: Norton, 1963), pp. 5, 9. For the "lively tradition of critical debate about the genre of *Father and Son,*" whether classic tragedy, comedy, documentary, or fiction, see Peterson (1986), pp. 219–20n. My personal favorite of all work on Gosse concerns his father, Philip: see Stephen Jay Gould, "Adam's Navel," in *The Flamingo's Smile: Reflections in Natural History* (New York: Norton, 1985), pp. 99–113. Philip Henry Gosse was the ideologically pre-Darwinian naturalist and notorious propounder in *Omphalos* [*Greek for navel*]: *An Attempt to Untie the Geological Knot* (1857) of the theory that there had been no gradual modification of the surface of the earth or slow development of organic forms, but that when the catastrophic act of creation took place the world instantly presented the structural appearance of a planet on which life had long existed. The theory was crudely represented as God's hiding fossils in rocks and giving Adam an "omphalos" in order to test human faith. Intended to reconcile Scripture with science, it was ridiculed and ignored by both religious and scientists. Gould argues for the unscientific character of *Omphalos.* Its fundamental false analogies and clever cogitation, for Gould, make the work "literary." For a confirmation of *Omphalos* as literature of a "monstrous elegance," see Jorge Luis Borges, "The Creation and P. H. Gosse," in *Other Inquisitions, 1837–1952,* trans. Ruth L. C. Simms (Austin: University of Texas Press, 1964).

22. Michel Foucault, *The Use of Pleasure,* Vol. 2 of *The History of Sexuality,* trans. Robert Hurley (New York: Pantheon, 1985).

23. John Ruskin, *Praeterita* (Oxford: Oxford University Press, 1985), "Author's Preface," p. 1.

24. Many Ruskin scholars have shared this specular approach to the art critic. See John D. Rosenberg, *The Darkening Glass: A Portrait of Ruskin's Genius* (New York: Columbia University Press, 1961); Elizabeth Helsinger, *Ruskin and the Art of the*

Beholder (Cambridge: Harvard University Press, 1982); Jay Fellows, *The Failing Distance: The Autobiographical Impulse in John Ruskin* (Baltimore: Johns Hopkins University Press, 1975); Robert Hewison, *John Ruskin: The Argument of the Eye* (London: Thames and Hudson, 1976); George Landow, *The Aesthetic and Critical Theories of John Ruskin* (Princeton: Princeton University Press, 1971); Richard L. Stein, *The Ritual of Interpretation: The Fine Arts as Literature in Ruskin, Rossetti, and Pater* (Cambridge: Harvard University Press, 1975); George L. Hersey, "Ruskin as an Optical Thinker," *The Ruskin Polygon: Essays on the Imagination of John Ruskin,* eds. John Dixon Hunt and Faith M. Holland (Manchester: Manchester University Press, 1982), pp. 44–46; John Dixon Hunt, "Ut pictura poesis, the Picturesque, and John Ruskin," *John Ruskin,* ed. Harold Bloom (New York: Chelsea House, 1986), pp. 51–68. I find Ruskin criticism to be of unusually high quality. Ruskin was an obsessive cross-referencer, and his scholars individually and collectively weave intricate webs of rich meaning, taking on some of the lost and labyrinthine wealth of their author.

25. For other passages on seeing, see *Praeterita* (1985), pp. 65, 68, 259, 264, 267, 397, 398.

26. John D. Rosenberg, *The Genius of John Ruskin* (Boston: Routledge Kegan Paul, 1963), p. 406. Page numbers for *Fors* and works other than *Praeterita* refer to Rosenberg's selection here.

27. Marcel Proust, "Preface to *La Bible d'Amiens,* in *On Reading Ruskin* Trans. and Ed. Jean Autret, William Burford, and Phillip J. Wolfe; Intro. Richard Macksey (New Haven: Yale University Press, 1987), p. 27.

28. For an excellent discussion of encomium, the rhetoric of praise, see Joel Fineman, *Shakespeare's Perjured Eye* (Berkeley: University of California Press, 1986), Ch. 2, 86–129.

29. John Stuart Mill, *Autobiography,* ed. Jack Stillinger (Boston: Houghton Mifflin, 1969), p.145. See also *The Early Draft of John Stuart Mill's "Autobiography,"* ed. Jack Stillinger, Urbana, 1961) and Michael St. John Packe, *The Life of John Stuart Mill* (London: Secker and Warburg, 1954). For variant interpretations of Mill's crisis, see Robert C. Cumming, "Mill's History of His Ideas," *Journal of the History of Ideas,* XXV (1964), pp. 235–56; John Durham, "The Influence of John Stuart Mill's Mental Crisis on His Thoughts," *American Imago,* XX (1963), pp. 369–84; Albert William Levi, "The 'Mental Crisis' of John Stuart Mill," *Psychoanalytic Review,* XXXII (1945), pp. 86–101 and "The Writing of Mill's Autobiography," *Ethics,* LXI (1951), pp. 284–96. For Mill and Harriet Taylor, see F. A. Hayek, *John Stuart Mill and Harriet Taylor* (Chicago: University of Chicago Press, 1951); Gertrude Himmelfarb, *On Liberty and Liberalism* (New York: Knopf, 1974); Victor Luftig, "The Mills: Work and Worship," in "'Intensities and Avoidances': Representing Friendship Between the Sexes in England 1850–1940" Ph.D. dissertation, Stanford University, 1988, pp. 25–38; Francis E. Mineka, "The *Autobiography* and the Lady," *University of Toronto Quarterly,* XXXII (1963), pp. 301–6; H. O. Pappe, *John Stuart Mill and the Harriet Taylor Myth* (Parkville: Melbourne University Press, 1961); John M. Robson, "Harriet Taylor and John Stuart Mill: Artist and Scientist," *Queen's Quarterly,* LXXIII (1966), pp. 167–86. Also see Robson's "Mill's 'Autobiography'—the Public and the Private Voice," *College Composition and Communication,* XVI (1965), pp. 97–101; Phyllis Rose, *Parallel Lives: Five Victorian Marriages* (New York: Vintage, 1984); Alice S. Rossi, Introduction to *Enfranchisement of Women and the Subjection of Women* (Chicago: University of Chicago Press, 1970); Kate Soper, Introduction to *Enfranchisement of*

Women and the Subjection of Women (London: Virago, 1983). For a reading of *The Autobiography* compatible with mine, on the rhetorical force of Mill's attribution of "masculine" intellectual capacity to Harriet in the context of Victorian gender stereo-typing, see Susan Groag Bell, "The Feminization of John Stuart Mill" in *Revealing Lives: Gender in Biography and Autobiography,* eds. Susan Groag Bell and Marilyn Yalom (New York: State University of New York Press, 1990). For an excellent recent article on Mill and freedom of speech, see Bruce L. Kinzer, "John Stuart Mill and the Irish University Question," *Victorian Studies* 31i (autumn 1987), pp. 59–78, and for a valuable scholarly attempt to answer the question, how did the great exponent of nine-teenth-century liberalism reconcile his employment as an official of a despotic govern-ment with his espousal of the principles of civil and political freedom?, see Abram L. Harris, "John Stuart Mill, Servant of the East India Company," *The Canadian Journal of Economics and Political Science* 30 (May 1964), pp. 185–202.

30. J. S. Mill, *Three Essays,* Introduced by Richard Wollheim, (Oxford: Oxford University Press, 1975), p.132.

31. *The Norton Anthology of English Literature,* Gen. ed. M. H. Abrams, fifth edi-tion, Vol. II (New York: Norton, 1986) p. 1032.

32. *Towards Socialism* (1966), p. 33.

33. Rose, *Parallel Lives* (1984), p. 140.

34. Introduction, *Praeterita,* p. xv.

35. Himmelfarb, *On Liberty and Liberalism* (1974).

36. Jurgen Habermas, *The Theory of Communicative Interaction,* Vol. I: *Reason and the Rationalization of Society,* trans. Thomas McCarthy (Boston: Beacon, 1984).

37. "The Subjection of Women" in *Three Essays,* p. 523.

38. Cited in Himmelfarb, *On Liberty and Liberalism* (1974), p. 222.

39. Cited in Gillian Beer, "Problems of Description in the Language of Discovery," in *One Culture: Essays in Science and Literature,* ed. George Levine with the assistance of Alan Rauch (Madison: University of Wisconsin Press, 1987), p. 39.

40. Thomas Henry Huxley, Charles Darwin, *Autobiographies,* ed. Gavin de Beer (London: Oxford University Press, 1974), p. 100.

41. Leonard Huxley, *Life and Letters of Thomas Henry Huxley,* 2 vols. (London: Macmillan, 1900), II, 410.

42. *The Autobiography of Charles Darwin 1809–1882,* ed. Nora Barlow (New York: Norton, 1969), p. 21.

43. No causal organic disorder was ever diagnosed for Darwin's long bouts of ill-ness, which Darwin himself associates with encounters with anyone beyond his imme-diate family circle, and recent writers on the subject seek in psychosomatic conditions. Nora Barlow includes an appendix on such speculation, in the *Autobiography,* pp. 240–43.

44. *The Life and Letters of Charles Darwin,* ed. Francis Darwin, 3 vols. (London: Murray, 1888); *Charles Darwin's Notebooks, 1836–1844,* ed. Paul H. Barrett (London: British Museum, 1987); *The Collected Papers of Charles Darwin,* 2 vols. (Chicago: University of Chicago Press, 1977); and especially *The Correspondence of Charles Dar-win,* eds. Frederick Burkhardt and Sydney Smith, 3 vols. completed (Cambridge and New York: Cambridge University Press, 1985–).

45. For a bibliography of Moore's work in ths area, see Robert M. Young, "Darwin and the Genre of Biography" in *One Culture,* esp. pp. 214–16, 219, 223. See also Young's *Darwin's Metaphor: Nature's Place in Victorian Culture* (Cambridge: Cam-

bridge University Press, 1985) and L. Robert Stevens, "Darwin's Humane Reading: The Unaesthetic Man Reconsidered" *Victorian Studies* 26 (Autumn 1982), pp. 51–63.

46. *Life and Letters,* I, pp. 84–85. Remaining references to Huxley's *Life and Letters* will be included in the text.

47. William Irvine, *Apes, Angels, and Victorians: A Joint Biography of Darwin and Huxley* (London: Weidenfeld and Nicolson, 1956), pp. 10–11.

48. Cited in Irvine, p. 20.

49. Beatrice Webb, *My Apprenticeship,* ed. Norman MacKenzie (Cambridge: University of Cambridge Press, 1979), p. 414. All further references are to this edition. I have also found useful Norman and Jeanne MacKenzie's lovely edition of *The Diary of Beatrice Webb,* 4 vols. (Cambridge: Belknap Press of Harvard University Press, 1982–1984) and *The Letters of Sidney and Beatrice Webb,* 3 vols., ed. Norman MacKenzie (Cambridge: Cambridge University Press, 1978).

50. Cited in Lepenies (1988), p. 142.

51. Elizabeth Barrett Browning *Aurora Leigh* (Chicago: Academy Chicago, 1979), p. 47.

52. Cited in Lepenies (1988), p. 135. For Woolf's own views of alternative relationships between men and women, see Victor Luftig, "Seeing Together: Woolf, Fry, and Friendship after the War" in "Intensities and Avoidances," pp. 213–301.

53. *The Turning Key* (1984), p. 45.

54. *Diary of Beatrice Webb,* Vol. 1, p. 118.

55. Mill, *Autobiography,* pp. 85–86.

56. Orwell, "Why I Write," p. 7.

57. *Diary,* vol. 1, pp. 329–30.

58. Ibid., p. 342.

59. Ibid., p. 371.

60. William Morris, *Political Writings of William Morris,* ed. A. L. Morton (New York: International Publishers, 1979), p. 200.

61. See *Contingency, Irony, and Solidarity,* p. 20 and chapters on Nietzsche and Derrida, and Harold Bloom, *The Anxiety of Influence* (New York: Oxford University Press, 1973).

62. Audre Lorde, *Zami: A New Spelling of My Name* (New York: Crossing Press, 1982); Kate Simon, *Bronx Primitive: Portraits in a Childhood* (New York: Harper and Row, 1982); Kim Chernin, *In My Mother's House: A Daughter's Story* (New York: Harper and Row, 1983); Sandra Cisneros, *The House on Mango Street* (Houston: Arte Público Press, 1984); Carolyn Kay Steedman, *Landscape for a Good Woman: A Story of Two Lives* (New Brunswick: Rutgers University Press, 1986); Joan Nestle, *A Restricted Country* (Ithaca: Firebrand Books, 1987); Gloria Anzaldúa, *Borderlands/La Frontera: The New Mestiza* (San Francisco: Spinsters/Aunt Lute, 1987). For a review essay of these and other recent autobiographical writings, see R. Gagnier, "Feminist Autobiography in the 1980s" in *Feminist Studies* 16/3 (Fall 1990).

Index